Models of Monetary Economies

Models of Monetary Economies

Editors

John H. Kareken and Neil Wallace

Proceedings and contributions
from participants of a December 1978 conference
sponsored by the Federal Reserve Bank of Minneapolis

January 1980

Published 1980
Federal Reserve Bank of Minneapolis

Copies available from the
Office of Public Information
Federal Reserve Bank
Minneapolis, MN 55480

Price: $5.00

International Standard Book Number 0-9603936-0-9

Printed in the United States of America

Participants
Conference on Models of Monetary Economies
December 7–8, 1978
Sponsored by the Federal Reserve Bank of Minneapolis

Robert Barro
University of Rochester

Truman Bewley
Northwestern University

William Brainard
Yale University

William Brock
University of Chicago and University of Wisconsin

John Bryant
Federal Reserve Bank of Minneapolis

Guillermo Calvo
Columbia University

David Cass
University of Pennsylvania

Robert Clower
University of California, Los Angeles

John Danforth
Federal Reserve Bank of Minneapolis

Stanley Fischer
Massachusetts Institute of Technology

Jerry Green
Harvard University

Frank Hahn
Cambridge University

Milton Harris
Carnegie-Mellon University

Leonid Hurwicz
University of Minnesota

Lewis Johnson
Board of Governors of the Federal Reserve System

James Jordan
University of Minnesota

Ira Kaminow
Federal Reserve Bank of Philadelphia

John Kareken
Federal Reserve Bank of Minneapolis and University of Minnesota

David Lindsey
Board of Governors of the Federal Reserve System

Robert Lucas
University of Chicago

Allan Meltzer
Carnegie-Mellon University

Preston Miller
Federal Reserve Bank of Minneapolis

Dale Mortensen
Northwestern University

Clarence Nelson
Federal Reserve Bank of Minneapolis

John Paulus
Federal Reserve Bank of Minneapolis

Edward Prescott
Carnegie-Mellon University

Arthur Rolnick
Federal Reserve Bank of Minneapolis

Thomas Sargent
Federal Reserve Bank of Minneapolis and University of Minnesota

José Scheinkman
University of Chicago

Karl Shell
University of Pennsylvania

Martin Shubik
Yale University

Christopher Sims
University of Minnesota

Ross Starr
University of California, Davis

James Tobin
Yale University

Robert Townsend
Carnegie-Mellon University

Neil Wallace
Federal Reserve Bank of Minneapolis and University of Minnesota

Charles Wilson
University of Wisconsin

Contents

1 Conference Proceedings

2 Post-Conference Contributions

Foreword

Mark H. Willes
President

The Federal Reserve System is charged with managing the nation's monetary system so as to promote economic efficiency, stability, and growth. Economists, however, are far from agreed on how to do that. Agreement would have to come from a well-developed theory of how money works in an economy, and there simply is no such theory. In an attempt to help fill this gap, in December 1978 the Federal Reserve Bank of Minneapolis provided a forum for new research on the theory of money. This volume, *Models of Monetary Economies,* contains the conference proceedings and some post-conference contributions by participants.

The research presented in this volume departs from standard monetary analysis in two fundamental ways. First, unlike some current approaches, it sticks strictly to the assumption that money is only useful because of what it can buy. That is, in itself money does not satisfy consumers, and it cannot be used to produce anything that does. Second, unlike virtually all current approaches, the research rigorously works out the implications of that assumption in various general equilibrium contexts.

While the Minneapolis Federal Reserve Bank does not necessarily endorse the views expressed at the conference or in this volume, we believe their publication makes a significant contribution to the literature on monetary economics. We hope it will stimulate further discussion and research and ultimately lead to improved monetary policies.

We are grateful to all conference participants, especially John Kareken and Neil Wallace, who planned the conference. We also thank Kathleen Rolfe and Arthur Rolnick, who made a volume out of the conference and other papers; Maureen O'Connor, who helped proofread; and Phil Swenson, who was responsible for the graphic design.

Introduction

John H. Kareken
Neil Wallace
Editors

In December 1978 the Federal Reserve Bank of Minneapolis was host to a conference entitled "Models of Monetary Economies," and this volume contains the papers presented and discussed at that conference. They will be found in part 1, along with the comments of the appointed discussants. The volume also contains several papers that were not presented at the conference. Long before the conference began, and again at its conclusion, conference participants were invited to submit notes or longer papers for inclusion in the conference volume. And, happily, some obliged. Their contributions will be found in part 2.

The papers in this volume are a part of the literature of "the new microfoundations of money." (That phrase was coined by Barro and Fischer in 1976.[1]) To put that observation another way, the models presented in this volume are all very different from, or alternatives to, those of the macroeconomics literature. Nor is that an accident. The Federal Reserve Bank of Minneapolis sponsored the "Models of Monetary Economies" conference precisely because some of its research staff were so doubtful about macroeconomic models, or about the monetary and fiscal policy implications of those models. The hope was that the Bank might, by financing the conference, help in the development of more satisfactory models. That hope has been in some measure realized, although the essential conclusion of this brief introductory essay is that monetary economists still have a way, possibly rather a long way, to go.

That conclusion emerges from a survey of various models of monetary economies, macroeconomic and other. The macroeconomic models, small- and large-scale, classical and Keynesian, are inconsistent; they yield contradictory implications. They do, that is, if what has been said about them is taken seriously: namely, that their common portfolio specification can be rationalized or defended by appeal to certain underlying models. And if that is not taken seriously, then the macroeconomic models are unsatisfactory on another count: they have too few implications; they do not provide answers to important questions.

This last statement applies as well to the money-in-the-utility-function and the money-in-the-production-function models. The sequence-economy or

[1] Author names and years refer to the works listed at the end of this book.

transaction-technology models, of which the so-called Clower-constraint models are a subset, also have too few implications. But even those models that are consistent and relatively rich in implications, the overlapping generations and the communication-cost models, are not entirely satisfactory. Why is explained later on. It could well be, though, that of all the models so far fashioned by monetary economists, those models are the most satisfactory. Developing them further may be the best research strategy for the period immediately ahead.

Macroeconomic Models

Virtually all of the models of the macroeconomics literature have a common portfolio specification, hereafter referred to as the *standard specification*. It says, and this is a definition, that desired asset quantities depend, by way of fixed functions, on current and lagged income, wealth, and yields to maturity or asset prices. (See, for example, Friedman 1956 and Tobin 1969 or almost any macroeconomics textbook, say, Dornbusch and Fischer 1978.) Few, though, regard that specification as primitive. With near-unanimity, it is held that the standard specification can be rationalized by appeal to some risk-aversion portfolio model, perhaps Tobin's (1958), and/or some inventory model of money demand, whether Baumol's (1952) or Tobin's (1956), that of Miller and Orr (1966), or one of a number of others. But that claim cannot be sustained.

What does it mean that the standard specification can be rationalized by appeal to some underlying model? Presumably, that the underlying model is a part of any model containing that specification. (After all, as a matter of logic, the assumptions of an underlying model are or are not accepted.) So no implication of any such model (that is, any macroeconomic model) can contradict any implication of the underlying model. The fact is, however, that macroeconomic models do have implications which contradict those of any risk-aversion portfolio model and those of any inventory model of money demand.[2]

Any risk-aversion portfolio model implies that desired asset quantities depend on wealth and on the parameters or moments of the joint distribution of asset yields. It follows that current and lagged yields can appear in the portfolio specification of a model of an ongoing economy only as conditioning variables or forecasters of the distribution of future asset prices. (If, for example, asset yields are identically and independently distributed over time, then those observed yields should not appear.) Thus, although risk-aversion portfolio models say that asset quantities may depend on observed yields, they also say that the nature of that dependence, how asset quantities and yields are related, is determined by the yield distribution. That dependence is not analogous to the static demand theory dependence of quantities on relative prices. There is, however, no acknowledgment of that in the models of the macroeconomics literature—or, more specifically, in the standard specification, with its fixed asset demand functions. That is why macroeconomic

[2]A vague appeal to some underlying model is implicit theorizing. And that macroeconomic models are contradictory reveals that that sort of theorizing is risky. What must be shown is that the underlying model is equivalent to (if and only if with) the assumptions that it justifies. If the implication has only been shown to go one way, then the underlying model may have other implications which contradict implications of the complete macroeconomic model. Moreover, to use some of the implications of the underlying model, rather than the underlying model itself, as a part of the macroeconomic model is to run the risk of missing those other implications.

models, those which include the standard specification, are contradictory.

When any such macroeconomic model is used to determine a nonstochastic equilibrium, there is an evident contradiction. More generally, nothing guarantees that the endogenous yield distribution implied by any particular macroeconomic model matches up with the distribution underlying the model's fixed relationships between asset quantities and yields. And note that there is a guaranteed contradiction when, as in Poole 1970 or Kareken, Muench, and Wallace 1973, a macroeconomic model is used to compare the consequences of alternative monetary instrument choices or when, as in Tobin and Brainard 1963, a macroeconomic model is used to determine how an unconstrained equilibrium compares with that which obtains under an effective Regulation Q ceiling. If the fixed asset demand functions of the model are right for one policy regime, they cannot be right for the other.

It is an implication of risk-aversion portfolio models that no fixed dependence of asset quantities on observed yields should fit any arbitrary time series. That may explain why researchers have not been able to identify an econometrically stable set of fixed functions relating asset quantities to yields (and income and wealth). Another possibility is that researchers have been looking for the wrong kind of dependence, that which is suggested by static demand theory.

Macroeconomic models also have implications which contradict those of the inventory models of money demand. An assumption common to all of the inventory models is that there are transaction costs. Those costs are what rescue currency (or any zero-interest means of payment) from being dominated by, for example, riskless bonds. But the inventory models have other implications, among them, that the total of resources used up in transacting changes with a change in the proportions in which the public holds means of payment and other assets. It is, however, an implication of macroeconomic models that the total of resources used in transacting is a constant. So there is an obvious contradiction, one which cannot simply be brushed aside. A change in the amount of resources used in transacting may be the principal effect of an open market operation. (See Bryant and Wallace 1979a.)

The conclusion is, then, that the standard portfolio specification cannot be rationalized or justified by appeal to some risk-aversion portfolio model and/or some inventory or transaction-cost model. The specification can only be regarded as a primitive assumption. But as most would agree, it is unsatisfactory simply to assume that asset quantities are unspecified fixed functions of observed yields, income, and wealth. Too little follows from that assumption.

It is suggestive that users of macroeconomic models have sought to justify the standard specification by invoking risk-aversion and inventory models. Those models would seem to be true to the postulate of intrinsic uselessness, which is surely accepted by all economists: No asset is ever wanted per se, but only for the future consumption it supports. To take the standard specification as one of the primitive assumptions of the model is, however, to give up that postulate and with it any hope of doing a traditional welfare analysis of alternative monetary and fiscal policies. (In that type of analysis alternative policies are ranked by their implied consumption allocations.) Then, too, the postulate is relatively rich in implications: to mention but one, the Modigliani-Miller theorem. Intrinsic uselessness is necessary for that result. (See, in particular, Stiglitz 1969.) Clearly, it could never be obtained by simply postulating separate and general demand functions for equities and bonds. So there is a strong case for not giving up the postulate of intrinsic uselessness, or for starting off not with the standard specification, but rather with that postulate.[3]

Money in Utility or Production Functions

There are many models in which a stock of something called money appears as an argument of utility functions (see, for example, Sidrauski 1967, Samuelson 1968, and Helpman and Sadka 1979) or of production functions (Levhari and Patinkin 1968 and Calvo 1979). As is evident, though, to assume that money is an argument of utility functions or of production functions is to indulge in implicit theorizing. No one regards either of these assumptions as primitive. To quote Samuelson (1968, p. 8),

> One can put *M* into the utility function, along with other things, as a real convenience in a world of stochastic uncertainty and indivisible transactions charges.
>
> If, however, one does put *M* directly into *U*, one must remember the crucial fact that *M* differs from every other good (such as tea) in that it is not really wanted for its own sake but only for the ultimate exchanges it will make possible.

And appended to the quoted passage there appears the following footnote:

> This is not the only way of introducing the real convenience of cash balances. An even better way would be to let *U* depend directly only on the time stream of [consumptions], and then to show that holding an inventory of *M* does contribute to a more stable and greatly preferable stream of consumptions. The present oversimplified version [putting *M* directly into *U*?] suffices to give the correct general picture.

But it does not do, making a vague appeal to "a world of stochastic uncertainty and indivisible transactions charges." More must be said of a model than that it may be consistent. Yet, unless the underlying world (environment) has been made explicit, consistency cannot be checked or therefore ensured. The criticism applies to all of the stories that have been told to justify including money among the arguments of utility and/or production functions.

As was noted above, the standard specification, as a primitive assumption, has too few implications. The assumption that something called money is one of the arguments of utility/production functions, which must also be regarded as primitive, does too. What is the thing called money? Some particular liability of government? Net outside indebtedness? Or is it some aggregate of government and private liabilities that can be spent? Suppose there are two countries. Is there some liability of the government or the private sector of one country that qualifies as money for the residents of the other? Anyone who starts off by putting money into utility/production functions must answer those questions, presumably by appealing to some implicit model or environment. Economists have for ever so long now been debating what ought to be lumped into an aggregate called money. And that is evidence enough that implicit theorizing has not served them well.

Seemingly, it is possible to avoid answering the questions of the previous

[3] It is not possible to prove the nonexistence of a set of assumptions which contains the postulate of intrinsic uselessness and which is equivalent to the standard specification. That, however, is hardly justification. Until a set has been found, the standard specification will remain largely without implications (except as ad hoc, and therefore unconvincing, restrictions are appended to it).

paragraph by including all assets as arguments of utility/production functions. What results, though, is an almost empty specification. About the only thing implied is that there are econometrically stable asset demand functions, precisely those of the standard specification. But time and again data have rejected that implication.

The alternative to putting money into utility/production functions is to make explicit use of the postulate of intrinsic uselessness. And although that may not always be easy, what results are considerably restricted asset demand functions. For to assume intrinsic uselessness is to in effect substitute profit or rate-of-return maximization for utility maximization. The contrast between standard demand theory and the demand theory of Lancaster (1966) is illustrative.

Imposing a Transaction Technology

On the surface at least, the sequence-economy models of Hahn (1973b) and others are consistent with intrinsic uselessness. There are two assumptions common to those models. The first is that there is a sequence of markets, one for each date $t = 1, 2, \ldots$, in which all goods, differing in physical characteristics and/or delivery times, may be traded. Presumably, something called money may be too. The second common assumption, one which distinguishes the sequence-economy models from the Arrow-Debreu model, is that exchange is costly. There is some resource cost associated with buying or selling any good at time t, for delivery at time $t + h$ $(h \geq 0)$. That cost may vary with what good is bought or sold, the individual doing the trading, the amount involved in the trade, and the delivery date.

If the right exchange-possibility and cost assumptions are imposed, sequence-economy models can yield positive equilibrium prices of money for all periods.[4] To quote Heller and Starr (1976, p. 203),

> Any durable good or futures contract can perform the function of shifting purchasing power forward or back, but transactions and storage costs associated with some commodities used for this purpose will be prohibitive. A distinguishing feature of money should be its low transactions and storage costs as compared to goods, bonds and futures contracts.

And by assumption the transaction technologies of the Heller-Starr and the other sequence-economy models conform to that characterization of money. (See Hahn 1973b, Starrett 1973, and Kurz 1974a, Heller 1974, and Honkapohja 1978.) That is the sense in which those technologies are right.

How, though, is the Heller-Starr transaction technology (or any of the others) to be regarded? As a primitive assumption? Or as an implication of some underlying model? The latter possibility seems ever so much more likely than the former. Implicitly, certain facts, aspects of the physical environment, are embedded in the technology. Milk depreciates very quickly. Land is not uniform. (How fertile a particular piece is requires too much checking.) And would anyone use the transaction technology appropriate for a Robinson Crusoe–Friday economy in, say, a model of the U.S. economy of 1979? But why not? Actually, it is only implicit theorizing, the appeal to some underlying model or environment, that saves transaction-technology models from being without implications. In the absence of explicit models, however, controversy

[4] For any finite-horizon version, though, a final-period price of money must in effect be imposed. See Heller and Starr 1976.

can, as was pointed out above, go on endlessly. In particular, what is assumed in sequence-economy models about the exchange efficiency of outside indebtedness may not seem convincing to everyone.

What has just been said applies—if anything, more strongly—to the Clower-constraint models. "Money buys goods and goods buy money; but goods do not buy goods." That is Clower's dictum (1967, p. 5); and it is an assumption, the distinguishing assumption, of a large number of models of monetary economies, including the Shubik and Lucas models of this volume. (With some justification, though, these models might be referred to as the Brunner-constraint models. See Brunner 1951.)

In the economy modeled by Shubik, exchange involves the use of redeemable claims on government and claims on private banks. The appeal is to an earlier paper by Shubik (1973). There he showed that with the strategic use of some physical thing as a means of payment, multilateral exchange of many goods can be modeled as a particular noncooperative game, the Nash equilibrium of which approaches the competitive equilibrium. Whether that justifies all of the details of Shubik's model in this volume is, however, unclear. Also, since, as we now know, there are several noncooperative games with equilibria which converge to the competitive equilibrium, some justification must be provided for that which is singled out. (See Hurwicz's comment in this volume.)

The Lucas model is of an economy populated by individuals of infinite life who discount. There is no capital, the consumption good being nonstorable. So saving is the accumulation of outside money. With regard to exchange, Lucas makes two assumptions: the first, that the proceeds (outside money) from the sale of current output can be used to acquire future but not current consumption, and the second, that there is no borrowing and lending. (Bewley, whose model is similar to Lucas', also rules out borrowing/lending, but does not impose the Clower constraint. Townsend gets no borrowing/lending as an implication of the spatial separation he imposes.)

Shubik's view would seem to be that use of a medium of exchange, or possibly the Clower constraint, is justified by exchange being (or being best represented as) a noncooperative game. That is an interesting possibility, although at this time hardly more. For Lucas, the justification is evidently to be found in the observation, which few would dispute, that exchange is really more difficult than it is in the Arrow-Debreu economy. There are barriers which would-be traders have to surmount, and the use of outside money helps in the surmounting of them. That may be. But imposing the Clower constraint, even after having offered a plausible intuitive explanation, is starting too far along.

The objection can be put another way. Clower-constraint models are all limiting versions of the Heller-Starr model. By assumption, the cost of buying one good with another, or with any asset save that called money, is infinite. Some may dispute this, arguing that it is only required that the cost be sufficiently great. But no Clower-constraint model determines endogenously what is used as a means of payment. That is given exogenously. So, independent of what happens to the physical environment, or, more specifically, to government policy, there is never any switching from one thing to another. Thus, whatever the inflation rate may be, the residents of one country never abandon the paper money of their government in favor of that of another.

The foregoing objection would be without force if no one had ever observed any variation in the means of payment. It is, however, a matter of record that different things have been used at different times and in different places.

Overlapping Generations Models

For quite a few years, monetary economists pretty much ignored the Samuelson (1958) pure consumption loan model. Cass and Yaari (1966a) are the conspicuous exceptions. Of late, however, the model has been the focus of considerable attention. Thus, versions of the Samuelson model will be found in two of the conference papers, those by Wallace and by Cass, Okuno, and Zilcha (COZ), and in two of the other papers, those by Brock and Scheinkman and by Townsend. Samuelson-type models (as models of monetary economies) are discussed by Bryant and by Cass and Shell.

Those models, referred to here as the *overlapping generations models,* are attractive because they are relatively explicit—perhaps not entirely so (see below) but more so than the models considered above. Why does this rather than that asset appear as an argument of utility functions? Why one transaction technology and not another? Why can individuals not borrow and lend? There is no need to ask such questions of any overlapping generations model.

Overlapping generations models may give an edge to outside indebtedness. Whether a particular model does would seem to depend on whether laissez-faire (no outside indebtedness and no tax-transfer or social security scheme) can be nonoptimal, and, more particularly, whether in equilibrium there is capital overaccumulation. (See, for example, Shell 1971.) And whether laissez-faire yields nonoptimal competitive equilibria depends on the structure of the economy: its natural growth rate, the age profile of endowments, and the technology for converting present into future consumption. As Wallace suggests, the overlapping generations models provide an interpretation of the widely held view, nicely articulated by Friedman (1960, pp. 5–6), that outside indebtedness is welfare-improving because it frees resources that would otherwise have to be used to provide a stock of commodity money. But overlapping generations models do not provide simple answers to how outside indebtedness should be managed. The policy that has received the most attention, herein referred to as *pseudo laissez-faire,* is the provision of a fixed nominal stock of such indebtedness.

Very generally, overlapping generations models have nonmonetary-like equilibria under pseudo laissez-faire, equilibria in which outside indebtedness is always without value, or in which the value of outside indebtedness converges to zero. That is true even though there may exist other optimal equilibria in which the value of outside indebtedness is bounded away from zero. If taken seriously (and the plausibility of the intrinsic uselessness postulate suggests that it should be), that conclusion implies that pseudo laissez-faire is defective. As a matter of government policy, it may be desirable to impose legal restrictions that bound the value of outside indebtedness away from zero. (See Scheinkman's comment in this volume.)

In some simple overlapping generations environments there does exist an optimal equilibrium under pseudo laissez-faire. (That conclusion is in sharp contrast to what is implied by models of infinitely lived agents who discount the future. In those models, any such equilibrium is in general nonoptimal. See the Bewley and Townsend papers.) In the COZ paper and the Cass addendum it is shown, though, that that is not generally true. Future research may further characterize the class of environments in which there is an optimal equilibrium under pseudo laissez-faire.

It has long been known that if all taxation is costly (distorting), then nothing recommends pseudo laissez-faire. A nonzero inflation tax is in general called for. (See Phelps 1973 and Helpman and Sadka 1979.) In that connection, there are very deep questions. Why should a society choose the social contrivance of outside indebtedness rather than a tax-transfer or social security scheme? And what keeps the outside indebtedness regime viable? Answers to those questions will presumably have other implications. The fact that overlapping generations models provide no answers suggests that even in them there are some implicit assumptions.

That, however, is not why many conference participants were skeptical of Wallace's claim that overlapping generations models must, by default perhaps, be the basis for analyses of monetary and fiscal policies. A common view is that overlapping generations models do not portray money as a medium of exchange. (See Tobin's comment.) That criticism is to be translated as follows. There is a clearly discernible real world pattern of transaction velocities, a pattern displayed by nearly all real-world economies, past and present. Some one thing has a large transaction velocity, or few things do, and all other things have small transaction velocities. And the only satisfactory models of monetary economies are those which yield this pattern.

There is a related, and perhaps more solidly grounded, suspicion about overlapping generations models: although they may provide reliable answers about fiscal policy, their monetary policy implications are not to be taken seriously. Nor is it irrelevant that in the preceding paragraphs the reference was exclusively to net outside indebtedness, the path of which is determined by fiscal policy (indeed, by the deficit on current account). Monetary policy determines the composition of that indebtedness and can therefore be of any consequence only if the components of the total sell at different prices. To address questions of monetary policy, it is then necessary to have a model which implies, inter alia, positive interest on default-free assets. There is such an overlapping generations model, that fashioned by Bryant and Wallace (1979a). But they too are guilty of having simply imposed a transaction technology.

In elaboration, it suffices to consider Federal Reserve notes and, as an instance of default-free assets, U.S. Treasury bills. The problem is that they are similar in the extreme. A note and a bill both promise known amounts of currency in the future, independent of the state of the world. So why do Treasury bills sell at discount? Why not at par? There is an explanation, obvious perhaps, but no less convincing for being so: Treasury bills are issued in inconvenient denominations. What if the U.S. Treasury or the Federal Reserve System stood ready, as the System does for currency, to exchange large- and small-denomination Treasury bills at no cost? Would large-denomination Treasury bills, those with par values of, say, $10,000, still sell at discount? That seems extremely unlikely. Or what if the System abandoned its policy of costless exchange of Federal Reserve notes of different denominations? Would large-denomination notes sell at par in a private market? That too seems extremely unlikely.

There is, then, a ready explanation for interest on riskless securities. Quantity discounts are offered on all kinds of things. And why not on Treasury bills? But it is not entirely satisfactory to modify the environment of an overlapping generations model by introducing a cost of intermediating large-denomination government liabilities. If it is costly for individuals to get together and share a government bond, then getting together for any other purpose, perhaps to exchange other things, cannot be costless. It is not, however, one of the assumptions of overlapping generations models that any communication or interaction among individuals is costly.

Costly Communication

It is important that the main assumption of the overlapping generations models be retained, for any model of a monetary economy must be able to address the issue of capital overaccumulation. Evidently, though, the (implicit) assumption of costless communication should be replaced. But how to model costly communication? The attempt to do so goes back only a little way in time. (To suggest that money eliminates the requirement that there be a double coincidence of wants is not to provide a model, nor, more importantly, an explanation from which anything at all follows.) Starr (1972), Ostroy (1973), and Feldman (1973) were among the first to enlist in the effort. But in the economy modeled by Ostroy and Starr (1974), all trades, although bilateral, take place at known Arrow-Debreu equilibrium prices. And their model is not dynamic; the trading process runs on in other than calendar time. Nor is Feldman's model dynamic.

In contrast, Harris' (forthcoming) model is dynamic. But, containing no outside indebtedness, it cannot be used to address present-day monetary policy questions. Townsend's models in this volume, also explicitly dynamic, do contain outside indebtedness. Also, although they do not and were never meant to explain quantity discounts on riskless securities, they may well be suggestive of models that can.[5]

If the majority view of the conference participants is a reliable guide, a model of a monetary economy, to be satisfactory, must explain not only valued fiat money but also the real-world pattern of transaction velocities. It must also explain interest on default-free assets. Seemingly then, as was observed at the beginning of this essay, monetary economists have some way to go. To say that is not in any way to belittle any of the postwar contributions to monetary economics, but only to acknowledge the extreme difficulty of the task that has confronted monetary economists.

Readers can, however, decide for themselves whether that rather somber judgement is justified. This volume contains a variety of models of monetary economies, as well as considerable informed discussion of different models. There is enough in it for readers to make up their own minds about the state of monetary economics.

[5]The equilibrium exchange ratio of any isolated market of the Townsend (or Harris) models is competitively determined. So presumably it is to be understood that there are many agents of each type in any such market. If, however, all agents of each type move together, as they do in the Townsend models, then nothing prevents all those of a type from sharing a large-denomination Treasury bill.

1 Conference Proceedings

The Role of Money in Supporting the Pareto Optimality of Competitive Equilibrium in Consumption Loan Type Models

David Cass, Masahiro Okuno, and Itzhak Zilcha*

1. Introduction and Summary

Perhaps the single most enduring theme in economics is that of the social desirability of the competitive mechanism. In its modern form, this theme occurs as the two basic theorems of welfare economics (see, in particular, Arrow 1951).[1] Our central concern in this paper is with the validity of the first of these two theorems — that every competitive equilibrium yields a Pareto optimal allocation — in idealized yet plausible models of intertemporal allocation in a market economy.

What is especially striking about the posture of the invisible hand is its apparent widespread reach; all that seems to be required in the well-known standard argument is that there be neither real externalities (in consumption and production) nor local satiation (in consumption). This is very misleading, quite aside from any questions of the existence of competitive equilibrium. One of the most important features of the maintained assumptions in that argument is that they implicitly impose some element of boundedness in order to offset the intrinsic one-directional, open-ended nature of time. In the commonly accepted paradigm, this element is simply imposed by postulating a bounded horizon (see, for example, Arrow and Hahn 1971). In another frequently recurring extension, it is effectively imposed by postulating the alternative — and equally implausible — assumption that there are essentially a finite number of infinitely lived agents (see, for example, Debreu 1954). In any case, it is not necessarily true that the invisible hand stretches over economies that evolve toward an unbounded horizon, even in the most favorable of circumstances otherwise.

This significant exception was first recognized, at least implicitly, in Malinvaud's (1953) classic paper on capital theory. However, it only received its first explicit elaboration in Samuelson's (1958) equally celebrated seminal contribution. Samuelson's discussion is the starting point for our own.

Samuelson showed that, in a simple model of a market economy charac-

*This paper, although prepared for the Federal Reserve Bank of Minneapolis conference, first appeared in the *Journal of Economic Theory* 20 (February 1979): 41–80. We gratefully acknowledge research support from the National Science Foundation.

[1] Author names and years refer to the works listed at the end of this book.

terized by an unbounded horizon; short-lived, overlapping, but essentially identical households; and a single, perishable physical commodity, without some extra-market institution there may be no competitive equilibrium which is Pareto optimal. He also showed that one natural extra-market institution which may set matters aright is fiat money initially owned (that is, cleverly invented) by the first generation of households and subsequently purchased with physical commodities (that is, expressly valued) by each succeeding generation — provided only that money trades for commodities at a sufficiently high (present value) price. A number of others have since refined and extended Samuelson's central argument (see, for example, Cass and Yaari 1966a, Diamond 1965, Gale 1973, Shell 1971, and Starrett 1972).

Even on his own grounds Samuelson dealt with a special case (boundary endowments) in a special way (stationary allocations). Expanding his analysis — much in the manner of Gale, but in different spirit — it is easy to show that in Samuelson's basic model (with two-period lifetimes) there is the following dichotomy. Without money, the competitive equilibrium is the initial endowment allocation itself, which may be Pareto optimal or not. Furthermore, upon the introduction of money, in the former case nothing is altered. The price of money must be zero and the allocation is again the initial endowments (in this instance, Pareto optimal). In the latter case, however, there now exists a continuum of potential competitive equilibria. Considering just the least complicated possibility, these range from the original autarkic equilibrium, where the price of money turns out to be zero and the allocation is once again the initial endowments (in this instance, not Pareto optimal), to the "fully" monetized equilibrium, where the price of money is at a maximum and the allocation turns out to be both stationary and Pareto optimal. In the intermediate range, that of the "partly" monetized equilibria, the price of money is positive, but the allocations are neither stationary nor Pareto optimal. In fact, in a "partly" monetized equilibrium, the allocation must be asymptotically the same as in the original autarkic equilibrium.

Thus, a complete analysis of Samuelson's basic model (now including consideration of more complicated possibilities for nonstationary equilibria) leads to several very strong conclusions. These can be summarized, in somewhat general fashion, by the following propositions. Consider the range of potential competitive equilibria with money, and call an equilibrium *barter* if the price of money is zero, *monetary* if it's positive. Then we have two propositions:

EXISTENCE PROPOSITION. *There is a monetary equilibrium if and only if there is no barter equilibrium which is Pareto optimal.*

OPTIMALITY PROPOSITION. *If there is a monetary equilibrium, then there is also a monetary equilibrium which is Pareto optimal.*

Note, in particular, that both propositions together imply that there is always some competitive equilibrium (barter or monetary) which is Pareto optimal.

The central issue we address in this paper is how robust these propositions (and their related implications) are to various generalizations of Samuelson's basic model and especially to relaxing the assumption that all households are essentially identical (that is, have the same tastes for and endowments of physical commodities except for date of birth).

It would hardly be surprising if such relaxation required some qualification or modification of the propositions. It is quite surprising, however, that with the introduction of what amounts to fairly routine variety in tastes and endowments — judged by that typically encountered in general equilibrium theory — neither proposition survives in any recognizable form. Specifically, we show that the consumption loan model with heterogeneous households (and, upon occasion, other extensions) yields the following sorts of counterexamples:

COEXISTENCE EXAMPLE. *There are both barter and monetary equilibria which are Pareto optimal.*

NONOPTIMALITY EXAMPLE. *There are both barter and monetary equilibria, but none which is Pareto optimal.*

While there is some degree of speciality to our examples, especially those exhibiting nonoptimality, this seems dictated more by our maintained simplifying assumptions — that there is effectively just a single common good (though perhaps more than one physical commodity) in each period and that each household survives at most two periods — than by any inherent feature of the issues involved.

The significance of the coexistence examples may not be immediately apparent. But in fact they do carry an important message. On the one hand, these examples clearly demonstrate that there is no observable criterion for determining whether the existence of fiat money as a store of value is necessary to support the Pareto optimality of competitive equilibrium. On the other hand, much more critically, they graphically illustrate one basic difficulty encountered in assigning a normative role to fiat money: the wide extent of nonuniqueness of monetary equilibrium. Even when the presence of money (trading for commodities at some suitable positive price) can surely guarantee the Pareto optimality of competitive equilibrium, the competitive mechanism by itself offers no assurance whatsoever that it will. *Indeed, our coexistence examples strongly suggest that in general something like continuous monitoring of the price level may be an indispensable component of an otherwise neutral monetary (or more accurately, fiscal) policy.*

It is the nonoptimality examples, however, which convey the central message we have to communicate. These examples dramatically highlight a second, even more fundamental difficulty with relying on the mere creation of fiat money to conjure up an effective appeal to the second basic theorem of welfare economics: the limited scope of once-and-for-all augmentation of initial wealth. Just the presence of money (trading for commodities at any conceivable positive price) may possibly not guarantee the Pareto optimality of competitive equilibrium. *Indeed, our nonoptimality examples strongly suggest that in general something like continuous redistribution by means of creation (or destruction) of fiat money may be an indispensable lubricant for the efficient operation of an evolving market economy.*

The plan of the paper is as follows. A partially generalized consumption loan model is described in section 2. Section 3 contains a review of the leading special case, Samuelson's basic model. The core examples, exhibiting the coexistence of both barter and monetary equilibria which are Pareto optimal and the nonexistence of any competitive equilibrium which is Pareto optimal, are presented in sections 4 and 5, respectively. Finally, the Appendix contains some technical results we require involving the construction of offer curves (or equivalently, indifference maps) exhibiting various special properties.

2. The Basic Model

The economy begins operation in period 1 and continues over periods extending indefinitely into the future $t = 1,2,\ldots$. In each period there are two commodities, one a perishable physical *good* (its various quantities are subscripted by the period in which it is available), the other an imperishable fiat *money*. Households or *consumers* (whose various attributes are superscripted by the order in which they are born, say, $h = 0,1,\ldots$) are either present at the inception of the economy, in which case they live out the balance of their lives during period 1, or born at the beginning of each period $t \geqq 1$, in which case they live out the whole of their lives during that and the succeeding period. Thus in each period there are always just two age groups of consumers, an older *generation* born in the preceding period, say, G_{t-1}, and a younger generation born in the current period G_t. For the most part we will only be concerned with one or the other of the two simplest conceivable demographic patterns, namely, that either $G_t = \{t\}$ for $t \geqq 0$ (each generation consists of a single consumer) or $G_0 = \{0\}$ and $G_t = \{2t-1,2t\}$ for $t \geqq 1$ (the oldest generation consists of a single consumer, and each succeeding generation consists of two consumers).[2]

Each consumer in each generation $h \in G_t$, $t \geqq 0$ (potentially) derives satisfaction or *utility* U^h from consuming goods during her or his lifetime $c^h = c_1^h$ for $h \in G_0$ and $c^h = (c_t^h, c_{t+1}^h)$ for $h \in G_t$, $t \geqq 1$. This fundamental economic hypothesis is represented by a utility function $U^h = U^h(c^h)$ for $c^h \geqq 0$, herein typically assumed to be at least continuous and quasi-concave (that is, to exhibit a diminishing marginal rate of substitution) and to have no local maxima (that is, to exhibit local nonsatiation).[3] Each consumer also has given endowments of the goods available during her or his lifetime $y^h = y_1^h > 0$ for $h \in G_0$ and $y^h = (y_t^h, y_{t+1}^h) \geqslant 0$ for $h \in G_t$, $t \geqq 1$, while each consumer in the oldest generation has a given endowment of money $m^h > 0$ for $h \in G_0$. We assume that the total amount of money in the economy consists of one unit $\Sigma_{h \in G_0} m^h = 1$ (so that if $G_0 = \{0\}$, then $m^0 = 1$), which amounts to defining the monetary unit. Finally, each consumer can buy and sell (within physical and temporal capabilities) either goods or money on both a spot and a one-period futures market at perfectly foreseen (present value) *prices*, denoted p_t and p_m, respectively.[4] Given these opportunities, each consumer chooses a

[2]Some asymmetry in treating the start of the economy is unavoidable, since, for example, consumers in the oldest generation have only themselves to deal with during their first period of life. For this reason we will typically streamline the various incarnations of our basic model by simply assuming that the oldest generation consists of just a single consumer. It can be easily verified that nothing we have to say depends critically on this particular simplification.

We should also emphasize at the outset that, unlike most of the literature, our specializations of the consumption loan model will always involve a stationary population (at least after period 1). Once again, nothing depends critically on this particular simplification, and it has the great virtue of completely avoiding the notational clutter inevitably associated with modeling a growing population.

[3]Except in one case (in section 5.2), we always maintain that these properties obtain for the tastes of consumers in the oldest generation. Since the relevant aspect of their lifetime consumption profiles is a single quantity, this simply means that they have utility functions which are continuous and strictly increasing.

Likewise, we will almost invariably assume that, for every good, there is some consumer who has a utility function which is everywhere strictly increasing in that good. The practical import of this hypothesis is that in a competitive equilibrium, every goods price will be positive (see the definition in the next paragraph and the subsequent discussion of the characterization of potential competitive equilibria).

[4]Generally, we should write the price of money p_{mt}. However, if we expand the budget con-

lifetime consumption profile rationally, that is, as some optimal solution to the budget constrained utility maximization problem

$$(1)\qquad \begin{aligned} &\text{maximize} && U^h(c_1^h) \\ &\text{subject to} && c_1^h \leqq y_1^h + p_m m^h \\ &\text{and} && c_1^h \geqq 0 \quad \text{for } h \in G_0 \end{aligned}$$

and

$$(2)\qquad \begin{aligned} &\text{maximize} && U^h(c^h) \\ &\text{subject to} && p_t c_t^h + p_{t+1} c_{t+1}^h \leqq p_t y_t^h + p_{t+1} y_{t+1}^h \\ &\text{and} && c^h \geqq 0 \quad \text{for } h \in G_t,\ t \geqq 1. \end{aligned}$$

Aggregate consistency in these choices completes the model. A *competitive equilibrium* is a set of positive goods prices, together with a nonnegative price of money, and optimal lifetime consumption profiles satisfying market clearing

$$(3)\qquad \sum_{h\in G_{t-1}\cup G_t} c_t^h = \sum_{h\in G_{t-1}\cup G_t} y_t^h \text{ or } \sum_{h\in G_{t-1}} (c_t^h - y_t^h) = \sum_{h\in G_t} -(c_t^h - y_t^h) \quad \text{for } t \geqq 1.$$

As suggested in the introduction, an important distinction will be that between a *barter equilibrium,* a competitive equilibrium in which $p_m = 0$, and a *monetary equilibrium,* a competitive equilibrium in which $p_m > 0$. Also, we will occasionally refer to the set of lifetime consumption profiles corresponding to some competitive equilibrium as a *competitive allocation*. In contrast, a *feasible allocation* (explicitly taking the notion of perishable physical goods to entail free disposal) is simply a set of nonnegative lifetime consumption profiles satisfying materials balance

$$(4)\qquad \sum_{h\in G_{t-1}\cup G_t} c_t^h \leqq \sum_{h\in G_{t-1}\cup G_t} y_t^h \quad \text{for } t \geqq 1.$$

To complete the list of standard definitions in this context, we define a particular feasible allocation (for instance, some competitive allocation), say, $\{c^{h\prime}\}$, to be *Pareto optimal* if there is no other feasible allocation $\{c^{h\prime\prime}\}$ such that

$$U^h(c^{h\prime\prime}) \geqq U^h(c^{h\prime}) \quad \text{for all } h \geqq 0$$

straint in (2) below to reflect such opportunities,

$$\begin{cases} p_t c_t^h + p_{t+1} c_{t+1}^h + p_{mt}\Delta m_t^h + p_{mt+1}\Delta m_{t+1}^h \leqq p_t y_t^h + p_{t+1} y_{t+1}^h \\ \Delta m_t^h \geqq 0 \\ \Delta m_{t+1}^h \geqq -\Delta m_t^h \end{cases}$$

where Δm_s^h represents the purchases (or sales, when negative) of money during period $s = t, t+1$ by consumer h, then an obvious arbitrage argument entails that in a competitive equilibrium $p_{mt} = p_m$ for $t \geqq 1$. For this reason we have chosen simply to adopt this requirement as a postulate and correspondingly (and legitimately) to ignore transactions on the money markets except insofar as they affect the oldest generation's demand for goods.

(5) and

$$U^h(c^{h''}) > U^h(c^{h'}) \quad \text{for some } h \geqq 0.$$

The foregoing description of an economy generally differs from the canonical consumption loan model in only one significant respect, namely, in admitting the possibility of heterogeneity in tastes for and endowments of goods both within and across generations. While it is this degree of freedom which plays a dominant role in our analysis, there are several additional, minor variations which we will also call upon for support.

- *Availability of a second perishable physical commodity*. Formally, such a commodity can be accounted for merely by reinterpreting c, y, and p as 2-vectors. However, for our particular purposes it will be less confusing to introduce a more clearly distinct notation for the quantity, endowment, and (present value, that is, with the first commodity in period 1 as numeraire) price of this second commodity, x, w, and q, respectively.
- *Shorter (or longer) lifetimes*. For this extension we will simply adopt the formality of reinterpreting c^h and y^h — or (c^h,x^h) and (y^h,w^h) — and their aggregate counterparts as needs be.
- *Money endowments to consumers in other than the oldest generation*. This extension is easily accomplished by specifying that such endowments occur in the second period of life $m^h = m^h_{t+1}$ for $h \in G_t$, $t \geqq 1$, and including their present value on the right-hand side of the budget constraint in (2). (In particular instances, some of these endowments may be negative, or may correspond to taxes rather than subsidies.)

The virtue — and, as with moral rectitude, limitation — of our basic model is that because there is only a single good available and a single period overlap the set of potential competitive equilibria can be succinctly characterized. In particular, define [presupposing (1), (2), and (3)]

z_t = excess demand by generation $t-1$ for the good in their second period of life

$$= \sum_{h\in G_{t-1}} (c^h_t - y^h_t)$$

$$= \sum_{h\in G_t} -(c^h_t - y^h_t)$$

= excess supply by generation t of the good in their first period of life

and

$$g_t = \Big\{(z_t,z_{t+1}) : (z_t,z_{t+1}) = \sum_{h\in G_t} [-(c^h_t - y^h_t), (c^h_{t+1} - y^h_{t+1})]$$

such that for some $(p_t,p_{t+1}) > 0$, (c^h_t,c^h_{t+1}) is an optimal solution to (2) for $h\in G_t\Big\}$

= *reflected generational offer curve* of generation t

for $t \geqq 1$. Now note that $z_1 = \Sigma_{h \in G_0} (c_1^h - y_1^h) = \Sigma_{h \in G_0} p_m m^h = p_m$ while, by suitable choice of the units for measuring the good in each period, $\Sigma_{h \in G_t} y_t^h = y > 0$ for $t \geqq 1$.[5] Then it is easily seen that the set of potential competitive equilibria is essentially equivalent to the set of solutions to the fundamental dynamical system

$$z_1 \geqq 0$$

(6) and

$$(z_t, z_{t+1}) \in g_t \text{ and } z_t \leqq y \text{ for } t \geqq 1.^6$$

In other words, given the basic data describing population structure G_t for $t \geqq 0$ and individual tastes and endowments U^h and y^h for $h \in G_t$, $t \geqq 0$, the potential evolution of the economy is completely captured, in terms of the reduced data describing reflected generational offer curves g_t for $t \geqq 1$ and aggregate first-period endowment y, by means of the system (6). For future reference, it will be useful to bear in mind that, except possibly for boundary endowments, $0 \in g_t$ for $t \geqq 1$ (so that typically $z_t = 0$ for $t \geqq 0$ is a solution to (6)—which means, of course, that there is some barter equilibrium), while if $(z_t, z_{t+1}) \in g_t$, then

$$z_{t+1} \begin{Bmatrix} > \\ = \end{Bmatrix} 0 \text{ according as } z_t \begin{Bmatrix} > \\ = \end{Bmatrix} 0$$

(so that every solution to (6) is nonnegative—which is, of course, our prime motivation for employing the reflected offer curve rather than the standard offer curve itself). Moreover, perhaps most importantly, points on the reflected generational offer curve which also represent competitive allocations must satisfy the equation

$$z_{t+1}/z_t = p_t/p_{t+1} = 1 + r_t = \text{one plus the } \textit{real rate of return} \text{ from period } t \text{ to period } t+1.^7$$

The core of our analysis involves focusing on a series of special cases, that is, detailed specifications of G_t, U^h, and y^h and hence g_t and y, and answering

[5]This maneuver presumes that $y_t^h > 0$ for some $h \in G_t$ for all $t \geqq 1$. Otherwise, the upper bound in (6) must be written $\bar{z}_t$, a $0 - y$ variable. We will refer to such a polar situation only once in the sequel (see the second example of nonstationarity, that involving only endowments, presented in section 5.1 below). In one other case (the third example in the same subsection) we will deliberately choose to streamline the description of a specific model by explicitly employing natural units for measuring the good in each period, so that the upper bound in (6) must also be written generally as $\bar{z}_t = \Sigma_{h \in G_t} y_t^h$.

[6]It should be immediately apparent from the definitions of z_t and g_t that a competitive equilibrium yields a solution to (6). But the reverse argument only requires observing that, in the definition of g_t, goods prices can be normalized so that they constitute a consistent sequence. This is because prices are assumed positive, while consumers are assumed rational [so that, among other things, those in each generation $t \geqq 2$ correctly perceive that they are unaffected by equiproportional shifts in the goods prices directly relevant to them (p_t, p_{t+1})].

[7]When $z_t = 0$ for $t \geqq 1$, this equation amounts to a definition of 0/0 (and it is obviously necessary to go back to the basic data to uncover the potential paths of the real rate of return r_t for $t \geqq 1$).

the following sorts of fundamental questions:

- What are the solutions to (6) and thus (1)–(3)? In particular (knowing that there is a barter equilibrium), is there a monetary equilibrium? In fact (assuming replication in the basic data), is there a stationary monetary equilibrium?
- What properties do these solutions exhibit? In particular, is some barter equilibrium Pareto optimal? If not, is some monetary equilibrium?

Partly as an exercise to gain familiarity with technique, but mostly as a review to provide foundation for comparison, we turn first to utilizing (6) to analyze the competitive equilibria in Samuelson's basic model.

3. Samuelson's Basic Model

Samuelson's central story (and more) can be fully elaborated in terms of the leading special case of our model, where each generation consists of just a single consumer, so that $G_t = \{t\}$ for $t \geqq 0$, and each consumer but the oldest has the same utility function, so that $U^t(c^t) = U(c^t)$ for $t \geqq 1$ — where $U = U(c_1,c_2)$ for $(c_1,c_2) \geqq 0$ is assumed to be differentiable (but, for simplicity, with $[\partial U(0,y)/\partial c_1] = [\partial U(x,0)/\partial c_2] = \infty$ for $(x,y) > 0$), strictly quasi-concave and strictly increasing — as well as the same positive endowments, so that $y^t = (y_1,y_2) > 0$ for $t \geqq 1$.[8] The critical feature of this case is that, besides being stationary, the reflected generational offer curve derives from the rational behavior of the representative consumer, so that

$$g_t = g = \Bigg\{(z_1,z_2) : \text{for some } (p_1,p_2) > 0\ (-z_1,z_2) \geqq -(y_1,y_2),$$

$$\frac{\partial U(-z_1 + y_1, z_2 + y_2)}{\partial c_1} \Bigg/ \frac{\partial U(-z_1 + y_1, z_2 + y_2)}{\partial c_2} = p_1/p_2,$$

$$\text{and } -p_1 z_1 + p_2 z_2 = 0\Bigg\}$$

for $t \geqq 1$, as illustrated in Figures 1 and 2.

From careful study of these figures, it becomes apparent that this particular feature has two important consequences for the structure of g, the solutions to (6), and thus the nature of competitive equilibrium. First, g intersects the origin just once. In other words, there is a unique (stationary) barter equilibrium, supported by prices $p_1 = 1$, $p_t/p_{t+1} = 1 + r_t = 1 + r$ for $t \geqq 1$ and $p_m = 0$, and yielding the autarkic allocation $c_1^0 = y_1^0$ and $(c_t^t, c_{t+1}^t) = (y_1,y_2)$ for $t \geqq 1$. (Here, as in what follows, we utilize notation which is either formally defined in the text or informally defined in the various accompanying fig-

[8] In this case, as in some others later on, there is no need to distinguish h from t, except insofar as the former appears as a superscript, the latter as a subscript.

It is also worth remarking that consumer 0's tastes and endowments (of goods) can also be assumed the same as any consumer t's, merely by reinterpreting $U^0(c_1^0) = U(y_1,c_1^0)$ and $y_1^0 = y_2$. More generally, in each of the special cases we treat later on in which both tastes and endowments are essentially stationary, we can reinterpret the model so that generation 0 is identical to generation $t \geqq 1$ except for date of birth and absence of ancestors (or, more accurately, ancestors who participate in the market economy). The possibility of such reinterpretation provides the main justification for the assertion made at the end of the first paragraph in footnote 2.

Figure 1
Potential Competitive Equilibria in Samuelson's Basic Model:
Just a Single Barter Equilibrium

$$\left(\frac{\partial U\,(y_1, y_2)}{\partial c_1} \bigg/ \frac{\partial U\,(y_1, y_2)}{\partial c_2} = 1 + r \geqq 1 \right)$$

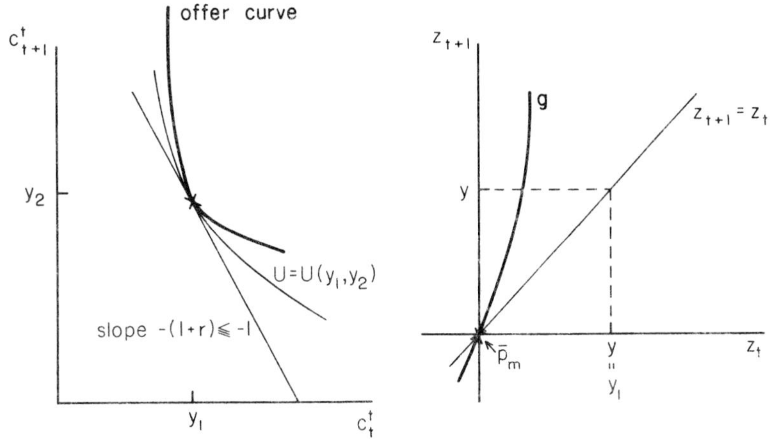

Ia. Consumer Behavior

Ib. Dynamical System

Figure 2
Potential Competitive Equilibria in Samuelson's Basic Model:
Also a Continuum of Monetary Equilibria

$$\left(\frac{\partial U\,(y_1, y_2)}{\partial c_1} \bigg/ \frac{\partial U\,(y_1, y_2)}{\partial c_2} = 1 + r < 1 \right)$$

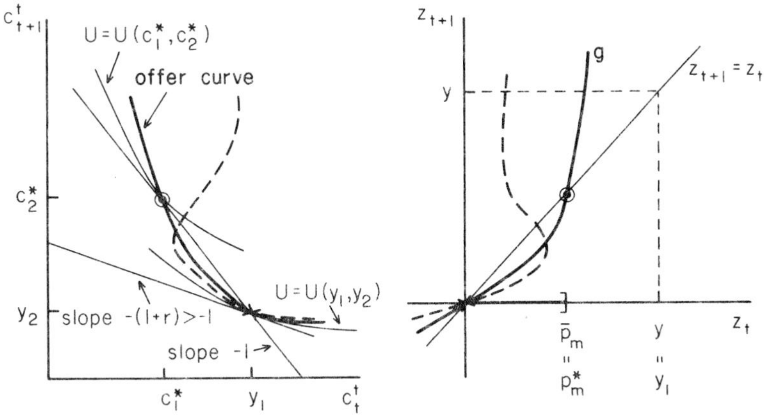

2a. Consumer Behavior

2b. Dynamical System

ures.) Second, in addition, g intersects the 45° line in the positive quadrant, just once, if and only if it has slope less than one at the origin. In other words, there will also be a unique stationary monetary equilibrium, supported by prices $p_1 = 1$, $p_t/p_{t+1} = 1 + r_t = 1$ for $t \geqq 1$, and $p_m = p_m^*$, and yielding the trading allocation $c_1^0 = y_1^0 + (y_1 - c_1^*)$ and $(c_t^t, c_{t+1}^t) = (c_1^*, c_2^*)$ for $t \geqq 1$—where $p_m^* = y_1 - c_1^* > 0$ or $c_1^* < y_1$ and $c_2^* > y_2$—if and only if $1 + r < 1$. In short, the dichotomy emphasized earlier in section 1 ultimately depends simply on the magnitude of the representative consumer's marginal rate of substitution at her/his endowments

$$\frac{\partial U(y_1,y_2)}{\partial c_1} \Big/ \frac{\partial U(y_1,y_2)}{\partial c_2} = 1 + r.$$

Continuing with an explicit description of that dichotomy, and with heavy reliance on graphical intuition and argument, we notice next that, in fact, there will be a whole range of monetary equilibria, corresponding to prices of money satisfying $0 < p_m \leqq \bar{p}_m$, if and only if there is a stationary monetary equilibrium, that is, once again, $1 + r < 1$.[9] This situation is suggestively exemplified in Figure 3, which contrasts the two possible cases. On the one hand, in the "normal" case (pictured in Figure 3a) we have $\bar{p}_m = p_m^*$, so that if $p_m = \bar{p}_m$, then competitive equilibrium is necessarily the stationary monetary one, while if $p_m < \bar{p}_m$, then competitive allocation necessarily converges monotonically to the representative consumer's endowments. On the other hand, in the "abnormal" case (pictured in Figure 3b) we have $\bar{p}_m > p_m^*$, so that evidently matters are not nearly so transparent. Indeed, in this case, there generally need not be just a single competitive equilibrium corresponding to each (sufficiently large) price of money, nor even any recognizable pattern to the asymptotic behavior of competitive allocation, even though we have chosen to depict a competitive equilibrium which replicates cyclically every two periods.[10]

These various cases (that is, $1 + r \geqq 1$ or $1 + r < 1$ and "normality" or "abnormality") have their counterparts in terms of welfare implications. In particular, using the fact that U is assumed strictly quasi-concave—so that transfers from consumer $t + 1$ to consumer $t - 1$ via consumer t, transfers which also (at least) maintain the intermediary consumer's welfare, necessarily involve increasingly unfavorable real terms of trade between good t and good $t + 1$—it can be easily demonstrated that if $1 + r \geqq 1$, then the barter equilibrium is Pareto optimal, while if $1 + r < 1$, then the stationary

[9] A note of warning. Here, as in the sequel, we take for granted that every solution to (6) must satisfy $z_1 \leqq \bar{p}_m \leqq y$, where $\bar{p}_m$ depends on both g_t and y in a way which should be obvious from the diagram representing the relevant dynamical system. Otherwise, when $z_1 > \bar{p}_m$, there will be some $\bar{t} < \infty$ such that either $z_{\bar{t}} > y$ or $z_{\bar{t}} \leqq y$, but there is no z such that $(z_{\bar{t}}, z) \in g_{\bar{t}}$, both of which are inconsistent with (6).

[10] Artistically inclined readers can surely sketch examples with much longer periodicity once they are reminded that the only significant restrictions on g's behavior in the positive quadrant are that it be continuous, when interpreted as a function of the variable $p_1/p_2 \geqq 1 + r$, and that it intersect each sufficiently positively sloped ray through the origin $z_{t+1} = (p_1/p_2)z_t$, but just once. (See too the introductory comments in the Appendix). We should also note that our labeling of this second case is not to be taken seriously (paranoically?). The "abnormal" case, which was apparently first mentioned in the literature by Gale (1973), seems just as likely as the "normal" case, even if it is much more bothersome, because it so clearly displays the ambiguity inherent in the actual evolution of monetary equilibrium. We shall have more to say about the implications of this characteristic sort of nonuniqueness in the following section.

Figure 3
Examples of Both Stationary (◉) and Nonstationary (• • •)
Monetary Equilibria in Samuelson's Basic Model

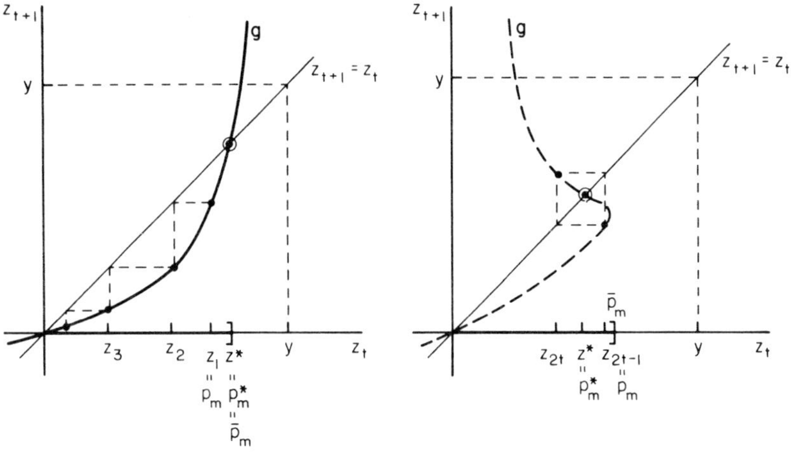

3a. The "Normal" Case   3b. The "Abnormal" Case

monetary equilibrium is Pareto optimal.[11] In contrast, but again explicitly using the fact that U is assumed strictly quasi-concave — so that $U(c_1,c_2) < U(c_1^*,c_2^*)$ for every $c_1 + c_2 \leqq y_1 + y_2$ such that $(c_1,c_2) \neq (c_1^*,c_2^*)$ — if $1 + r < 1$, then in the "normal" case the allocation corresponding to each competitive equilibrium (barter or monetary) except the stationary monetary one is strictly dominated by that corresponding to the latter. In other words, in this case, neither the barter equilibrium nor any nonstationary monetary equilibrium is Pareto optimal.

For the same basic reason, in the "abnormal" case neither the barter equilibrium nor any nonstationary monetary equilibrium yielding the same (endowments) allocation asymptotically — that is, such that $\lim_{t\to\infty} z_t = 0$ — is Pareto optimal. But in this case, the general welfare status of the nonstationary monetary equilibria is mixed, since every competitive equilibrium such that $\limsup_{t\to\infty} z_t > 0$ is in fact Pareto optimal — including, for instance, the specific periodic equilibrium depicted in Figure 3b. (For the sake of brevity we forego justifying this assertion, which is also referenced in the following section; the argument is quite straightforward but rather tedious.)

Given our present purposes, the foregoing descriptive analysis of Samuelson's basic model has already been aptly summarized by the two propositions stated in section 1. We now proceed to the heart of the paper, to the demonstration that these properties are actually very model-bound. Before doing so, however, we might well underline that in each of the following arguments we will utilize essentially the same graphical heuristic utilized here (though

[11]These results (and their parallels in the subsequent sections) are so well-known that they hardly require documentation; for completeness' sake, however, we refer skeptically minded readers to Starrett's (1972) neat general argument. Note also that such results may be falsified (in case $1 + r \leqq 1$) when U is not assumed to be strictly quasi-concave, as in Shell's (1971) nice expository piece.

bolstered now and then by analytical means). We take this rehearsal as providing license to be somewhat terse in presentation, if not also in interpretation.

4. Coexistence of Both Barter and Monetary Equilibria Which Are Pareto Optimal

The model underlying the two examples presented in this section differs in only one essential respect from Samuelson's basic model, to wit, in that there are two distinct types of consumers in every generation but the oldest. More specifically, suppose now that $G_0 = \{0\}$ and $G_t = \{2t-1, 2t\}$ for $t \geqq 1$ and that the odd-numbered consumers are of α-type, so that $U^h(c^h) = U^\alpha(c^h)$ and $y^h = y^\alpha > 0$ for $h = 2t-1$, $t \geqq 1$, and the even-numbered of β-type, so that $U^h(c^h) = U^\beta(c^h)$ and $y^h = y^\beta > 0$ for $h = 2t$, $t \geqq 1$—where generally $U^\alpha \neq U^\beta$ and $y^\alpha \neq y^\beta$. Even this seemingly minor modification, by permitting greater freedom in specifying the reflected generational offer curves (which are, as before, stationary over time $g_t = g$ for $t \geqq 1$), entails fundamentally contrary consequences for the conclusions outlined in the preceding section. The most important of these, and the one we detail here, is illustrated by the two examples shown in Figures 4 and 5.

The key feature of these counterexamples is that in the first (respectively, second) when the real rate of return is zero, $p_1/p_2 = 1$, the β-type consumer wants to save more (less) than the α-consumer wants to dissave during their mutual first period of life, that is, in Figure 4, $a < b$ (in Figure 5, $a > b$), and when the real rate of return is—within an appropriate bound—higher, $1 \leqq p_1/p_2 \leqq \bar{R}$ (lower, $\underline{R} \leqq p_1/p_2 \leqq 1$), the α-type consumer has a vertical segment on the offer curve, and the β-type a horizontal, that is, c_t^h is constant for $h = 2t - 1$, and c_{t+1}^h for $h = 2t$.[12] Thus, in order to simplify their presentation, these specific examples embody somewhat extreme behavior, since (partly) vertical or horizontal offer curves implicitly require a region of inferiority for the good with unchanged consumption. Verification that this specialization is only a convenient simplification we leave as an exercise; verification that it is also a legitimate simplification we leave to the Appendix.

The critical similarity in these counterexamples is that they each display multiple stationary barter equilibria,[13] ranging from one which is Pareto optimal (corresponding to goods prices $p_t = (1 + \bar{r})^{-(t-1)}$ for $t \geqq 1$) to one which isn't (corresponding to goods prices $p_t = (1 + \underline{r})^{-(t-1)}$ for $t \geqq 1$). Their critical dissimilarity is that the first (in this sense analogous to that pictured in Figure 2) also has a single stationary monetary equilibrium—which is, of course (by virtue of its corresponding zero real rate of return), Pareto optimal—while the second (in this sense analogous to that pictured in Figure 1) hasn't. Reflecting on these two considerations, mainly by literally drawing their

[12]The upper bound $\bar{R}$ respectively, lower bound $\underline{R}$) is chosen so that the length of the vertical and horizontal segments of the respective consumers' offer curves is greater than $b - a$ $(a - b)$. This choice guarantees (see directly below) that there are at least two stationary barter equilibria with positive (negative) real rate of return.

[13]Since in consumption loan type models with only a single-period overlap between generations barter involves just trade between contemporaries, this also means that barter equilibria needn't be stationary, nor even periodic (see, however, the closing remark to this section). For instance, there is an irregular barter equilibrium corresponding to goods prices which satisfy

$$p_t/p_{t+1} = \begin{cases} 1 + \bar{r} & \text{for } t = 2^s,\ s \geqq 0 \\ 1 + \underline{r} & \text{otherwise.} \end{cases}$$

Figure 4
Coexistence With Stationary Monetary Equilibrium ($a < b$)

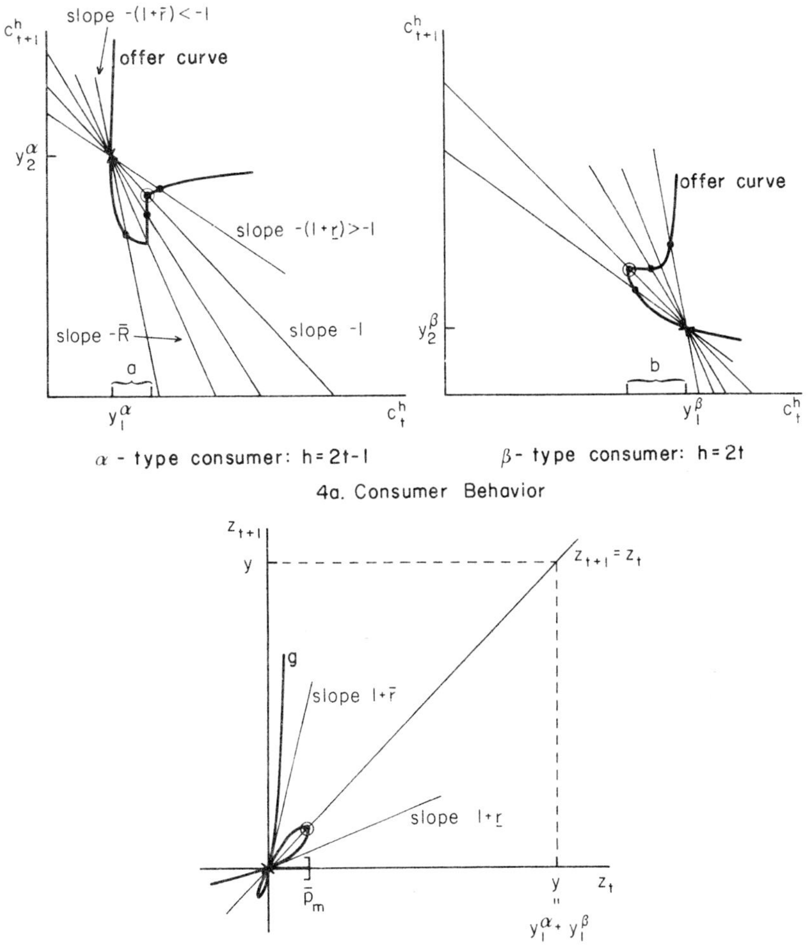

4b. Dynamical System

implications for the solutions to (6) (in diagrams like Figures 4b and 5b), leads to the following important conclusions. On the one hand, in general, there is no direct connection between the level of the price of money and any descriptive or prescriptive properties of competitive equilibrium. On the other hand, in particular, there is no necessary relationship between the potentiality for monetary equilibrium and the optimality of barter equilibrium.

Moreover, the second example suggests an even more striking conclusion. Suppose we ignore the possibility of barter equilibrium (especially the possibility of any which is Pareto optimal)—either on practical grounds (observing that monetary institutions are intrinsic to all but the most primitive societies) or, perhaps better, on theoretical grounds (appealing to the extensions of Samuelson's basic model employed to construct the examples elaborated in the last two parts of the following section). Then this economy has the property that, though there are competitive equilibria which are Pareto optimal (again, as in the "abnormal" case of Samuelson's basic model, essentially characterized by the condition lim $\sup_{t\to\infty} z_t > 0$), these may be neither easily discernible nor, on any reasonable grounds, expectedly laissez-faire. In particular, it is straightforward to establish that for large enough

Figure 5
Coexistence With Nonstationary Monetary Equilibrium ($a > b$)

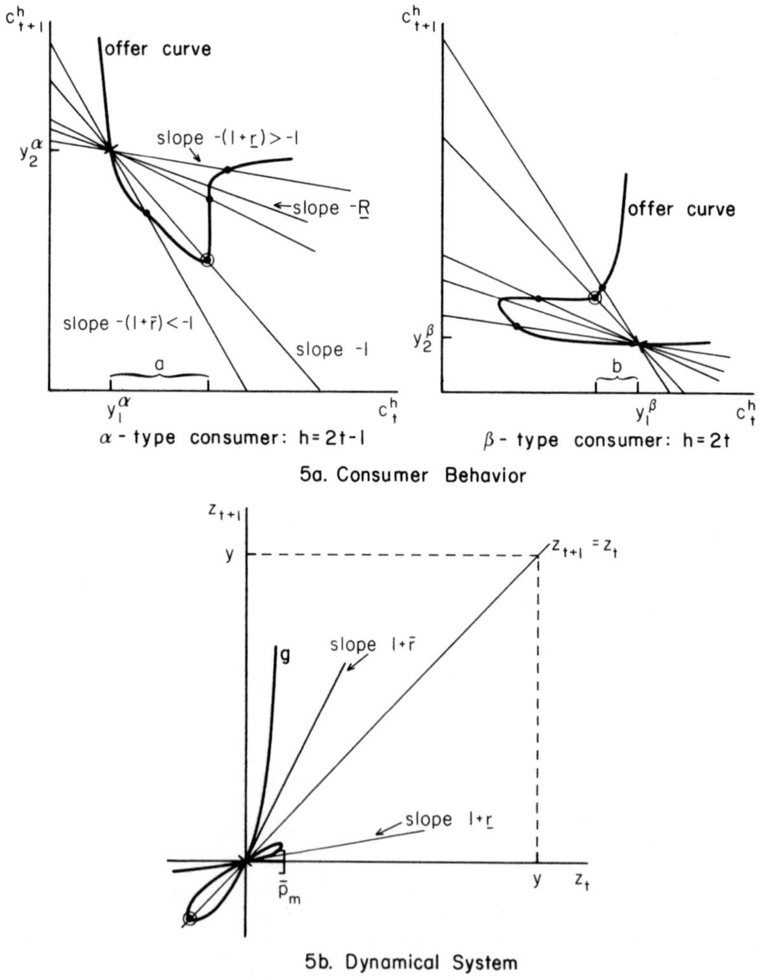

values of $\overline{r} > 0$ (or $\underline{r} < 0$), the smallest periodicity of any competitive equilibrium which replicates cyclically and which is also Pareto optimal may be arbitrarily large.[14]

In thus emphasizing the importance of periodicity (of which stationarity is the simplest realization) we are tacitly embracing the widely held professional belief that, in order for perfect foresight (or, more fashionably, rational expectations) to be a reasonable description of individual accommodation to uncertainty, there must be sufficient regularity of aggregate outcomes—so that, for example, correct information about the past provides a sound basis for accurate prediction of the future.

5. Nonexistence of Any Competitive Equilibrium (Barter or Monetary) Which Is Pareto Optimal

Merely enlarging on Samuelson's basic model by permitting heterogeneity within each generation does not alter its central welfare implication. In such an economy, there is always some competitive equilibrium which is Pareto optimal, in fact, one which is also stationary (or, alternatively, monetary, provided that such equilibria exist). Here we present a recital of examples denying even the generality of this proposition, counterexamples which depend, in order of their appearance at center stage, on nonstationarity in tastes and endowments (or heterogeneity across succeeding generations), nonmonotonicity in tastes (or satiation from immoderate consumption), and nonconvexity in tastes (or enhancement from unbalanced consumption).

Among these examples we can distinguish a core (specifically, the subset including only those pictured in Figures 7, 9, 10, and 11), the significance of which extends far beyond their immediate bad tiding. In brief, these particular examples suggest a potentially persuasive argument in favor of continued, conscious government intervention in the competitive market process, one which doesn't rely on paucity of information, singularity of externalities, or any of the other standard reasons for market failure. Rather, this case rests squarely on their general, fundamental welfare implication: *There may be no once-and-for-all redistribution of wealth between the members of any finite number of generations which will permit the competitive mechanism unaided to attain a socially desirable allocation.*

The validity of this assertion can be easily established simply by formalizing all such restricted wealth transfers in terms of alternative distributions of money endowments (referring for details to the comment following our description of the basic model in section 2). Now, each of the core examples, including that which depends on nonstationarity, has a very important characteristic: The particular period during which markets first open (heretofore always taken as period 1) is essentially immaterial to the behavior of the economy in that and each succeeding period—provided that only the then current older generation has a money endowment. Moreover, given any finite

[14]Formally, periodic monetary equilibrium requires that for some finite span of periods, or periodicity $1 \leqq \tau < \infty$, goods prices must exhibit the property that $p_{t+\tau} = p_t$ or $\Pi_{s=0}^{\tau-1} (p_{t+s}/p_{t+s+1}) = \Pi_{s=0}^{\tau-1} (1+r_{t+s}) = 1$ for $t \geqq 1$. But in this case, any such periodicity must therefore also satisfy the inequality

$$\min_{1 \leqq \tau' \leqq \tau} (1+\overline{r})^{\tau'} (1+\underline{r})^{\tau-\tau'} = (1+\overline{r})(1+\underline{r})^{\tau-1} < 1$$

from which the assertion in the text follows immediately.

distribution of money endowments, there must always come a period after which the creation (or destruction) of money ceases, or equivalently, in which relative to all later generations only the then current older generation has a money endowment. A fortiori, the demonstration of nonexistence when only the oldest generation has a money endowment, suffices also when, only to some limited extent, other generations have as well.[15]

Having this point always clearly in mind, we are then well prepared to review the various types of counterexamples.

5.1. *Nonstationarity*

The simplest stories involving nonstationarity require only slight perturbations of the most familiar example from Samuelson's basic model, already previously sketched in Figure 2. Explicitly building on that example, suppose now that some maverick consumer $t' \geqq 1$ has either completely inflexible tastes $U^{t'}(c^{t'}) = \min\{c^{t'}_{t'}/y_1, c^{t'}_{t'+1}/y_2\}$ or completely skewed endowments $y^{t'} = (0, y_2)$, while every other consumer is just as before.[16] Then the dynamical system characterizing competitive equilibrium is as shown in Figure 6, which has as its only solution $z_t = 0$ for $t \geqq 1$. In other words, under either of these hypotheses the only competitive equilibrium is the barter one, which is obviously not Pareto optimal since it is possible to improve the welfare of every consumer $t > t'$ (without affecting the welfare of any other consumer $1 \leqq t \leqq t'$) by switching to the alternative allocation

$$c^t = \begin{cases} y^t & \text{for } 1 \leqq t \leqq t' \\ [y_1, y_2 + (y_1 - c_1^*)] & \text{for } t = t' + 1 \\ c^* & \text{otherwise.} \end{cases}$$

Though these examples do illustrate the essential idea underlying the whole argument in this section (namely, to structure tastes and endowments so as to bar any stationary equilibrium which is also Pareto optimal), they have at least two objectionable features. In the first place, the least complicated redistribution schemes which will permit attainment of a socially desirable allocation are all but indistinguishable from the origination of fiat money itself (albeit at some appropriate later date $t > t'$ in the economy's history). In the second place, there is no room left for the existence of any monetary equilibrium (precisely for the same reason there is no room left for the existence of any Pareto optimal equilibrium). A necessarily more complicated example without either of these limitations—so, in particular, with both

[15]This argument is not quite complete, since it implicitly requires that every competitive allocation can be strictly improved upon generation by generation. However, we will in fact demonstrate that this stronger form of Pareto superiority is feasible in each of the core examples.

In this context, it is an interesting problem (though not one we will pursue further here) to characterize the simplest wealth transfers that can be achieved, for instance, by assigning just nonnegative money endowments (that is, ostensibly, by disbursing subsidies rather than collecting taxes) and also that can be instrumental in supporting the Pareto optimality of competitive equilibrium.

[16]Thanks are due Charles Hulten of Johns Hopkins University for pointing out the relevance of the first of these hypotheses for our present purpose. This hypothesis, of course, already introduces an element of satiation. Note too that, for the second hypothesis to be consistent with the existence of competitive equilibrium, we require the boundary condition

$$\frac{\partial U(0,y_2)}{\partial c_1} \bigg/ \frac{\partial U(0,y_2)}{\partial c_2} < \infty.$$

Figure 6
Nonexistence Due to Nonstationarity: Two Examples
With Singularly Shifting Tastes or Endowments

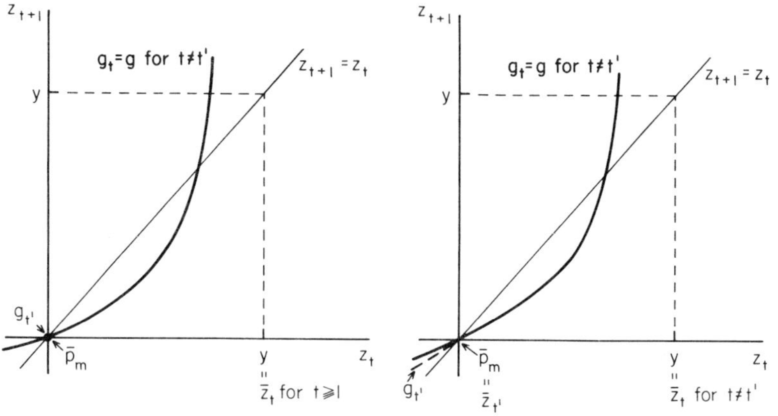

6a. Inflexible Tastes   6b. Skewed Endowments

Figure 7
Nonexistence Due to Nonstationarity: An Example
With Regularly Shifting Tastes and Endowments

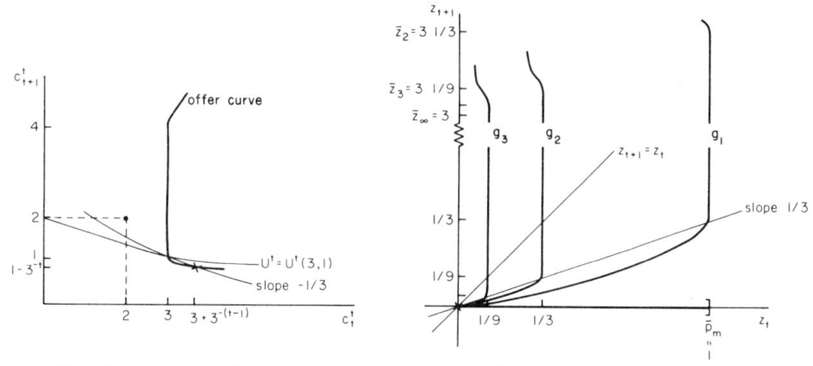

7a. Consumer Behavior   7b. Dynamical System

barter and monetary equilibria—is depicted in Figure 7. Here again we have $G_t = \{t\}$ for $t \geqq 0$, but now U^t is such that it yields an offer curve which has a vertical segment between (3,1) and (3,4) and that it satisfies U^t (2,2) > U^t (3,1),[17] while $y^t = (3 + 3^{-(t-1)}, 1 - 3^{-t})$ for $t \geqq 1$. Close examination of Figure 7

[17]Once again, see the Appendix for detailed instructions on how to lay out an indifference map which yields such an offer curve and yet at the same time satisfies such an additional restriction. In fact, this example doesn't require quite such extreme behavior. The subsequent argument remains true, for instance, provided each offer curve has a segment from (3,1) to (·,4) with slope dc^t_{t+1}/dc^t_t [or average $(c^t_{t+1} - 1)/(c^t_t - 3)$] greater than minus one.

reveals that, although $\bar{p}_m = 1$, every solution to (6) (with the upper bound y suitably replaced by $\bar{z}_t = y_t^t$) must satisfy

$$\frac{\partial U^t(y^t)}{\partial c_t^t} \bigg/ \frac{\partial U^t(y^t)}{\partial c_{t+1}^t} \leqq p_t / p_{t+1} = z_{t+1} / z_t \leqq 1/3 \text{ for } t \geqq 1$$

since otherwise typically there will be some $\bar{t} < \infty$ such that although $z_{\bar{t}} < \bar{z}_{\bar{t}}$, there is no z such that $(z_{\bar{t}}, z) \in g_{\bar{t}}$, which is inconsistent with (6). But from this it follows directly that every competitive allocation is strictly dominated by the stationary allocation

$$c^t = \begin{cases} y_1^0 + 2 & \text{for } t = 0 \\ (2,2) & \text{otherwise} \end{cases}$$

since $U^0(y_1^0 + 2) > U^0(y_1^0 + \bar{p}_m) \geqq U^0(c_1^0)$ for every $c_1^0 \geqq 0$ such that $c_1^0 \leqq y_1^0 + p_m$, and if

$$\frac{\partial U^t(y^t)}{\partial c_t^t} \bigg/ \frac{\partial U^t(y^t)}{\partial c_{t+1}^t} \leqq p_t / p_{t+1} \leqq 1/3,$$

then

$$U^t(2,2) > U^t(3,1) \geqq U^t(c_1, c_2) \text{ for every } (c_1, c_2) \geqq 0$$

$$\text{such that } p_t c_1 + p_{t+1} c_2 \leqq p_t y_t^t + p_{t+1} y_{t+1}^t$$

for $t \geqq 1$ (so that the welfare of every consumer is improved), while $y_1^1 = 4$ and $y_{t+1}^t + y_{t+1}^{t+1} = 4$ for $t \geqq 1$ (so that the allocation is feasible).

5.2. *Nonmonotonicity*

It is well-known that local (and hence global) satiation already raises difficulties for the first basic theorem of welfare economics within the barest standard framework usually employed in expositing the principles of general equilibrium theory. Figure 8 illustrates an example of precisely the same type of difficulty within the present context, an example again patterned after that introduced earlier in Figure 2. Here, because consumer 0 is satiated at the consumption level $\bar{c}_1^0$—well below $y_2 + (y_1 - c_1^*)$—every competitive allocation is dominated by one or the other of two alternatives. On the one side, if $p_m \leqq \bar{c}_1^0 - y_2$, then the competitive allocation converges monotonically to the representative consumer's endowments and is therefore dominated by the stationary allocation (which entails some free disposal of good 1, and hence is itself, for this reason alone, not Pareto optimal)

$$c^t = \begin{cases} \bar{c}_1^0 & \text{for } t = 0 \\ (c_1^*, c_2^*) & \text{otherwise.} \end{cases}$$

On the other side, if $\bar{c}_1^0 - y_2 < p_m \leqq \bar{p}_m$, then—because consumer 0 is "wasting" an amount $p_m - (\bar{c}_1^0 - y_2) > 0$ of good 1—it is dominated by augmenting the first-period consumption of consumer 1 by some (possibly smaller) amount, everything else remaining the same (a feasible allocation which also may fail to be Pareto optimal).

Figure 8
Nonexistence Due to Nonmonotonicity: An Example
With Global Satiation, Especially for the Oldest Generation

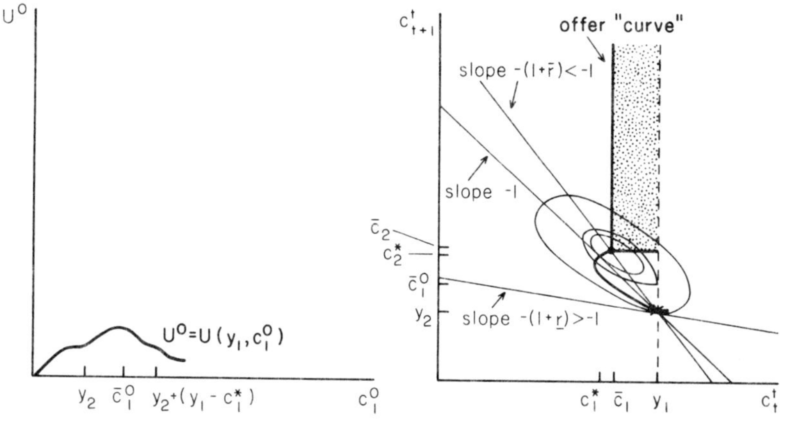

8a. Consumer Behavior

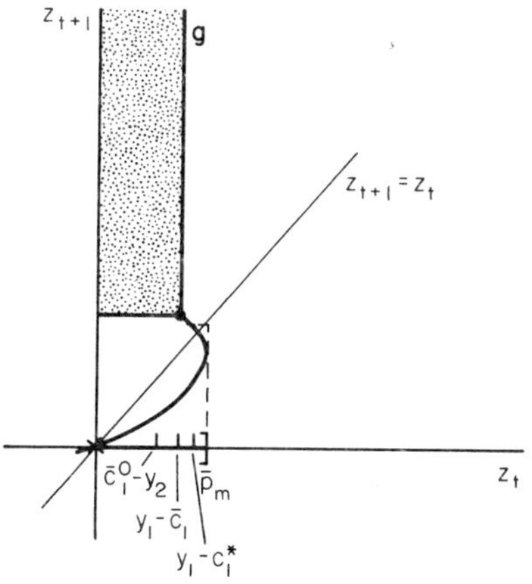

8b. Dynamical System

Since all that this particular argument really requires is that U^0 have a global maximum at a sufficiently low level of consumption, one might sensibly wonder why we've chosen to depict such an apparently unnecessarily complicated example. The sort of intergenerational symmetry consideration remarked in the second paragraph in footnote 8 provides some rationale. A more compelling justification, however, is that the general structure of tastes pictured on the right-hand side of Figure 8a and reflected in Figure 8b suggests the possibility of constructing an example in which some lesser degree of satiation naturally puts a damper on the real rate return, and hence, on the efficacy of the mere presence of money as a restorative for Pareto optimality.

In order to follow up this suggestion, we need first to introduce a second perishable physical commodity. So, as outlined in section 2, suppose now that there is another commodity, the quantity of which is denoted x, the endowment w, and the price q. Furthermore, suppose once more that in each generation but the oldest there are two consumers $G_t = \{2t - 1, 2t\}$ for $t \geqq 1$ whose tastes for and endowments of the two commodities depend only on whether they are odd- or even-numbered. In particular, odd-numbered consumers $h = 2t - 1$ for $t \geqq 1$ are of α-type and have tastes of the form

$$U^h(c^h, x^h) = U^\alpha(c^h) + V(x_t^h)$$

and endowments of the form

$$(y^h, w^h) = (y_1, y_2, w, 0);$$

U^α is differentiable, strictly quasi-concave, and has a global maximum at $(\bar{c}_1^\alpha, \bar{c}_2^\alpha)$, where $\bar{c}_1^\alpha < y_1$, $\bar{c}_2^\alpha > y_2$, and

$$-\frac{\bar{c}_2^\alpha - y_2}{\bar{c}_1^\alpha - y_1} = 1 + \bar{r} < 1,$$

while V is differentiable, concave, and strictly increasing, so that

$$\frac{dV(x)}{dx} > 0.$$

In contrast, even-numbered consumers $h = 2t$ for $t \geqq 1$ are of β-type and have both simpler tastes of the form

$$U^h(c^h, x^h) = U^\beta(c^h)$$

and simpler endowments of the form

$$(y^h, w^h) = (y_1, y_2, 0, 0);$$

U^β is differentiable, strictly quasi-concave, and strictly increasing and also satisfies the condition

$$\frac{\partial U^\beta(y_1, y_2)}{\partial c_1} \Big/ \frac{\partial U^\beta(y_1, y_2)}{\partial c_2} = \frac{\partial U^\alpha(y_1, y_2)}{\partial c_1} \Big/ \frac{\partial U^\alpha(y_1, y_2)}{\partial c_2}$$

$$= 1 + \underline{r} < 1 + \bar{r}.$$

(This last assumption merely eases description of the appropriate reflected generational offer curve.)

After modifying (2) and (3) in an obvious way to accommodate this second commodity (duly noting that all commodity prices must still be positive in order to be consistent with market clearing), we find that for all practical purposes, this example reduces to a very special case of our basic model, by virtue of the following considerations. Only α-type consumers own and value the second commodity. Hence, in every competitive equilibrium it must be true that $x_t^{2t-1} = w$ and $q_t > 0$ for $t \geqq 0$. But such market clearing conditions for the second commodity will be a consequence of rational behavior on the part of α-type consumers only if

$$p_t / p_{t+1} < -\frac{\bar{c}_2^\alpha - y_2}{\bar{c}_1^\alpha - y_1} = 1 + \bar{r} < 1$$

and

$$q_t = \left(\frac{dV(w)}{dx_t^{2t-1}} \bigg/ \frac{\partial U^\alpha (c^{2t-1})}{\partial c_t^{2t-1}} \right) p_t$$

for $t \geqq 1$.[18] In other words, in this example, the appropriate reflected generational offer curve for the purpose of characterizing the set of potential competitive equilibria is derived from the two representative consumers' offer curves under the hypothesis that the price of the second commodity can and does adjust so as to maintain each α-type consumer's demand for the commodity equal to that consumer's supply. This result and its ramifications are pictured in Figure 9.

Two conclusions are immediately deducible from this figure. First, every competitive allocation necessarily converges monotonically to the representative consumers' endowments. Second, and the more significant of the two from our present perspective, every competitive allocation is thus strictly dominated by the stationary allocation

$$c^h = \begin{cases} y_1^0 + (y_1 - \bar{c}_1^\alpha) + (y_1 - c_1^{\beta *}) & \text{for } h = 0 \\ (\bar{c}_1^\alpha, \bar{c}_2^\alpha) & \text{for } h = 2t - 1 \\ [c_1^{\beta *}, c_2^{\beta *} + (y_1 - \bar{c}_1^\alpha) + (y_2 - \bar{c}_2^\alpha)] & \text{otherwise} \end{cases}$$

and

$$x^h = \begin{cases} 0 & \text{for } h = 0 \\ (w, 0) & \text{for } h = 2t-1 \\ 0 & \text{otherwise} \end{cases}$$

for $t \geqq 1$.[19]

[18]The first condition must hold because otherwise, that is, when

$$p_{t'}/p_{t'+1} \geqq -\frac{\bar{c}_2^\alpha - y_2}{\bar{c}_1^\alpha - y_1} = 1 + \bar{r} \text{ for some } t' < \infty$$

consumer $2t' - 1$ would demand $x_{t'}^{2t'-1} > w$. This is because under these circumstances the budget constraint encompasses the lifetime consumption profile

$$(\bar{c}_1^\alpha, \bar{c}_2^\alpha, x) \text{ with } x = w + \frac{p_{t'}(y_1 - \bar{c}_1^\alpha) + p_{t'+1}(y_2 - \bar{c}_2^\alpha)}{q_{t'}} \geqq w$$

while at this particular profile the consumer is completely satiated in both periods' consumption of the first commodity, but not the first-period consumption of the second commodity.

The second condition is then essentially just the first-order requirement for the optimal solution to (2) (suitably expanded) to satisfy $x_{t'}^{2t'-1} = w$ given the first condition.

[19]This assertion implicitly requires that $\bar{p}_m < y_1^0 + (y_1 - \bar{c}_1^\alpha) + (y_1 - c_1^{\beta *})$, a restriction which is easily satisfied, for instance, by specifying the β-consumer's choice of first-period consumption at the real rate of return 0 small enough relative to that same choice at every real rate of return $r \leqq \bar{r} < 0$, everything else unchanged.

Notice especially that this example does in fact presume all consumers being locally nonsatiated, that is, always capable of increasing their utility with some arbitrarily small perturbation in their lifetime consumption profile. Thus, it clearly does not have the common feature of most familiar counterexamples to the first basic theorem of welfare economics. However, it is also clear that the example depends critically on having just the right combination of some consumption satiation together with some boundary endowments; for instance, this special kind of combination is well-known to create problems just for the existence of competitive equilibrium within essentially atemporal models of the allocation of consumption goods. Furthermore,

Figure 9
Nonexistence Due to Nonmonotonicity: An Example
With Global Satiation in the First of Two Commodities

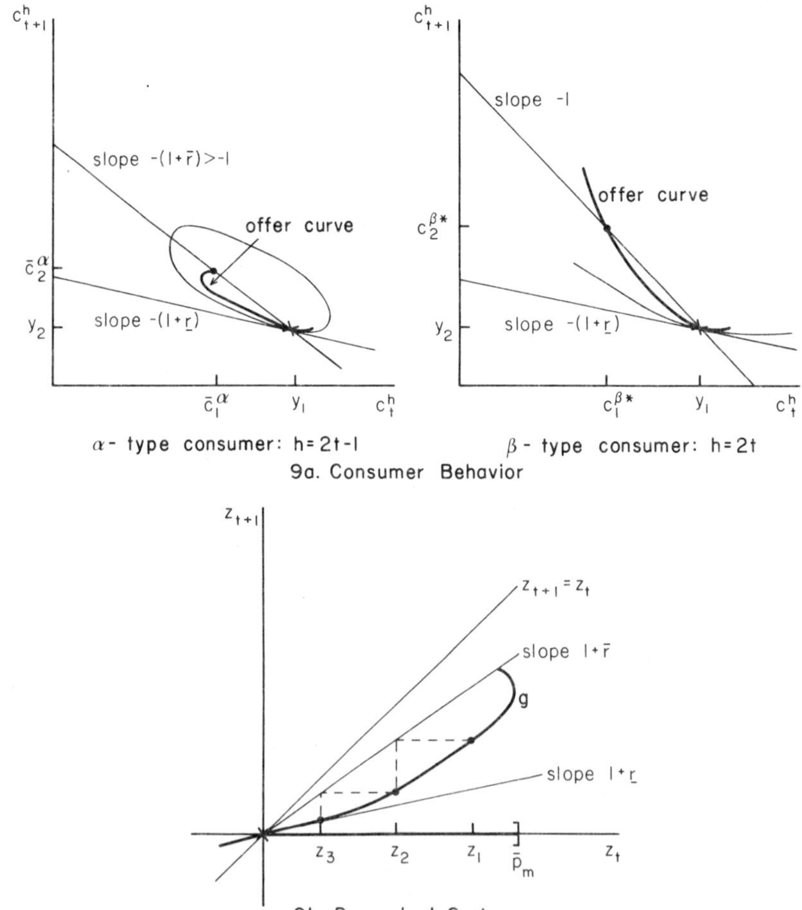

9b. Dynamical System

since such a concatenation obviously hangs in very delicate balance, it has usually been considered somewhat of an anomaly in that context, so that one could quite rightly ask whether it should also be so viewed in this. While we believe that the speciality of our particular counterexample (and its kin) is dictated more by our technical procedures than by our substantive objectives, this position remains to be satisfactorily buttressed. More to the point, there is a critically important distinction between the two situations being modeled. Indeed, it would probably be hard to overemphasize the fact that a large measure of consumption satiation and related endowment sparsity is intrinsic to accurately portraying the essence of the intertemporal allocation of consumption goods—both because individuals are inherently finite-lived and because their lives are naturally several-staged.[20]

An even more extreme degree of satiation cum sparsity can be utilized to model an economy in which, *though there is a stable, stationary monetary equilibrium, there is still no competitive equilibrium which is Pareto optimal.* In outline, this counterexample runs as follows. Suppose now that in each generation but the oldest there are three consumers $G_t = \{3t-2, 3t-1, 3t\}$ for $t \geqq 1$ whose tastes and endowments are described by

$$U^h(c^h, x^h) = \begin{cases} U^\alpha(c^h_{t+1}, x^h_t) \\ U^\beta(c^h_t, c^h_{t+1}) \\ U^\gamma(x^h_t) \end{cases} \quad \text{and} \quad (y^h, w^h) = \begin{cases} (0, y^\alpha_2, w^\alpha_1, w^\alpha_2) & \text{for } h = 3t-2 \\ (y^\beta_1, y^\beta_2, 0, 0) & \text{for } h = 3t-1 \\ (0, 0, w^\gamma, 0) & \text{otherwise} \end{cases}$$

where $U^\alpha(c^h_{t+1}, x^h_t) = \min\{c^h_{t+1}, x^h_t\}$ and $(0, y^\alpha_2, w^\alpha_1, w^\alpha_2)$ satisfies $w^\alpha_1 + w^\alpha_2 - y^\alpha_2 > 0$ but ≈ 0,[21] U^β is differentiable, strictly quasi-concave, strictly increasing, and also satisfies the condition

$$\frac{\partial U^\beta(y^\beta_1, y^\beta_2)}{\partial c_1} \Big/ \frac{\partial U^\beta(y^\beta_1, y^\beta_2)}{\partial c_2} = 1 + r^\beta \approx 0,$$

and U^γ is (like U^0) continuous and strictly increasing. Also, to simplify exposition, suppose that the oldest generation's endowment includes the second commodity in amount w^α_2 (so that p_m must be reinterpreted as the present value of 1 unit of money together with w^α_2 units of the second commodity).

For such an economy, after making necessary amendments to (1)–(3), it is easily seen that the γ-type consumers' tastes entail $q_t > 0$ for $t \geqq 1$, while their endowments entail $x^h_t = w^\gamma$ for $h = 3t$, $t \geqq 1$, so that the α-type consumers' tastes and endowments entail both

[20] In this connection, it is also worth remarking that we have developed variants of the counterexample depicted in Figure 9 which are grounded only on having heterogeneity across generations—but heterogeneity which is repeated regularly (so that, for instance, generations are alternately thrifty and spendthrifty)—and in which it is inevitable that some consumers possess the only endowments of some goods which they alone value. We have chosen to present the more artificial construct since these alternatives necessarily involve introducing a third stage of the life cycle and since introducing a specialized second commodity also admits yet another variety of quite interesting counterexample (as we shall now proceed to demonstrate).

[21] The α-type consumers could be assumed to have more flexible tastes; all that is required in the following argument is that their choices of second-period consumption satisfy the lower bound $c^h_{t+1} \geqq y^\alpha_2 + \epsilon$ for $t \geqq 1$, for some fixed positive number $\epsilon > 0$.

Here and below $\approx$ *0* means something like small enough so that Figure 10 is qualitatively accurate.

$$c_{t+1}^h = x_t^h = w_1^\alpha + w_2^\alpha > y_2^\alpha$$

and

$$q_{t+1} = q_t + \frac{w_1^\alpha + w_2^\alpha - y_2^\alpha}{w_2^\alpha} p_{t+1} > q_t$$

for $h = 3t - 2$, $t \geqq 1$. (All this, of course, is based on the provisional supposition that the economy is in competitive equilibrium.) The crucial upshot of these implications is that the appropriate reflected generational offer curve now has a very special form, since the representative α-type consumer's offer curve is just a single point, independent of all commodity prices, while the representative β-type consumer's offer curve is just the same as in Samuelson's basic model. Hence, the set of potential competitive equilibria can be represented as shown in Figure 10 (which explicitly assumes the least complicated, but yet still nonempty possibility, that there are only two stationary monetary equilibria). From this figure it is evident that every solution to (6) must satisfy

$$\frac{z_{t+1} - (w_1^\alpha + w_2^\alpha - y_2)}{z_t} = p_t/p_{t+1} \leqq 1 + \bar{r}^* < 1$$

and hence, in fact, that every competitive equilibrium either coincides with the (unstable) stationary monetary equilibrium corresponding to (the first) commodities prices

$$p_t = (1 + \bar{r}^*)^{-(t-1)} \text{ for } t \geqq 1$$

or, typically, converges to the (stable) stationary monetary equilibrium corresponding to (the first) commodities prices

$$p_t = (1 + \underline{r}^*)^{-(t-1)} \text{ for } t \geqq 1.$$

Thus it is also immediately apparent that every competitive allocation is therefore dominated, since every sequence of one-for-one forward transfers of the first commodity between only β-type consumers which satisfies the bounds

$$0 < \Delta c_{t+1}^{3t-1} = -\Delta c_{t+1}^{3(t+1)-1} = \Delta c^\beta < \bar{c}_1^{\beta *} \text{ for } t \geqq 1$$

is both feasible and—from each of their viewpoints (by virtue of the fact that at best they face a uniformly negative real rate of return $p_t/p_{t+1} - 1 \leqq \bar{r}^* < 0$ for $t \geqq 1$)—preferable.

5.3. *Nonconvexity*

This counterexample is nothing more than a straightforward variation of the example presented previously in Figure 5, and beyond simply displaying its structure, as we do in Figure 11, it requires only justifying its construction, as we do in the Appendix.

Note, however, that this same device, namely, introducing some nonconvexity into the upper reaches of the β-type consumer's indifference map, can also be employed to provide a solid theoretical foundation for our earlier

Figure 10
Nonexistence Due to Nonmonotonicity: An Example
With Local Satiation in the Second of Two Commodities

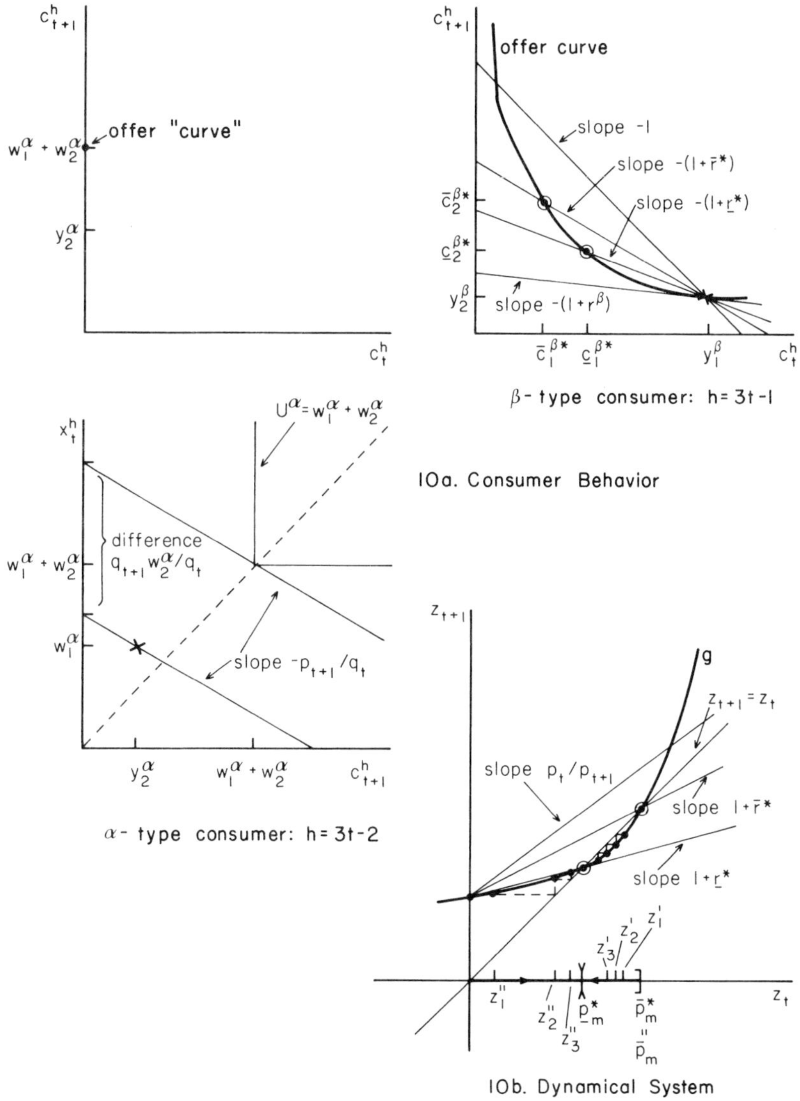

emphasis on the inherent difficulties attendant on nonuniqueness of monetary equilibrium (at the end of section 4). The doggedly persevering reader should, by now, be able to follow the dots.

Figure 11
Nonexistence Due to Nonconvexity

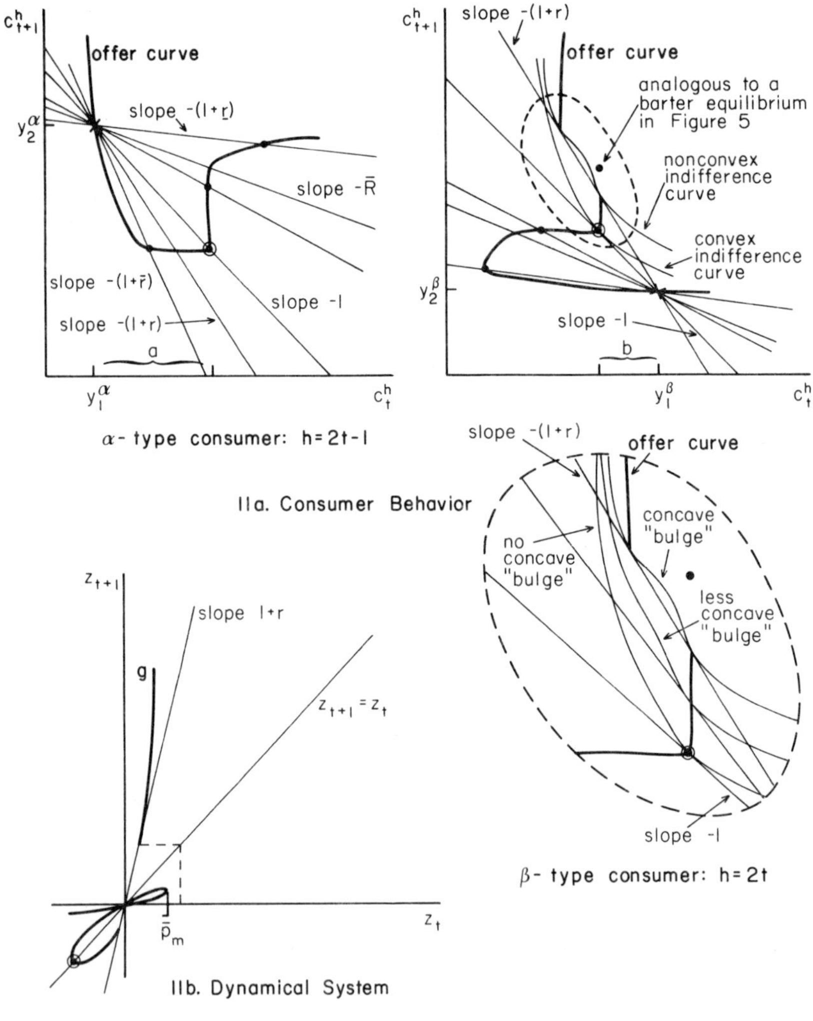

Appendix
Construction of Vertical or Truncated Offer Curves

A1. Introduction and Background

The purpose of this appendix is to substantiate the several claims made in the text (both explicitly and implicitly) regarding the possibility of constructing various types of individual offer curves. In accomplishing this purpose, it essentially amounts to an elementary exercise in demand theory.

The following central result is well-known. Consider the typical consumer in our basic model, and suppose that her/his utility function U^h is continuous, strictly increasing, and strictly quasi-concave, while her/his endowment vector (y_t^h, y_{t+1}^h) is nonnegative and nontrivial. Then, if (c_t^h, c_{t+1}^h) represents the unique optimal solution to the consumer's budget constrained utility maximization problem (2) as depending on (positive, finite) relative prices—or, in common parlance, her/his *demand functions*—these are (nonnegative and) continuous and satisfy the consumer's (relative price) budget constraint

$$(p_t / p_{t+1})\, c_t^h + c_{t+1}^h = (p_t / p_{t+1})\, y_t^h + y_{t+1}^h.$$

Moreover, even if U^h has a strict global maximum, say, at $(\bar{c}_t^h, \bar{c}_{t+1}^h)$ (but is elsewhere strictly increasing or decreasing), the same result remains true provided, in addition, either the consumer's endowment vector is weakly dominated, $(y_t^h, y_{t+1}^h) \leqq (\bar{c}_t^h, \bar{c}_{t+1}^h)$, or she/he is not satiated at the endowment vector, $(y_t^h, y_{t+1}^h) \not\geqq (c_t^h, c_{t+1}^h)$, and relative prices are limited in range,

$$p_t / p_{t+1} \begin{Bmatrix} \leqq \\ \geqq \end{Bmatrix} - \frac{\bar{c}_{t+1}^h - y_{t+1}^h}{\bar{c}_t^h - y_t^h} \text{ according as } \bar{c}_t^h \begin{Bmatrix} < \\ > \end{Bmatrix} y_t^h .$$

The converse to these propositions is already falsified by simple examples of the sort pictured in Figures 4 and 5 (assuming their validity, which follows from an argument similar to that presented explicitly in the next section). In particular, under either alternative set of maintained assumptions, the optimal consumption vector will coincide with the endowment vector for at most a single relative price [except in the singular situation where $(y_t^h, y_{t+1}^h) = (\bar{c}_t^h, \bar{c}_{t+1}^h)$, in which case they obviously coincide at every relative price]. Hence, it would be accurate to say that the general problem (but posed in terms of more specifically formulated questions) we are addressing here is, To what extent does the property of representing the demand functions (c_t^h, c_{t+1}^h)—or, equivalently, the *excess* demand functions $(c_t^h - y_t^h, c_{t+1}^h - y_{t+1}^h)$ composing the offer curve, for short, simply the *offer curve*—impose further restrictions beyond just continuity and satisfaction of a budget constraint?

In a very elegant development initiating with Sonnenschein (1972, 1973) and culminating with Mantel (1974) and Debreu (1974), it has recently been established that, under analogous maintained assumptions for $n \geqq 2$ commodities and $m \geqq n$ individuals, aggregate excess demand functions are completely characterized by continuity (in uniformly positive simplicial prices) and Walras' law. While this fundamental result obviously has some indirect bearing on the topic of this essay, especially on the conclusions exemplified by Figures 4 and 5, even in these examples it is not decisive for our purposes. Indeed, from the main line of argument in the text it should be clear that both continuity and (the analogue of) Walras' law play crucial roles in delimiting the set of potential competitive equilibria in our basic model. Thus, for instance, the former rules out the possibility that there is no Pareto optimal stationary equilibrium, the latter that there are multiple stationary monetary equilibria in section 4.

Moreover, it almost goes without saying that the requirement of market clearing is always at center stage in our presentation. This condition is especially important, for instance, in ruling out the possibility that there is some Pareto optimal stationary equilibrium—and, hence, any Pareto optimal competitive equilibrium—in section 5.

A2. Vertical Offer Curves

We concentrate attention on the details of the nonstationarity example described in Figure 7. Also, in order to simplify the discussion, here we will employ somewhat more conventional notation, namely, (x,y) for the consumption vector, (again) U for the utility function, and $(\tilde{x},\tilde{y})$ for the endowment vector. Exactly the same basic principles apply to rationalizing the preference structure underlying the heterogeneity examples described in Figures 4 and 5, except that, roughly speaking, the roles of x and y become reversed.

What we propose to show, then, is that given $(\underline{x},\underline{y}) > 0$ such that $\underline{x} < \tilde{x}$ and $\underline{y} > \tilde{y}$, $\bar{y} > \underline{y}$, and $(x^*,y^*) > 0$ such that $x^* < \underline{x}$ and $y^* > \underline{y}$, it is possible to construct $\bar{U}: R^2_+ \rightarrow R$ which is continuous, strictly increasing, strictly quasi-concave, and such that

- *The offer curve originating at $(\tilde{x},\tilde{y})$ is vertical between $(\underline{x},\underline{y})$ and $(\bar{x},\bar{y}) \equiv (\underline{x},\bar{y})$.*†

- *The indifference curve passing through $(\underline{x},\underline{y})$ lies strictly below (that is, to the southwest of) (x^*,y^*).*

The idea of this construction is wholly geometric and is fully elucidated by Figure A1. An algorithm for the construction proceeds as follows. Pick two functions $\underline{f}: R_+ \rightarrow R$ and $\bar{f}: R_+ \rightarrow R$ which are differentiable, strictly decreasing, and strictly convex, which satisfy $\underline{f}(x) < \bar{f}(\underline{x})$ for $x \geqq 0$ and which yield $\underline{f}(x^*) < y^*$, $\underline{f}(\underline{x}) = \underline{y}$, $\underline{f}'(\underline{x}) = (\underline{y} - \tilde{y}) / (\underline{x} - \tilde{x})$, and $\bar{f}(\bar{x}) = \bar{y}$, $\bar{f}'(\bar{x}) = (\bar{y} - \tilde{y}) / (\bar{x} - \tilde{x})$, respectively. In particular, this choice entails that the curves $y = \underline{f}(x)$ and $y = \bar{f}(x)$ for $x \geqq 0$ have the following relationships to the budget constraints

$$-\frac{\underline{y}-\tilde{y}}{\underline{x}-\tilde{x}}\,x + y = -\frac{\underline{y}-\tilde{y}}{\underline{x}-\tilde{x}}\,\tilde{x} + \tilde{y} \text{ or } y = \frac{\tilde{y}\underline{x}-\underline{y}\tilde{x}}{\underline{x}-\tilde{x}} + \frac{\underline{y}-\tilde{y}}{\underline{x}-\tilde{x}}\,x$$

†Thus, for the sake of symmetry in various expressions, we will interchangeably use the notation $\bar{x} = \underline{x}$, and later on, $x' = \underline{x}$ as well.

(A1) and

$$-\frac{\bar{y}-\tilde{y}}{\bar{x}-\tilde{x}}x + y = -\frac{\bar{y}-\tilde{y}}{\bar{x}-\tilde{x}}\tilde{x} + \tilde{y} \text{ or } y = \frac{\tilde{y}\bar{x}-\bar{y}\tilde{x}}{\bar{x}-\tilde{x}} + \frac{\bar{y}-\tilde{y}}{\bar{x}-\tilde{x}}x,$$

respectively:

$$\underline{f}(x)\left\{\begin{matrix} > \\ = \end{matrix}\right\}\frac{\tilde{y}\underline{x}-\underline{y}\tilde{x}}{\underline{x}-\tilde{x}} + \frac{\underline{y}-\tilde{y}}{\underline{x}-\tilde{x}}x \text{ according as } x\left\{\begin{matrix} \neq \\ = \end{matrix}\right\}\underline{x}$$

(A2) and

$$\bar{f}(x)\left\{\begin{matrix} > \\ = \end{matrix}\right\}\frac{\tilde{y}\bar{x}-\bar{y}\tilde{x}}{\bar{x}-\tilde{x}} + \frac{\bar{y}-\tilde{y}}{\bar{x}-\tilde{x}}x \text{ according as } x\left\{\begin{matrix} \neq \\ = \end{matrix}\right\}\bar{x}.$$

Generally, such functions $\underline{f}$ and $\bar{f}$ can be found in the parametric class $f(x) = a + be^{\beta x} + ce^{\gamma x}$ with $a + b + c > 0$, $a < 0$, $(b,c) > 0$, and $(\beta,\gamma) < 0$. So, without any loss of generality, assume in addition that $\lim_{x\to\infty} \underline{f}(x) \leqq \lim_{x\to\infty} \bar{f}(x) < 0$, so that, in particular, both functions also intersect the x-axis.

Figure A1
Construction of a Utility Function
Which Yields a Vertical Segment on the Offer Curve
and Satisfies an Additional Dominance Condition

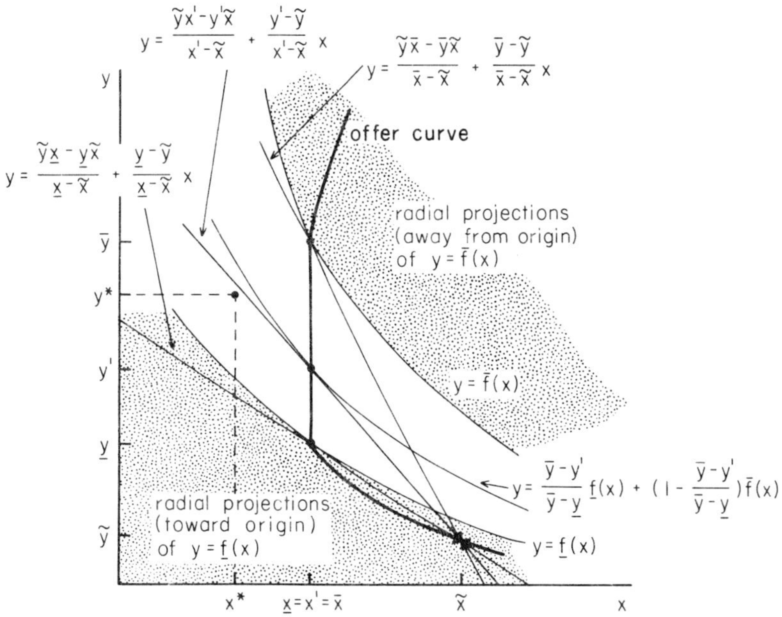

Next, define indifference curves (covering the whole nonnegative quadrant) in terms of the two functions $\underline{f}$ and $\bar{f}$ thusly:

- For $(x',y') \geqq 0$ and $0 \leqq y' \leqq \underline{f}(x')$, the indifference curve is the appropriate segment (that is, that lying in the nonnegative quadrant) of the radial projections of $(x, \underline{f}(x))$ (that is, as x varies over the nonnegative halfline) toward the origin in proportion

$$\text{(A3)} \qquad \alpha = \begin{cases} 0 & \text{if } x' = y' = 0 \\ y'/\underline{f}(x') & \text{if } x' = 0, y' > 0 \\ x'/x'' & \text{otherwise} \end{cases}$$

where x'' is defined by $\underline{f}(x'')\,/\,x'' = y'\,/\,x'$ if $x' > 0$.

- For $(x',y') \geqslant 0$ and $\underline{f}(x') \leqq y' \leqq \bar{f}(x')$, the indifference curve is the appropriate segment of the convex combinations of $(x, \underline{f}(x))$ and $(x, \bar{f}(x))$ using weights

$$\text{(A4)} \qquad \alpha = \frac{\bar{f}(x')-y'}{\bar{f}(x') - \underline{f}(x')} \quad \text{and} \quad 1 - \alpha = 1 - \frac{\bar{f}(x')-y'}{\bar{f}(x') - \underline{f}(x')},$$

respectively.

- For $(x',y') \geqslant 0$ and $y' \geqq \bar{f}(x')$, the indifference curve is the appropriate segment of the radial projections of $(x, \bar{f}(x))$ away from the origin in proportion

$$\text{(A5)} \qquad \alpha = \begin{cases} y'/\bar{f}(x') & \text{if } x' = 0, y' > 0 \\ x'/x'' & \text{otherwise} \end{cases}$$

where now x'' is defined by $\bar{f}(x'')\,/\,x'' = y'/x'$ if $x' > 0$.

Finally, simply label each indifference curve with the value of its y-intercept.

Establishing that the utility function so constructed has the requisite continuity, monotonicity, and convexity properties is a routine matter. To begin with, observe that, given our particular choice of labeling for the indifference curves, in each of the three regions delineated by $\underline{f}$ and $\bar{f}$ the various definitions of α (A3)–(A5) can be recast in terms of U, $\underline{f}(0)$, and $\bar{f}(0)$. For instance, (A4) is equivalent to

$$\text{(A4}'\text{)} \qquad \alpha = \frac{\bar{f}(0)-U}{\bar{f}(0) - \underline{f}(0)} \quad \text{and} \quad 1 - \alpha = 1 - \frac{\bar{f}(0)-U}{\bar{f}(0) - \underline{f}(0)}$$

where U is related to (x',y') implicitly by the equation

$$\text{(A6)} \qquad y' = \frac{\bar{f}(0)-U}{\bar{f}(0) - \underline{f}(0)}\underline{f}(x') + \left(1 - \frac{\bar{f}(0)-U}{\bar{f}(0) - \underline{f}(0)}\right)\bar{f}(x').$$

Following this lead through, it is easy to show that, in general, U is defined implicitly in terms of its indifference curves by the formulae

$$\text{(A7)}\quad y = \begin{cases} (U / \underline{f}(0))\,\underline{f}(x\,\underline{f}(0)/U) \text{ for } x \geqq 0,\ \underline{f}(x\,\underline{f}(0)/U) \geqq 0, \text{ and } 0 \leqq U \leqq \underline{f}(0) \\ \dfrac{\bar{f}(0)-U}{\bar{f}(0)-\underline{f}(0)}\underline{f}(x) + \left(1 - \dfrac{\bar{f}(0)-U}{\bar{f}(0)-\underline{f}(0)}\right)\bar{f}(x) \text{ for } x \geqq 0, \\ (\bar{f}(0)-U)\,\underline{f}(x) + (U - \underline{f}(0))\bar{f}(x) \geqq 0, \text{ and } \underline{f}(0) \leqq U \leqq \bar{f}(0) \\ (U/\bar{f}(0))\bar{f}(x\bar{f}(0)/U) \text{ for } x \geqq 0, \bar{f}(x\bar{f}(0)/U) \geqq 0, \text{ and } \bar{f}(0) \leqq U. \end{cases}$$

But by virtue of the specification of $\underline{f}$ and $\bar{f}$, each of the functions on the right-hand side of (A7) is differentiable, strictly decreasing in x, strictly increasing in U, and strictly convex in x on its respective domain. Hence, the desired properties follow directly upon application of well-known, elementary results from functional analysis.

Utilizing yet another simple reformulation of (A4), it is also easy to verify the first additional property motivating this whole exercise—that the offer curve originating at $(\tilde{x},\tilde{y})$ is vertical between $(\underline{x},\underline{y})$ and $(\bar{x},\bar{y})$. In particular, from (A6) we see that

$$\frac{\bar{f}(0)-U}{\bar{f}(0)-\underline{f}(0)} = \frac{y'-\bar{f}(x')}{\underline{f}(x')-\bar{f}(x')} = \frac{\bar{f}(x')-y'}{\bar{f}(x')-\underline{f}(x')}.$$

Thus, by fixing $x' = \underline{x} = \bar{x}$ [so that, as in Figure A1, $\underline{f}(x') = \underline{f}(\underline{x}) = \underline{y}$ and $\bar{f}(x') = \bar{f}(\bar{x}) = \bar{y}$], and considering only the nonnegative region lying between the prespecified curves $y = \underline{f}(x)$ and $y = \bar{f}(x)$ for $x \geqq 0$, the indifference curves described in (A7) can equally well be described by

$$\text{(A8)}\qquad y = \frac{\bar{y}-y'}{\bar{y}-\underline{y}}\underline{f}(x) + \left(1 - \frac{\bar{y}-y'}{\bar{y}-\underline{y}}\right)\bar{f}(x) \quad \text{for } x \geqq 0, \underline{y} \leqq y' \leqq \bar{y}.$$

Since the budget constraint

$$-\frac{y'-\tilde{y}}{x'-\tilde{y}}x + y = -\frac{y'-\tilde{y}}{x'-\tilde{y}}\tilde{x} + \tilde{y} \quad \text{or} \quad y = \frac{\tilde{y}x'-y'\tilde{x}}{x'-\tilde{x}} + \frac{y'-\tilde{y}}{x'-\tilde{x}}x$$

is identical to that obtained by taking the same convex combination of the two budget constraints described in (A1), that is,

$$y = \left(\frac{\bar{y}-y'}{\bar{y}-\underline{y}}\right)\left(\frac{\tilde{y}\underline{x}-\underline{y}\tilde{x}}{\underline{x}-\tilde{x}} + \frac{\underline{y}-\tilde{y}}{\underline{x}-\tilde{x}}x\right) + \left(1 - \frac{\bar{y}-y'}{\bar{y}-\underline{y}}\right)\left(\frac{\tilde{y}\bar{x}-\bar{y}\tilde{x}}{\bar{x}-\tilde{x}} + \frac{\bar{y}-\tilde{y}}{\bar{x}-\tilde{x}}x\right)$$

$$= \frac{\tilde{y}x'-y'\tilde{x}}{x'-\tilde{x}} + \frac{y'-\tilde{y}}{x'-\tilde{x}}x$$

(A8), together with (A2), immediately entails

$$\text{(A9)}\qquad \frac{\bar{y}-y'}{\bar{y}-\underline{y}}\underline{f}(x) + \left(1 - \frac{\bar{y}-y'}{\bar{y}-\underline{y}}\right)\bar{f}(x) \begin{Bmatrix} > \\ = \end{Bmatrix} \frac{\tilde{y}x'-y'\tilde{x}}{x'-\tilde{x}} + \frac{y'-\tilde{y}}{x'-\tilde{x}}x$$

$$\text{according as } x \left\{ \begin{matrix} \neq \\ = \end{matrix} \right\} x' = \bar{x} = \underline{x} \text{ for } \underline{y} \leqq y' \leqq \bar{y}$$

which is the precise statement of the desired conclusion, shown in Figure A1.

The second additional property—that the indifference curve passing through $(\underline{x},\underline{y})$ lies strictly below (x^*,y^*)—was already guaranteed by the value restrictions on $\underline{f}$, specifically, that $\underline{f}(\underline{x}) = \underline{y}$ and $\underline{f}(x^*) < y^*$, also shown in Figure A1.

There are two additional points related to the foregoing construction which merit at least passing comment. First, the same basic technique can be employed to justify the offer curve originating at $(\tilde{x},\tilde{y})$ having a nonvertical linear segment, say,

$$y = a + bx \text{ for } 0 < x^1 \leqq x \leqq x^2 < \tilde{x},$$

provided, for instance, that $b < (y^2-\tilde{y})/(x^2-\tilde{x}) < 0$. Since the details of such a construction are not especially material to any of our present objectives, we will not elaborate them here. Second, the utility function implicitly defined by (A7) is not differentiable when either $(x,y) = (x,\underline{f}(x)) \geqq 0$ or $(x,y) = (x,\bar{f}(x)) \geqq 0$. Wayne Shafer has suggested an alternative procedure for defining a utility function which exhibits all the same properties, but which is also both differentiable and homothetic. The essence of Shafer's clever idea is displayed in Figure A2, and in bare outline (that is, without any subtleties)

Figure A2
Construction of a Utility Function
Which Yields an Essentially Vertical Offer Curve
and Yet Is Both Differentiable and Homothetic

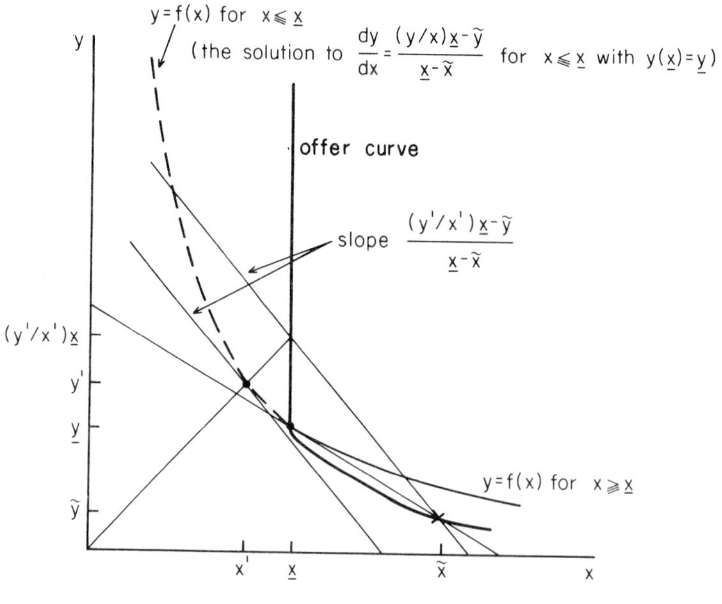

goes as follows. Pick a function $f : \{x : x \geqq \underline{x}\} \to R$ which is differentiable, strictly decreasing, and strictly convex and which yields $f(\underline{x}) = \underline{y}$ and $f'(\underline{x}) = (\underline{y}-\tilde{y})/(\underline{x}-\tilde{x})$. Next, extend this function leftward from $x = \underline{x}$ by solving the ordinary differential equation

$$\frac{dy}{dx} = \frac{(y/x)\underline{x}-\tilde{y}}{\underline{x}-\tilde{x}} \quad \text{for } x \leqq \underline{x}$$

with initial condition $y(\underline{x}) = \underline{y}$; the solution is (no surprise) basically a power function

$$y = f(x) = \frac{\tilde{y}}{\tilde{x}}x + \left(\frac{\underline{y}\tilde{x}-\tilde{y}\underline{x}}{\tilde{x}}\right)\left(\frac{x}{\underline{x}}\right)^{\frac{\underline{x}}{\underline{x}-\tilde{x}}} \text{for } x \leqq \underline{x}.$$

Finally, define the indifference curves as appropriate radial projections of $(x,f(x))$ from 0, and label them in some smooth, monotonic fashion, for instance, according to the y-coordinate of their intersection with the ray $y = (\underline{y}/\underline{x})x$.

Our particular algorithm has two advantages over Shafer's, the first minor, the second not so minor. In the first place, it conveniently enables satisfying the additional dominance condition $U(x^*,y^*) > U(\underline{x},\underline{y})$ (or, more generally, satisfying various other additional restrictions on the indifference map).

In the second place, and more importantly, it can be used virtually unaltered to construct the sort of indifference map underlying the nonconvexity example described in Figure 11. In fact, the only significant change required is in the choice of $\bar{f}$: Given $(\hat{x},\hat{y}) > 0$ such that $\hat{x} < \bar{x}$ and $(\hat{y}-\tilde{y})/(\hat{x}-\tilde{x}) = (\bar{y}-\tilde{y})/(\bar{x}-\tilde{x})$, $\bar{f}$ now needs simply be specified, for instance, to be differentiable and to satisfy

$$\text{(A10)} \qquad \bar{f}(x) \begin{Bmatrix} > \\ = \end{Bmatrix} \frac{\tilde{y}\bar{x}-\bar{y}\tilde{x}}{\bar{x}-\tilde{x}} + \frac{\bar{y}-\tilde{y}}{\bar{x}-\tilde{x}}x \text{ according as } x \begin{Bmatrix} \neq \\ = \end{Bmatrix} \bar{x} \text{ or } \hat{x}$$

as shown in Figure A3. [Compare with the second inequality in (A2) and its representation in Figure A1.] Given such a specification, the earlier argument (where relevant) is identical down to the bottom line (A9), which only need be slightly modified to correspond with (A10)

$$\text{(A9}'\text{)} \qquad \cdots x \begin{Bmatrix} \neq \\ = \end{Bmatrix} x' = \bar{x} = \underline{x}\left(x \begin{Bmatrix} \neq \\ = \end{Bmatrix} \bar{x} \text{ or } \hat{x}\right) \text{ for } \underline{y} \leqq y < \bar{y}\,(y=\bar{y}).$$

In other words, the offer curve must now have the vertical segment with an upper endpoint discontinuity as depicted in Figure A3. (A separate argument, not spelled out here, establishes that the offer curve in the nonnegative region lying strictly above the prespecified curve $y = \bar{f}(x)$ for $x \geqq 0$ must have the single-valuedness property shown as well, provided that $\bar{f}$ is strictly convex on the interval $[0,\hat{x}]$.)

Figure A3
Construction of a Utility Function
Which Yields a Vertical Segment—With a Discontinuity
at its Upper Endpoint—on the Offer Curve

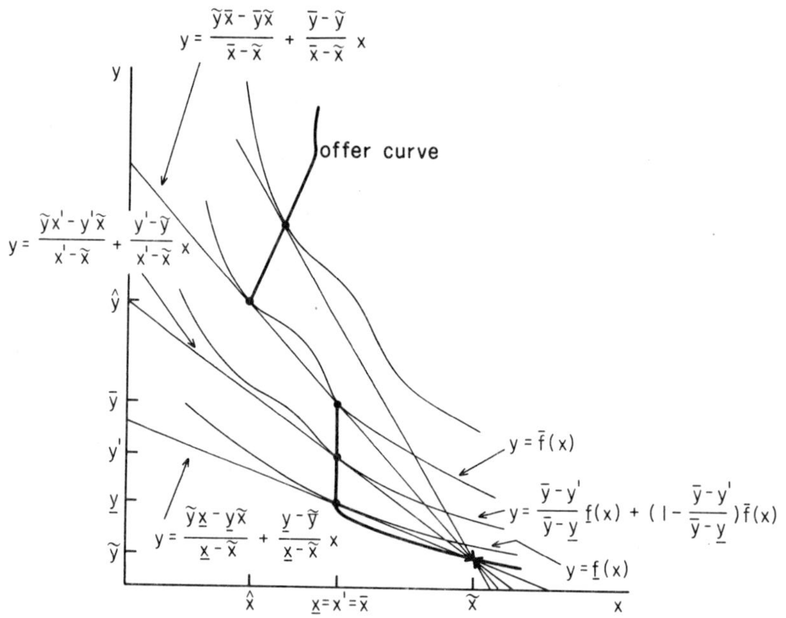

A3. Truncated Offer Curves

It is worth briefly sketching an explicit procedure for obtaining the satiation example described in Figure 9; an obvious elaboration then yields that described in Figure 8. Thus, again employing the neutral notation (x,y), U, and $(\tilde{x},\tilde{y})$, we show here that it is possible to construct a well-behaved utility function which achieves a global maximum at a consumption vector $(\bar{x},\bar{y})$ such that $\bar{x} < \tilde{x}$ and $-1 < (\bar{y}-\tilde{y})/(\bar{x}-\tilde{x}) < 0$. Again, the basic nature of the construction is geometric and can be completely captured in a diagram, as illustrated by Figure A4. An algorithm for this particular construction runs as follows. Pick an ellipse lying wholly within the positive quadrant, say, $f(x,y) = 0$. Then, let

$$x^{\infty} = \min\{x : f(x,y) = 0 \text{ for some } y > 0\}$$

and

$$y^{0} = \min\{y : f(x,y) = 0 \text{ for some } x > 0\},$$

with corresponding abscissa y^{∞} and ordinate x^{0}, respectively, and let (x^{1},y^{1}) be such that $x^{\infty} < x^{1} < x^{0}$, $y^{0} < y^{1} < y^{\infty}$, $f(x^{1},y^{1}) = 0$ and

$$-\frac{\partial f(x^1,y^1)}{\partial x}\bigg/\frac{\partial f(x^1,y^1)}{\partial y} = -1.$$

(Refer to Figure A4; in this case the picture is surely much more informative than any accompanying algebra!) Next, pick any $(\tilde{x},\tilde{y})$ such that $x^1 < \tilde{x} < x^0$, $y^0 < \tilde{y} < y^1$ and $f(\tilde{x},\tilde{y}) = 0$, so that

$$-1 < -\frac{\partial f(\tilde{x},\tilde{y})}{\partial x}\bigg/\frac{\partial f(\tilde{x},\tilde{y})}{\partial y} < 0,$$

and given $(\tilde{x},\tilde{y})$, any $(\bar{x},\bar{y})$ lying strictly inside $f(x,y) = 0$ but strictly below $y = (\tilde{y}-\tilde{x}) - x$, so that also

$$-1 < \frac{\bar{y}-\tilde{y}}{\bar{x}-\tilde{x}} < -\frac{\partial f(\tilde{x},\tilde{y})}{\partial x}\bigg/\frac{\partial f(\tilde{x},\tilde{y})}{\partial y}.$$

Finally, once again define the indifference curves as radial projections, but here of the ellipse $f(x,y) = 0$ from the point $(\bar{x},\bar{y})$, and label them in some smooth, monotonic fashion, but here so that $(\bar{x},\bar{y})$ has the highest value, for instance, according to the lower y-coordinate of their intersection with the ray $y = (\bar{y}/\bar{x})x$.

Figure A4
Construction of a Utility Function
Which Yields a Truncated Offer Curve

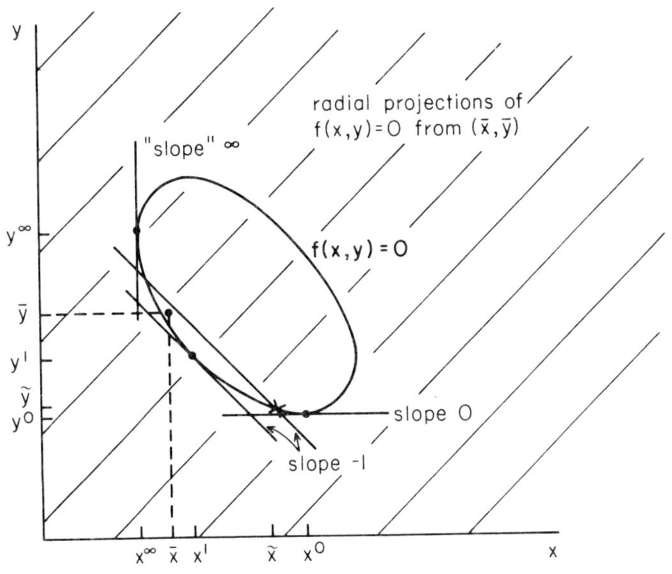

Notice a couple of additional features of the utility function and endowment vector so constructed. The corresponding offer curve will be backward bending (as drawn in Figures 8 and 9) if and only if

$$-\left.\frac{\partial f(x,y)}{\partial x} \bigg/ \frac{\partial f(x,y)}{\partial y}\right|_{(x,y)\,=\,(\bar{x},\ \min\{y\,:\,f(\bar{x},y)\,=\,0\})} > \frac{\bar{y}-\tilde{y}}{\bar{x}-\tilde{x}}.$$

Furthermore, the relationship between particular points on the corresponding offer curve and other strategically chosen points on the indifference map (as drawn, for instance, in Figure 8) can within limits be determined by suitably varying f, $(\tilde{x},\tilde{y})$, and $(\bar{x},\bar{y})$.

The Overlapping Generations Model of Fiat Money

Neil Wallace

1. Introduction

There are two widely accepted defining characteristics of fiat money: inconvertibility and intrinsic uselessness. *Inconvertibility* means that the issuer, if there is one, does not promise to convert the money into anything else—gold or wheat, for example. *Intrinsic uselessness* means that fiat money is never wanted for its own sake; it is not legitimate to take fiat money to be an argument of anyone's utility function or of any engineering production function. Stated somewhat differently, intrinsic uselessness means that one person gives up goods (objects that appear as arguments of utility functions, directly or indirectly) for fiat money only because the person believes that someone else will subsequently give up goods for fiat money at an acceptable rate of exchange.

The argument for intrinsic uselessness is that too much is sacrificed by abandoning it. The principal way of abandoning intrinsic uselessness is to make money an argument of utility functions or engineering production functions. But this begs too many questions. Is it fiat or commodity money that appears in these functions? What if there are several fiat moneys, those of different countries? Do all appear, and if so, how? Does Robinson Crusoe have fiat money as an argument of his utility function? And what about other pieces of paper? Most economists would be unhappy with a theory of the value of shares in the XYZ Corporation that starts out making such shares an argument in utility functions. Why is it better to do this for fiat money? All of this is to say that theories that abandon intrinsic uselessness will be almost devoid of implications.

In contrast to intrinsic uselessness one might say that inconvertibility is not something to be argued about. Either the institution under investigation displays this property or it does not. But some care must be taken. As I use it, *inconvertibility* means that it is known with certainty that the issuer does not now and will never in the future stand ready to convert fiat money into a commodity. Viewed this way, fiat money systems have, I think, been rare. Specie suspensions during wars do not in general qualify. In most such instances—for example, Great Britain during the Napoleonic wars and World War I and the United States during the Civil War—convertibility was subsequently restored. That being so, it seems sensible to suppose that individuals had always attached some positive probability to such restoration, which is enough to violate what I mean by inconvertibility. But now restoration of convertibility seems unlikely. So, and perhaps for the first time, theories of inconvertible money are of practical importance.

If inconvertibility and intrinsic uselessness are taken seriously, there is an immediate and long-standing problem: the devices usually invoked to prove that an object has value in equilibrium—basically, that supply is limited and that utility is increasing in the amount consumed—cannot be used for fiat money. Since getting fiat money to have value is necessary for any nontrivial theory of it, three options seem to be available: first, one can abandon inconvertibility and intrinsic uselessness; second, one can impose legal restrictions that give fiat money value; and third, one can attempt to model explicitly the notion that fiat money facilitates exchange. For good reasons, monetary theorists are almost unanimous in pursuing the third option.

In order to pursue the notion that fiat money facilitates exchange, one must abandon the costless multilateral market clearing implicit in the Walrasian (or Arrow-Debreu) general equilibrium model. Since exchange works perfectly in that model, there can be no role for a device that is supposed to facilitate exchange. In order to get a theory of fiat money, one must generalize the Walrasian model by including in it some sort of *friction,* something that will inhibit the operation of markets. On that there is agreement.

But what sort of friction? On that there is no agreement, which is to say there is no widely accepted theory of fiat money. I will try to alter this situation by arguing that the friction in Samuelson's 1958 consumption loan model, *overlapping generations*, gives rise to the best available model of fiat money.

That this needs arguing is clear. It is now 20 years (a generation!) since Samuelson described the role of fiat money in the overlapping generations model. Yet neither he nor most economists seem to take it seriously as a model of fiat money. (See, for example, Samuelson 1968.[1]) One claim seems to be that the overlapping generations friction accounts for the store-of-value function of money only. As a consequence, it is argued, models built on it are quite misleading. In particular, the tenuousness of equilibria in which fiat money has value in models built on the overlapping generations friction is due, according to this claim, to the fact that this friction does not account for the medium-of-exchange role of money. But this claim fails to recognize that tenuousness is an implication of the two defining properties of fiat money, inconvertibility and intrinsic uselessness, and not of the overlapping generations friction.

One of the most important, although obvious, implications of inconvertibility and intrinsic uselessness is that if fiat money has value in an equilibrium, then there cannot be another asset with a rate-of-return distribution in that equilibrium which dominates that of fiat money. For suppose this were not true. Then someone gives up goods for fiat money in this equilibrium even though the person could instead buy an alternative asset that in all circumstances would give more goods subsequently. Why? Any reason that one could give would violate intrinsic uselessness.

Another implication says, in effect, that an economy can work (although maybe not so well, as we will see) without fiat money, or equivalently, without it having value. In other words, there are *nonmonetary equilibria*,

[1]Author names and years refer to the works listed at the end of this book.

equilibria in which fiat money is without value at any date.

These implications of inconvertibility and intrinsic uselessness imply that *monetary equilibria*, equilibria in which there is valued fiat money, are tenuous.

Also implicit in the definition of fiat money is the idea that in an equilibrium with valued fiat money its value exceeds its cost of production. But this rules out a competitive monetary equilibrium with free entry into the production of fiat money. Put differently, wealth is greater in the monetary equilibrium than in the nonmonetary equilibrium. Somehow this wealth must be allocated among individuals. The market cannot do that.

All these problems, if problems they be, show up in the models built on the overlapping generations friction. But all of them—absence of dominance, existence of a nonmonetary equilibrium, and wealth creation—have to be addressed by any model of fiat money that maintains inconvertibility and intrinsic uselessness. The fact that they come up in models built on the overlapping generations friction is not, therefore, a defect of that friction.

In a way, it is precisely those problems that give rise to a rich theory of fiat money. That is the message of what follows and constitutes my principal argument for taking seriously models built on the overlapping generations friction. I will show how models built on this friction can be made to confront virtually every long-standing problem in monetary economics.

The first problem I take up—and perhaps the most basic—concerns the efficiency of fiat and commodity money systems. One notion is that fiat money helps by freeing resources that would otherwise be used to produce a commodity money. In section 2, I show how models built on the overlapping generations friction give precise content to this notion. Roughly speaking, the results tie the existence of an optimal fixed-supply monetary equilibrium to the nonoptimality of the nonmonetary equilibrium.

The second problem I address concerns fiat money–financed deficits. In section 3, I show how overlapping generations models allow us to present simple public finance analyses of fiat money issue as a taxation device. Not surprisingly, fiat money issue turns out to be an excise tax.

The third problem I consider concerns paradoxical time series correlations between the quantity of fiat money and other variables. In section 4, I review, by way of a simple example, Lucas' (1972) incomplete information theory of nonstructural time series correlations. This theory shows what happens if information barriers (another friction?) force individuals to make imperfect inferences from observations on the equilibrium value of fiat money. The theory is the key building block in the current attempt to bring cyclical phenomena within the purview of ordinary economic theory. An understanding of Lucas' theory forces one to a radical reinterpretation of many of the macroeconomic time series correlations that are currently treated as structural.

The fourth problem I deal with concerns open market operations, or monetary policy narrowly conceived. The main result comes from nothing more than a careful consolidation of the balance sheets of the monetary authority and the public: without additional frictions, the portfolio of the monetary authority does not matter even for the value of fiat money. What counts is asset creation and destruction, not asset exchanges, or in other words, outside money, not inside money, or in still other words, fiscal policy, not monetary policy.

The fifth and last problem I take up concerns country-specific fiat moneys. In section 6, I summarize my work with Kareken (1978) on the relationship between national budget policies and international monetary relationships. The theme, which grows directly out of the defining properties of fiat money, is that while one may get a theory of one valued fiat money by explicit modeling of how fiat money facilitates exchange, in order to get a theory of several valued fiat moneys one must in addition invoke legal restrictions (other frictions?) that prevent one fiat money from being substituted for another. One implication is that a laissez-faire international monetary system with many national fiat moneys makes no sense.

2. Efficiency of Fiat and Commodity Money Systems

As noted above, one widely held view is that fiat money is an efficient form of money; since fiat money can be produced costlessly, there is a gain from using it instead of something else that is both costly to produce and has alternative uses. (See Friedman 1953, pp. 204–50; 1960.) While this seems plausible, several questions must be answered. Since the gain does not exist in every economy—for example, it does not exist in the world of the Walrasian general equilibrium model or in that of Robinson Crusoe—in what sort of economies does it exist? And does the gain depend on how fiat money is managed? I will provide answers to these questions in the context of a particular overlapping generations model and will then consider generalizations of it.

2.1. *Commodity Money Equilibria*

Before describing the model, a confession is in order. I suggested above that while a model may or may not have a monetary equilibrium, one in which fiat money has value, it will, in general, have a nonmonetary equilibrium, one in which fiat money has no value. The confession is that I will not distinguish between nonmonetary equilibria and commodity money equilibria. For me they are simply different names for the same thing.

While any given model may have several nonmonetary equilibria, there will in general be no basis for classifying these into two distinct classes—one called *commodity money equilibria* and the other called, say, *barter equilibria*. (This is true vacuously if the given model has a unique nonmonetary equilibrium.) Nor is it obvious that anything is to be gained from attempting to classify the nonmonetary equilibria of different models into those that, in some sense, look like commodity money equilibria and those that look like barter equilibria. True, some models may display transaction patterns such that no object is playing a special role in exchange (all objects have roughly the same transaction velocity), while other models may display patterns such that one object has a quite special role in exchange (its transaction velocity is much higher than that of any other object). But most models with friction are likely to display some intermediate pattern in which a ranking of objects by transaction velocity produces a hierarchy. I doubt that a fruitful qualitative distinction will emerge from attempting to classify models by the nature of their transaction-velocity pattern. Nor, as I hope to demonstrate, is it fruitful to group together all objects with transaction velocities greater than some number and to call the collection *money*.

2.2. *A Model With Constant Returns-to-Scale Storage*

This model, a slight variant of the one studied by Cass and Yaari (1966a), is a discrete-time, one-good economy. At any date t, the population consists of $N(t)$ young (or age 1), the members of generation t, and $N(t-1)$ old (or age 2), the members of generation $t-1$. Each young person at t maximizes $u[c^h(t)]$; $c^h(t) = [c_1^h(t), c_2^h(t)]$, where $c_j^h(t)$ is age j consumption of member h of generation t, and u is twice differentiable with convex upper contour sets. The c_j are normal goods, and u_1/u_2, the marginal rate of substitution function, approaches infinity as c_1/c_2 approaches zero and approaches zero as c_1/c_2 approaches infinity. Each old person at t maximizes $c_2^h(t-1)$.

Each young person is endowed at t with y units of the consumption good. The good may be exchanged, consumed, or stored; if $k \geq 0$ units are stored, the result is xk units of $t+1$ consumption where $x > 0$. I assume that $N(t)/N(t-1) = n > 0$ for all t.

I will study the evolution of this economy from some arbitrary initial date labeled $t=1$ for convenience. In the aggregate, the $t=1$ old, the members of generation 0, are endowed with $K(0) \geq 0$ units of the consumption good and with $M(1)$ units of fiat money.

For all t, $M(t)$, the post-transfer time t stock of money, obeys $M(t) = zM(t-1)$, $z > 0$. The time t transfer (or tax), $(z-1)M(t-1)$, is divided equally at time t among the $N(t-1)$ members of generation $t-1$. The handouts are fully anticipated and are viewed as lump-sum, as not dependent on saving or portfolio behavior.

Our two main questions about this economy are, Under what circumstances does a monetary equilibrium exist? and When it exists, under what circumstances does it improve matters?

2.2.1. *Equilibria*

Let $p(t)$ be the price of a unit of fiat money at time t in units of time t consumption. Then, letting $c(t) = [\ldots, c^h(t), \ldots]$, $k(t) = [\ldots, k^h(t), \ldots]$, $m(t) = [\ldots, m^h(t), \ldots]$ be the vectors of generation t's lifetime consumption, time t storage, and time t money purchases, respectively, an equilibrium is a sequence $[c(t-1), k(t), m(t), p(t)]$, $t=1, 2, \ldots$ that is consistent with

- $c^h(t)$, $m^h(t)$, and $k^h(t)$ being optimal for the perfect-foresight competitive choice problem of the young to be described below
- $c_2^h(0)$ being maximal for the (trivial) competitive choice problem of the current old
- $M(t) = \Sigma m^h(t)$, which, like all other unindexed summations, is over all h in generation t.

2.2.2. *The Choice Problem of the Young*

The young choose nonnegative values of $c^h(t)$, $k^h(t)$, and $m^h(t)$ to maximize $u[c^h(t)]$ subject to

(1) $$c_1^h(t) + k^h(t) + p(t)\, m^h(t) - y \leq 0$$

(2) $$c_2^h(t) - xk^h(t) - p(t+1)\, \{m^h(t) + (z-1)\, M(t)\, /\, [N(t)]\} \leq 0$$

for $p(t) \geq 0$ and $p(t+1) \geq 0$.

The necessary and sufficient conditions for an optimum are (1) and (2) at equality and

(3) $$u_1 - \ell_1^h \leq 0 \qquad \text{with} = \text{if } c_1^h(t) > 0$$

(4) $u_2 - \ell_2^h \leqslant 0$ with = if $c_2^h(t) > 0$

(5) $-\ell_1^h + x\ell_2^h \leqslant 0$ with = if $k^h(t) > 0$

(6) $-\ell_1^h p(t) + \ell_2^h p(t+1) \leqslant 0$ with = if $m^h(t) > 0$

where ℓ_j^h is the nonnegative multiplier associated with constraint j and where, by our nonsatiety assumption about u and the boundedness and nonemptiness of the feasible $c^h(t)$, $\ell_j^h > 0$ and finite in any equilibrium.

2.2.3. *Nonmonetary Equilibrium*

By definition, $p(t) = 0$ for all t in such an equilibrium. This implies that (3)–(5) hold with equality. So, letting $v[c^h(t)] \equiv u_1/u_2$ be the marginal rate of substitution function, which by normality of the $c_j(t)$ satisfies $v_1 < 0$, $v_2 > 0$, (3)–(5) give us

(7) $v[c^h(t)] = x.$

Thus, there is a unique $k^h(t)$, say, k^*, for which (7) holds. [To prove this, use (1) and (2) at equality to write the $c_j^h(t)$ as functions of $k^h(t)$.]

2.2.4. *Monetary Equilibria*

By definition, $p(t) > 0$ and $m^h(t) > 0$ for some t in such an equilibrium. But by (6), this implies $p(t) > 0$ for all t. Therefore, by (3)–(6)

(8) $v[c^h(t)] = p(t+1)/p(t) \geqslant x$ for all t

is necessary and sufficient in order that choices be optimizing in a monetary equilibrium. I can now prove

PROPOSITION 1. *$xz/n \leqslant 1$ is necessary and sufficient for the existence of at least one monetary equilibrium.*

Proof (Necessity). Suppose to the contrary that there is a monetary equilibrium and $xz/n > 1$. Then, by the rule generating $M(t)$ and the equilibrium condition, $M(t) = N(t)\,\overline{m}(t)$, where $\overline{m}(t) = \Sigma m^h(t)/N(t)$, we have for all t

(9) $$\frac{p(t+1)}{p(t)} = \frac{M(t+1)\,p(t+1)}{zM(t)\,p(t)} = \frac{N(t+1)\,\overline{m}(t+1)\,p(t+1)}{zN(t)\,\overline{m}(t)\,p(t)} = \frac{nq(t+1)}{zq(t)}$$

where $q(t) \equiv p(t)\,\overline{m}(t)$. Then, by the inequality part of (8), we have for all t

(10) $q(t+1)/q(t) \geqslant xz/n > 1.$

But since $q^h(t) = m^h(t)\,p(t) < y$ for all h and t, the same bound applies to $q(t)$. And no bounded $q(t)$ sequence can satisfy (10).

Proof (Sufficiency). I will prove that $xz/n \leqslant 1$ implies the existence of a monetary equilibrium with $k^h(t) = 0$ and $q^h(t) = q(t)$ for all h and $t \geqslant 1$. By (1), (2), and (8), it suffices to find a positive $q(t)$ sequence that satisfies

(11) $v[y - q(t), q(t+1)\,n] = [q(t+1)/q(t)]\,(n/z) \geqslant x.$

If there is a $q \in (0,y)$ such that $q(t) = q(t+1) = q$ satisfies the equality part of

(11), then the inequality part is implied by $xz/n \leqslant 1$. But the existence (and uniqueness) of such a q, denoted q^*, is trivial. Let $v^*(q) \equiv v(y-q, nq)$. Then v^* is continuous (strictly increasing), with $0 = \lim v^*(q)$ as $q \rightarrow 0$ from above and $\infty = \lim v^*(q)$ as $q \rightarrow y$ from below.

2.2.5. *Other Monetary Equilibria*

In the borderline case $xz/n = 1$, there exists a continuum of monetary equilibria. As is easily shown, if $xz/n = 1$, then for any $\hat{q} \in (0, q^*)$, there exists a $\hat{k} \in (0, k^*)$ such that $\hat{q}^h(t) = q$, $k^h(t) = \hat{k}$ for all $t \geqslant 1$ and h is a monetary equilibrium.

In the rest of this paper, special attention will be paid to monetary equilibria that are the analogues of the q^* and $\hat{q}$ equilibria, equilibria that I call *stationary*. But there are, in general, other monetary equilibria. Without additional restrictions on preferences, there may exist nonconstant $q(t)$ sequences that satisfy (11). Also, independent of whether preferences are further restricted, if $xz/n < 1$, then for any $q(1) \in (0, k^*)$, there exist monetary equilibria with $q^h(1) = q(1)$ for all h and $q^h(t+1) / q^h(t) = xz/n$ for all $t \geqslant 1$ and h. This is to say that if individuals in every period act on the basis of the view that per capita real money holdings decline exponentially at the rate xz/n, then there are equilibria in which this occurs.

The existence of multiple perfect-foresight or *rational expectations* equilibria has been taken by some to be a weakness of this equilibrium concept. (See Shiller 1978.) But a weakness relative to what? In models of money, actions depend on beliefs about the future. One option is to leave matters there; actions and, hence, equilibria depend on unexplained beliefs. By requiring that beliefs be tied to objective features of the environment, rational expectations equilibria allow us to focus on a subset of the equilibria consistent with all possible unexplained beliefs. The fact that this subset turns out to contain more than one equilibrium does not provide an argument for abandoning the rational expectations equilibrium concept. Instead, it suggests that we look for a principle that justifies focusing on a subset of the rational expectations equilibria. We know already that we will not be able to justify focusing on equilibria not in the subset of rational expectations equilibria.

One argument for focusing on the k^*, q^*, and $\hat{q}$ equilibria starts out by requiring that equilibrium values depend only on relevant state variables, or, equivalently, by requiring that agents forecast on this basis. In the model we are studying, each member of generation t for $t \geqslant 1$ must forecast $p(t+1)$. But since the evolution of the money supply and the population are known, it is enough to forecast $q(t+1)$. If each young person acting like a competitor responds to the calling out of an arbitrary current price $p(t) \geqslant 0$ with a money demand based on a forecast of $p(t+1)$ that satisfies $q(t+1) = q(t)$, then such demands are consistent with the k^*, q^*, and $\hat{q}$ equilibria only. This forecasting scheme must be justified by some appeal to relevant state variables; since the relevant physical environment for each young person in this economy does not depend on when the young person appears, the person's real portfolio behavior ought not to depend on time. In monetary equilibria other than the $\hat{q}$ and q^* equilibria, the variable time plays a significant role.

2.2.6. *A Stability Result*

I will now present for this model a sort of stability result adapted from the argument presented by Lucas and Prescott (1974).

First note that without additional assumptions, the equality part of (11) is equivalent to

$$q(t) = H[q(t+1)] \tag{12}$$

where H, a continuous function, is defined on $(0,\infty)$, is such that $0 < H < y$, and has a unique fixed point, denoted $\tilde{q}$. (The range of H is limited to the shaded area in Figure 1.) It is an implication that $H'(\tilde{q}) < 1$. For the stability argument I assume $\ell < H' < 1$ for some $\ell \in (-\infty, 1)$, which aside from boundedness is to impose globally the restriction on H' that necessarily holds at the fixed point.

For the forecasting scheme, I assume that every member of generation 1 acts on the basis of some positive forecast of $p(2)$, denoted $\bar{p}(2)$, and that every member of generation $t \geqslant 2$ acts on the basis of a point forecast $\bar{p}(t+1)$ given by

$$\bar{p}(t+1) = [\lambda \bar{p}(t) + (1-\lambda) p(t)](n/z), \quad \lambda \in [0,1). \tag{13}$$

Here generation $t \geqslant 2$ forms a forecast of $p(t+1)$ by taking a weighted average of the previous generation's forecast of $p(t)$ and the realization of $p(t)$ and "updating" it. The "updating" is accomplished by multiplying by n/z. Note that the scheme discussed above is the special case $\lambda = 0$. In the Appendix I prove

PROPOSITION 2. *If forecasts are given by (13) for some $\bar{p}(2) > 0$ and H [see (12)] satisfies $H' \in (\ell, 1)$ for some $\ell \in (-\infty, 1)$, then*

Figure 1
The Range of H

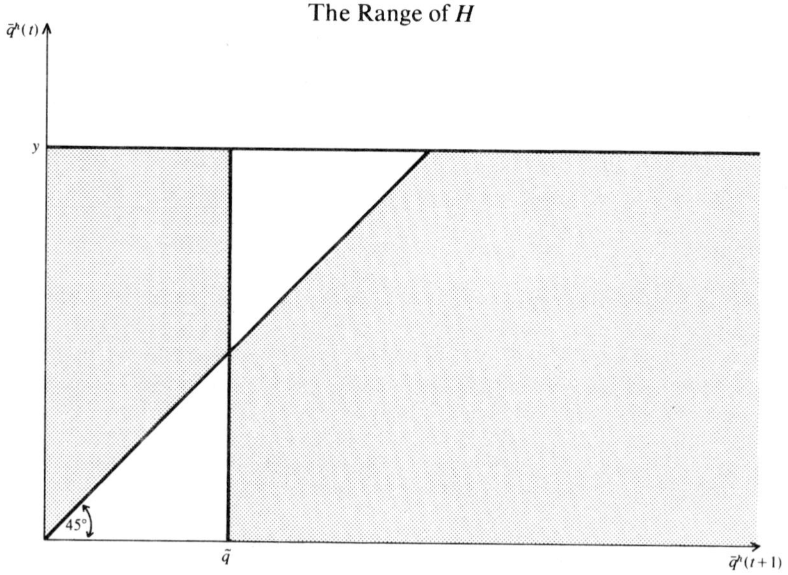

a. *If $xz/n < 1$, then $\lim q^h(t) = q^*$*

b. *If $xz/n = 1$ and $\bar{q}(2) \geqslant q^*$, then $\lim q^h(t) = q^*$*

c. *If $xz/n = 1$ and $\bar{q}(2) < q^*$, then $q^h(t) = \bar{q}(2)$*

d. *If $xz/n > 1$, then $\lim q^h(t) = 0$*

where $\bar{q}(2) = \bar{p}(2)\, M(2)\, /\, N(2)$.

This proposition establishes that the q^* and $\hat{q}$ equilibria—when they exist—and the k^* equilibrium—when the q^* and $\hat{q}$ equilibria do not exist—are in a sense robust with regard to mistakes about the future.

It is worth emphasizing, though, that while the proposition would no doubt hold for some ways of generalizing of (13), the "updating" by n/z seems essential. Such "updating" must be justified by appealing to relevant state variables. Thus, this stability argument cannot be used, for example, to dispose of equilibria with $q^h(t+1)\, /\, q^h(t) = xz/n$ when $xz/n < 1$. For if (n/z) in (13) is replaced by x, then the same sort of stability argument could no doubt be made for those equilibria.

2.2.7. *Optimality*

Letting $C_j(t)$ be total age j consumption of members of generation t and $K(t) \geqslant 0$ be the total of time t output that is stored, a consumption allocation—$c_2(0)$, $c(1)$, $c(2)$, ..., $c(t)$, ...—is *feasible* if for all $t \geqslant 1$ there exists $K(t) \geqslant 0$ that satisfies

$$(14) \qquad C_1(t) + K(t) + C_2(t-1) \leqslant N(t)y + xK(t-1)$$

with $K(0)$ given by initial conditions.

An allocation with a bar ($\bar{}$) over it is *Pareto superior* to one with a caret ($\hat{}$) if $\bar{c}_2^h(0) \geqslant \hat{c}_2^h(0)$ and $u[\bar{c}^h(t)] \geqslant u[\hat{c}^h(t)]$ for all h and all $t \geqslant 1$ with strict inequality somewhere. An allocation with a caret is *Pareto optimal* if there does not exist a feasible allocation that is Pareto superior to it.

Our question about the gain from using fiat money is answered in part by the following propositions.

PROPOSITION 3. *If $x > n$, then any equilibrium allocation is optimal.*

PROPOSITION 4. *If $x \leqslant n$, then the k^* (the nonmonetary) and the $\hat{q}$ equilibria are nonoptimal.*

PROPOSITION 5. *If $xz/n \leqslant 1$ and $z \leqslant 1$, then the q^* equilibrium is optimal.*

PROPOSITION 6. *If $xz/n \leqslant 1$ and $z > 1$, then the q^* equilibrium is nonoptimal.*

The proofs of Propositions 3 and 5 are given in the Appendix.

Proof of Proposition 4. Let $(\bar{c}_1, \bar{c}_2)$ and $\bar{k} > 0$ be the equilibrium lifetime consumption vector and storage of each member of generation $t \geqslant 1$ in any given k^* or $\hat{q}$ equilibrium. By feasibility [see (14)] these quantities satisfy

$$\bar{c}_1 + \bar{c}_2/n \leqslant y + (x/n - 1)k.$$

Since $x \leqslant n$, it follows from (14) that the same consumption allocation for members of generation $t \geqslant 1$ is feasible with $K(t) = 0$ for all $t \geqslant 1$. But this makes it possible to give more to members of generation 0 at $t = 1$ because in any k^* or $\hat{q}$ equilibrium, total consumption of generation 0 at $t = 1$ satisfies

$$N(1)\,\bar{c}_1 + N(1)\,\bar{k} + C_2(0) = N(1)y + xK(0)$$

while under the proposal it satisfies the same equation with $\bar{k}$ replaced by zero.

Q.E.D.

Proof of Proposition 6. By (14), if $K(t) = 0$ for all $t \geq 1$, the class of feasible consumption allocations such that $c^h(t) = (c_1, c_2)$, a constant for all h and $t \geq 1$, is given by

(15) $$c_1 + c_2/n \leq y.$$

It follows that $c^h(t)$ for all h and $t \geq 1$ in any q^* equilibrium satisfies (15) and with equality. Denote $c^h(t)$ in this equilibrium by (c_1^*, c_2^*). It is also the case [see (1) and (2)] that (c_1^*, c_2^*) is preference-maximizing in the set

(16) $$c_1 + c_2\,(z/n) \leq y + (z-1)\,q^*.$$

In Figure 2, let $(\hat{c}_1, \hat{c}_2)$ be the preference-maximizing point that satisfies (15). Transitivity and the fact that the boundary of (16) is steeper than that of (15) imply that (c_1^*, c_2^*) lies northwest of $(\hat{c}_1, \hat{c}_2)$. By revealed preference, then, $(\hat{c}_1, \hat{c}_2)$ is preferred to (c_1^*, c_2^*). And since $c^h(t) = (\hat{c}_1, \hat{c}_2)$ for all h and $t \geq 1$ is feasible with $K(t) = 0$ for all $t \geq 1$, it is feasible under the caret allocation to have total consumption of generation 0 at $t = 1$ satisfy

$$\hat{C}_2(0) = xK(0) + N(1)\,(y-\hat{c}_1) > xK(0) + N(1)\,(y-c_1^*) = C_2^*(0)$$

where $C_2^*(0)$ is total generation 0 consumption at $t = 1$ under the q^* equilibrium.

Q.E.D.

Propositions 3–6 imply no connection between the path of the value of fiat money in an equilibrium and the optimality of that equilibrium. Thus there may be an optimal monetary equilibrium with a declining value of fiat money—for example, if $x < n < z \leq 1$—and there may be a nonoptimal monetary equilibrium with an unchanging value of fiat money—for example, if $z = n > 1 > x$. What counts is the path of the quantity of fiat money.

Propositions 3–6 suggest that the quantity of fiat money should not be increased. For those propositions imply that if $z \leq 1$, then an optimal monetary equilibrium exists whenever the nonmonetary is nonoptimal. If we limit consideration to $z = 1$, a fixed money supply, then the converse is also true.

But several comments are in order. First, note that we have studied changes in fiat money brought about in a particular way. These changes satisfy

$$-\tau(t) = p(t)\,[M(t) - M(t-1)] = p(t)\,(z-1)\,M(t-1)$$

where $\tau(t)$ is the national income accounts definition of taxes minus transfers in real terms and where the tax or transfer is lump-sum.

So this conclusion holds for fiat money supply increases that come about

Figure 2
The Nonoptimality of $z > 1$

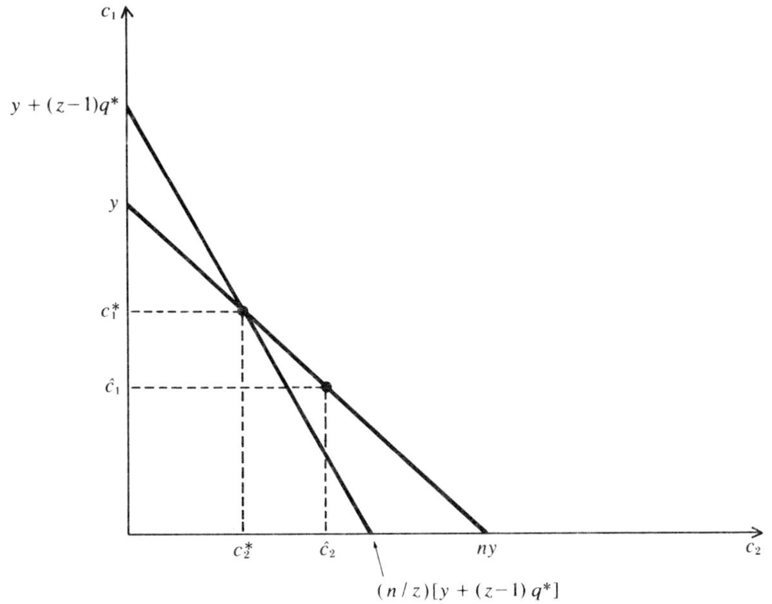

by way of deficits. They are most definitely not to be confused with changes that come about through open market operations, a class of policies discussed in section 5. The conclusion also holds only for purposeless deficits, a point taken up in section 3.

That the tax or transfers are viewed by individuals as unrelated to their saving and portfolio choices is also critical. To take an extreme example, if the scheme is instead one in which each person knows that her or his money purchases when young, $m^h(t)$, say, will be augmented by $(z-1)\, m^h(t)$ when old, then, as is well known, the equilibrium consumption allocation does not depend on z.

It must also be emphasized that we have studied only very special time paths of $M(t)$. In a sense, only the limiting behavior of the supply of fiat money is crucial. For, still considering the same transfer mechanism, suppose

$$M(t) = \begin{cases} z_1\, M(t-1) & t = 1, 2, \ldots, T \\ z_2\, M(t+1) & t \geq T+1. \end{cases}$$

Then it is easily shown that Propositions 5 and 6 hold with z replaced by z_2 and q^* replaced by a monetary equilibrium path with $q^h(t) = q^*$ for all h and $t \geq T$. In other words, both the existence and optimality of monetary equilibria depend only on the limiting behavior of the supply of fiat money. (The equilibrium consumption allocation does, however, depend on z_1.)

Finally, this model does not deal kindly with the prescription that money ought to be managed so that its rate of return is equal to that on real capital. In most models, this is not even a well-defined prescription since the equilibrium rate of return on capital depends on the monetary policy followed.[2] In this model, the technology is such that this prescription is well defined; namely, set z so that $xz/n = 1$. But if $x < n$, then such a policy guarantees that any equilibrium is nonoptimal.

2.3. *Absence of a Dominating Asset and the Sign of the Real Rate of Interest*

In the model so far analyzed, individuals hold a single asset except in the borderline case $xz/n = 1$. In any case, individuals do not diversify in a determinate way. It is important to note that the basic message of Propositions 1–6 carries over to other models.

Thus suppose that the gross return on storage x is random in the following way. The gross return on the consumption goods stored from t to $t+1$ is $x(t) > 0$ where $x(t)$ is a drawing from a probability distribution. For some utility functions, probability distributions, and values of n and z, there exist monetary equilibria with equilibrium portfolios that are diversified in a determinate way. (See Bryant and Wallace 1979b.) More to the point, though, versions of Propositions 1–6 can be expected to hold.[3] And, for any z and n, if the probability distribution of returns to storage is too favorable, then there will not exist a monetary equilibrium. Thus the absence of dominance requirement still obtains.

Since this requirement is foreign to so many so-called models of money, I want to comment on it in some detail. And to simplify the discussion, I will abstract from growth.

Economists are used to working with models in which there are real assets with a positive net yield in equilibrium. Put differently, most economists seem automatically to assume a positive real rate of interest implied by the presence of something like the "land" of the Hecksher-Ohlin model (Henry George land)—a uniform, productive, nonreproducible form of capital.[4] But real land is quite different from the land of the Hecksher-Ohlin model. If it were not, why have titles to physical quantities of land rarely if ever served as commodity money? (And why does it prove so difficult to implement Henry George's tax?) Indeed, one suspects that the transaction velocity of real land is not very high (relative, say, to that of shares in GM). The point,

[2]Tobin's (1965) is one of the first models with this property. The model described in the text could easily be converted to one in which the equilibrium rate of return on storage of the consumption good depends on the monetary policy followed. One need only assume that x depends on the aggregate amount stored.

[3]A model that allows for intergeneration risk sharing via markets arises from assuming that generation $t+1$ appears prior to the realization of $x(t)$. One that precludes such risk sharing arises from assuming that the realization of $x(t)$ occurs after generation $t-1$ disappears and before generation $t+1$ appears. Moreover, since in the latter instance, the young of generation t maximize expected utility conditional on $x(t)$ while in the former they maximize unconditionally, the definition of Pareto superiority should take this difference into account. (See Muench 1977.)

I suspect that Muench's result in his appendix on the nonoptimality of nonstochastic growth rate rules according to his conditional Pareto optimality criterion is due to his scheme for allocating old people across markets. This scheme is not necessarily part of Lucas' model.

[4]For a detailed model of traded land of this sort, see Kareken and Wallace 1977.

of course, is that real land is nonuniform, is reproducible, and may not be productive. To abstract from these features for some purposes may be harmless. To abstract from them in thinking about fiat money is probably disastrous.

Also, one should not be misled by the role of physical appreciation in the model analyzed above. In that model $x > n$ is enough to drive out fixed-supply fiat money. But this does not mean that the existence of any good that appreciates physically would do. The $x > n$ results found above depend on all aspects of the model—that there is only one good, that the population and its endowment of that good are nonrandom, and so on. Physical appreciation does not imply dominance of fixed-supply fiat money if there are other sources of supply and demand disturbances that in a multigood model make the price of the physically appreciating good random. Thus, for example, the possibility of gold discoveries makes gold a less perfect commodity money than would otherwise be the case.

All of this is not to say that the world we live in, without various legal restrictions, necessarily has room for valued fixed-supply fiat money. It is meant to suggest that the possibility cannot be easily dismissed by casual empiricism that appeals to the existence of a positive (net of growth) real rate of interest given by the technology. Hahn dismisses the possibility in his discussion of the overlapping generations model when he says (1973a, p. 232), "But money is not the only means of storage nor the only costless means (recall Keynes's remarks on land)."

2.4. *Private Borrowing and Lending and So-Called Inside Money*

Models built on the overlapping generations friction imply a sharp distinction between what used to be called *inside money* and *outside money*. I will present one aspect of this distinction here by considering a version of the model we have been studying that has room for private borrowing and lending. Another aspect of this distinction will come up in the discussion of open market operations.

I will proceed by describing an example. Let $n = z = 1$ (an unchanging population and money supply), $x = 0$ (no storage), and let generation t consist of two groups: $N_1(t) = \alpha N$ and $N_2(t) = [1-\alpha]\, N$, $0 < \alpha < 1$, where $h \in N_1(t)$ is endowed with y units of the consumption good when young and $h \in N_2(t)$ is endowed with y units when old. For all h and $t \geqslant 1$, assume that $u[c^h(t)] = c_1^h(t)c_2^h(t)$.

A quick route to the study of equilibria for this economy analogous to the k^*, q^*, and $\hat{q}$ equilibria is to find equilibria consistent with there being a single, unchanging equilibrium gross rate of return on saving denoted R. In such an equilibrium we have, for the logarithmic utility function,

$$v(y-s_1, Rs_1) = Rs_1 / (y-s_1) = R \tag{17}$$

$$v(-s_2, y + Rs_2) = (y + Rs_2) / (-s_2) = R \tag{18}$$

where $v = u_1 / u_2$ and s_i is real saving of each member of group N_i.

A nonmonetary equilibrium of this type must satisfy (17), (18), and $\alpha s_1 + (1-\alpha)\, s_2 = 0$, the last condition being the nonmonetary equilibrium condition for this economy: net saving must be zero. Clearly the solution is unique and implies $R = (1-\alpha) / \alpha$ and

$$c^h(t) = \begin{cases} [y/2, y(1-\alpha)/2\alpha] & \text{if } h \in N_1 \\ [\alpha y/2(1-\alpha), y/2] & \text{if } h \in N_2. \end{cases}$$

The proofs of Propositions 3 and 4 imply that this equilibrium is optimal if $\alpha \leqslant 1/2$ and nonoptimal otherwise. Those proofs apply because in terms of resources and preferences this economy is a special case of the one studied in those proofs.

A monetary equilibrium consistent with an unchanging rate of return must satisfy (17), (18), $R = 1$, and $\alpha s_1 + (1-\alpha) s_2 > 0$, the last condition being a positive net saving requirement. Since $s_1 = -s_2 = y/2$ at $R = 1$, this exists if and only if $\alpha > 1/2$. Moreover, $p(t)M$, the equilibrium aggregate real value of fiat money is $N[\alpha s_1 + (1-\alpha) s_2] = y(2\alpha-1) N/2$. Clearly, when this equilibrium exists, it is optimal.

Now, suppose that there are K such economies identical except that $1/2 < \alpha_1 < \alpha_2 < \ldots < \alpha_K < 1$. In particular, let the fixed supply of fiat money be the same in all these economies.

Viewed as a cross section, then, the price of fiat money varies directly with α_K. And since M/N, the per capita supply of fiat money, is the same for all these economies, it necessarily bears no relationship to the equilibrium value of $p(t)$ in the different economies. But if for some reason we try to find some nominal asset total that is related to $p(t)$ across these economies, then we will succeed. In a monetary equilibrium, members of group N_1 in the aggregate in economy k hold assets with real value of $\alpha_k Ny/2$. Therefore, the nominal value of their assets is $M/(2-\alpha_k^{-1})$, real assets divided by the price of fiat money in economy k. This nominal asset total is decreasing in α_k, as is $1/p(t)$, the price level.

It is also the case that similar relationships can be generated for the time paths of asset totals and the price level in a single economy by studying economies in which $\alpha(t)$ varies through time.

But what is to be inferred from such relationships? The economy just examined is one in which members of group 1, the only holders of assets, are indifferent between holding fiat money and holding promises of members of group 2. (It is, of course, easy to destroy this indifference. One way is to make the endowment of group 2 random.) But so what? That does not justify aggregating the two into something called M_i and ignoring the distinction between fiat money and the debt of group 2. Since versions of Propositions 3–6 apply to this class of economies, the distinction is critical. The point, of course, is that α influences the demand for fiat money in a way not all that different from the influence exerted by $N(t)$ or x in the model of section 2.2. Even though variations in the demand for fiat money affect the value of a fixed stock of it, no response in the form of a value of $z \neq 1$ is called for.

3. Fiat Money Issue as Taxation

One of the basic propositions of public finance asserts that if endowment taxation is costless, then it is best. I will begin by establishing a version of this proposition for a no-storage ($x=0$) version of the model studied in section 2.2.

PROPOSITION 7. *If $N(t)\beta y$ for $0 < \beta < 1$ can be raised each period through fiat money issue, then with costless taxation of endowments there exists a monetary equilibrium with a constant money supply that is Pareto superior to* *any stationary equilibrium with $N(t)\beta y$ raised through fiat money issue.*

Proof. Let $(\hat{c}_1, \hat{c}_2)$ be the q^* equilibrium allocation with a fixed money supply and with each young person subject to endowment taxation of βy. It follows from (1) and (2) that $(\hat{c}_1, \hat{c}_2)$ satisfies

$$c_1 + c_2/n \leqslant (1-\beta)y \tag{19}$$

with equality and is preference-maximizing in this set. Let $(\bar{c}_1, \bar{c}_2)$ be any stationary equilibrium with $N(t)\beta y$ raised through fiat money issue. [Bryant and Wallace (1979a) prove that the existence of any equilibrium with $N(t)\beta y$ raised through fiat money issue implies the existence of a stationary equilibrium in which this occurs.] By feasibility $(\bar{c}_1, \bar{c}_2)$ also satisfies (19). And being an equilibrium, it satisfies (19) with equality and, by (1) and (2), is preference-maximizing in the set

$$c_1 + c_2/R \leqslant y \tag{20}$$

where R equals $p(t+1)/p(t)$, a constant in a stationary equilibrium.

But these facts imply that $(\hat{c}_1, \hat{c}_2)$ does not satisfy (20), which is to say that $(\bar{c}_1, \bar{c}_2)$ lies northwest of $(\hat{c}_1, \hat{c}_2)$. (See Figure 3.) If this were not true, transitivity or smoothness of preferences would be violated. It follows that the caret allocation is Pareto superior to the bar allocation because $(\hat{c}_1, \hat{c}_2)$ is preferred to $(\bar{c}_1, \bar{c}_2)$ by all members of all generations $t \geqslant 1$ and $\hat{c}_1 < \bar{c}_1$ implies

Figure 3
Costless Endowment Taxation
vs. a Fiat Money–Financed Deficit

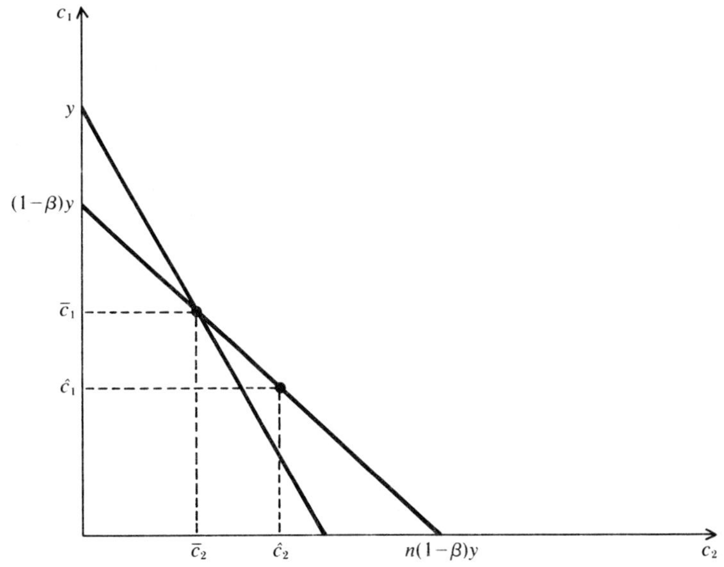

that the current old get more under the caret allocation than under the bar allocation.

Q.E.D.

Note, of course, that there may not be such a bar allocation and that there may be more than one. (For an excise tax on any commodity, there may be no tax that raises a given revenue or there may be many.) Note also that although in this simple model fiat money issue is a tax on saving, the nonoptimality of such taxation does not require that saving depend on the rate of return in any systematic way. In particular, the proof holds for a Cobb-Douglas utility function which implies no dependence of saving on the rate of return. Nor does the nonoptimality depend on there being inflation in the sense of a falling value of fiat money. But if there is an equilibrium bar allocation, then the equilibrium value of R is less than n. Thus, the growth-corrected rate of return must be negative. If it were not, the government could not succeed in financing its deficit.

Of course, in general, fiat money issue is not a tax on all saving. It is a tax on saving in the form of money. But it is important to emphasize that the equilibrium rate-of-return distribution on the equilibrium portfolio does depend on the magnitude of the fiat money–financed deficit. This is true, for example, in a model with a risky real asset that gives rise to diversified equilibrium portfolios and is true in a model in which the rate of return on money is random because the size of each generation is random.

In all these models, the real rate-of-return distribution faced by individuals in equilibrium is less favorable the greater the fiat money–financed deficit. Many economists seem to ignore this aspect of inflation because of their unfounded attachment to Irving Fisher's theory of nominal interest rates. [According to this theory, (most?) real rates of return do not depend on the magnitude of anticipated inflation.] The attachment to Fisher's theory of nominal interest rates accounts for why economists seem to have a hard time describing the distortions created by anticipated inflation. The models under consideration here imply that the higher the fiat money–financed deficit, the less favorable the terms of trade—in general, a distribution—at which present income can be converted into future income. This seems to be what most citizens perceive to be the cost of anticipated inflation.

Of course, Proposition 7 is only the start of an analysis of fiat money issue as a taxation device. The modern public finance literature often starts by ruling out endowment taxation.[5] And, as has often been noticed, if all taxes are distorting, then the optimal tax structure may involve taxation through fiat money issue.

A simple way to amend the model of section 2.2 to allow for this possibility is to impose costs of raising revenue through endowment taxation. Thus $(\hat{c}_1, \hat{c}_2)$ in Figure 3 is not feasible if it is assumed that $(\beta+g)y$ must be turned over by each young person in order that the government get βy—$gy > 0$ being enforcement costs. It follows, then, that the fixed-supply–monetary-equilibrium allocation satisfies (19) with strict inequality and that no qualitative comparison between endowment taxation and fiat money–issue taxation is possible. Indeed, it is easy to make assumptions that guarantee that the optimal tax structure involves some of both forms of taxation.

[5]See Helpman and Sadka 1979 for an analysis of fiat money issue as a taxation device when only commodity taxes are allowed.

4. Lucas' Incomplete Information Model

So far nothing has been said about business cycles. Among the aspects of business cycles that call for explanation are time series relationships between, on the one hand, nominal aggregate demand variables like the deficit and, on the other hand, real variables like total output. These relationships appear paradoxical from at least two points of view. First, ordinary market-clearing models with behavior generated by optimization free from various kinds of money illusion do not seem to generate them. Second, such relationships do not seem to be invariant; they do not hold in cross sections where the observations are averages over time of the same variables for different countries, and they do not seem to persist over time. Lucas' (1972) model shows how relationships with these properties can arise if ordinary market-clearing models are altered so that individuals are faced with incomplete information in a way that induces them to make inferences from observations on the value of money. I will present a very simple version of Lucas' model.

4.1. *The Model*

The model is a variant of that in section 2.2. The size of each generation is random: $N(t) = N_i > 0$ with probability $\pi_i > 0$, $i=1, 2$. The tax-transfer scheme is that of section 2.2 except that it too is random: $M(t) = z(t)M(t-1)$ where $z(t) = z_j > 0$ with probability $\theta_j > 0, j=1, 2$. $N(t)$ and $z(t)$ are independent of one another. Moreover, $N_1/N_2 = z_1/z_2 < 1$, the equality being a very special assumption, the need for which is discussed below. There is a common von Neumann–Morgenstern utility function $u[c^h(t)]$, the expected value of which is maximized by each young person. And, as above, each young person is endowed with y units of the single consumption good when young. Storage is ruled out.

Two versions of this model will be studied. One is a *complete* information version. In it, the young at time t choose money holdings knowing $M(t-1)$, $z(t)$, and $N(t)$; that is, they know the money supply, $M(t)$, and the size of their generation, a demand variable. They also know the distributions of $z(t+1)$ and $N(t+1)$. In the *incomplete* information version, the young at t choose money holdings knowing only $M(t-1)$ and the distributions of $z(t)$, $z(t+1)$, $N(t)$, and $N(t+1)$. They do, however, draw inferences about $z(t)$ and $N(t)$ from observing $p(t)$, the time t value of money.

It is convenient to begin by rewriting constraints (1) and (2) as

$$c_1^h(t) \leq y - q^h(t) \tag{21}$$

$$c_2^h(t) \leq \{q^h(t)+\bar{q}(t)[z(t+1)-1]\}p(t+1)/p(t) \tag{22}$$

where $q^h(t) = p(t)m^h(t)$ is the choice variable, $\bar{q}(t) = p(t)M(t)/N(t)$ is per capita real money holdings, which the individual treats parametrically, and where, by the definition of $\bar{q}(t)$,

$$p(t+1)/p(t) = N(t+1)\bar{q}(t+1)/N(t)\bar{q}(t)z(t+1). \tag{23}$$

In order to proceed, the distribution of $c_2(t)$, which depends on the information restrictions, must be specified. The procedure to be followed is, first, to in effect make a guess about certain properties of the equilibrium $c_2(t)$ distribution, and, second, to show that there is in fact an equilibrium satisfying these properties.

4.1.1. *Complete Information*

Here the guess is that there is an equilibrium in which for each value of $N(t)$ there is at most one value of $\bar{q}(t)$, that is, an equilibrium such that $\bar{q}(t) = q_i$ if $N(t) = N_i$.

Now if $N(t) = N_i$ and individuals forecast on the basis of $\bar{q}(t) = q_i$, then by (23) the distribution of $p(t+1)/p(t)$ is given by $p(t+1)/p(t) = N_j q_j / N_i q_i z_k$ with probability $\pi_j \theta_k$, there being four possible values of $p(t+1)/p(t)$. This implies a distribution for the right-hand side of (22), namely,

$$(24) \qquad c_{2i}(j,k) \leq [q_i^h(t) + q_i(z_K - 1)] N_j q_j / N_i q_i z_k$$

with probability $\pi_j \theta_k$ where $c_{2i}(j,k)$ is second-period consumption if $N(t) = N_i$, $N(t+1) = N_j$, and $z(t+1) = z_k$. Given $N(t) = N_i$, for each value of $q_i^h(t)$, the choice variable, there are four possible values of $c_{2i}(j,k)$ as j and k each range over 1 and 2.

Thus, if $N(t) = N_i$, $q_i^h(t)$ is chosen to maximize $\Sigma_j \Sigma_k \pi_j \theta_k u[c_{1i}, c_{2i}(j,k)]$ subject to (21) and (24) with q_i and N_i known and treated parametrically. It follows that for $i=1, 2$ the optimal value of $q_i^h(t)$ satisfies (21) and (24) with equality and

$$(25) \qquad 0 = \sum_j \sum_k \pi_j \theta_k \{u_1[c_{1i}, c_{2i}(j,k)] - u_2[c_{1i}, c_{2i}(j,k)] N_j q_j / N_i q_i z_k\}.$$

Since all members of generation t are identical, for equilibrium we must have $q_i^h(t) = q_i$ for $i=1, 2$. Therefore, for each i the equilibrium q_i satisfies

$$(26) \qquad 0 = \sum_j \sum_k \pi_j \theta_k \{u_1(y - q_i, q_j N_j / N_i) - u_2(y - q_i, q_j N_j / N_i) N_j q_j / N_i q_i z_k\}$$

giving us a pair of equations in q_1 and q_2. Letting $\eta = \Sigma_k \theta_k / z_k$, the mean of z_k^{-1}, we may rewrite (26) as

$$(27) \qquad 0 = \sum_j [\pi_j u_1(y - q_i, q_j N_j / N_i)] - \eta \sum_j [\pi_j u_2(y - q_i, q_j N_j / N_i) N_j q_j / N_i q_i], \quad i = 1,2.$$

Notice that for any equilibrium of this kind, η is the only aspect of the distribution of $z(t)$ that matters for real variables and, hence, for expected utility. It follows that in an equilibrium of this kind, there is no correlation between $z(t)$ and real variables.

4.1.2. *Incomplete Information*

Here the young choose $q^h(t)$ knowing only $M(t-1)$ and the current value of fiat money, $p(t)$. The surmise is that there is an equilibrium in which for given $M(t-1)$, $p(t)$ and $N(t)/z(t)$ are in one-to-one correspondence with $p(t)$ strictly increasing in $N(t)/z(t)$. Note that $N(t)/z(t)$ may be thought of as a measure of the demand for money at t relative to the supply at t and that for our specification there are three distinct values of $N(t)/z(t)$.

In such an equilibrium, knowledge of $p(t)$ implies knowledge of $N(t)/z(t)$. And for two of the possible values of $N(t)/z(t)$—namely, N_1/z_2 and N_2/z_1—knowledge of the ratio $N(t)/z(t)$ implies knowledge of both $N(t)$ and $z(t)$. But because $N_1/N_2 = z_1/z_2$, if $N(t)/z(t) = N_i/z_i$, its intermediate value, then either

$N(t) = N_1$ and $z(t) = z_1$ or $N(t) = N_2$ and $z(t) = z_2$. In other words, if $p(t)$ takes on its intermediate value, then either both demand and supply are low or both are high. This is what gives rise to more uncertainty in this version than in the complete information version.[6]

The hypothesized correspondence between $p(t)$ and $N(t)/z(t)$ implies that an observation on $p(t)$ is equivalent to an observation on $\bar{q}(t)$ since $\bar{q}(t) = p(t)M(t-1)[z(t)/N(t)]$ and $M(t-1)$ is known. We further hypothesize that the equilibrium is such that $\bar{q}(t)$ is a function of $N(t)/z(t)$, namely, that $\bar{q}(t) = q_{ij}$ if $N(t) = N_i$ and $z(t) = z_j$ with $q_{11} = q_{22}$. This is equivalent to hypothesizing that the equilibrium sample space for the price level, $1/p(t)$, is proportional to the known pretransfer stock of money, $M(t-1)$.

The distribution of $c_2(t)$ conditional on $N(t)/z(t)$ can now be described. If $N(t)/z(t) = N_i/z_j$ with $i \neq j$, then for all k and r

$$c_{2ij}(k,r) \leqslant [q^h_{ij}(t)+q_{ij}(z_r-1)]N_k q_{kr}/N_i q_{ij} z_r \tag{28}$$

with probability $\pi_k \theta_r$. Aside from different subscripting, this is the same as (25). Thus, if $i \neq j$, then for each value of the choice variable, $q^h(t)$, there are four possible values of second-period consumption. If $N(t)/z(t) = N_i/z_i$, then for all i, k, r

$$c_{2ii}(k,r) \leqslant [q^h_{ii}(t)+q_{ii}(z_r-1)]N_k q_{kr}/N_i q_{ii} z_r \tag{29}$$

with probability $\rho_i \pi_k \theta_r$, where $\rho_i = \pi_i\theta_i/(\pi_1\theta_1+\pi_2\theta_2)$ is the probability that $N(t) = N_i$ given that $[N(t),z(t)]$ is either (N_1,z_1) or (N_2,z_2). In this case, the value of $N(t) = N_i$ cannot be identified so there are eight possible values for second-period consumption for each value of the choice variable, $q^h_{ii}(t)$.

Therefore, if $N(t)/z(t) = N_i/z_j$ with $i \neq j$, then expected utility is $\Sigma_k\Sigma_r\pi_k\theta_r u[c_{1ij},c_{2ij}(k,r)]$. This is maximized by choice of $q^h_{ij}(t)$ subject to (21) and (28). Thus for $(i,j) = (1,2)$ and $(i,j) = (2,1)$, the optimal choice satisfies (21) and (28) with equality and

$$0 = \sum_k \sum_r \pi_k\theta_r\{u_1[c_{1ij},c_{2ij}(k,r)] - u_2[c_{1ij},c_{2ij}(k,r)]N_k q_{kr}/N_i q_{ij} z_r\}. \tag{30}$$

If $N(t)/z(t) = N_i/z_i$, then expected utility is $\Sigma_i\Sigma_k\Sigma_r\rho_i\pi_k\theta_r u[c_{1ii},c_{2ii}(k,r)]$. This is maximized by choice of $q^h_{ii}(t)$ subject to (21) and (29). The optimal choice satisfies the constraints with equality and

$$0 = \sum_i \sum_k \sum_r \rho_i\pi_k\theta_r\{u_1[c_{1ii},c_{2ii}(k,r)] - u_2[c_{1ii},c_{2ii}(k,r)]N_k q_{kr}/N_i q_{ii} z_r\}. \tag{31}$$

Since for equilibrium we must have $q^h_{ij} = q_{ij}$, (30) and the relevant constraints at equality give us two equilibrium conditions: for $i \neq j$

$$0 = \sum_k \sum_r \pi_k\theta_r[u_1(y-q_{ij},N_k q_{kr}/N_i) - u_2(y-q_{ij},N_k q_{kr}/N_i)N_k q_{kr}/N_i q_{ij} z_r] \tag{32}$$

[6]The special assumption $N_1/N_2 = z_1/z_2$ is needed because in arbitrary discrete sample spaces an observation on a ratio is in general equivalent to an observation on both the numerator and the denominator. Lucas avoids the equivalence by working with continuous sample spaces.

while (31) and the relevant constraints at equality give us one condition

$$(33) \qquad 0 = \sum_i \sum_k \sum_r p_i \pi_k \theta_r [u_1(y-q_{ii}, N_k q_{kr}/N_i) \\ - u_2(y-q_{ii}, N_k q_{kr}/N_i) N_k q_{kr}/N_i q_{ii} z_r].$$

Together, (32) and (33) are three equations in the three values of q_{ij}: q_{12}, q_{21}, and $q_{11} = q_{22}$.

4.2. *A Numerical Example*

I will display the incomplete information solution for the following example: $y = 1.0$, $u[c^h(t)] = (c_1^h)^{1/2} + (c_2^h)^{1/2}$, $z_1 = 1.0$, $z_2 = 1.1$, and $\pi_k = \theta_r = 1/2$ for all k and r.

For these parameter choices, (32) can be written as

$$(34) \qquad q_{ij}(y-q_{ij})^{-1/2} = (.25) \sum_k \sum_r [(N_k q_{kr}/N_i)^{1/2}/z_r], \quad i \neq j$$

while (33) can be written as

$$(35) \qquad q_{ii}(y-q_{ii})^{-1/2} = (.125) \sum_i \sum_k \sum_r [(N_k q_{kr}/N_i)^{1/2}/z_r].$$

The solution for the q_{ij}'s, which satisfies the hypothesized correspondence between $p(t)$ and $N(t)/z(t)$, is as shown in Table 1. In a long time series for this economy, each of these cells turns up one-quarter of the time. Therefore, observations on the pairs $[q(t), z(t)]$—per capita real saving or real money holdings and the gross growth rate of the money supply—give rise to the scatter diagram shown as dots (●) in Figure 4. (Each dot represents one-quarter of the observations.)

Table 1

N \ z	$z_1 = 1.0$	$z_2 = 1.1$
N_1	.477	.485
N_2	.469	.477

I said above that Lucas' model is one of noninvariant time series relationships. In this context, *noninvariant* means that the distribution of $q(t)$ implied by a different distribution for $z(t)$ cannot be inferred by simple extrapolation from the dots in Figure 4.

Thus, for the same economy but $z_i' = (1.2)z_i$, $i=1, 2$, which represents a more expansionary fiscal policy, the solution for the q_{ij}'s is as shown in Table 2. The implied $[q(t), z'(t)]$ time series scatter is represented by triangles (▲) in Figure 4.

I can also describe the equilibria for some degenerate $z(t)$ distributions. In such cases, the equilibrium is given by the complete information model since if $z(t)$ is nonrandom, an observation on $p(t)$ is equivalent to an observation on

Table 2

$N \backslash z'$	$z'_1 = 1.2$	$z'_2 = 1.32$
N_1	.388	.395
N_2	.381	.388

$N(t)$. For the economy of the numerical example, but $z(t) = z$ for all t, (27) can be written as

$$q_i(y-q_i)^{-1/2} = (\eta/2)\sum_j(q_jN_j/N_i)^{1/2}, \quad i=1, 2. \tag{36}$$

If $z = 1$ ($\eta=1$), then $q(t) = .508$ when $N(t) = N_1$ and $q(t) = .492$ when $N(t) = N_2$. This solution and that for $z = 1.1$ ($\eta=1/1.1$) are shown in Figure 4 as circles (○).

As these examples demonstrate, the regression equation between $q(t)$ and $z(t)$ that shows up for realizations under a given distribution for $z(t)$ is not one that continues to hold if that distribution is replaced by another distribution. The same is true of regressions of $q(t)$ on $p(t+1)/p(t)$ or on $p(t)/p(t-1)$. Being

Figure 4
Alternative $[q(t), z(t)]$ Time Series Distributions

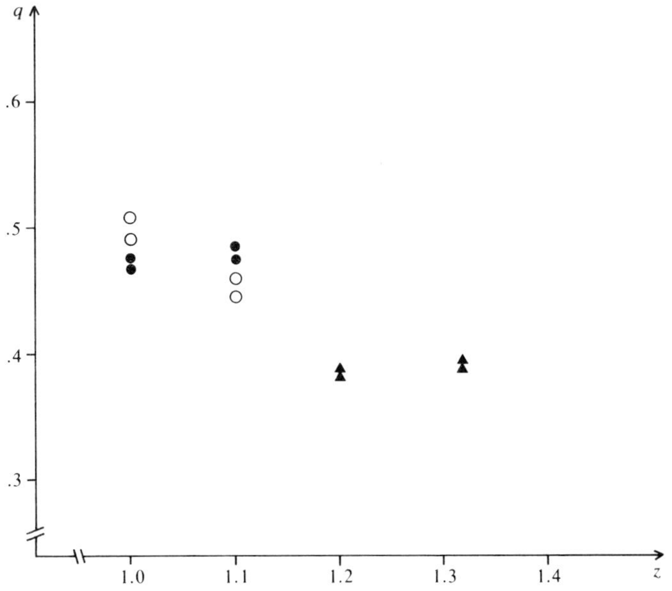

regressions of a choice variable on a rate of return, one may be tempted to call these *demand functions*. But this would be a mistake, as the reader can verify by studying the distributions of these variables in the examples. This is not to suggest, though, that observations on $[q(t),z(t)]$ are useless. If everything about the economy of the example were known except for the value of γ in $u(c^h) = (c_1^h)^\gamma + (c_2^h)^\gamma$ and the distribution of $z(t)$, then observations on $[q(t),z(t)]$ would permit estimation of γ. This, in turn, would allow predictions to be made about outcomes under different $z(t)$ distributions.

4.3. *General Implications*

Two features of Lucas' model should be kept distinct. One is the nature of the relationships implied under a particular regime. The other is the absence of invariance of these relationships.

With regard to the first feature, Lucas produces a model in which aggregate output is higher the higher is the realized deficit, $z(t)$. This is accomplished by generalizing the model above in two directions. One involves endowing the young with productive, nonstorable labor instead of output and making leisure an additional argument in the utility function. With gross substitution between first- and second-period utility, a positive correlation between per capita output and $z(t)$ is implied.[7] This correlation is converted to one between aggregate output and $z(t)$ by treating the aggregate as a sum over separate subeconomies, each of which is like the economy just described. The subeconomies are related in two ways: at any date t their $N(t)$ realizations sum to a constant and their $z(t)$ realizations are identical.

With regard to the second feature, noninvariance of price-quantity time series correlations is a general property of models in which individuals face uncertainty. In such models, individuals act on the basis of the distributions they think they face.[8] They respond to observations on prices only to the extent that these are relevant as conditioning variables for subsequent distributions they will face. In particular, the individual terms in a time series of prices and quantities implied by such a model are not the outcomes of a sequence of separate conceptual experiments in which individuals are faced with alternative nonstochastic budget sets. Yet despite the fact that macroeconomics is concerned almost entirely with saving and portfolio decisions in which uncertainty and dynamics are acknowledged to play crucial roles, macroeconometric models and, indeed, the macroeconomic paradigm that flows from Keynes' (1936) *General Theory* via Hicks (1937) consist of nothing more than interpreting each term in a time series as the outcome of a separate, static, nonstochastic experiment.

As this discussion suggests, one does not need anything as subtle as Lucas' incomplete information model in order to produce noninvariant time series correlations. The role of the incomplete information model is to produce positive correlations between variables like the government deficit and total output. It is worth noting that Keynes defined the existence of involuntary unemployment as no more than the existence of such Phillips curve correlations.[9]

[7]See Lucas 1977 for a defense of the assumed labor supply response.

[8]One well-known example is the Tobin (1958) portfolio model. For other examples, see Lucas 1976.

[9]According to Keynes (1936, p. 15), people are "involuntarily unemployed if, in the event of a small rise in the price of wage-goods relatively to the money-wage, both the aggregate supply of

5. The Insignificance of Open Market Operations

In the models so far examined, there is a close association between the time path of the supply of fiat money and the time path of its value. Moreover, the usual neutrality proposition holds for those models in the following sense. If $[\hat{c}(t-1),\hat{k}(t),\hat{p}(t)]$ for $t=1, 2, \ldots$ is an equilibrium for a given $M(t)$ sequence, then $[\hat{c}(t-1),\hat{k}(t),\hat{p}(t)/\lambda]$ is an equilibrium for the sequence $\lambda M(t)$ for any $\lambda > 0$.

But those results imply nothing about the effects of changes in the money supply that are brought about through asset exchanges. For asset exchanges, it will be shown that the following is true: If fiscal policy is held fixed (in a way to be made precise below) and government and private transaction costs are the same, then the portfolio of the government—that of a consolidated Federal Reserve–Treasury, say—does not matter, even for the value of fiat money.[10]

The need for a proviso about fiscal policy is clear. If the Federal Reserve makes a loan or buys a security that pays interest, some assumption must be made about what happens to the interest. My assumption corresponds to assuming that the interest goes to the Treasury which uses it to reduce other taxes or to increase other transfers.

I will first ignore transaction costs and consider a model in which the asset purchased in an open market operation is real capital or, equivalently, a title to it. I will then turn to the special case in which open market operations are conducted in government bonds. I will close the section by arguing that there is no obvious evidence that contradicts the view that asset exchanges hardly matter.

5.1. *Government Holdings of Risky Real Assets*

I will work with the model of section 2.2 except that here x, the return on storage, is in each period an independent drawing from a discrete probability distribution: $x(t) = x_i > 0$ with probability $\pi_i > 0$, where $i=1, 2, \ldots, I$ and where $\Sigma_i \pi_i x_i > n$. Moreover, the realization of $x(t)$—the gross return on goods stored from t to $t+1$—occurs after generation $t-1$ disappears and after generation t commits itself to a portfolio, but before generation $t+1$ appears. Thus, intergeneration risk sharing via markets is precluded.

I will also assume that the common utility function u is von Neumann–Morgenstern and that each young person maximizes expected utility. I continue to assume $N(t)/N(t-1) = n$.

5.1.1. *Possible Stationary Equilibria With a Fixed Money Supply and No Government Storage*

It is convenient to describe the choice problem and, hence, equilibrium conditions in terms of demands and supplies for contingent claims on second-period consumption. Thus, let s_i be the price in units of first-period consumption of one unit of second-period consumption in state i, state i being the outcome $x(t) = x_i$. I will denote by c_{2i} second-period consumption in state i.

labour willing to work for the current money-wage and the aggregate demand for it at that wage would be greater than the existing volume of employment."

[10]It may be helpful to note that this is nothing but a Modigliani-Miller irrelevance-of-financial-structure result in which the government is a financial intermediary in the same way as is the corporation in the Modigliani-Miller theory.

Each young person chooses c_1 and c_{2i} for each i to maximize $\Sigma_i \pi_i u(c_1, c_{2i})$ subject to

$$(37) \qquad c_1 + \sum_i s_i c_{2i} \leq y$$

treating the s_i's as parameters. The necessary and sufficient conditions for a maximum are (37) at equality and for each i

$$(38) \qquad \pi_i u_2(c_1, c_{2i}) = s_i \sum_{j=1}^{I} \pi_j u_1(c_1, c_{2j}).$$

These conditions are implicit demand functions.

Supplies are generated by competitive firms. Profits from storing $k \geq 0$ units of consumption good are $k(\Sigma_i s_i x_i - 1)$ and must be nonpositive in any competitive equilibrium. Thus, $\Sigma_i s_i x_i = 1$ in an equilibrium with positive storage. Profits from storing m units of money are $m[p(t+1)\,\Sigma_i s_i - p(t)]$, it being taken for granted that there is an equilibrium in which $p(t+1)$ does not depend on i. Moreover, anticipating that in a stationary monetary equilibrium with a fixed money supply $p(t+1) = np(t)$, it follows that $n\Sigma_i s_i = 1$ in such an equilibrium.

Thus, a stationary nonmonetary equilibrium for this economy consists of nonnegative values of k, c_1, and c_{2i} and s_i for each i that satisfy (37) at equality, (38), the nonpositive profit condition, $\Sigma_i s_i x_i \leq 1$, and

$$(39) \qquad c_{2i} = x_i k, \quad i = 1, 2, \ldots, I$$

where k is per capita storage of the consumption good. It is easy to show that such an equilibrium with $k > 0$ exists and is unique. We denote the equilibrium values by adding a star (*).

A stationary monetary equilibrium for this economy consists of nonnegative values of k, c_1, c_{2i}, and s_i for each i and a positive value of q that satisfy (37) at equality, (38), two nonpositive profit conditions, $\Sigma_i s_i x_i \leq 1$ and $n\Sigma_i s_i = 1$, and

$$(40) \qquad c_{2i} = x_i k + nq, \quad i = 1, 2, \ldots, I$$

where $q = p(t)M/N(t)$ for all t. I will denote any such equilibrium by adding two stars (**).[11]

5.1.2. *Stationary Monetary Equilibria With Government Storage*

Let k_g be per capita storage by the government. I will study equilibria in which the government acquires k_g by a new issue of money and in which it maintains these holdings in every period but does not alter its consumption because it is storing k_g. This implies that the government must transfer the amount $x(t)N(t)k_g - N(t+1)k_g$ in period $t+1$. I assume that each of the $N(t)$ members of generation t receives $(x_i - n)k_g$ if $x(t) = x_i$ in the second period of her or his life. Moreover, this transfer (or tax, if negative) is viewed as lump-sum. These assumptions imply

PROPOSITION 8. *If the stationary monetary equilibrium exists, then the contingent claims prices, the consumption allocation, and the value-of-money*

[11]The condition $\Sigma_i \pi_i x_i > n$ insures that $K^{**} > 0$ in any stationary monetary equilibrium.

sequence of that equilibrium, and the per capita portfolio, $k = k^{**} - k_g$ *and* $q = q^{**} + k_g$, *are an equilibrium for any* $k_g \leqslant k^{**}$.

Proof. At $s_i = s_i^{**}$ for all i, the value of taxes $k_g \Sigma_i s_i (x_i - n)$ is zero. Thus, (37) remains the budget set, while in place of (40), we have

$$(41) \qquad c_{2i} = x_i k + nq + (x_i - n) k_g.$$

Thus, if $k = k^{**} - k_g$ and $q = q^{**} + k_g$, then $c_{2i} = c_{2i}^{**}$. To verify that the $p(t)^{**}$ sequence is an equilibrium value-of-fiat-money sequence, we must show that for this price sequence, the amount of money, M, that satisfies the government budget constraint for the purchase of k_g, namely,

$$(42) \qquad p(t)^{**}(M - M^{**}) = N(t) k_g$$

also satisfies $q = q^{**} + k_g$. But this is immediate and completes the proof.

Proposition 8 is not a liquidity-trap result. It is not the case that private sector demands for storage and money holdings are perfectly elastic. The result arises because of the way profits and losses on the government's portfolio are passed back to individuals by way of transfers and taxes.

It is crucial for Proposition 8 that taxes and transfers be passed back on an equal per capita basis. Thus, for example, if instead, any taxes $(x_i < n)$ are levied on, say, the odd-numbered members of generation t and any transfers $(x_i > n)$ are given to the even-numbered members of generation t, then Proposition 8 does not hold. It is not necessary, however, that individuals be identical in tastes and endowments.

The upper bound on k_g is also crucial. If government storage exceeds what would otherwise be undertaken by the private sector in a monetary equilibrium, $(k^{**} < k_g \leqslant k^*)$, then since private storage is nonnegative, private holdings cannot simply offset government holdings. The larger is k_g in this range, the closer is the economy pushed toward a nonmonetary equilibrium. In other words, in this range the more the government stores, the lower is the value of fiat money.[12] Whether this is to be regarded as monetary policy is debatable; the equilibrium value of transfers implied by unchanged government consumption is negative if $k_g > k^{**}$.

5.2. *Government Bonds and the Optimal Financing of Deficits*[13]

In the United States, open market operations are conducted mainly in government bonds. For a given fiscal policy, one may approach the study of such open market operations by posing the following question: For a given time path of total (outside) government debt, the time path implied by fiscal policy, what are the effects of varying the proportions of the total between fiat money and so-called interest-bearing debt?

Any theory of the composition of total government debt must explain positive interest on safe government debt, where *safe* means free of default risk. Bryant and Wallace (1979a) argue that transaction costs must be invoked to explain positive nominal interest on such debt. One transaction-cost

[12]To find a stationary monetary equilibrium for $k_g \in (k^{**}, k^*)$, solve (37) at equality with y replaced by $y + k_g \Sigma_i s_i (x_i - n)$, (38), and (41) with $k = 0$ for c_1, q, c_{2i}, and s_i with $\Sigma_i s_i = 1/n$ and $\Sigma_i s_i x_i \leqslant 1$. Then the value of money, $p(t)$, is found from $q - p(t) M^{**}/N(t) = k_g$ and the money supply, M, from $q = p(t) M$.

[13]This section summarizes Bryant and Wallace 1979a,b.

model posits that government bonds (Treasury bills and so forth) are issued in denominations so large that most potential holders cannot or do not want to hold them directly. They must be broken up or intermediated by way of a resource-using intermediation technology.[14] But the detailed model of transaction costs is probably less important than the recognition that if safe bonds bear nominal interest, then it must be that the bonds are somehow more costly for the private sector to absorb than is fiat money.

By itself, nothing is implied for the optimal composition of total debt from such relative costliness of bonds. If the private sector costs of absorbing bonds are precisely matched by government real resource savings from issuing bonds (instead of issuing fiat money), then a version of Proposition 8 would hold; that is, the composition of the total of net or outside debt would not matter. Bryant and Wallace do not assume such symmetry of transaction costs. Instead, they assume that the government—a consolidated Treasury–Federal Reserve in the United States—is indifferent in terms of real resource costs between issuing fiat money and issuing and selling bonds.

This particular asymmetry implies a very simple result. Barring special circumstances having to do with price discrimination or particular second-best situations, if bonds bear interest, then too many are outstanding. Indeed, if bonds bear interest whenever the public holds any, then—and again barring special circumstances—the only efficient composition of total outside debt is one composed entirely of fiat money.

That the possibility of price discrimination could vitiate this result is obvious. If by issuing different kinds of debt, the government, a monopolist in issuing safe titles to fiat money, can face groups with different demand functions for nominally safe debt with different rates of return, then efficiency does not call for all debt to be zero-interest debt. Recall that perfect price discrimination is consistent with efficiency.

One potentially relevant second-best situation concerns the role of currency reserve requirements in limiting the size of insured intermediation. (See Bryant and Wallace 1979b.) Given a system of improperly priced deposit insurance—and, on the face of it, both that provided by the FDIC and that provided by Federal Reserve lender-of-last-resort activity would seem to be improperly priced—portfolio restrictions, including reserve requirements, play a potentially important role in limiting the effects of the distorting incentives produced by the insurance.

But neither of these special circumstances can be expected to validate the usual analysis of open market operations. From a macroeconomic point of view, there is a sense in which such special circumstances—including the sort of transaction-cost asymmetry assumed by Bryant and Wallace—are only wrinkles on Proposition 8. The theoretical presumption is that the value of fiat money is not much affected by the composition of the total of the net or outside debt of the government.

5.3. *Casual Remarks on Evidence*

As with the absence-of-dominance implication, the implication that the composition of the government's portfolio is largely irrelevant for the value of fiat money cannot be dismissed easily by casual empiricism.

[14]To invoke transaction costs to explain positive nominal interest on safe assets is not new. This is done in the inventory models of money demand. See Baumol 1952, Tobin 1956, and Miller and Orr 1966.

While there are many historical episodes in which measures of money and measures of total nominal income and/or the price level move up and down together, the implied simple correlations by themselves say nothing about the effects of government asset exchanges.

Most, if not all, of these episodes are ones in which increases in the amount of money are accompanied by asset creation and decreases by asset destruction. Throughout history, the major increases in the amount of money have come about by way of coinage debasements, discoveries of the commodity money, and budget deficits; the major decreases have come about by way of banking panics and, to a lesser extent, budget surpluses. None of these qualify as asset exchanges. Moreover, from the point of view of the models described above, such changes in the amount of money ought to be accompanied by price level changes.

Some would take the implications of macroeconometric models to be a second source of evidence against the view that asset exchanges do not matter. But this would be a mistake. As has long been recognized, the implications for monetary policy that flow from such models depend in a crucial way on the estimated so-called money-demand functions imbedded in the models. But these estimated relationships consist of little more than the simple correlations between measures of money and measures of total nominal income referred to above. And like them, they may well take the form they do only because they are estimated on observations generated by policies under which changes in the measure of money are accompanied by changes in asset totals in the same direction.

A third purported body of evidence is designed to overcome the objection just raised to simple correlation studies. It consists of time series regressions of variables like the price level, total nominal income, real income, and the unemployment rate on measures of both monetary policy and fiscal policy and perhaps some other variables. Examples are recent studies by Stein (1976) and Perry (1978). These investigators treat their regression equations as invariant relationships, as relationships that would continue to hold no matter what rules for the monetary and fiscal policy variables were put into effect. For a host of reasons, many of which already appear in the literature, such a view is preposterous. Yet these authors proceed as if invariance is obvious and does not even require a defense.

I will cite just a few reasons why the invariance view of such regression equations is farfetched. In any sensible model, the correlation (simple or partial) that turns up in time series between a measure of the deficit and other variables under a policy regime in which the deficit is in part random says little about what the response of the economy would be to alternative permanent levels of the deficit. (This is true in both the complete and incomplete information versions of the model described in section 4.) One reason is that a deficit viewed as temporary and likely to be offset by some future surplus gives rise to quite different expectations about future tax liabilities and future prices than does a new level of the deficit that is viewed as permanent. In a similar vein, can it be that the regression that turns up is independent of the sort of policy that the Federal Reserve was following? In particular, can it be independent of whether the Federal Reserve was focusing on interest rates or monetary aggregates? Finally, the invariance view of these regressions implies that nothing happens at time t if it is then announced that a huge permanent deficit will be run starting at time $t+1$. Is that believable?

Unfortunately, I am not clever enough to end these remarks with a description of the right set of tests of the view that the government's portfolio hardly matters. It is even conceivable that the relevant experiment has not yet been performed![15]

6. Country-Specific Fiat Moneys[16]

So far I have considered economies with one government and at most one fiat money. I now turn to a world economy with many governments and, at least potentially, many fiat moneys. The main result is that the market left to itself cannot cope with more than one fiat money.

Consider two economies (countries) of the kind described in section 2.2. For simplicity, let these be identical except that each country has its own tax-transfer scheme. (Think of country 1 as issuing red pieces of paper and country 2 green pieces of paper.) If residents the world over are free to choose to hold whatever money they want, then it follows that if there is an equilibrium in which at least one money has value, then the value of one relative to that of the other (the exchange rate) is constant over time. This is an instance of the absence-of-dominance implication. Moreover, for any unchanging exchange rate, there are equilibria. Why? Name an exchange rate. This allows us to aggregate the red and green pieces at any date into an equivalent number of red pieces, say. Put differently, the named exchange rate and the time paths of the separate money supplies imply a time path of the world money supply. And for any such path, we can display the possible equilibria. Since this is true for any named exchange rate, it follows that there is no market-determined exchange rate. Nor can this result be avoided by simply adding uncertainty. The indeterminacy will not go away by making the deficit in one or both of the countries random.

The indeterminacy just described arises in a regime in which there is no intervention in exchange markets and in which there is unfettered international borrowing and lending; that is, there are no capital controls. It is a regime in which each government does no more than operate its own tax-transfer scheme. Kareken and Wallace (1978) argue that only two kinds of regimes can be expected to prevail. If governments insist on autonomy of budget policies — different values of z in the context of the model of section 2.2 — then the relative values of the two currencies must change over time with that of the country with the higher value of z falling relative to that of the other country, and there must be controls that prevent residents of one country from freely borrowing and lending internationally. But if governments coordinate budget policies—have identical z's—then there can be unfettered international borrowing and lending if the exchange rate is fixed either cooperatively or by one country acting on its own.

These results are established in two steps. The first is a standard argument. If the budget policies differ, then the exchange rate cannot be constant. If it were, residents of the country with the smaller deficit (smaller value of z) would eventually be permanently subsidizing residents of the other country. [To argue that there is no subsidy if the country with the smaller deficit holds

[15]Surely one cannot take the view that history has necessarily generated enough observations to allow us to decisively test every proposition of interest. If this is true for propositions in economics, why not also for those in every other science?

[16]This section consists of a brief summary of Kareken and Wallace 1978.

its reserves in the form of interest-bearing assets is fallacious since it depends on the Fisherian notion that (most?) real interest rates do not depend on the anticipated inflation rate.] The second step simply invokes absence of dominance. The exchange rate can change only if residents are restricted in their portfolio choices.

7. Concluding Remarks

Stanley Fischer (1975, p. 159) concluded the section of his survey paper devoted to microeconomic foundations of money as follows:

> This work [that on the foundations of monetary theory] is obviously both difficult and only a beginning. It is not clear where, if anywhere, it will lead. It will no doubt provide more convincing and carefully worked out explanations for the use of a medium of exchange than we now have, but it appears that those explanations will not be fundamentally different from the traditional verbal explanations, and that they will not have any major consequences for the way in which macromodels are built.

Fischer's pessimism is due, in part, to the fact that the work he surveyed was not carried to the point where it could confront most practical problems in monetary theory and policy and, in part, to the notion that the only practical implications that could possibly flow from such work are a suggested list of arguments and a functional form for the demand function for money.

From our vantage point, the pessimism seems unwarranted. While the reader may find much to quarrel with in what I have presented, two points must be conceded. First, models built on the overlapping generations friction do meet the criteria for being models of money with a microeconomic foundation. (In slightly different words, those models do successfully integrate value and monetary theory.) Second, they do confront and have radical implications for practical issues in monetary theory and policy. Moreover, I would hazard two conjectures, the first with more confidence than the second. Any microeconomic model of money that maintains intrinsic uselessness will have implications sharply at variance with currently held views. Furthermore, any such model will have implications not all that different from those described in the body of this paper.

Yet many readers, I surmise, remain unconvinced. Many, I suspect, still hold to the view that the overlapping generations model is defective because it captures only the *store-of-value* function of money and, in particular, does not capture the *medium-of-exchange* function of money.

Presumably, the medium-of-exchange function is meant to be an additional function of money. (Since money must be held in any model of it, any model of money displays the store-of-value function.) But what is this additional medium-of-exchange function? One hopes that giving money this additional role is not the same as abandoning intrinsic uselessness and is not tantamount to requiring that we find a role for money in a nondynamic setting. But if not, then what does it mean? To say that money plays a medium-of-exchange role if it facilitates trade or is traded relatively frequently is not very helpful. After all, money gets traded in the overlapping generations model; in some versions it is the only thing traded, in others not. And, of course, it facilitates trade; in some versions, the old and the young cannot trade at all except via money. Could it be that this distinction between roles of money is not all that useful? The possibility should be taken seriously. After all, although this distinction has been around for a long time, not a single proposition in monetary theory makes use of it. At a minimum, this should make us question whether saying that a model gives money this or that role is a serious criticism of the model.

But none of this is to suggest that the overlapping generations model is, as it were, the last word in models of money. (I would say it is the first word in models of money.) As noted above, there is general agreement that one needs to introduce some sort of friction into the Walrasian (Arrow-Debreu) general equilibrium model in order to get from it a model of money. But some friction is also needed for a more general problem; the explanation of the form that interactions take among agents where interactions via Walrasian markets is a limiting special case. The obvious goal is a specification of friction that simultaneously provides insights into many forms of interaction, not just market interactions via fiat money.

A related limitation of the overlapping generations model is that money, in a way, works too well in that model. Money completely overcomes the friction. Given a real friction, there is no reason why it should be feasible to overcome it completely.[17] A somewhat trivial way to overcome this defect is to make running the monetary system costly, for example, by making it costly to print money and to prevent counterfeiting. A less trivial way of dealing with this defect involves a theory of the social management of fiat money. Such a theory may also eliminate either the nonmonetary or the monetary equilibrium when both exist. All we have now in the face of these multiple equilibria are the propositions, established for some versions that connect the nonoptimality of the nonmonetary equilibrium with the existence and optimality of some monetary equilibrium.

[17]This is related to if not identical with Hahn's (1973a) distinction between essential and inessential monetary equilibria.

Appendix

A1. Proof of Proposition 2

Letting $\bar{q}(t) = \bar{p}(t)M(t)/N(t)$ for all t, the forecasting scheme (13) is equivalent to

(A1) $$\bar{q}(t+1) = \lambda\bar{q}(t) + (1-\lambda)q(t) \quad \text{all } t \geqslant 2.$$

But $q(t)$ as a function of $\bar{q}(t+1)$ is given by

(A2) $$q(t) = \begin{cases} H[\bar{q}(t+1)] & \text{if } (n/z)\bar{q}(t+1)/q(t) > x \\ \bar{q}(t+1)(n/zx) & \text{otherwise} \end{cases}$$

where, recall, $\bar{p}(t+1)/p(t) = (n/z)\bar{q}(t+1)/q(t)$ is the predicted rate of return on money.

I will use (A1) and (A2) to find $\bar{q}(t+1)$ as a function $\bar{q}(t)$.

If $q(t)$ is given by the upper branch of (A2), then by (A1)

(A3) $$\bar{q}(t+1) = \lambda\bar{q}(t) + (1-\lambda)H[\bar{q}(t+1)].$$

But by the hypothesis on H', $\bar{q}(t)$ and $\bar{q}(t+1)$ satisfy (A3) if and only if

(A4) $$\bar{q}(t+1) = G[\bar{q}(t)]$$

where $G' = \lambda/[1 - (1-\lambda)H'] \in (0,1)$ and where $\tilde{q}$ is the unique fixed point of both H and G. It follows that $\bar{q}$ sequences that satisfy G converge monotonically to $\tilde{q}$.

If $q(t)$ is given by the lower branch of (A2), then by (A1)

(A5) $$\bar{q}(t+1) = \bar{q}(t)\lambda/[1-(1-\lambda)n/zx].$$

To prove parts a and b of Proposition 2 we consider two cases:

1. $xz/n \leqslant 1$, $\bar{q}(t) \geqslant \tilde{q}$. Suppose at least one of the hypotheses holds with strict inequality. We first show that, then, only the upper branch of (A2) is consistent with the hypotheses. To verify consistency, note that $\bar{q}(t) \geqslant \tilde{q}$ implies $G[\bar{q}(t)] \geqslant \tilde{q}$ which implies $H\{G[\bar{q}(t)]\} \leqslant G[\bar{q}(t)]$ which, in turn, implies satisfaction of the proviso for the upper branch of (A2). To verify inconsistency with the lower branch of (A2), note that (A5) implies $\bar{q}(t+1) > \tilde{q}$ which implies choosing greater second-period consumption at the rate of return x than at the rate of return $n/z \geqslant x$, a violation of our normal goods assumption on preferences. Thus, with strict inequality in one of the hypotheses, we have monotone convergence of $\{\bar{q}(t)\}$ to $\tilde{q}$ via (A4). If both hypotheses hold with equality, then $\bar{q}(t+1) = \tilde{q}$ by (A5).
2. $xz/n < 1$, $\bar{q}(t) < \tilde{q}$. Here either branch of (A2) may be consistent with the hypotheses. But whichever is we get $\bar{q}(t+1) > \bar{q}(t)$ and convergence of $\bar{q}$ to $\tilde{q}$. [Note that (A5) is exponential increasing with $xz/n < 1$.]

Now since $xz/n \leqslant 1$ implies that $\tilde{q} = q^*$ and since convergence of $\{\bar{q}(t)\}$ to $\tilde{q}$ implies convergence of $\{q(t)\}$ to $\tilde{q}$ cases 1 and 2 give us parts a and b of the proposition.

To prove part c we consider $xz/n = 1$ and $\bar{q}(t) < \tilde{q}$. Here $\bar{q}(t+1)$ can only be taken from (A5), that is, $q(t)$ and $\bar{q}(t+1)$ can satisfy only the lower branch of (A2). But (A5) implies $\bar{q}(t+1) = \bar{q}(t)$ and, hence, part c of the proposition.

To prove part d we again consider two cases:

1. $\bar{q}(t) > \tilde{q}$. Here $\bar{q}(t+1)$ and $q(t)$ may be consistent with either branch of (A2). But both imply $\bar{q}(t+1) < \bar{q}(t)$. We cannot get convergence to $\tilde{q}$ because for $\bar{q}(t)$ close enough to $\tilde{q}$, $xz/n > 1$ implies that $\bar{q}(t+1)$ and $q(t)$ cannot satisfy the upper branch of (A2). Thus, we eventually get some $\bar{q} < \tilde{q}$, which brings us to the second case.
2. $\bar{q}(t) \leqslant \tilde{q}$. Here $\bar{q}(t+1)$ must satisfy (A5) which implies convergence of $\{\bar{q}(t)\}$ to 0 and hence convergence of $q(t)$ to 0, as we set out to prove.

A2. Proof of Proposition 3

Let a caret (ˆ) over a term denote an equilibrium allocation and a bar (¯) over a term a feasible Pareto superior (P.S.) allocation. I will show that the assumed existence of the latter gives rise to a contradiction.

Without loss of generality, assume that the P.S. allocation satisfies (14) with equality and that for all $t \geqslant 1$, $v[\bar{c}^h(t)] = v[\bar{c}^{h'}(t)]$ for all h and h' in generation t. (Given an allocation P.S. to the equilibrium allocation that does not satisfy these conditions, one can easily construct the P.S. allocation that is P.S. to the former and, hence, to the latter.)

I will prove in detail that $\bar{K}(t) = \hat{K}(t)$ for all t and will then refer the reader to published results on pure exchange economies for the rest.

Suppose $\bar{K}(t) \neq \hat{K}(t)$ for some t. Then there is a smallest $t \geqslant 1$ at which this happens. I first rule out

A first departure of the form $\bar{K}(t) > \hat{K}(t)$.

Being a first departure, it follows from (14) with equality that either (a) $\bar{C}_2(t-1) < \hat{C}_2(t-1)$ or (b) $\bar{C}_1(t) < \hat{C}_1(t)$ or both.

Case (a): This is easy. Since t is the first departure of $\{\bar{K}\}$ from $\{\hat{K}\}$, we have for $i = 1, 2, \ldots, t-1$

$$\text{(A6)} \qquad \bar{C}_1(t-i) + \bar{C}_2(t-i-1) = \hat{C}_1(t-i) + \hat{C}_2(t-i-1).$$

But by (a) and the properties of a P.S. allocation, $\bar{C}_1(t-1) > \hat{C}_1(t-1)$. One then proceeds backward from $t-1$ to $t-2$ and so on using (A6) to conclude that $\bar{C}_2(0) < \hat{C}_2(0)$, a contradiction.

Case (b): This is more demanding. Under a feasible P.S. allocation, the members of generation t must have more second-period consumption than under an equilibrium allocation. And since $v[\hat{c}^h(t)] \geqslant x$, the extra storage does not produce enough. Therefore, it follows by (14) at equality that

$$\text{(A7)} \qquad \hat{C}_1(t+1) + \hat{K}(t+1) - [\bar{C}_1(t+1) + \bar{K}(t+1)] \equiv N(t+1)d(t+1) > 0.$$

I now show by induction that the d sequence is increasing and unbounded. Since $[\hat{C}_1(t+1) + \hat{K}(t+1)]/N(t+1) \leqslant y$, this will rule out $\bar{K}(t) > \hat{K}(t)$ under case (b).

For the induction step, we use (A7) as an initial condition and consider the following problem.

Choose $c(t+1)$—an allocation for members of generation $t+1$—to minimize $C_2(t+1)$ subject to

$$\text{(A8)} \qquad \hat{C}_1(t+1) + \hat{K}(t+1) - [C_1(t+1) + \bar{K}(t+1)] \geq N(t+1)d(t+1)$$

$$\text{(A9)} \qquad u[c^h(t+1)] \geq u[\hat{c}^h(t+1)].$$

Since $\bar{c}\,(t+1)$ is feasible for this problem—that is, satisfies (A9) and (A8) [see (A7)]—we have $\bar{C}_2(t+1) \geq \tilde{C}_2(t+1)$, where a tilde (˜) over a term denotes a solution value for this minimization problem. Before we use this inequality, though, we want to derive a convenient expression for $\tilde{C}_2(t+1)$ in terms of $d(t+1)$.

It is easily verified that there is a unique solution to this minimization problem that satisfies (A8) and (A9) with equality and, since $\hat{c}^h(t+1) = \hat{c}^{h'}(t+1)$,†

$$\text{(A10)} \qquad \hat{c}_1^h(t+1) - \tilde{c}_1^h(t+1) = d(t+1) + \Delta(t+1), \text{ all } h$$

where

$$\Delta(t+1) = [\bar{K}(t+1) - \hat{K}(t+1)]/N(t+1).$$

But in general, along a contour of u, $c_2^h = g(c_1^h)$ where $g' = -u_1/u_2 = -v$ and $g'' > 0$. Therefore, applying the intermediate value theorem to g, we have

$$\text{(A11)} \qquad g(c_1^h) = g(\hat{c}_1^h) + (\hat{c}_1^h - c_1^h)\,[-g'(\hat{c}_1^h) + f_{\hat{c}}(\hat{c}_1^h - c_1^h)]$$

where the function $f_{\hat{c}}$, whose argument is $(\hat{c}_1^h - c_1^h)$, is strictly increasing and such that $f_{\hat{c}}(0) = 0$.

Now since $\tilde{c}^h(t)$ and $\hat{c}^h(t)$ are on the same contour of u, we may use (A10) and (A11) to write

$$\text{(A12)} \qquad \tilde{c}_2^h(t+1) = \hat{c}^h(t+1)$$
$$+ [d(t+1) + \Delta(t+1)]\,\{v[\hat{c}^h(t+1)] + f_{\hat{c}(t+1)}[d(t+1) + \Delta(t+1)]\}$$

or since

$$\bar{C}_2(t+1) \geq \tilde{C}_2(t+1) = N(t+1)\,\tilde{c}_2^h(t+1),$$

$$\text{(A13)} \qquad [\bar{C}_2(t+1) - \hat{C}_2(t+1)]\,/\,N(t+1)$$
$$\geq [d(t+1) + \Delta(t+1)]\,\{v[\hat{c}^h(t+1)] + f_{\hat{c}(t+1)}[d\,(t+1) + \Delta(t+1)]\}.$$

But since the P.S. and equilibrium allocations satisfy (14) at equality, we have

$$\hat{C}_1(t+2) + \hat{K}(t+2) - [\bar{C}_1(t+2) + \bar{K}(t+2)] \equiv N(t+2)d(t+2)$$
$$= \bar{C}_2(t+1) - \hat{C}_2(t+1) - xN(t+1)\Delta(t+1)$$

†We could get by without this last assumption. See Kareken and Wallace 1977.

or

(A14) $d(t+2) = [\bar{C}_2(t+1) - \hat{C}_2(t+1)] / N(t+1)n - x\Delta(t+1) / n.$

Then using (A13)

(A15) $d(t+2) \geqslant d(t+1)\, v[\hat{c}^h(t+1)] / n + \Delta(t+1)\, \{v[\hat{c}^h(t+1)] - x\} / n$

$+ [d(t+1) + \Delta(t+1)] f_{\hat{c}(t+1)}\, [d(t+1) + \Delta(t+1)] / n.$

The right-hand side consists of a sum of three terms. The last term has the form $(\cdot) f(\cdot) / n$ which is nonnegative by the properties of f. The second term is also nonnegative since $v[\hat{c}^h(t+1)] \geqslant x$ with strict equality if $\Delta(t+1) < 0$. [If $\Delta(t+1) < 0$, then $\hat{K}(t+1) > 0$.] Thus (A15) implies

(A16) $d(t+2) \geqslant d(t+1)\, v[\hat{c}^h(t+1)] / n \geqslant d(t+1)\, (x/n).$

Thus the d sequence is bounded below by a strictly increasing exponential and hence is unbounded.

Next I quickly rule out

A first departure of the form $\bar{K}(t) < \hat{K}(t)$.

If there is such a P.S. allocation, then by (14) either

(A17) $\bar{C}_1(t+1) + \bar{K}(t+1) < \hat{C}_1(t+1) + \hat{K}(t+1)$

or

(A18) $\bar{C}_2(t) < \hat{C}_2(t)$

or both. If (A17) holds, we have an initial condition for the induction proof just given. If (A18) holds, then $\bar{C}_1(t)$ must exceed $\hat{C}_1(t)$ by more than $x[\hat{K}(t) - \bar{K}(t)]$ because $\bar{K}(t) < \hat{K}(t)$ implies $\hat{K}(t) > 0$ and hence $v[\hat{c}^h(t)] = x$. But then we can work backward as under case (a) above.

We have now proven that if there is a P.S. allocation, $\bar{K}(t) = \hat{K}(t)$ for all t. Therefore, by (14) at equality, any such P.S. allocation satisfies

(A19) $\bar{C}_1(t) + \bar{C}_2(t-1) = \hat{C}_1(t) + \hat{C}_2(t-1)$ for all $t \geqslant 1$.

Then, since $v[\hat{c}^h(c)] \geqslant x > n$, one can derive a contradiction from assuming that somebody is strictly better off under a P.S. allocation than under an equilibrium allocation. To prove this the reader can either adapt the case (a) and (b) arguments above or can consult the proof in Kareken and Wallace 1977, which itself is similar to the case (a) and (b) arguments made above.

A3. Proof of Proposition 5

Here I outline a proof that follows closely the proof of Proposition 3.

First, one rules out the existence of a feasible P.S. allocation with a first date $t \geqslant 1$ at which $\bar{K}(t) > 0$. In such a proof one gets to an expression like (A15), but in this case with $\Delta(t+1) \geqslant 0$. And since $v(\hat{c}^h) = n$, one must use the fact that the relevant f function in the third term on the right-hand side of (A15) is strictly increasing. Then, any feasible P.S. allocation—that is, any bar allocation—satisfies (A19) and one can proceed as indicated there.

Discussion by James Tobin

1. Introduction
Why does fiat money, consisting of intrinsically worthless tokens, have positive value? What determines its value? These are classical questions of monetary theory. This conference, at least its first session, seems to be based on two premises. One is that the two questions have not been satisfactorily and rigorously answered. The other is that the answer to the second question, the determination of the value of money, can be achieved if and only if a precise answer to the first question, the economic function of money, can be obtained. I am dubious of both premises.

2. Overlapping Generations and the Theory of Money
Starting from the presumption that fiat money should have neither value nor real consequence but confronting the fact that it does, some theorists have been grasping for straws. They have discovered the mortality of human beings, formalized in the *overlapping generations model*. Ever since Samuelson's (1958)† seminal exposition of this parable, we have known that providing for consumption in old age solely by personal accumulation of goods might be inefficient. A permanent arrangement by which retired workers can claim part of the output of active workers may make all generations better off. There are a number of such arrangements conceivable. One is a fiat store of value—intrinsically useless, costless to produce, somehow acceptable and known to be acceptable to all generations. Workers can acquire it by saving when young and then sell it for consumption goods when old. It is tempting to call this asset *money* and to exclaim, Eureka, here is the reason for the existence and value of money. Neil Wallace says it is the only model of money extant.

I do not believe that the overlapping generations model is the key to the theory of money. The "consumption loan" parable is valuable and instructive, but it should not be taken seriously as an explanation of the existence of money in human society. There is a semantic problem here. One can call the fiat store of value of the model *money*, but it bears little resemblance to the money of common parlance or the money that economists and policymakers argue about.

†See the reference list at the end of this book.

Here are six of my reasons for doubting that the model is the way to explain money in those customary meanings.

First, the overlapping generations model does not inevitably imply the necessity or desirability of an arrangement alternative to or supplementary to reliance on age-related endowments and on accumulation and decumulation of goods. The examples of the Cass, Okuno, and Zilcha paper (in this volume) remind us of this fact. Even if we confine ourselves to the simplest models, in which generations are internally homogeneous and alike in tastes, endowments, and so forth, we know that goods suffice as a store of value unless total reliance upon them would lead to an interest rate below the natural growth rate of the economy. But money is a universal phenomenon, surely not observed solely in societies or eras in which the net marginal product of capital has not exceeded the growth rate.

Second, if a nonreproducible asset has been needed for intergenerational transfers of wealth, land has always been available. Quantitatively it has been a much more important store of value than money.

Third, as the Cass-Okuno-Zilcha paper also makes clear, an alternative arrangement is needed in the overlapping generations model only if the life cycle is one of saving followed by dissaving. But in many, probably most, societies throughout history the dominant sequence was the reverse. The young lived off the production of the old, most of whom died before they stopped working and became dependent on their children. Those who did outlive their capacity to earn their own living were supported in kind by their children. They did not have to buy their excess consumption by dissaving. Until relatively recently the family was the social institution that smoothed out life cycle discrepancies between endowments and consumptions and did so without a lot of monetary transactions. Yet there was money in those societies nonetheless.

Fourth, as Robert Barro has argued, mortal individuals may behave as if their horizons were infinite, internalizing the utilities and anticipating the endowments of their descendants and benefiting or suffering from similar behavior on the part of their predecessors. Under some circumstances, gifts from young to old and bequests from old to young can overcome the inefficiencies that might otherwise result from reliance on barter and storage of goods. While I do not regard constructive immortality as realistic, I don't believe that the rationale of money depends on whether it is or not. If there were a society of ageless and immortal consumers, I would expect to find them using money.

Fifth, isn't it slightly ridiculous to identify as money the asset that the typical agent of the model would hold for an average of 25 years, say, from age 40 to age 65? The average holding period of a dollar of demand deposits is about 2 days.

Sixth, staying within the overlapping generations model and assuming that some arrangement other than barter and storage is called for, fiat money does not appear to be the most effective or likely mechanism of intergenerational transfer of consumption goods. Another mechanism —widely adopted in societies where fiat money already existed—is a social security scheme. The government promises more or less definite per capita real benefits to each old cohort and raises the needed real resources by taxes on their young contemporaries. I would rather grow old and feeble under that regime than be dependent on the price my young contemporaries may be prepared to pay for my holdings of fiat money.

The reason for my preference is the following. The market price of fiat money will reflect decentralized decisions by agents, each estimating what the price will be when it becomes her or his turn to sell the money. The more I pondered the Cass-Okuno-Zilcha paper, the more doubtful I became that the fiat money solution would ever leave the starting gate and the more likely it seemed that the barter solution, with no intergenerational trade, would prevail. Why should young G^1 surrender consumption goods for money, knowing that what they get later in return depends on young G^2's guess of young G^3's guess of young G^4's guess . . . of young G^N's guess . . . of what young G^Z will pay for money? The uncertainty is not merely about what those generations' intertemporal marginal rates of substitution will be, but about what each preceding generation will think they will be. With no history as guide, G^1 is supposed to estimate—rationally!—these probabilities and to display no risk aversion.

Why, you may ask, should a young generation as skeptical as I have just described be willing to pay the taxes necessary to provide the promised social security benefits to its contemporary elders under the arrangement I said I would prefer to fiat money? The answer is that explicit governmental promise carries more conviction than the decentralized market expectation; there is no governmental commitment to the value of fiat money. The willingness or obligation individual young workers feel to the social security commitment is enhanced not only by the association of the tax with their own future benefits but also by the knowledge that their contemporaries will be taxed too. The social compact is clear and compelling. There is no social compact involved in market exchanges of goods for fiat money.

To these points may be added the central message of the Cass-Okuno-Zilcha paper, as I understand it. This is the fragility of the "monetary" rectification of a nonoptimal barter or no-exchange equilibrium. The appealing idea that an initial fiat money endowment of one aged generation suffices to fix things up—that is, leads to a Pareto-optimal competitive intergenerational equilibrium—proves to be a mirage. It is model-bound, dependent on assumptions other than mortality and overlap—for example, homogeneity of tastes and endowments within and across generations. Even with those assumptions, the stationary "monetary" equilibrium featured in Wallace's paper (in this volume) is only one of many Pareto-optimal competitive equilibria, one that will not prevail unless the initial price of money is just right. The Cass-Okuno-Zilcha counterexamples are ingenious and instructive. I interpret them to show in yet another context that general equilibrium theory contains little information about empirical observations; it is compatible with a vast range of histories. One may doubt that a social institution as basic and universal as money owes its existence to a process so unpredictable in its social and distributional consequences.

To summarize thus far, overlapping generations of mortal agents do not constitute either a sufficient or necessary explanation for money. The model does capture, as Cass, Okuno, and Zilcha have emphasized, one feature of money that any theory of money must confront: Its value to me today depends on its value to you tomorrow, which depends on its value to someone else the next day, and so on into the endless future. But the model does not capture other essential attributes of money connected with its use as a transactions medium and unit of account.

3. Fiat and Commodity Money

Before turning to that subject, I interject my opinion that Wallace and Cass, Okuno, and Zilcha, as well as many others, somewhat exaggerate the uniqueness of fiat money. Clearly enough, the value of paper money does not derive from the beauty of the engravings; the practice of putting money stocks in utility functions is reprehensible. But money is not the only asset more durable than human beings—consider land. It is not the only asset valued in a bootstrap or chain letter way—consider precious metals. And it is not the only asset valued more as a social than an individualistic phenomenon—consider telephones.

Moreover, the line between fiat and commodity money is not as sharp as many imply. There is a strong fiat element in the designation, whether by formal government mandate or informal social consensus, of any commodity as numeraire and means of payment. That is true of gold, cigarettes, boulders in lagoons, as well as paper. Demand for additions to the monetary stocks of the designated commodity is added to the demand for the commodity as a consumption or capital good. Unless the commodity is subject to constant real costs in production, its value is bound to be different because of its monetary use. The fact that dentists and hoarders pay the same price for gold, in labor and other commodities, does not mean that the marginal utility of gold dental crowns controls the value of monetary gold. Furthermore, commodity moneys have generally been supplemented by paper or fountain-pen promises to pay the commodity, issued privately or publicly with only fractional backing and circulated for long periods without tests of convertibility. Incidentally, those who are worried about instability of government supply of fiat money are advised to recall the nonpolicy volatility of supplies of commodity and representative moneys in the past.

4. Money as a Public Good Facilitating Multilateral Exchange

The traditional explanation of money is the division of labor, the daily recurring need to exchange specialized endowments or products for diversified consumption goods and services. Long, long ago our precursors pointed out that the use of a common medium of payment facilitates multilateral trade among members of an economy. Barter, in contrast, would restrict transactions to "double coincidences of wants," Jevons' famous phrase. The insight tells us why the social institution of money has been observed throughout history even in primitive societies. An insight is not a model, and it does not satisfy the trained scholarly consciences of modern theorists who require that all values be rooted, explicitly and mathematically, in the market valuations of maximizing agents. But I must say in all irreverent candor that as yet I do not feel significantly better enlightened than by the traditional insight.

Social institutions like money are public goods. Models of general equilibrium — competitive markets and individual optimizing agents — are not well adapted to explaining the existence and quantity of public goods. Another time-honored observation of monetary economists is the analogy of money and language. Both are means of communication. The use of a particular language or a particular money by one individual increases its value to other actual or potential users. Increasing returns to scale, in this sense, limits the number of languages or moneys in a society and indeed explains the tendency for one basic language or money to monopolize the field. Theory must give way to history in explaining which language and what money — English and the dollar for our country — are adopted in any given community. Government itself is a public good, and one of its principal functions is to provide other public goods to its citizens. Naturally enough, nation-states regard the definition and coinage of money as one of their prerogatives and responsibilities.

Another classical observation is the triad of money's functions: unit of account, means of payment, store of value.

The public good characteristic of money certainly applies to the use of a common unit of account. In an economy of N commodities, the number of relative prices is $(N^2/2) - (N/2)$, and the number of price quotations on any given day when markets have not cleared will be much larger. Reduction of the information set to N money prices obviously facilitates calculation and comparison by buyers and sellers. For example, sellers exchanging their one commodity endowment during a particular period can simply set for themselves a reservation price in terms of money rather than in terms of every other commodity. Even the Walrasian auctioneer found it necessary to adopt a numeraire and impose it on bidders.

As this reference illustrates, the use of a common numeraire or unit of account does not logically compel the use of a common money in transactions. Commodity-for-commodity barters could be and are made with values equated by reference to numeraire or unit-of-account prices. But it is hard to imagine, and I suspect even harder to illustrate historically, a unit of account disembodied from a generally accepted means of payment. The dollar is our unit of account because physical dollars are generally acceptable in transactions.

The public good argument applies to acceptability as a means of payment. Indeed, there is, as the language analogy suggests, arbitrariness and circularity in acceptability. Dollar bills and coins are acceptable because they are acceptable; of course, the state has a lot to do with making them acceptable, by defining them as acceptable for settlement of private contracts and for tax payments. Dollar bills and coins are not the only means of payment in the United States; they do not even enter the bulk of transactions. Credible promises to pay those dollars, or to convey other such promises, also serve as generally acceptable media, or as widely acceptable media. Those that gain general acceptability are rarely actually converted into the currency they promise; the circularity of acceptability applies once again. But the ultimate fiat refers to the basic medium that also defines the unit of account.

The conventional story I have just rehearsed begins to explain the doubts I expressed at the outset. General equilibrium theory is not going to explain the institution of a monetary unit of account associated with a basic common means of payment. The public good characteristics that do explain the institution do not tell us much about what will determine the values of the unit of account in terms of various commodities. One reason this is not a simple matter is the multiplication and pyramiding of derivative circulating media. Not only is this process subject to the arbitrary circularity of acceptability already mentioned. It also involves a mixture of institutional history, legal regulation, technology, and private enterprise.

5. Limitations of Contracts and Markets

Why do most commodity transactions involve the exchange of money, basic or derivative? Money is not the only way of avoiding the restrictions of "double coincidences." Individuals can exchange their endowments for commodities they do not wish to consume at once and hold those for later consumption or exchange. The social costs of the procedure are the resources employed in trading, the stocks tied up in inventories, the failure to make mutually advantageous exchanges. These are magnified by agents' uncertainties about their own future preferences and endowments, trading opportunities, storage gains and losses.

Contracts for future delivery, and for contingent future delivery, are another way to mesh the endowment and consumption paths of various agents without the intermediation of money. In the ideal Arrow-Debreu world, the point of presumptive reference for so much economic theory, all transactions are handled this way. An economic history is just a realization of contracts made once and for all time and every contingency; no money is needed or used. We all know the essential reasons why futures markets, and especially contingent future contracts, are so limited in coverage in time, commodities, and contingencies. Those reasons include the costs of making and executing such contracts, the intrinsic difficulties, often impossibilities, of enforcing performance, the moral hazards involved in defining relevant states of nature.

Money, a basic or derivative acceptable means of payment, takes the place of insurance for a host of risks that are insurable, if at all, only at very high cost. This is true even of risks that are small for the economy at large though significant for individuals. If you are stranded in a strange town, it is unlikely that the taxi driver or innkeeper happens to want a lecture or offprint on general equilibrium. It is also unlikely that you previously had or seized the opportunity to contract for the delivery of their services in the precise contingency. Note, moreover, that the insurance you want is not so much against a high price for the services you urgently need as against the possibility that you cannot buy them at all. The holding of money provides the latter insurance, not the former.

Uncertainty of the future spot price of a commodity an agent will or may wish to buy, relative to the current spot price of what the agent has to sell, is inevitable except in an Arrow-Debreu world. That is to say, it is inevitable. Where the stakes are so high that price uncertainty is a large consideration, we frequently do resort to futures contracts and insurance. The greater the uncertainty, the less useful is money proper as "a temporary abode of purchasing power." For long holding periods, the liquidity and acceptability of money are outweighed by the uncertainties of its purchasing power.

It is surely a misunderstanding of a monetary economy to model it as if currency, or promises to pay currency, were the only stores of value or even the predominant vehicles of saving. Land and durable goods, or claims upon them, are the principal stores of value other than human beings themselves. Money is a very transient abode of purchasing power, not designed to be a lifetime store of value. For long-term bridges between sales and purchases, the capital and financial markets provide assets that offer higher returns and better hedges against risk. That is why choices among money, other assets denominated in money, and real capital appear to me to be central to monetary theory, absent though they are in the overlapping generations model.

That is why I think that Wallace should not conclude that because bonds would be redundant in his model they are either redundant or just another form of money in the fact or in other models.

One way to explain the function and value of money is the absence of some markets. In the ideal general equilibrium world, a complete and connected battery of markets would handle all transactions without circulation of any money. In the overlapping generations model, markets are necessarily incomplete because unborn generations cannot make contracts, and money substitutes for the missing futures markets.

But that is only one illustration of a general phenomenon. Markets are much rarer and much more restricted than economists, especially general equilibrium theorists, like to admit. Maybe the Walrasian auctioneer solicits multivariate excess demand schedules for all N commodities from all agents and clears the N markets simultaneously. Working for Arrow-Debreu, the auctioneer's list of "commodities" expands by orders of magnitude. In fact, most markets, even those most highly organized, are bilateral markets, one commodity versus money. Even the stock exchange is a collection of bilateral markets of this kind, with a specialist for each issue separately trying to find the market-clearing price. For most commodities, no organized market exists at all. Often there is bilateral bargaining. Often one party, usually the seller, sets a price at irregular intervals and accommodates willing transactors at the prevailing price.

When economists speak of these arrangements as markets, they are using a metaphor, an abstraction useful for many purposes but not for illuminating the functions of money. True markets are rare and restricted in scope because the operation of such markets is expensive. The number of spot commodities in the U.S. economy is a large multiple of the human population. Rarely do two suppliers produce the same homogeneous commodity, and most firms sell an ever-changing menu of products. It is simply inconceivable that there could be organized competitive markets for them, let alone Walrasian multicommodity market clearing, that would dispense with the need for money.

Failure of the conditions necessary for Arrow-Debreu equilibrium is one way to describe the reasons societies adopt, use, and value money—a contorted and contrived way, to be sure, but one that comes naturally to economic theorists. So a monetary economy will not achieve such an equilibrium. Neither will barter, given the costs of commodity exchange markets and bilateral transactions. A monetary economy reaches a different second best, presumably a better second best, than a barter economy. After all, it does not preclude barter or futures transactions but adds other options.

Questions of this kind, about alternative regimes, should be distinguished from questions about quantitative variations within any one regime. For example, given a monetary economy and its institutions, markets, and intermediaries, how does its equilibrium depend on the quantity of money? To say that real magnitudes don't depend on that quantity is not to say that money is a veil in the sense that the economy achieves the same equilibrium that it would in the absence of any monetary institutions. Nor is it to say that variation or evolution of the institutions of the monetary economy will be neutral. Indeed, all it really does say is that once you have money it doesn't matter how you label the unit of account: If quarters were dollars, prices would be four times as high. (Remember, however, that lots of assets, some public and some private liabilities, some means of payment but most not, are denominated in the monetary unit. A valid quantity theorem or neutrality proposition really requires that all of them change in the same proportion, not just currency or some arbitrary M_j.) My point here is to elaborate my doubt, expressed at the beginning, that understanding why we have a monetary regime will tell us much about what determines the value of money within it.

6. Concluding Remarks: Constant Velocity and Superneutrality

I guess that the authors of tomorrow's papers, Shubik and Lucas, may share this feeling. They simply assume rules of the game that require use of money to purchase goods. They do not explain the origins of these rules but rigorously derive the value of fiat money from them and from other assumptions. These are interesting and instructive exercises. But caution is advised in applying their conclusions to the live issues of monetary theory and policy. In particular, any institutional rule or technological assumption that fixes the velocity of money—for example, that limits a dollar to changing hands just once per period—evades all the macroeconomic issues that hinge on the endogenous variation of velocity, questions which involve in turn the menu of money substitutes provided by government or by private agents and intermediaries.

A final word. I have argued that the life cycle, or overlapping generations, model is miscast as the hero of the great fiat money mystery. But I do believe that a life cycle or finite-horizon model of saving and asset demands has significantly different implications from a model of infinitely lived consumers. One example is the issue of superneutrality, the alleged invariance of real outcomes with respect to variations in the rates of monetary growth and of inflation. This *might* be true of an economy of identical immortal consumers who will accumulate every asset independently in whatever amount yields their common rate of time discount. This discount will control their consumption paths and capital goods holdings, independently of the real money balances they choose to hold alongside. Mortal consumers, however, have finite demands for wealth in general and in any specific form. They face a problem of portfolio choice; and if inflation lowers the return on money, their consumption and capital accumulation paths will be altered. Thus life cycle models will not be superneutral.

Discussion by José Alexandre Scheinkman*

1. Introduction

My purpose here is not to provide a general discussion of Wallace's paper in this conference but to concentrate on two points raised by him to which I think I have something to contribute.

The first of these points concerns what Wallace calls the "tenuousness of equilibria in which fiat money has value." In an overlapping generations model of fiat money, the equilibria in which fiat money has value (also called *monetary* equilibria) coexist with equilibria in which fiat money has no value (*nonmonetary* equilibria), and there are usually many monetary equilibria in which the economy behaves asymptotically, as in the nonmonetary equilibria. Furthermore, there seems to be no mechanism to insure that even small perturbations would not lead the economy into one of the class of monetary equilibria that converge toward a nonmonetary equilibrium. Wallace claims that "tenuousness is an implication of the two defining properties of fiat money, inconvertibility and intrinsic uselessness, and not of the overlapping generations friction."

In particular, he dismisses the criticism that such behavior is a consequence of the lack of a medium-of-exchange role for money in such models. Part of this note concentrates on examining this claim. In section 2 I develop a model in which money has a role as a medium of exchange. By comparing the overlapping generations model with it and with results known in the case in which real balances are assumed to enter directly in the utility function of agents, I show that tenuousness of equilibria in which fiat money has positive value seems to be related to the possibility of the economy operating in the absence of fiat money. The mathematical conditions that insure the absence of tenuousness are very similar in all three classes of models. While section 2 develops a model of money as a medium of exchange, section 3 studies more closely the issue of tenuousness in the overlapping generations model and in models where real balances enter the utility function.

The second point I discuss is the issue of government bonds. In a two-period model, as Wallace correctly points out, if money has a positive price there cannot exist any asset with a distribution of rates of return that domi-

*I thank the Instituto de Matemática Pura e Aplicada and the E.P.G.E. of Fundacão Getúlio Vargas for use of their research facilities and the National Science Foundation for support of this research through Grant SOC 74-19692 to the University of Chicago.

nates money. This observation is then used to derive implications for the role of government bonds in macro models. I point out in section 4 how these results are no longer valid in models in which one treats individuals that live for more than two periods.

As mentioned above, this comment is restricted to just a few of the points raised by Wallace. In particular, nothing is said here about the interesting implications of the model, developed in sections 1.4 and 3 of the paper, concerning what certain statistical relationships really mean (not much!). In general, I find this a provocative and interesting piece that should start some good discussions.

2. A Model of Money as a Medium of Exchange

2.1. *Necessary Conditions for Equilibrium*

In his paper at this conference, Lucas presents a Clower-type model that yields a unique equilibrium in which money has a positive value. This is obtained by requiring agents to sell their goods for money one period ahead in order to obtain other goods. If agents cannot survive with their own endowment, a unique equilibrium obtains and money has a positive value. Let us consider, however, a generalization of the model in which agents may barter as well as exchange goods for money and money for goods as in the Clower type of model.

Each period individual consumers receive y units of one of a list of nonstorable commodities. They want to consume a mix of goods with fixed relative prices. They can trade their endowment in two markets. In one they can sell in exchange for fiat money and buy the composite good with fiat money carried over from the previous period. In the other (the barter market) they can exchange part of their endowment for the composite good; but if they deliver $\bar{y}$ to that market, they get $g(\bar{y}) > 0$ units of the composite good, where g is a strictly concave function with $g(0) = 0$, $g'(0) = 1$.[1] Notice that we can rationalize the fixed relative prices in the same way as Lucas did in his conference paper. We could also view our model as one in which labor can be sold for fiat money or used directly in home production of goods, provided home production is less efficient.

Formally, a consumer solves

$$(1) \qquad \max \sum_{t=0}^{\infty} \delta^t u(c_t)$$

subject to

$$c_t = \frac{m_t - (m_{t+1} - h_{t+1})}{P_t} + y$$

provided $yP_t \leq m_{t+1} - h_{t+1}$ and

$$c_t = \frac{m_t}{P_t} + g\left(y - \frac{m_{t+1} - h_{t+1}}{P_t}\right)$$

[1]The condition $g'(0) = 1$ is convenient from the mathematical viewpoint since it preserves the smoothness of the trading opportunities. In general, one wants $g'(0) \leq 1$.

if $yP_t \geqslant m_{t+1} - h_{t+1}$, where m_0 is given, $c_t \geqslant 0$, $m_t \geqslant 0$, $m_t - h_t \geqslant 0$, and h_t is government transfers at time t, m_t the amount of money the consumer holds at t (post transfers), and P_t the price of the composite good in terms of money.[2] The utility function u is c^2 and concave.

By defining $f(z) = z$ for $z \leqslant 0$ and $f(z) = g(z)$ for $z \geqslant 0$, we may rewrite (1) for $(m_0, \{h_t\}, \{P_t\})$ as

$$\text{(2)} \qquad \max \sum_{t=0}^{\infty} \delta^t \, v(m_t, m_{t+1}, t)$$

where

$$v(m_t, m_{t+1}, t) = u\left[\frac{m_t}{P_t} + f\left(y - \frac{(m_{t+1} - h_{t+1})}{P_t}\right)\right]$$

subject to

$$m_t \geqslant 0, \frac{m_t}{P_t} + f\left(y - \frac{m_{t+1} - h_{t+1}}{P_t}\right) \geqslant 0$$

$$m_t - h_t \geqslant 0.$$

A necessary condition for optimality is given by

$$\text{(3)} \qquad \frac{-u'(c_{t-1})}{P_{t-1}} f'\left(y - \frac{m_t - h_t}{P_{t-1}}\right) + \frac{\delta \, u'(c_t)}{P_t} \gtreqless 0$$

with ($\leqslant$) if $c_t > 0$ and ($\geqslant$) if $m_t > 0$, $m_t - h_t > 0$, $t = 1, 2, \ldots$.

Given a sequence of money supplies $\{\overline{m}_t\}_{t=0}^{\infty}$ with $\overline{m}_t \geq 0$, an equilibrium is a sequence $\{P_t\}_{t=0}^{\infty}$ such that $\overline{m}_t$ is a solution to (2) where $\overline{h}_t = \overline{m}_t - \overline{m}_{t-1}$.

In an equilibrium $c_t \geqslant g(y)$ and since $\overline{m}_t > 0$, $\overline{m}_{t-1} = \overline{m}_t - h_t > 0$, we must have

$$\text{(4)} \qquad \frac{u'(c_{t-1})}{P_{t-1}} f'\left(y - \frac{\overline{m}_{t-1}}{P_{t-1}}\right) = \frac{\delta \, u'(c_t)}{P_t}$$

where $c_t = (\overline{m}_t / P_t) + f[y - (\overline{m}_t / P_t)]$.

2.2. *The Structure of the Equilibrium Set*

We will restrict ourselves to the case of a fixed money supply, which illustrates most of the properties of the model. In particular, we will show how this model shares the tenuousness property with the overlapping generations model. We start by fully characterizing the equilibria.

LEMMA. *A sequence $\{P_t\}_{t=0}^{\infty}$ is an equilibrium if and only if $\overline{m}_t \equiv \overline{m}$ solves (4) and*

[2] In order to save in notation, we have stated the consumers' problem already requiring them not to use the barter market whenever they want to take for the future at least as much as they get when they sell in the money market all of their initial endowment. The reader can see that this is in fact optimal by simply observing that $g(x) < x$.

(5) $$\lim_{t\to\infty} \delta^t \frac{u'(c_t)}{P_t} = 0.$$

Proof (Necessity). We know that (4) is a necessary condition. Now let $V_s(x)$ denote the value function of a consumer who starts at time s with an initial money endowment of x and faces prices $\{P_t\}_{t=s}^{\infty}$ and transfers $h_t \equiv 0$, $t=s, s+1, \ldots$.

Since $\{P_t\}_{t=0}^{\infty}$ is an equilibrium, $m_t \equiv \overline{m}$ solves the optimization problem of the consumer. Since $\overline{m} > 0$, the result of Benveniste and Scheinkman (1979)[3] implies that V_t is differentiable at $\overline{m}$ and furthermore

$$V_t'(\overline{m}) = \delta^t \frac{u'(c_t)}{P_t} f'\left(y - \frac{\overline{m}}{P_t}\right) = \delta^{t+1} \frac{u'(c_{t+1})}{P_{t+1}}.$$

Also, $V_t(\alpha\overline{m}) \geqslant \Sigma_{s=t}^{\infty} \delta^s u[g(y)]$. Thus $\lim_{t\to\infty} \inf V_t(\alpha\overline{m}) \geqslant 0$. Furthermore, $\lim_{t\to\infty} \sup V_t(\overline{m}) \leqslant 0$, since $V_t(\overline{m}) \leqslant \Sigma_{s=t}^{\infty} \delta^s u(y)$. Thus, for $0 < \alpha < 1$, the concavity of V_t implies that

$$V_t(\alpha\overline{m}) - V_t(\overline{m}) \leqslant (\alpha-1)\overline{m}\,\delta^{t+1} \frac{u'(c_{t+1})}{P_{t+1}} < 0.$$

Thus,

$$\lim_{t\to\infty} (\alpha-1)\overline{m}\,\delta^{t+1} \frac{u'(c_{t+1})}{P_{t+1}} = 0.$$

Proof (Sufficiency). This follows from the fact that $\overline{m}$ satisfies the Euler equation and the transversality condition (5) by a standard argument. (See, for example, Benveniste and Scheinkman 1976.)

Q.E.D.

It is now immediate that if there exists $\overline{P}$ *with* $f'(y - \overline{m}/\overline{P}) = \delta$ then such $\overline{P}$ is an equilibrium. The strict concavity of g guarantees that such $\overline{P}$, if it exists, is unique. We will assume its existence since otherwise no monetary equilibria will exist. Furthermore, there is no equilibrium in which $c_t \equiv y$. For if there were such an equilibrium, then from (4) we would have $P_t = \delta P_{t-1}$, and (5) would be violated.

In order to study other equilibria, let us define $\sigma(P) = P/u'(c)$ where $c = (\overline{m}/P) + f[y - (\overline{m}/P)]$. Thus (4) may be rewritten as

(6) $$\sigma(P_t) f'\left(y - \frac{\overline{m}}{P_{t-1}}\right) = \delta\,\sigma(P_{t-1}).$$

Notice that since u is C^2, σ is C^1 and

$$\sigma'(P) = \left\{u'(c) + \frac{\overline{m}u''(c)}{P}\left[1 - f'\left(y - \frac{\overline{m}}{P}\right)\right]\right\} \frac{1}{[u'(c)]^2}.$$

[3] Author names and years refer to the works listed at the end of this book.

Thus $\lim_{P\to\infty} \sigma'(P) = 1/u'[f(y)] > 0$, since $f(y) > 0$.

The figure shows the general properties of σ. Notice that $\lim_{P\to 0} \sigma(P) = 0$. Since for large P, $f'[y - (1/P)] < \delta$, it is obvious from the figure that if we choose $\bar{P}$ large enough we may obtain a solution to (6) such that $\lim_{t\to\infty} P_t = \infty$ and P_0 is any real number $\geqslant \bar{P}$. From the lemma, this is an equilibrium. Along such equilibria we have $\lim_{t\to\infty} c_t = f(y)$. That is, the economy becomes demonetized in the limit.

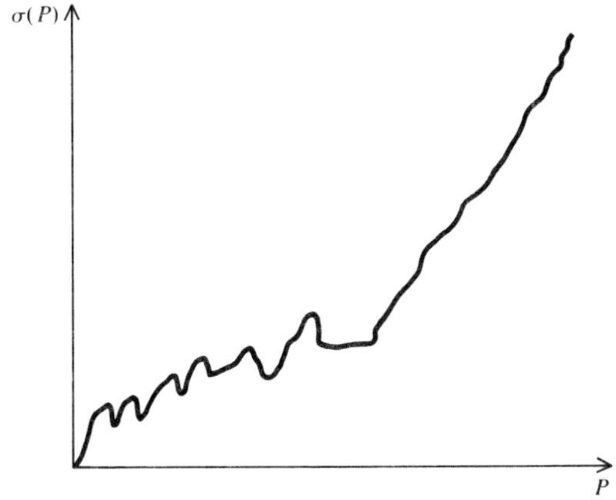

The Clower-type model discussed by Lucas corresponds to the case where $f(z) = 0$, $z \geqslant 0$. Even in this limit case we could still get equilibria in which the economy becomes demonetized if the consumer has utility for and can survive with the initial endowment. Thus only in the case where money is essential does this phenomenon disappear.

The model discussed in this section does have some implications which are different from those of the overlapping generations model that Wallace treats. One example consists of the optimal quantity of money which in this model is any policy that drives out barter from the system and thus would require a contraction of the money supply.[4] But in regard to the issue of tenuousness, this model does have a lot in common with the overlapping generations model, as I will show in the next section.

3. Tenuousness in the Overlapping Generations Model and in Models Where Real Balances Enter the Utility Function

Tenuousness can be avoided even in an overlapping generations model if one makes special assumptions about endowments, technology, and utility functions. In a pure trading model, a sufficient condition for this is that the endowment of old agents be zero and, if the utility function can be written as $u(c_1, c_2) = u(c_1) + \delta u(c_2)$, that

$$\lim_{x\to 0} x u'(x) > 0. \tag{7}$$

This condition turns out also to be necessary for a large class of models

[4] This conclusion depends on $g'(0) = 1$.

(compare Brock and Scheinkman 1977). The interpretation of (7) is that traders badly need to trade consumption when young for consumption when old, and since money is the only way to do so this will avoid equilibria in which real balances converge to zero. Those are precisely the equilibria in which the economy becomes asymptotically demonetized. It is interesting to notice that the analogue of (7) is also needed to eliminate equilibria in which real balances converge to zero in models where real balances directly enter the utility function of agents (compare Brock 1978). Thus tenuousness seems to be related to how much importance fiat money has in the operation of the economy. Another way to see this point is to see what (7) implies about the inflation tax collected along the stationary equilibria as the rate of inflation goes to infinity. The first-order condition written in real balance form is

$$u'(w_y - x_\mu) = \frac{\delta}{1 + \mu} u'(x_\mu) \tag{8}$$

if w_y is the endowment when young (endowment when old is zero), μ is the rate of creation of money, and x_μ is the real balances associated with the equilibrium which is stationary in real balances. Equation (8) may be rewritten as

$$\frac{u'(w_y - x_\mu)}{x_\mu u'(x_\mu)} = \frac{\delta}{x_\mu + \mu x_\mu}. \tag{9}$$

Since $\lim_{\mu\to\infty} x_\mu = 0$, (7) holds if and only if $\lim_{\mu\to\infty} \mu x_\mu > 0$, that is, if the inflation tax collected along stationary equilibria as the rate of creation of money goes to infinity is bounded away from zero. Brock (1978) shows the same point in a model with real balances in the utility function. The condition $\lim_{\mu\to\infty} \mu x_\mu > 0$ also has the interpretation that no matter how expensive it becomes to hold money people still hold a large quantity of it; that is, money is very necessary to the system. Since inconvertible fiat money seems only to appear in economic systems in which the division of labor has led to tremendous costs to pure barter, it may well be that assumptions such as (7) or (9) are not unnatural in a highly aggregated model.

4. The Role of Government Bonds

Wallace notices that in the context of his model, if fiat money has value in an equilibrium, then in that equilibrium there cannot be any asset with a rate of return distribution which dominates fiat money. This conclusion does not continue to hold if we consider a model in which agents live for more than two periods. For consider a tree that matures in two periods, and suppose there are very high costs in transacting in one-period-old trees. Then agents may hold trees in order to trade consumption when old for consumption when young but hold money in order to consume in middle age. Martins (1975) considers a model in which two-period-old bonds are issued and transaction costs on one-period-old bonds are infinite. In his model, bonds are much like another type of money and the nominal interest rate on bonds is positive and determined by the supply of bonds relative to the supply of money.

Thus Bryant and Wallace's (1979a) point that the private sector must incur transaction costs to offset the nominal interest rate on bonds is invalidated in models with more than two periods.

The Capital Stock Modified Competitive Equilibrium

Martin Shubik*

1. Introduction

The general equilibrium model is static. Even when defined for T time periods the true flavor of the dynamics of an ongoing economy is missed. At the end of the Tth period, any stock left over is of zero worth.

The model presented here contains the usual general equilibrium model as a special case of an economy which uses money and which has an interest rate of $\rho = 0$. When $\rho > 0$, capital stock is left over with positive worth to the future generations.

Even the model suggested here, which follows the dynamic programming idea of a salvage value for leftover stock, fails to capture some of the basic aspects of a multigenerational economy. We would like to consider the implications of an overlap such as is shown in Figure 1a where several generations whose lives overlap have to take care of the young and the old. Setting aside the extra problems posed by such a model, we may regard our treatment as covering the case with successive but not overlapping generations. When one generation dies, the next is born and begins life with the capital stock left behind.

There are several different ways we can explain the transfer of capital stock to successive generations. We may consider interlinked utility functions, love or altruism; the external imposition of law; or the design of a self-policing noncooperative game. The example presented in this paper is closest to the latter two approaches and is a direct extension of the type of models constructed previously by Shubik (1973), Shapley and Shubik (1977), and Dubey and Shubik (1977a,b).[1]

2. The Model

2.1. *Competitive Equilibrium*

Since in what follows there is a considerable amount of notation and tedious

*This work relates to U.S. Department of the Navy Contract N00014-77-C-0518 issued by the Office of Naval Research under Contract Authority NR 047-006. However, the content does not necessarily reflect the position or the policy of the Department of the Navy or the U.S. Government, and no official endorsement should be inferred.

[1]Author names and years refer to the works listed at the end of this book.

Figure 1

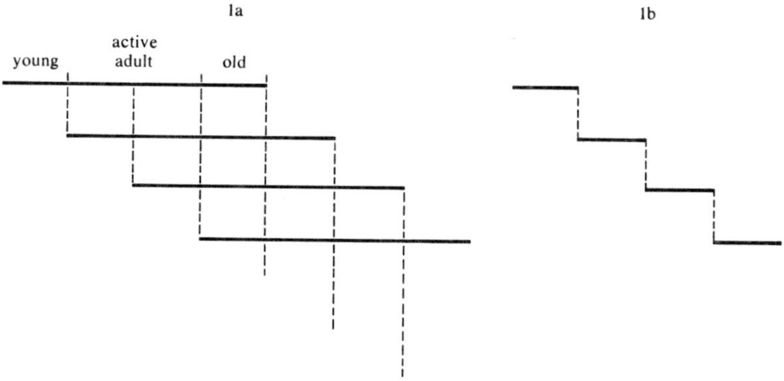

detail concerning accounting conventions, we present a specific example in full detail.

Consider a society with a continuum of small traders who live for three periods. All traders are identical, and all firms are identical. Each trader i has a utility function of the form

$$U^i = \sum_{t=1}^{T} \beta^{t-1}\phi(c_t^i) \text{ specified to } \sum_{t=1}^{3} \beta^{t-1}\sqrt{c_t^i} \tag{1}$$

where

c_t^i = amount consumed by i at time t
β = a natural discount factor.

At $t = 1$ the economy is organized, a central bank comes into being, and private banks and corporations are set up.

Because our prime purpose is the study of the rate of interest for money, the quantity of money, and the flows of money, we make some heroic simplifications. All these simplifications have been considered and for the main purpose at hand can be defended.

- There is no exogenous uncertainty.
- We consider a single-commodity world.
- The managers of the firms are automata who maximize long-run (finite-horizon) profits.
- All traders are alike and small.
- All firms are alike and small.
- All inside banks are alike and small.
- We consider only relatively simple strategies.[2]
- We consider only finite-period economies.

We are primarily concerned with comparing our monetary economies at equilibrium with a related general equilibrium model, so we first solve for the

[2]The reader not interested in the delicate aspects of historical strategies in multistage games should ignore this comment. However, it is noted as a warning that equilibria other than those noted may exist.

latter. Because of the extreme symmetry imposed on our model, we may drop identifying superscripts on variables and parameters of the firms, individuals, and banks.

Let us assume that the typical firm has a production function of the form

(2) $$k_t = g(I_{t-1}) \text{ specified to } k_t = \sqrt{\alpha I_{t-1}}$$

where

I_t = the amount invested in time t
k_t = the amount of capital at the start of time t.

We have

(3) $$k_t = I_t + c_t.$$

Let A = the initial supply of capital at time t; hence $k_1 = A$. At the start of any period, capital is eaten or used to produce more capital at the start of the next period (inventorying is ruled out).

Each individual has shares in the firms. Individual i holds the shares of firm j with a density of $f^i_{j,t}$ at time t. Since all firms and individuals are the same, in equilibrium there will be no trade in shares, and we can denote the typical portfolio of an individual by

f = the portfolio of an individual in stock of the firms.

The competitive equilibrium is given by prices p_1 $(=1)$, p_2, p_3 satisfying

(4) $$\max \sqrt{c_1} + \beta\sqrt{c_2} + \beta^2\sqrt{c_3}$$

subject to

$$c_1 + p_2 c_2 + p_3 c_3 = f\Pi$$

and

(5) $$\max \Pi = A - I_1 + p_2\left(\sqrt{\alpha I_1} - I_2\right) + p_3\sqrt{\alpha I_2}$$

where

(6) $$c_1 = A - I_1$$

(7) $$c_2 = \sqrt{\alpha I_1} - I_2$$

(8) $$c_3 = \sqrt{\alpha I_2}.$$

The equilibrium prices are p_1, p_2, p_3. We may set $p_1 = 1$. The total profit for any firm is Π. In (4) it refers to total industry profit. Thus $f\Pi$ is the income of an individual. The marginal utility of income (the Lagrangian multiplier) is μ.

We have these six conditions on the maximization of welfare and profits:

$$(9) \qquad \frac{1}{2\sqrt{c_1}} = \mu$$

$$(10) \qquad \frac{\beta}{2\sqrt{c_2}} = \mu p_2$$

$$(11) \qquad \frac{\beta^2}{2\sqrt{c_3}} = \mu p_3$$

$$(12) \qquad c_1 + p_2 c_2 + p_3 c_3 = f\Pi$$

$$(13) \qquad \frac{p_2 \alpha}{2\sqrt{\alpha I_1}} = 1$$

$$(14) \qquad \frac{p_3 \alpha}{2\sqrt{\alpha I_2}} = p_2 .$$

Fixing $\alpha=400$, we calculate the cases $A = 100, 200, 400$ with $\beta = 1$ and $A = 100$ with $\beta = 1/2$ (see Table 1).

Table 1

A	β	c_1	c_2	c_3	p_1	p_2	p_3	μ	k_1	k_2	k_3
100	1	46.81104	88.00820	152.1228	1	.729311	.5547206	.073080	100	145.8616	152.1228
200	1	108.96850	119.77190	168.5800	1	.953834	.8039840	.047898	100	190.8200	168.5800
400	1	246.76040	161.03033	186.0620	1	1.237890	1.1516200	.031830	100	247.5780	186.0620
100	½	60.32134	100.84180	100.2800	1	.386710	.5013990	.064378	100	125.9820	100.2800

2.2. *The Noncooperative Game: Modeling Considerations*

We may attempt to model the same economic problem as a game of strategy. In order to do so we must specify the structure of trade. A natural consideration in defining a game of strategy is to introduce a money.

A *money* is defined as a good or item which can be traded directly for all other items which are traded. Given m commodities to be traded, depending on the number of markets which exist, there may be 0, 1, 2, . . . , $m-2$, or m moneys. For $m = 4$, Figure 2 shows cases with 0, 1, 2, and 4 moneys. If we allow for the existence of all pairwise markets, then there will be $m(m-1)/2$ markets and m moneys. (In Figure 2 a point is a good and a line joining two points symbolizes a market between the two goods at either end.)

If all items are moneys, then there is no need for credit because all the wealth of all individuals can be used in direct exchange. This is not so if there are few markets. A difference between the total wealth of an individual and that person's cash or immediate money position appears.

There are many reasons (involving such things as search, transportation, and trust) why considerably fewer than all markets exist in any economy. Without further discussion, we assume that in the economies we examine if

Figure 2

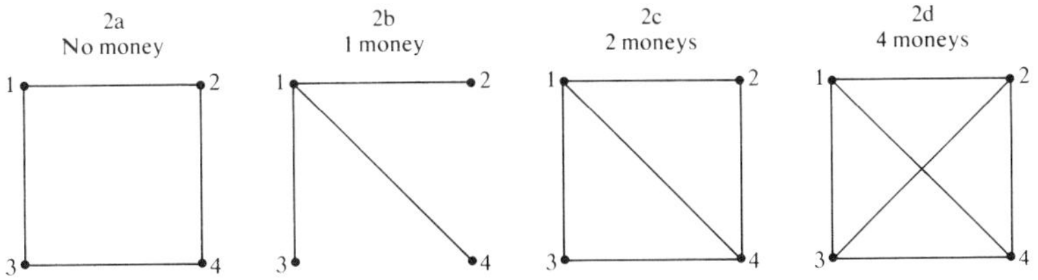

there are m commodities then there will be m markets and one money.

If the money is also a commodity, its value in consumption or production serves as its backing. In that case, we are examining an economy with $m+1$ commodities, one of which serves as money. (Figure 2b shows such a structure, with the first commodity acting as a money.) If the money is fiat, or some form of credit with no direct physical properties of a commodity, then rules must be supplied as to how it enters the economy and how it is redeemed at the end of trade. This will call for a specification of rules concerning failure to repay debts.

In essence, the model constructed below is based on the following factors, which are explained in more detail subsequently:

1. A satisfactory model of a competitive economy must have a mechanism for price formation which depends on the strategies of the agents.
2. A modern economy has at least one money, that is, one commodity or financial instrument which can be exchanged directly for any other economic good.
3. In an economy with trade in m goods with less than $m(m-1)/2$ markets, a necessary and sufficient condition for the competitive allocations to be feasible given only one round of trade is that at least one commodity is a money which is in sufficient supply.
4. A sufficient supply of a money can always be guaranteed by the societal specification of rules of issue and rules concerning penalties for failure to repay.
5. The use of a money and credit system provides a strategic decoupling which enables individuals to move independently simultaneously in equilibrium or disequilibrium. Thus the aggregate economic process may appear to take place at the same time whereas individual behavior is sequential.
6. Even if we model time as continuous, the individual sequential process of trade in money creates a transactions holding or float which is positive over the finite period of time during which trade takes place.
7. For an economy which exists for a finite number of time periods, a necessary condition for individuals to be able to achieve a competitive outcome is that the money rate of interest $\rho = 0$. If $\rho > 0$, this implies that individuals are taxed for using money. If the original issue of money is from the government or outside bank, this implies that there will be a positive drain from the system, and the usual income-equals-expenditure condition of the competitive allocation cannot hold.

8. If the penalties for failure to repay loans are set appropriately, individuals will be motivated to avoid ending in debt.
9. Assume that an economy lasts T time periods. We introduce the fiction of a $T+1$ period in which the referee punishes those who end in debt and also offers to buy at given prices any inventories which are left over. Then for any set of positive prices p_{T+1} set for the purchase of leftover capital, there will be associated a positive rate of interest for money which balances the residual debt of the economy at time $T+1$ against the value of the remaining capital stock.
10. If the prices p_{T+1} are set to zero, then the noncooperative equilibria of the nonatomic game include the competitive equilibria, there is no value to capital stock left over, and the rate of interest $\rho = 0$.
11. The money rate of interest needed to call forth any residual capital stock is also a function of the trading technology.
12. In a multistage economy without trust or other credit and without uncertainty, money serves at least two purposes. It serves to finance transactions and to finance intertemporal trade. In a single-stage economy, money is needed only to finance transactions. A simple exchange of personal IOU notes for government notes serves to provide money to finance transactions. This, however, will not cover the financing called for by intertemporal trade. In particular, different quantities of money may be required at different periods.
13. We may consider a system with two types of money which exchange on a one-for-one basis but differ in their way of entry into and exit from the system. In particular, we may create an internal or privately held banking system by having bank shares issued and sold after the issue of outside money. This may provide for a flexible system to finance intertemporal trade and, if the rate of interest is positive, result in the profits of the banking system being paid back to the traders.

2.3. *The Noncooperative Game: Description and Notation*

2.3.1. *Initial Conditions*

At the start of the economy we imagine a set of traders with an initial endowment of capital with density A. No further input comes into the economy, so their ownership can be characterized by $(A,0,0)$—A being the exogenous endowment for the first period and 0, the endowment for the subsequent two periods.

In a slightly more complex model we might wish to consider a vector of initial resources A of m dimensions plus a unit of time. Thus we might imagine both production and consumption as nothing more than a mapping of $(A_t,1) \rightarrow A_{t+1}$ with time being used up and replenished exogenously. A_t is the vector of resources at the start of time t, excluding time. $(A_t,1)$ is the vector of all resources including time.

It is useful to regard all economic entities as existing in pairs for accounting purposes. Thus at the start of this economy the accounts of the individuals appear as in Figure 3.

In general, individuals do not bother to issue themselves with ownership paper for any assets except land, houses, and major durables. Thus frequently the amount of ownership paper in an economy is less than the ownership.

2.3.2. *The Organization of the Economy*

We must describe the formation of and rules for guiding the outside bank, inside banks, and firms. There are many different ways in which they can be formed. It is my belief that a useful way to proceed is to select one way, thereby producing a completely well-defined model, and then to investigate the changes caused by considering variations in the formation of institutions.

Figure 3

Individuals

Assets	Debt, Equity
A	
	A

Figure 4 shows one possible pattern in the formation and liquidation of the institutions in an economy. The institutions we need are an outside bank, inside banks, and firms. The financial instruments are outside money, bank money, bank and corporate shares, and personal IOU notes or credit.

2.3.3. *The Outside Bank*

We imagine a society which has decided to trade using only money and spot markets. A central banking system is formed as follows.

The central bank issues an amount of money M which it sells for personal IOU notes to be paid back at the end of the economy, that is, at the financial settlement at the start of period $T+1$.

Figure 4

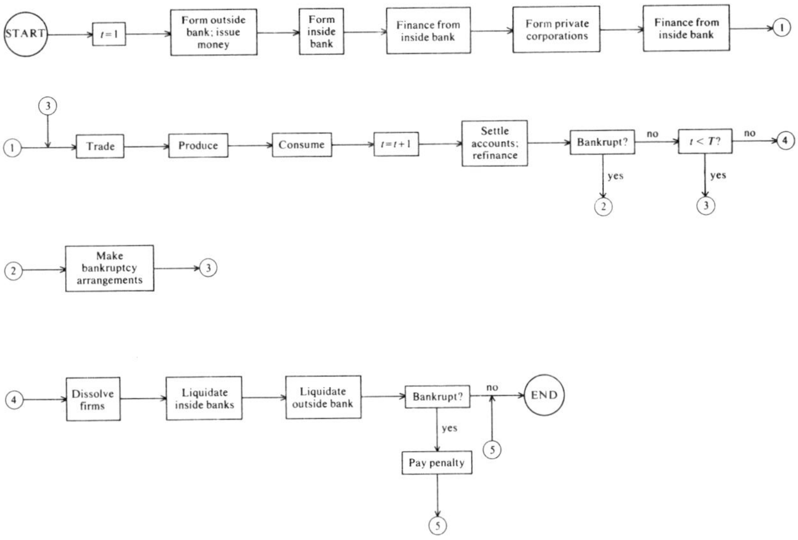

An individual i is permitted to bid any amount of personal credit in order to obtain a share of M. Suppose i bids u^i. Then if $u = \int_{i \in I} u^i$ (where I is the set of all traders), then that individual obtains $s^i = u^i M/u$ (where s^i = the amount of outside money individual i obtains). The equation determining the rate of interest in the economy for loans of T periods is

$$\frac{u}{M} = (1 + \rho)^T. \tag{15}$$

Strategically we may view the outside bank as part of the rules of the game. Fixing M is fixing the outside money supply; fixing ρ leaves the outside supply to be determined by the strategic behavior of the traders. In general, if both ρ and M are fixed, credit rationing must be considered.

The initial accounts appear as in Figure 5. The contract u reads, "In return for M obtained at the start of $t = 1$, u will be returned at the start of $t = T+1$. At time t it has a present value of $M(1+\rho)^{t-1}$."

At this point we need to make a decision concerning accounting practices and economic analysis. Should the books be kept on an accrual or cash basis? In an economy without uncertainty and with perfect trust it does not matter. They will both reflect the same economic reality. Otherwise this is not necessarily true.

Figure 5

Outside Bank

u	M

Individuals

A	u
M	A

2.3.4. *Failure to Repay and Bankruptcy*

Closely related to accounting practices are practices concerning the rollover and refinancing of loans or other payments due. If it is always possible to refinance, then any failure may be put off until the end of the economy.

In order to make final indebtedness unattractive, there must be penalties for those who fail to settle accounts. The simplest yet quite general rule is to imagine that at the end of the economy positive amounts of money have no utility, but debt has negative utility. Thus we may modify the utility function suggested in (1) to become

$$U^i = \sum_{t=1}^{T} \beta^{t-1} \phi(c_t^i) + \lambda \min[0, D_{T+1}] \tag{16}$$

where

D_{T+1} = final cash balances
λ = a penalty parameter.

We could make the form of the penalty term far more complex, but as we have shown elsewhere qualitatively the same results are obtained (see Shapley and Shubik 1977). Essentially, if credit is granted, then in a game of strategy, rules must be specified to cover the contingencies of failure to repay. Figure 6 shows the approach adopted here.

At the end of the economy the holding of positive amounts of money has no value, as is indicated by the vertical indifference curves. However, ending in debt has negative utility, as is indicated by the curvature of the indifference curves in the negative orthant. The specific form used in (16) is indicated by the straight lines with slope λ in the negative orthant.

Qualitatively, it is simple to state our previous results. If the penalty λ is made high enough, then in the noncooperative game using money no one attempts to take strategic advantage of the possibility of being able to go bankrupt and the resultant noncooperative equilibria include the competitive allocations.

In terms of the special model already described in section 2.1, all we need is that $\lambda > \mu$ and we obtain a noncooperative equilibrium with $u = M$ and $\rho = 0$. This will be considered more elaborately below.

2.3.5. *Inside Banks*

Given that the outside bank has been formed and has supplied M units of outside money to the traders, we now consider the sale of shares in a set B of inside banks. We may save on notation by normalizing the number of shares to one.

Assume that an individual i bids v_j^i for shares of bank j where $\int_{j \in B} v_j^i = v^i \leqslant s^i$ and v_j^i is in outside bank money. Bank j will have a capital of $v_j = \int_{i \in I} v_j^i$ resulting from the sale of its shares.

We assume that the banks stand to lend and accept deposits. We distinguish between lending and depositing. We assume that private individuals with surplus cash do not lend it directly to others. They either hoard it or deposit it with a bank. If no one bids for shares of the inside banks, they do not come into existence.

Figure 6

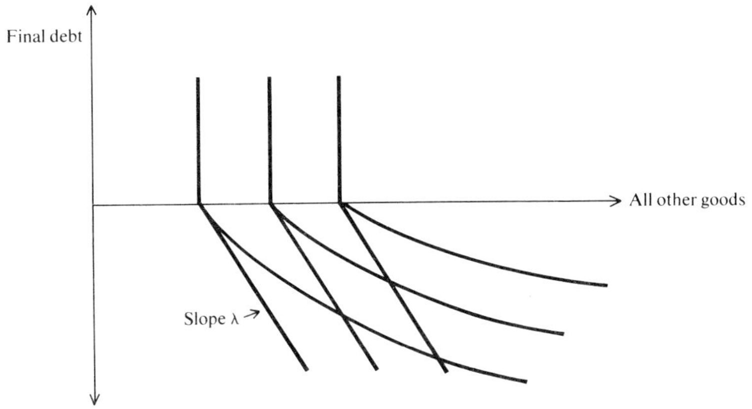

We defer a discussion of the strategies of the individuals, inside banks, and firms until section 2.4, so the specification of the loan policy is delayed until then.

2.3.6. *The Creation of Firms*
In this formulation, firms are created after the financial system. Even so, there are alternatives in the creation of firms, each of which may have different financial implications in terms of the volume of trade and cash needs of different entities.

Case 1. Firms are created by an exchange of resources for stock.
Case 2. Firms are created by a sale of stock for money, after which money is used to buy resources offered for sale by individuals.
Case 3. Firms are created by a sale of stock for money, after which the money is used to buy resources. However, individuals must offer all resources for sale. They are permitted to buy back resources, but every item must pass through a market at least once prior to its consumption.

Although the last case may appear to be the most unrealistic, it has the advantage that all of consumption is monetized. The only barter possible is that which occurs when a firm sells itself its own assets and avoids incurring any actual transaction while doing so.

Assume that individual i bids z_k^i for the shares of firm k, where z_k^i is in outside or inside bank money or a combination of both. We normalize the number of shares of any firm to be one.

Firm k will have a capital of $z_k = \int_{i \in I} z_k^i$.

2.3.7. *Trade, Production, and Consumption*
Given the existence of all institutions, we consider a standard cycle where individuals and firms refinance, then trade in a market for goods for production and consumption.

We assume that (after the first period) the firms will hold all capital which at time t will be divided into goods for sale c_t and for reinvestment I_t. An individual i will bid b_t^i for the product of the firm offered at time t. Thus price will be given by

$$p_t = b_t / c_t .$$

The firms take their capital $k_t - c_t$ and produce new capital

$$k_{t+1} = g(k_t - c_t) = g(I_t).$$

2.3.8. *The Accrual Accounting, Roll-Over Loan, Assessible Stock Finesse*
For purposes of simplification, in our initial study to investigate the money rate of interest, we make assumptions frequently not borne out in reality.

- Firms and banks pay out their profits only at the end of time.
- Loans can always be rolled over.
- All shares are fully assessible, so given the accrual of profits we do not need to worry about interim corporate or bank failure; losses are eventually flowed through to individuals who will have to face up to the penalty of indebtedness at the end of the economy.

2.4. *Strategies of Firms, Banks, and Individuals*

2.4.1. *Firms*

A strategy by a firm consists of buying resources in the first period;[3] producing, and then dividing further capital into that retained for production and that placed on sale for consumption. As money income is received, the firm will deposit it in the bank and let it accrue until the end. After the last period, the firm liquidates and pays out the total to the stockholders while retiring its stock.

In equilibrium, since no firm is large enough to influence the market, a firm will apparently face fixed prices $p_1, p_2, \ldots, p_{T+1}$ and interest rates $\rho_1, \rho_2, \ldots, \rho_T$. Thus a firm starts by borrowing from (depositing in) the bank an amount d_1 and buying capital $I_1 = p_1(A-c_1)$. Then it produces k_2 and divides it into $I_2 = (k_2-q_2)$ and q_2 for sale. At the start of the third period, the firm banks $\gamma_2 \ldots$. Thus a strategy is described by

$$(d_1, I_1, k_2-q_2, q_2;\ \gamma_2, k_3-q_3, q_3;\ \ldots, \gamma_T, k_{T+1})$$

where

$$\gamma_t \leqslant p_t q_t .$$

2.4.2. *Banks*

We may consider several variations for the strategy of a bank. The first and simplest is the fixed passive 100 percent reserves policy. The bank is permitted to lend up to its total capital. This capital may include accrued or received interest. Deposits are essentially brokered costlessly, that is, they are loaned out at the going rate, but the earnings are paid to the depositors.

A second variation includes the possibility of a variable reserve ratio. Thus at any time t the central bank specifies a number r_t such that an inside bank is permitted to lend up to r_t times its total capital. This leverage could be so large that capital requirements are negligible.

If the banks are so small that they cannot influence the rate of interest, in the first instance the money supply cannot be increased faster than by the previous rate of interest. In the second instance the supply of money is varied exogenously by changing the reserve ratio.

A small competitive bank in an environment with no uncertainty will always operate without excess reserves. It will always be loaned up. Thus in both formulations suggested above the banks act passively. They lend all that they have to lend. If equilibrium rates of interest exist, then the demand for the banks' funds equals their supply. (Banking is discussed further in section 4.)

In reality, banks are not necessarily small with respect to their markets, and costs are not constant.

2.4.3. *Individuals*

A strategy by an individual is first to bid for outside money and bank shares; then to borrow, bid for shares in the firms, buy consumption goods, and refinance; and in all subsequent periods to buy consumption goods and refinance. It may be represented by

[3] If we assume a concave production function such as $k_t = \sqrt{\alpha I_{t-1}}$, this implicitly covers the presence of a limited second resource and we are required to consider the sale of the production function in order to balance the books and account for profits.

$$(u, v, e_1, z, b_1, e_2, b_2, \ldots, e_T, b_T)$$

where

u = bid for outside money
v = bid for inside bank shares (a vector)
e_t = borrow from or deposit in inside banks at t
z = bid for shares in firms (a vector)
b_t = bid for consumer goods (a vector).

Since our purpose is limited to the examination of equilibrium points of the capital stock modified competitive equilibrium and associated noncooperative games, the above description of what constitutes strategies is somewhat informal, leaves out a discussion of information condition, and cuts corners on notation. These points have been discussed in detail in Dubey and Shubik 1977a,b.

3. The Capital Stock Modified Competitive Equilibrium

In this section we take a direct extension of the competitive equilibrium model noted in section 2.1, and without going into the detail called for by the noncooperative game we solve a model closely related to that in 2.1 for different growth rates. (See also Dubey and Shubik 1977a,b.) In particular, we consider four cases: no capital stock left over, initial and final capital stock constant, 10 percent growth, and maximum growth.[4]

Using the model of section 2.1 with the modifications indicated below, we calculate four different levels of growth for the case $A = 100$ and $\beta = 1$ (see Table 2).

Table 2

	c_1	c_2	c_3	p_1	p_2	p_3	μ	k_1	k_2	k_3
No ending capital	46.81104	88.0082	152.1228	1	.729311	.554724	.073080	100	145.8616	152.1228
Stationary capital	41.06995	69.6929	83.1272	1	.767658	.702895	.078020	100	153.5318	183.1272
10 percent growth	40.17960	67.2762	76.9800	1	.772809	.722460	.078880	100	154.6800	186.9800
Maximum growth	0	0	0	no price system				100	200.0000	282.8400

The capital stock modified equilibrium conditions have instead of (4) and (5)

$$\max \sqrt{c_1} + \beta\sqrt{c_2} + \beta^2\sqrt{c_3} + \lambda \min\{0,[\Pi/1+\rho - (c_1 + p_2c_2 + p_3c_3)]\} \tag{4'}$$

$$\max A - I_1 + p_2\left(\sqrt{\alpha I_1} - I_2\right) + p_3\left(\sqrt{\alpha I_2} - I_1\right) + p_4\sqrt{\alpha I_3} \tag{5'}$$

where Π in equation (4′) indicates the profit paid to the consumer which in this highly symmetric example is the amount given by equation (5′). The parameter p_4 is set exogenously and determines the growth of the economy.

[4]We could also consider depletion in general.

It is easiest to carry out all calculations in terms of present values. Hence, although in the noncooperative game we consider only spot markets for goods, here we consider p_1, p_2, p_3, p_4 to be the present values of spot prices in the future.

In (4′) Π is divided by $(1+\rho)$ indicating that there is a time lag in the receipt of income. It is easy to see that if $p_4 = 0$ then $\rho = 0$ and there is 0 ending capital which corresponds to the Arrow-Debreu general equilibrium solution.

In addition to equations (4′) and (5′) and equations (6) to (16) we have

$$(9') \qquad \frac{1}{2\sqrt{c_1}} = \lambda$$

$$(10') \qquad \frac{\beta}{2\sqrt{c_2}} = \lambda p_2$$

$$(11') \qquad \frac{\beta^2}{2\sqrt{c_3}} = \lambda p_3$$

$$(12') \qquad \frac{\Pi}{1+\rho} = c_1 + p_2c_2 + p_3c_3$$

$$(13') \qquad \frac{p_2\sqrt{\alpha}}{2\sqrt{I_1}} = 1$$

$$(14') \qquad \frac{p_3\sqrt{\alpha}}{2\sqrt{I_2}} = p_2$$

$$(17) \qquad p_3 = \frac{p_4\sqrt{\alpha}}{2\sqrt{I_3}}.$$

For the stationary economy[5] we require $p_4 = p_3 = .702895$ and $\lambda \geqslant .078020$.

3.1. *Monetization of the Economy and Creation of Firms*

In section 2.3 we noted several variations in the creation of firms. Each variant requires a different amount of money (normalizing $p_1 = 1$ in all cases) for the economy. In particular, if individuals are the original owners of all resources, including production technologies (or institutions), then if we form firms by exchanging stock for resources we will use far less money than if stock is sold for money and then money is used to purchase resources.

Although three cases were noted previously, we note a two-by-two breakdown which leads to four cases and includes the situations requiring the least and most money. Table 3 shows the total expenditures of an individual in a stationary economy lasting T time periods under the different arrangements. In each instance the real goods aspects of the economies are the same, but the monetization is different. *Exchange, hold back* uses the least money, and

[5]This formulation is not fully correct. We have not included the income obtained from the profits of the banking sector. We defer this until section 6.

buy stock, sell all uses the most money. Given that some money is used for transactions and a pool or float of noninterest-earning money is formed, for any finite-horizon model (as can be seen from Table 3) there will be a difference in the money interest rate when compared with a different finite-horizon model when the trading technology calls for different amounts of working capital or transaction reserves or bank float in the circuit not earning interest.

We would suspect that over an infinite horizon the differences caused by initial conditions should ameliorate.

The important feature to appreciate, however, is not the details of initial conditions or the trading technology, but the fact that if outside money exists, that is, if money is supplied by the government or any agency beyond private members of the economy, then for a positive rate of interest there must be a drain of money from the economy.

Table 3 is calculated as follows. Given a natural discount rate of β, the optimal stationary state consumption of an individual is $100\beta(2-\beta)$ given initial assets of 200β. The individual must supply the corporation with its raw materials in the amount of $100\beta^2$. The firm must also purchase its production function at price V. This cost will reflect the allocation of profits or quasi-rents earned from a firm with decreasing returns to scale.

Table 3

	Individuals hold back	Individuals sell or exchange all
Exchange	$100\beta^2 (2-\beta)\left(\frac{1-\beta^{T-1}}{1-\beta}\right)$	$100(2-\beta)\left(\frac{1-\beta^{T}}{1-\beta}\right)$
Buy stock	$V + 100\beta^2 + 100\beta^2(2-\beta)\left(\frac{1-\beta^{T-1}}{1-\beta}\right)$	$V + 100\beta^2 + 100\beta^2(2-\beta)\left(\frac{1-\beta^{T}}{1-\beta}\right)$

In an exchange of resources for stock, individuals take ownership paper directly for $100\beta^2 + V$. Starting with period 2, the individuals then buy $100\beta(2-\beta)$ from the firm which produces 200β per period. Thus individuals spend

$$100\beta(2-\beta)\sum_{t=2}^{T}\beta = 100\beta^2(2-\beta)\left(\frac{1-\beta^{T-1}}{1-\beta}\right). \tag{18}$$

The other three cases are calculated in a similar manner.

3.2. *Policy and Profits of Firms*

The firms are assumed to be run by profit-maximizing automata who consider the maximization of the present value of the expected total income stream including final liquidation value of the firm.

We consider a T time period world with a final settlement and liquidation period at $T+1$. In period $T+1$ an outside agency (the government, god, or referee) announces prices for all leftover resources. In particular, here we assume a price p_{T+1} is announced that motivates the firms to leave 200β at $T+1$. Since production functions are neither destroyed nor augmented in this economy, a price of $V/(1+\rho)^T$ is offered for redemption where ρ is the money rate of interest.

If the prices $p_1, p_2, \ldots, p_{T+1}$ and $V/(1+\rho)^T$ are all regarded as futures prices, then we have two cases representing the present worth of the firm. They correspond to the *hold back* and *sell all* cases. In the original period of formation the owners hold back their first period of consumption rather than place the resources in the firm and buy back consumption. In the second instance all resources go to the firm. Thus in Case 1 (hold back), less is invested and the firm is worth less. In Case 2 (sell all), the firm is worth more.

Case 1. (Hold back)

$$V + 100\beta^2 = 100\beta^2 (2-\beta) \left(\frac{1-\beta^{T-1}}{1-\beta}\right) + 200\beta^{T+1} + V/(1+\rho)^T \tag{19}$$

Case 2. (Sell all)

$$V + 200\beta = 100\beta (2-\beta) \left(\frac{1-\beta^{T}}{1-\beta}\right) + 200\beta^{T+1} + V/(1+\rho)^T \tag{20}$$

paid in capital = income + liquidation value

3.3. *Income and Expenditure of Consumer Owners*

Let I and E stand for income and expenditures of a consumer. In a general equilibrium analysis, $I-E = 0$ and there is no worth attached to leftover capital stock. Denoting that by K, we have $K = 0$.

If we have a lag between income and expenditure such that income is obtained after expenditure, we have

$$E - I/(1+\rho) \leqslant E - I = 0 \quad \text{for } \rho \geqslant 0. \tag{21}$$

When $\rho = 0$, the use of money is costless and the equality is satisfied. When $\rho > 0$, instead of (21) we may consider

$$E - I/(1+\rho) = K \tag{22}$$

which links the money rate of interest with the remaining capital stock.

3.4. *The Rate of Interest and the Value of Capital*

Setting aside until section 4 the problem of financing the inside banks and controlling their behavior, we may calculate the money rate of interest and the value of capital as a function of growth in the economy.

We will have four cases of which the least and most money utilization are shown.

(23) Consumer Balance[6] (Exchange/Hold back)

$$100\beta^2 (2-\beta) \left(\frac{1-\beta^{T-1}}{1-\beta}\right) \left(\frac{\rho}{1+\rho}\right) = 200\beta^{T+1} + V/(1+\rho)^T$$

[6]An adjustment to account for bank profits must be made for this equation. It is done in section 6.

This is combined with (19) to solve for V and ρ.

(24) Consumer Balance (Buy stock/Sell all)

$$\left[V + 100\beta(2-\beta)\left(\frac{1-\beta^T}{1-\beta}\right) + 100\beta^2\right]\left(\frac{\rho}{1+\rho}\right) = 200\beta^{T+1} + V/(1+\rho)^T$$

This is combined with (20) to solve for V and ρ.

3.4.1. *The Infinite Horizon*

From (23) with (19) and from (24) with (20) we may derive

$$(25) \qquad \lim_{T\to\infty} \frac{\rho}{1+\rho}\{(1+\rho)^T - 1\} = \frac{1-\beta}{2-\beta}$$

which for $\beta = 1$ gives $\rho \to 0$ and

$$(26) \qquad \lim_{T\to\infty} \frac{1+\rho}{\rho}\left[\frac{1-\rho(1+\rho)^{T-1}}{(1+\rho)^T - 1}\right] = \frac{(2-\beta^2)}{\beta(1-\beta)}$$

which for $\beta = 1$ gives $\rho \to 0$. Thus for a stationary state with no natural discount rate we have for the infinite horizon a money rate of interest of zero and constant money prices.

For $\beta = 0$, only $T = 1$ is relevant. If, however, $0 < \beta < 1$, then ρ approaches zero as the horizon lengthens. For example, for $T = 19$, $\rho = 1$ percent; for $T = 397$, $\rho = .1$ percent; for $T = 6190$, $\rho = .01$ percent when $\beta > 0$, given the exchange/hold back case.

3.4.2. *The Finite Horizon*

Using the data displayed in Table 2 for four levels of growth over three periods, we calculate the values for ρ and V given the most monetized economy, that is, one in which shares are bought and all trade is monetized.

As we see from Table 4, the interest rate for zero ending capital is zero, for stationary growth is high, and for 10 percent growth is higher. Maximum growth calls for no consumption and an essentially unboundedly high interest rate.

In the case of 10 percent growth, the redemption price of the firm drops from V to $.95346V/(1+\rho)^3$ where the first term reflects the decline in mar-

Table 4

	ρ	$\hat{p}_1c_1$	$\hat{p}_2c_2$	$\hat{p}_3c_3$	I_1	I_2	I_3	λ	p_1	V
No ending capital	0	46.81104	64.18535	84.38571	53.18896	57.85332	0	.073080	0	142.194
Stationary capital	.4755	41.06995	78.93971	124.48809	58.93005	83.83891	100.0	.078020	.702895	178.931
10 percent growth	.5180	40.17960	78.92330	128.15490	59.82040	87.40380	110.0	.078880	.757722	183.632
Maximum growth	—	—	—	—	100	200	282.8	—	—	—

ginal productivity at level 110 compared with 100.

The stationary and 10 percent growth calculations can be made from the data of Table 2, giving

(27) $$V + 100 = 223.2875 + V/(1+\rho)^3$$

and

(28) $$\frac{\rho}{1+\rho}[V + 211.87] = 70.2895 + V/(1+\rho)^3$$

for the stationary economy and

(29) $$V + 100 = 231.1352 + .95346V/(1+\rho)^3$$

and

(30) $$\frac{\rho}{1+\rho}[V + 207.6064] = 83.3492 + .95346V/(1+\rho)^3$$

for 10 percent growth.

In this model unbounded growth is not possible. Even without consumption, investment cannot exceed 400, or where $z^2 = 20\sqrt{z}$.

4. Outside and Inside Banks

4.1. *Creation of Inside Banks*

In a one-period economy which uses fiat money, an outside bank or agency can fix an arbitrary amount which will suffice to finance all transactions. If, however, we wish to consider a multiperiod economy using fiat money, then in order for the appropriate price ratios to exist between periods the supply of money used in transactions may vary from period to period.

If the money rate of interest $\rho = 0$, then there is no problem in having an outside bank issue enough money for any finite number of periods. At zero interest rate there is no distinction between hoarding and saving, so if M units of fiat money are issued they will only all be actively used at the period of maximum transactions. At other times, part of the money supply will be in hoard or inactive balances.

If the economy has a money interest rate greater than zero, then the amount of money is not automatically conserved within the system. A mechanism for the variation of the money supply is called for. The creation of an inside banking system (that is, a privately owned system) serves to enable intertemporal exchanges to take place by borrowing, saving, and lending.

It is important to note the institutional aspect of intermediation which differentiates saving from lending. In actuality firms extend credit to each other, friends lend each other money directly, credit is manufactured informally, and much trade involves barter or informal nonmonetary quid pro quo arrangements. The simplest model to stress the properties of monetary trade rules out the granting of credit between individuals and considers no futures markets except for money. Thus banks are given a special role, as indicated in Figure 7. In particular, individual deposits are aggregated. Loans and deposits are between individuals and the bank, thus aggregation of saving and disaggregation into lending takes place. A loan will depend on the aggregate of deposits of the bank, its capital, and the specifics of the demands by those requesting the loans.

Figure 7

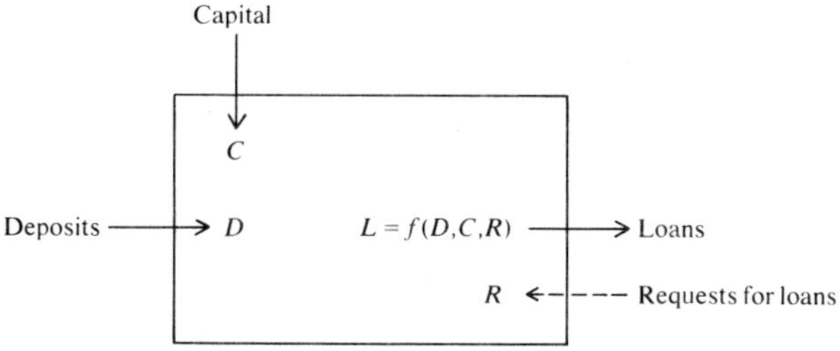

Before we discuss how the money supply is varied (see section 4.2 below), we consider the earnings of the inside banks and the price paid for their shares. As has already been indicated in Tables 3 and 4, we have been able to determine a money interest rate and value of capital consistent with the individual consumers maximizing subject to a budget involving transaction costs and the firms maximizing in such a way that the present value of the firm precisely equals what is paid for its stock. We may write an extra equation for the inside bank on the basis that its shares must equal the present value of all earnings plus liquidation. Denote the amount paid for inside bank shares by B. Then for the two extreme cases from Table 3 involving the least and the largest money requirements we have for the stationary state

$$B = \frac{\rho}{(1+\rho)^2} \sum_{t=2}^{T} p_t c_t + \frac{B}{(1+\rho)^T} \tag{31}$$

and

$$B = \frac{\rho}{(1+\rho)} \left\{ \sum_{t=1}^{T} p_t c_t + V + I_1 \right\} + \frac{B}{(1+\rho)^T} . \tag{32}$$

In the economy which uses the least money, the first borrowing takes place during the second period. Thus the first income earned is discounted by $(1+\rho)^2$. In section 6 we utilize these extra conditions to evaluate the worth of bank shares.

It must be noted that all of the outside money can be regarded as being used immediately to buy the shares of the inside banks without any loss of generality. This is because the earnings from bank shares and the outside interest rate must be the same in an economy with no uncertainty and no frictions or barriers to borrowing.

4.2. *Problems With Competitive Banking and the Money Supply*

In the model described above, the firms use the money capital raised to buy resources. The banks, however, make loans which do not necessarily equal the capital of the bank. Furthermore, the banks do not invest their idle funds. A natural question to ask is, What controls or information must be supplied for the functioning of a competitive banking system? We may even question whether it is possible to have the inside banks competitively determine the money supply and/or the rate of interest efficiently.[7]

The system we have solved in the examples has the government specify the outside money supply, the salvage value for goods, a redemption rate for firms,[8] and the bankruptcy penalty.[9] The money rate of interest is determined by the bidding for outside money [see equation (15)].

Given the outside rate of interest and liquidation values, competition by individuals and/or firms will determine the quantity of inside money issued by a passive banking system with unlimited rights to create money, but only on request.

At time t given ρ_t, individuals can determine the amount D_t of loans they would like, where D_t is a function of ρ_t and the liquidation conditions. If banks can issue on demand and are required to both accept deposits and make loans at the specified rate ρ_t, then supply always equals demand. Furthermore, the payout on deposits cannot exceed income from loans since the bank shares would not be sold otherwise.

The system described has passive nonstrategic banks. Could we have an efficient banking system with price (that is, interest rate) or quantity competition? If as a first approximation we assume that banking is a constant returns to scale industry[10] (say, costs are zero), then price competition in general cannot determine an efficient interest rate (see section 4.3) unless the quantity of money is exogenously controlled each period. This follows essentially from the Bertrand-Edgeworth duopoly (or oligopoly) model. (See Shubik 1959.) If the central bank or referee sets the rules on what a private bank can loan according to some reserve ratio formula such as a function of capital and deposits, then all banks will always be loaned up if the interest rate is greater than zero. But the example in section 3.4 provides an instance where the reserve ratio formula needed to avoid excess reserves at the appropriate interest rate would be essentially as complex as fitting a function to a series of T points; that is, it would be equivalent to announcing a money supply constraint each period.

If a strategy by a bank is to announce an amount of loanable funds, L less than or equal to some bound, then we would have interest rates determined by

$$1+\rho = D/L$$

where D is the amount of money due one period hence offered for L. If there are many banks, then limiting Cournot oligopoly behavior gives rise to the same problem as with the price model; that is, banks will not have excess reserves at positive rates of interest.

In summary, it is suggested here that we cannot have a competitive[11]

[7]For a discussion of what is meant by efficiency, see section 4.3.

[8]For production functions homogeneous of order 1, $V = 0$.

[9]The full significance of the bankruptcy penalty has been discussed in Dubey and Shubik 1977a and is not central to the discussion here.

[10]With increasing returns to scale, competition would be eliminated anyhow.

[11]In actuality there may be room for competition in terms of services and cost efficiency.

inside banking system which determines both the quantity of money and the interest rate.

In our model competitive bidding for outside money determines the (long-run) interest rate for outside money. Competitive bidding for shares in inside banks, together with the rule that an inside bank must accept deposits and pay the going rate on them, guarantees that the outside money rate of interest is greater than or equal to the inside money rate of interest. Hence we have a system in which the outside rate of interest is determined competitively and is linked to inside bank earnings and the inside banks are a passive mechanism constrained to fill loans and accept deposits. Thus the money supply is varied.

4.3. *On Modified Pareto Optimality*

In section 4.2 and elsewhere we have referred to efficient banking and efficient allocations. For the classical competitive equilibrium model of T time periods with no liquidation values, our definition remains as usual. When there is an outside agency which has announced liquidation conditions and either an interest rate or money supply conditions for each period, then by *efficient allocations* we mean the Pareto optimal set of this constrained feasible set of outcomes.

4.4. *Multistage Financing and Working Capital*

In section 3.4 several models of the economy with different transaction needs for money were considered. It was observed that if outside money is issued and a positive interest rate exists then the economy must be cash consuming.

In different economies the technological and strategic features of trade and production determine the needs for working capital, the size of the float and lags and biases in the pattern of payments. Some individuals are paid in advance; others wait for months. The velocity of payments is clearly partly influenced by the rate of interest; it is also determined by technology and custom.

Some individuals may try to live off the float, indulge in check kiting or strategic manipulation of the paying of bills. All of these activities would have quantitative but not qualitative effects on the models in 3.4.

Working capital needs are influenced both by the number of stages in production and by the level of integration. Thus, as is suggested by Figure 8, the consolidation of two firms in a buyer-seller relationship is tantamount to introducing a barter exchange.

Horizontal integration merely poses minor accounting problems (if com-

Figure 8

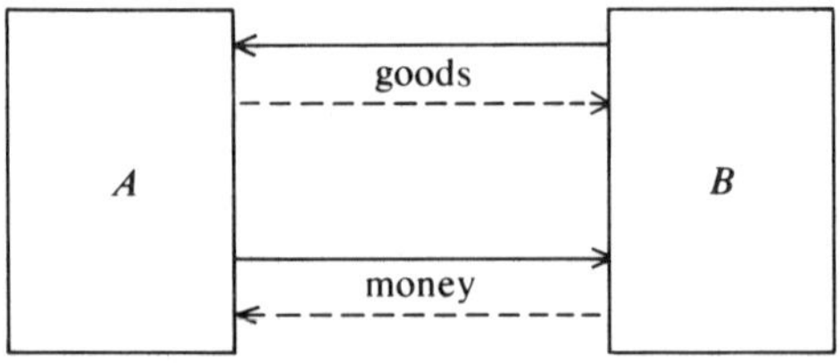

plex taxation is not present), in that the payments pattern between A and B may be biased in favor of one or the other. But when they are considered as a whole, the possible nonsymmetry is no longer visible.

The more important feature is reflected in the possibility that as the number of stages of production for a given output are increased—if we fix the price of the final output (which for a single product or aggregate we can do without loss of generality) for purposes of comparison—the economy with many stages of production will require more capital and hence more money to finance it than the one with fewer stages.

We illustrate the multistage financing by a simple extension of the example given in section 3. In particular, instead of having only a single production function of the form $x_{t+1} = 20\sqrt{x_t}$ we introduce an intermediate good such that before the product of the first stage of production can be used for consumption or production it must be stored (or otherwise processed) for a period. We have

$$y_{t+1} = 20\sqrt{x_t}$$

followed by

$$x_{t+2} = y_{t+1}.$$

It is straightforward to check that all the previous conditions for a stationary state are the same except for the introduction of extra initial conditions and variables for the intermediate good. In particular, the solution is illustrated for $\beta = 1$ and $T = 3$. The new initial conditions require $A_1 = 200$ and $A_2 = 200$, where A_1 is the initial supply of output from the first stage and A_2 the initial supply of output from the second stage. Thus, although final consumption is the same in this economy as in the previous one, more capital is required. (See Böhm-Bawerk 1959 or more easily Lutz 1968 for a simple exposition of Böhm-Bawerk.)

In the start of the economy we can consider the setting up of vertically integrated firms or two sets of firms, one of which sells to the other. If we adopt the former convention, then trade between the two firms is not monetized because it is taken care of by internal accounting. Either convention of forming a set of vertically integrated firms or of forming two sets of firms will yield the same new equations which are modifications of equations (20) and (24).[12]

Given $\beta = 1$, the salvage prices are β^T, β^T, and $V/(1+\rho)^T$. Then we have

$$(20')\qquad V + 200\beta + 200\beta = 100\beta(2-\beta)\left(\frac{1-\beta^T}{1-\beta}\right) + 200\beta^{T+1} + 200\beta^{T+1} + V/(1+\rho)^T$$

$$(24')\qquad \left[V + 100\beta(2-\beta)\left(\frac{1-\beta^T}{1-\beta}\right) + 100\beta^2 + 100\beta^2\right]\left(\frac{\rho}{1+\rho}\right) = 200\beta^{T+1} + 200\beta^{T+1} + V/(1+\rho)^T.$$

[12] The residual values of the firms $V_1 + V_2 = V$ the value of the integrated firm. In this example $V_2 = 0$.

Setting $T = 3$ we reduce (20′) and (24′) to

$$4(1+\rho)^3(\rho-1) = 4\rho - 1.$$

Hence, $\rho = 141.3$ percent and $V = 322.989$.

For $T = 70$ we obtain $\rho = 4.83$ percent and $V = 7267.545$.

5. Multigenerational Economies

5.1. *Finite and Infinite Stationary Economies*

In the previous sections we have examined finite economies of arbitrary length with one generation. We may extend our analysis to consider overlapping generations. The simplest model is as shown in Figure 1b. Suppose that each generation is active for T periods after which it dies and settles accounts with society at the start of period $T+1$. Society passes on the capital to the new individuals at the start of that period, and this process is continued indefinitely.

Although the process may continue indefinitely, each individual has a finite life and hence faces a final settlement date.

The example from the previous sections is continued. Suppose

$$A = 200 \qquad \text{with } \beta = 1$$

$$T = 70$$

$$\lambda = \mu = 1$$

$$p_{70g+1} = 1$$

V_g valued at $V_g/(1+\rho)^{70}$.

From equations (20) and (24) we obtain

$$V + 200 = 7000 + 200 + V/(1+\rho)^{70}$$

or

$$V = 7000\left[\frac{(1+\rho)^{70}}{(1+\rho)^{70} - 1}\right] \tag{33}$$

and

$$\frac{\rho}{1+\rho}\{V + 7100\} = 200 + \frac{V}{(1+\rho)^{70}} \tag{34}$$

giving

$$(1+\rho)^{70}\{139\rho - 2\} = 139\rho + 68.$$

Hence

$$\rho = 4.276 \text{ percent and } V = 7394.46.$$

Since the corporations may have indefinite life, we may interpret the first generation as one in which the corporations are set up, but at $t = 71$, instead of considering the liquidation of the inside banks and the corporations, we may consider that inside bank shares and corporate shares are redeemed and immediately redistributed to the new generation.

From (32) we obtain $B = 627.85$.

Unlike our previous observation in section 3.4.2, that as the horizon of the economy lengthens the rate of interest approaches zero, here we have a stationary state with a positive rate determined by the life of a single generation. Although all physical quantities are stationary, the prices inflate constantly given $\beta = 1$; as β decreases, we may verify that we switch from inflation to deflation.

We may observe two somewhat different types of stationarity. One is *full* stationarity, as shown above, where each period is a replica of the last. The other is *periodic* stationarity, as in Tables 2 and 4, where initial conditions are reproduced after T periods.

If we consider K generations, we do not need to supply liquidation conditions for each generation. If we specify conditions at $KT+1$, the other values are determined by the requirement that the books balance every T periods.

A somewhat more satisfactory model of many generations has them overlapping as is shown in Figure 1a or in the Lexis diagram shown in Figure 9. We can see a stationary population in which each individual lives three periods. At the end of time at KT, one-third of the population has just been born, one-third is middle-aged, and one-third is about to die. Thus, in order to fully specify terminal conditions, we must take a generation for full liquidation. What happens at the six points denoted by dots in Figure 9 must be specified. (Similarly, for full specification of the model, initial conditions for generations 1, -1, and -2 must be given, that is, conditions for those alive before the start of time and for those just born.)

Figure 9

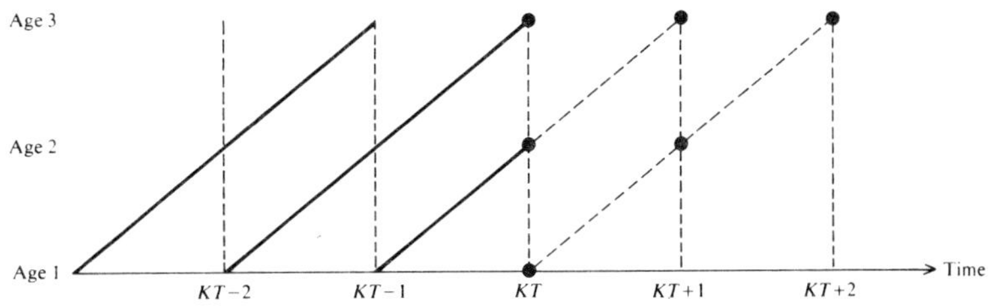

5.2. *Pareto Optimality*

As long as births are exogenous to the model and the fixing of the terminal conditions are regarded as exogenous, then the comments made in section 4.3 apply to this multigenerational model. Except for the requirements of the ending conditions, there is no essential difference between the multigenerational economy and the standard closed system with production and trade. An economy in which individuals live for T periods, which is active for

K full generations, will have $T(K+2) - 2$ cohorts [that is, individuals born at $-(K-1)$, $-(K-2)$, ... up until $TK + (K-1)$]. Thus an imputation is a vector of $T(K+2) - 2$ components, and the usual definition of Pareto optimality can be applied.

If births are considered to be in any way endogenous to the model, then the definition of optimality depends delicately upon the assumptions made concerning the strategic control one generation has upon others.

5.3. *The Interlinking Mechanisms*

In the models of section 5.1, the outside bank or state provides the linkage between otherwise completely selfish generations. The money loss experienced by each generation is enough to pay for the capital stock that the next generation starts with.

When we view this process strategically, we may imagine that the population alive at $t = 1$ owns the original resources, bids for outside money, and sets up the inside banks and firms. However, from then on the state transfers the shares redeemed from the dead to the newly born.

We could modify this model to take into account the possibility of intergenerational concern. Thus we could attach a utility to the leaving of bequests. The form of the desired bequest and the way it is transferred may both influence the economic outcome. In particular, we need to modify the utility function to show intergenerational concern. There are several different relatively natural assumptions which can be made.

- Generation A is concerned with generation B's enjoyment of what it gets.
- A wishes to leave B a specific array of goods.
- A's utility depends on leaving B a sum of money.
- A's utility depends on leaving B a sum of money corrected by an inflation/deflation index.

The first convention leads to an unnecessary and not overly economically relevant complication in interlinked utilities. The second assumption, that individuals desire to leave bequests manifested in arrays of goods, may have some limited merits in the leaving of family heirlooms. But the last two assumptions appear to be far more reasonable in terms of the coding of information and simplicity. Furthermore, much of the intergenerational transfer is not primarily economic; value systems, home education, tastes, political views, and the like remind us how limited pure economic views of life are.

Let us consider as our simplest model one in which the first generation attributes θ percent of the money value of its initial assets to inheritance and $(1-\theta)$ percent to the state. Suppose some individuals wish to leave the next generation enough to be in real terms as well off or k percent better off than themselves, taking into account what will be received from the state.

For purposes of illustration, we select essentially the simplest functional forms we can without trivializing the example. We modify (4) to become

$$(4'') \qquad \sum_{t=1}^{T} \beta^{t-1} \sqrt{x_t} + \lambda \min [0, D_{T+1}] + \omega \max [0, h(D_{T+1})]$$

where λ is a penalty against debt and ω is a parameter reflecting the desirability of leaving an inheritance.

Two problems must be faced. The first concerns sequencing. Can an individual both end in debt and leave an inheritance? Or does the payment of debt take precedence over the inheritance? Although on occasion assets are siphoned off, leaving creditors unpaid, here we assume creditors are paid first. The second problem concerns the precise form of $h(D_{T+1})$. In fact, monetary intergenerational transfers (except possibly for the very rich) do not appear to be as important as the transfers which take place during life (Guthrie 1963).

Consider the endowment of the first generation. In the example of section 3 this amounts to $A+V$ at the market price at the start, of which from the initial conditions $\theta(A+V)$ is from inheritance and the remainder from the state. Suppose that the individuals wish to leave the next generation as well off as their generation. The specific strength and nature of this desire is reflected in $h(D_{T+1})$. For example

$$h(D_{T+1}) = \theta(A+V)\left[1 - \left(\frac{D_{T+1} - (A+V)}{(A+V)}\right)^2\right]$$

indicates that leaving too large an inheritance is considered as unfavorable as leaving too small an inheritance. For purposes of calculating an example, we use

$$h(D_{T+1}) = \min\,[D_{T+1}, \theta(A+V)].$$

Thus (4″) becomes

$$(4''') \qquad \sum_{t=1}^{T} \beta^{t-1}\sqrt{x_t} + \lambda \min\,[0, D_{T+1}] + \omega \max\left\{0, \min\,[D_{T+1}, \theta(A+V)]\right\}$$

which indicates that utility increases linearly up to the point of funding the next generation for the private contribution to the same standard of living. Beyond that level no extra benefits accrue to the donor.

We now return to the original example using the stationary state with $T = 70$ as in section 5.1. Equation (35) is now modified, giving[13]

$$(36) \qquad (1+\rho)^{70}\{[141 - 2(1-\theta)\rho - 2(1-\theta)]\} = 68(1-\theta) + [141 - 2(1-\theta)]\rho.$$

For $\theta = 0$ we obtain (35). For $\theta = 1$ this becomes

$$(1+\rho)^{70}\{141\rho\} = 141\rho.$$

Hence $\rho = 0$. For $\beta = 1$, V is not well defined. For $\theta = 1/2$ we obtain

$$(37) \qquad (1+\rho)^{70}\{140\rho - 1\} = 34 + 140\rho$$

$\rho = 3.39$ percent, and $V = 7751.422$.

Comparing this with the result from (35), we see that the more individuals are innately willing to leave to the next generation, the lower will be the rate of interest.

[13]Given $\lambda = \omega = 1$ and $p_T = 1$, it can be checked that equilibrium is as before, with the difference being a smaller component by the government.

6. Taxation and Corporate Reality

6.1. *Central Bank Profits, Taxes, and Interest*

In the models presented here, there is a money drain from the system as a whole which is measured by the profits of the outside or central bank. The system loses $M(1+\rho)^T - M$ to the central bank, where M is the outside money issue and ρ the money rate of interest. This loss is made up or balanced at period $T+1$ by the purchase of residual assets at the final settlement date. Thus the rate of interest is essentially a money transactions tax or, over the full life of an individual, an income tax.

Money flows out of the system, but in order to obey conservation it must be balanced. This is done with the balancing of the worth of final assets. In the Arrow-Debreu general equilibrium, the value of assets is zero and there is either no money or, if the model is interpreted as having money, the rate of interest is zero or is not determined.

All other things being equal, taxation could be used directly as an alternative to having all capital financed through central bank profits or through altruism. The effect of an income tax will be to introduce a different leak in the economy and hence lower the rate of interest needed to produce the financing of the capital goods.

We reconsider the example of section 3, taking into full account inside and outside banking profits and income and capital gains taxes. Before the original equations are modified, we must digress into a consideration of accounting conventions and profits.

6.2. *Accounting, Profits, and Taxes*

In many actual modern economies the individuals and enterprises are confronted with an array of different taxes, and the tax bills are highly dependent on accounting conventions and law. (See, for example, U.S. Internal Revenue Code of 1954, June 1, 1976, edition.) In particular, key considerations are the definition of a taxable event, profits, and income.

In particular, in the United States there are at least three critical tax distinctions: individual, corporate, and capital gains.

According to economic theory, the income of an individual or corporation in an economy which lasts for T periods is given by the total discounted income stream and liquidation value of the investment. To the tax collector, income is usually defined over a period of a year, and in general for individuals, income is an actual cash flow to the individual caused by transactions. For the firm, income will frequently be on an accrual basis, thus not matching cash. Furthermore, for both firms and individuals, unpaid profits, unrealized capital gains, and other forms of increase in wealth not matched by actual transactions are not recorded as income.

The microeconomic theorist wishing to reconcile microeconomic theorizing with macroeconomic approaches and with corporate reality must appreciate the full implications of the relationship among economic, accounting, and legal definitions of items such as income. With the three different types of taxes noted above and with interest payments being deductible from gross income as an expense but dividends not being deductible, the conditions for Modigliani-Miller equivalence (Modigliani-Miller 1958) between debt and equity finance do not hold even without uncertainty.

In particular, it is of interest to note that the concept that the firm should maximize the present value of profits for the good of its stockholders is not necessarily reasonable, given different tax structures. The timing of the booking of profits and the paying of dividends to individuals may be critical to the welfare of the stockholders.

We must return to the basic optimization equations to appreciate this. We study the stationary state with a government which intends to finance the stationary state primarily through taxation and slightly through central bank earnings. We consider three taxes, all proportional to the sum taxed:

η_1 = individual income tax
η_2 = capital gains tax
η_3 = corporate income tax.

Because all taxes are proportional, in spite of the usual convention that they are not indexed (that is, they are paid on spot not inflation corrected incomes or capital gains), we can work with present values (futures prices) without distortion.

We now set up the new full (nonatomic) noncooperative game. We need to be explicit about extra rules concerning taxation planning.

Individuals bid u for the supply of outside money M. The u is to be paid back at time $T+1$. Thus

$$\frac{u}{M} = (1+\rho)^T.$$

Inside banks are formed. Since they are essentially strategic dummies, numbers do not matter. The individuals using inside money $v \leqslant M$ buy shares of the inside banks. (We can assume there is only one without loss of generality.)

If the government is controlling the economy for a stationary state, then if B is the capital of the bank, $B/(1+\rho)^T$ will be offered as the salvage value of the bank's paid in capital (in present value terms).

In competition, if E_t is the present value of earnings during t, then the value of bank shares will be

$$B = \sum_{t=1}^{T} E_t(1 - \eta_3) + B/(1+\rho)^T \tag{38}$$

after-tax income + return of capital.

The bank has no capital gains tax to pay when it liquidates.[14] Furthermore, if it has to book the payment of interest on an accrual basis, it has no strategic freedom in reporting income. Hence we may write (38) to evaluate the bank shares. We note that the value is directly influenced by the level of corporate taxes.

After the inside banking system exists, individuals borrow and buy shares in corporations which are being formed. The different possibilities in equity financing have been already noted in section 3.1 (debt finance was not discussed). However, the number of firms to be formed was not noted. Given that the assumption was made that production functions are individually

[14]This is true if inflation is less than the money rate of interest.

owned, an upper bound for the number of firms is one per consumer (leaving out layers of intermediate good firms as in 4.4). For purposes of the argument here, as long as there are many firms, the relative densities of consumers and firms do not matter. The simplest is to consider the same densities.

In our analysis so far we have not discussed debt finance. It has two important features: one associated with taxation, the other with uncertainty. We first consider equity finance, then comment on the difference made by considering debt.

As can be seen from equation (39), a firm needs to raise money to buy its initial assets plus its production technology. However, its income will be taxed, so its present value must reflect this. Hence

$$V + 200\beta = 100\beta(2-\beta)\left(\frac{1-\beta^T}{1-\beta}\right)(1-\eta_3) + 200\beta^{T+1} + V/(1+\rho)^T. \tag{39}$$

If the stationary state exists with taxation, then consumer spending will be

$$V + 200\beta + 100(2-\beta)\beta\left(\frac{1-\beta^T}{1-\beta}\right). \tag{40}$$

Offsetting the consumer's spending is income after taxes

$$\frac{1}{1+\rho}\left[V + 200\beta + 100\beta(2-\beta)\left(\frac{1-\beta^T}{1-\beta}\right)(1-\eta_2)(1-\eta_3)\right] \tag{41}$$

obtained from the firm. The factor $1/(1+\rho)$ indicates that we have attributed the transaction money holding and float loss to the consumer. This has to net out to the consumer because any payments advantage among firms is reflected to the consumer in income.

We must account for consumer income derived from inside banking profits. We may consider the presence of a float between the consumer and the bank, that is, a lag in payments in which the consumer must pay debts promptly but has a lag in payments of income. Alternatively, we may assume that profits are credited instantly to the consumer. Adopting the last convention, if W is borrowed from the bank, then

$$\rho W(1-\eta_3) \tag{42}$$

is paid back as after-tax profits. Hence total consumer income after taxes is

$$\frac{1}{1+\rho}\left[V + 200\beta + 100\beta(2-\beta)\left(\frac{1-\beta^T}{1-\beta}\right)(1-\eta_2)(1-\eta_3)\right] + \rho W(1-\eta_2)(1-\eta_3) \tag{43}$$

plus at the end a return of capital from liquidation of

$$\frac{200\beta^T}{1-\eta_3} + V/(1+\rho)^T + B/(1+\rho)^T. \tag{44}$$

We note that in expression (43) above the consumer has been taxed at the capital gains rate η_2 rather than the individual income tax rate η_1. This follows immediately from the choices of the firm and weak Pareto optimality. As income flows in, if the firm is actually trying to maximize the present value of dividends plus liquidation of residual assets after taxes, it does not matter whether the firm pays dividends or not. If capital gains taxes are lower than income taxes, the firm here should never pay dividends. Instead, earnings will be returned as part of increased equity at the end and will be taxed less. This will be generally true for firms not facing exogenous or strategic uncertainty.

The total debt that must be financed by a consumer is calculated from (40) and (43). The difference between them equals W or

$$W = \frac{\rho(V + 200\beta) + (\rho + \eta_2 + \eta_3 - \eta_2\eta_3)I}{(1+\rho)[1 + \rho(1 + \eta_2)(1 + \eta_3)]} \tag{45}$$

where

$$I = 100\beta(2-\beta)\left(\frac{1 - \beta^T}{1-\beta}\right).$$

Hence the value of the bank shares is given by

$$B = \rho W(1 - \eta_3) + B/(1+\rho)^T$$

or

$$B = \rho W(1 - \eta_3)\left(\frac{(1+\rho)^{70}}{(1+\rho)^{70} - 1}\right). \tag{46}$$

If we let θ be the percentage of the worth of initial assets (in present value terms) that a consumer wishes to leave in her or his estate, then the balancing of the consumer accounts calls for

$$W = (1-\theta)[200\beta^{T+1} + V/(1+\rho)^T + B/(1+\rho)^T]. \tag{47}$$

For simplicity, set

$$k_1 = \rho + \eta_2 + \eta_3 - \eta_2\eta_3$$
$$k_2 = (1 - \eta_2)(1 - \eta_3)$$
$$\omega = 1 - \theta.$$

We may then write (47) for $\beta = 1$, $T = 70$

$$\left[\rho\left(\frac{7000(1 - \eta_3)(1+\rho)^{70}}{[(1+\rho)^{70} - 1]} + 200\right) + 7000k_1\right]\left(1 - \frac{\omega(1 - \eta_3)}{[(1+\rho)^{70} - 1]}\right) \tag{48}$$

$$= \omega\left(\frac{7000(1 - \eta_3)}{(1+\rho)^{70} - 1} + 200\right)(1+\rho)(1 + k_2\rho).$$

A few specific cases are explored for comparison. In particular we consider

(i) $\eta_1 = \eta_2 = \eta_3 = \theta = 0$: no taxes or bequests.
(ii) $\eta_1 = \eta_2 = \eta_3 = 0$ and $\theta = .5$ and $.9$: no taxes but high bequests.
(iii) $\eta_1 > \eta_2 = .25$, $\eta_3 = .5$, and $\theta = 0$ and $.1$: capital gains of 25 percent, corporate income taxes of 50 percent, and bequests of 0.

For (i) and (ii) we may simplify (48) to

$$\rho[71(1+\rho)^{70} - 36]\left(1 - \frac{\omega\rho}{[(1+\rho)^{70} - 1]}\right) = \omega[(1+\rho)^{70} + 34](1+\rho)^2. \tag{49}$$

For (i), $\rho \simeq 4.33$ percent, $V = 7379.7$, $W = 5989.6$, and $B = 273.42$. For $\theta = .5$, $\rho \simeq 3.4$ percent, $V = 7745.8$; $\theta = .9$, $\rho \simeq 1.816$ percent, $V = 9772.6$. For $\eta_1 > \eta_2 = .25$, $\eta_3 = .5$, $\theta = 0$, $k_1 = \rho + .625$, $k_2 = 1.875$, $\rho \simeq .873$ percent, $V = 15{,}357.4$, $W = 4459.37$, $B = 42.705$.

6.2.1. *On Debt Financing*
The key legal economic distinction caused by debt financing in a world without uncertainty is the possibility that interest payments may be regarded as business expenses whereas dividends are not. Thus, all other things being equal, a firm maximizing its present value will select debt finance and in a world without uncertainty will pay no taxes, having no profits. However, the debt holders will pay income tax. If the firm used equity finance and did not pay dividends, the equity holders would only pay capital gains while the firm might pay income taxes.

6.3. *Private Capital and Social Capital*
It is argued here that the simple individualistic model does not provide us with a description of motivation for the formation of even private capital in an economy. By considering trade in money, a society can use the rate of interest as a means of covering the costs of investment. But there are clearly other considerations and techniques for promoting capital formation. In particular, we have

- The desire to leave bequests—altruism
- Corporate and individual income taxes
- Wealth taxes and capital gains taxes
- Other taxes, such as sales taxes
- Earnings of the central bank via interest
- Government debt.

In actuality, much of the revenues gathered by the government go to pay for the governmental bureaucratic infrastructure which may be regarded as a public good or they go for transfer payments to the old and poor, but not to newborn capitalists.

If economists are willing to limit their scope to economics rather than to the whole of social, political, or other choice, then the problem of efficient economic choice can be well formulated. We take the array of public goods desired by society together with the leftover capital stock at the end of time as a datum. Then efficiency is measured in terms of the feasible set of actions in a finite economy.

The question of how much planning and control is needed by a government to obtain the desired amount of capital goods and public goods must be resolved. We return to this in section 8.

6.4. *Turnover, Velocity of Trade, and Taxes*
As a crude approximation, we might consider the life-span of an individual to be around 70 years. We have used $T = 70$ in several of the examples above. The two basic relations of time span are life cycle to manufacturing cycle and life cycle to tax cycle. Income and capital gains taxes are levied on an annual basis, but much manufacturing has a cycle shorter than a year. Thus if we were to consider an economy with five turnovers per annum or a manufacturing length of ten weeks, the individual would live for 350 manufacturing cycles. This correction to equation (48) would cut the interest rate considerably. As was noted in section 4.4, vertical integration or capital deepening, which is a characteristic of much of modern production, would increase the need for financing and raise the interest rate. A depth of from three to five appears reasonable for an economy with extraction, raw material fabrication, manufacturing, wholesaling, and retailing.

6.5. *Heavy Money and Earnings on Deposits and Bank Reserves*
The rate of return on bank reserves will only coincide with the rate of interest on inside money if there is no variability in money supply. Let the rate of return be δ. Then as we have $M = B$ we may write (in present value terms at the end of the economy)

$$M[(1+\delta)^T - 1] = 200(1+\rho)^T + V + B \qquad (50)$$

$$\underset{\text{outside money}}{\text{cost of}} = \underset{\text{capital stock.}}{\text{end value of}}$$

For illustration we consider the case with no taxes or bequests, $T = 70$, and $\beta = 1$. This instance was studied in section 6.2, yielding $\rho = 4.33$ percent. Solving (50) for this instance we obtain $\delta = 5.53$ percent. Thus when inside banks can create money, bank reserves yield a higher return than bank money does. Outside money is a *heavy money* compared with inside money.

Institutionally, coin and other currency are issued by the treasury, mint, or central bank, and they circulate without earning interest. In the structure noted here, as long as the name of a private controlled bank were held as prime as the name of the central bank, then there would be no need for any issue of government notes or coin.

The system could function with interest payments made on both bank reserves and demand deposits (that is, money used for transactions). These require a modification of (48) with these two features treated parametrically.

7. On Unbounded Growth
Phelps (1966), Solow (1963), Koopmans (1977), and many others have been concerned with economies with unbounded growth, economies in which population grows along with other resources. Ramsey (1928), Koopmans (1960, 1972), and others have been concerned with optimality and ethical considerations about the treatment of future generations. It is suggested here that if the assumption of exogenous population growth is made and financial rules of the game are provided for the economy, then Pareto optimality for a

series of generations can be well defined in the conventional way.

We continue our example, introducing labor and population growth explicitly. As before, we assume $A_1 = 200$; we add $L_1 = 100$ as initial population with an exogenous growth rate of n. Thus

$$L_t = 100(1+n)^{t-1}. \tag{51}$$

The full production function becomes

$$z_{t+1} = 2\sqrt{k_t\, L_t} \tag{52}$$

or

$$z_{t+1} = 20\sqrt{k_t\,(1+n)^{t-1}}\,.$$

We modify the starting stock to be $z_1 = 200(1+n)^{-2}$ in order to obtain the golden rule growth where $k_1 = 100(1+n)^{-2}$ and initial per capita consumption is $(1+n)^{-2}$.

Modifying equation (39) we obtain

$$V + \frac{200\beta}{(1+n)^2} = \frac{100\beta(2-\beta)}{(1+n)^2}\left(\frac{1-[\beta(1+n)]^T}{1-\beta(1+n)}\right) + 200\beta\,\frac{[(1+n)\beta]^T}{(1+n)^2} + V/(1+\rho)^T \tag{53}$$

and modifying (47) we obtain

$$\frac{\rho}{(1+\rho)^2}\left[V + \frac{200\beta}{(1+n)^2} + \frac{100\beta(2-\beta)}{(1+n)^2}\left(\frac{1-[\beta(1+n)]^T}{1-\beta(1+n)}\right)\right] \tag{54}$$

$$= \frac{200\beta}{(1+n)^2}[(1+n)\beta]^T + V/(1+\rho)^T + B/(1+\rho)^T.$$

For $T \to \infty$ we obtain

$$\frac{2\rho}{(1+\rho)^2}\left[\frac{200\beta}{(1+n)^2} + \frac{100\beta(2-\beta)}{\beta n(1+n)^2}\right] = \frac{200\beta}{(1+n)^2}$$

or

$$\frac{\rho}{(1+\rho)^2}\left[2 + \frac{2-\beta}{\beta n}\right] = 1$$

or

$$\rho^2 - \left[\frac{2-\beta}{\beta n}\right]\rho + 1 = 0. \tag{55}$$

We need $\beta(1+n) \geqslant 1$ to avoid some basic problems in the interpretation of the motivation of the stationary state.

Solving for $\beta = 1$ and $n = .02$ and $.05$ we obtain

$$\rho = .020008 \text{ and } .050126.$$

For $\beta = .98$ and $n = .04$, we have

$$\rho = .038488.$$

We see that the money rate of interest is not quite the same as the growth rate but for $\beta = 1$ is slightly higher.[15]

8. Concluding Remarks

In many ways, many of the basic problems involving money also involve uncertainty. In spite of the attractiveness of immediately examining money in the context of uncertainty, it has been suggested in the analysis above that money and the rate of interest can be integrated into economic analysis without uncertainty or even a natural time discount. In doing so, a finite-horizon model for a multigenerational economy can be specified as a noncooperative game.

The extension of the competitive market to include capital stock provides a determination of the money rate of interest and a transaction demand for money. Liquidity preference and a structure of rates of interest call for the consideration of uncertainty. This is not dealt with here.

8.1. *Many Capital Goods and Societal Goals*

The examples presented in this paper have one capital good which is also the consumer good. It is conjectured that for any number of goods, given that technology and population size is fixed and that all consumption processes involve the use of the individual's time and no better than constant returns hold for production processes, then for $0 < \beta \leq 1$ an upper bound stationary state exists. This is defined in the sense that the referee selects an initial vector of resources, A, and a vector of prices to be paid for all resources at period $T+1$, such that the system at $T+1$ will produce A.

It is further assumed that the life-span and preferences of each generation are identical.

From a practical point of view the calculation of all ending prices in an ongoing economy is out of the question in a noncentralized economy. The motivation for production provided by a wealth-maximizing enterprise is not well defined in actuality without specifying expectations of future prices, demands, and interest rates. The larger the governmental sector and the more clearly enunciated its policy is, the easier and more accurate will be the estimating of the future.

Leaving aside technological change and shifts in taste, then the operational equivalent of the models in the previous sections is that of a society in which individuals believe that policy is designed for a specific level of growth.

8.2. *The Interest Rate as a Control Variable*

The influence of the central bank on the rate of interest is one of the key

[15] It is also of interest to note that in this model with taxes individuals will pay income taxes on labor sold. They will not be able to shelter all of their income in capital gains.

controls in monetary policy. A lowering of the rate of interest in general will increase the demand for bank money and stimulate investment. Yet in the model suggested here the growth rate and rate of interest go in the same direction.

In the models suggested, once the banking system is erected and prices for ending capital given, the interest rate is endogenously determined. If instead we fix it as a control variable, this does not provide enough guidance to the economy to determine prices for ending capital.

8.3. *Statics, Laissez-Faire, and Institutions*

It is suggested here that an attempt to introduce residual capital stock into the static general equilibrium model of an economy immediately raises many basic problems concerning the design and limits of competitive economic mechanisms for an ongoing society. Specifically, unless considerable individual altruism is postulated, the goals and guidance for overall capital formation appear to lie outside of the competitive economy. Furthermore, in a society which uses money it does not appear to be possible to determine both the rate of interest and the money supply competitively.

A passive banking system can be used to provide a variable money supply.

8.4. *A Note on Methodology*

The analysis here is based on two basic premises concerning methodology.

First, a model purporting to explain the functioning of an economy with competitive elements needs to be explicitly *game theoretic* in structure. The discipline called for in fully formulating a well-defined game of strategy forces attention on rules of the game such as methods of payment and bankruptcy rules which have direct counterparts in economic and financial life. The noncooperative equilibrium solution is a far more general solution concept than is the competitive equilibrium of Walrasian analysis. The former contains the latter as a special case.

The second point concerns the role of *gaming,* the construction of playable games which can be used for experimentation. The economy is part of our society and is run by individuals acting through institutions. These have structure and rules. The design of an economic model as a playable game forces on the designer a degree of care and specificity that offers a virtually automatic test of the completeness, consistency, and complexity of the model proposed.

The models presented here do not fully meet the two stringent conditions noted above. The decision of bankruptcy and positions of disequilibrium is skimpy. Yet the attempt to convert the models into playable games appears to be a fruitful approach to the eventual construction of an economic dynamics.

Equilibrium in a Pure Currency Economy

Robert E. Lucas, Jr.*

1. Introduction

This paper studies the determination of the equilibrium price level in a stationary economy in which all exchange involves the trade of fiat money for goods. The use of money in exchange is guaranteed by the imposition of a constraint, as suggested by Clower (1967),[1] which requires that purchases of goods must necessarily be paid for by currency held over from the preceding period. The models examined also resemble closely that studied by Friedman (1969, first part). Individual behavior resembles that captured in inventory-theoretic models of money demand, as studied by Baumol (1952) and Tobin (1956), so that another way to think of the paper is as an attempt to study the transaction demand for money in as simple as possible a general equilibrium setting.

In section 2, an example with perfect certainty is analyzed, with a digression to motivate the cash-in-advance constraint. In this example, which is a special case of the much more general setup treated by Grandmont and Younes (1972, 1973), equilibrium velocity is determined in an entirely mechanical way by the assumed payments period. In section 3, individual uncertainty is introduced, giving rise to a precautionary motive for holding currency and a nontrivial problem of equilibrium determination, in which velocity depends on the kinds of economic factors long thought to be important in reality. The analysis of this latter case is continued in sections 4–6.

I think of this exercise not so much as an end in itself, but as an analytical step toward models which capture more and more features which monetary economists believe to be important in understanding actual monetary systems. In the concluding section, then, I will go well beyond the results developed in the paper to venture some opinions on some of these other issues.

2. An Economy With Certainty

Throughout the paper, I will study an economy with a continuum of identical

*Although prepared for the Federal Reserve Bank of Minneapolis conference, this paper will also appear in *Economic Inquiry*. The paper was revised in January 1979. I thank Milton Harris for his helpful criticism.

[1]Author names and years refer to the works listed at the end of this book.

traders. Each trader is endowed with one unit of labor each period, to which no disutility is attached, which yields y units of a nonstorable consumption good. In the present section, preferences over consumption sequences $\{c_t\}$, $c_t \geqslant 0$, are

$$\sum_{t=0}^{\infty} \beta^t U(c_t) \tag{1}$$

where $0 < \beta < 1$, and $U{:}R^+ \rightarrow R$ is bounded, twice differentiable, with $U'(\cdot) > 0$ and $U''(\cdot) < 0$.

Considering only allocations in which identical traders are identically treated, it is clear that an optimal allocation is $c_t = y$ for all t. Nothing more will be done in this section than to propose a monetary arrangement which will bring this allocation about and to determine the money price of goods under this arrangement.

In order to motivate the need for any monetary arrangement (indeed for any arrangement other than autarchy, in which agents consume their own produce y), I will first reinterpret this model economy as one involving many goods, as follows. Let the good come in n colors, where items of each color are produced under the technology assumed above: one unit of labor yields y units of any color. Consumption is now a vector $(c_{1t},\ldots,c_{nt})$, where c_{it} is consumption of color i in period t. Let current period utility be

$$V(c_1,\ldots,c_n) = U\left[\prod_{i=1}^{n} \left(\frac{c_i}{\alpha_i}\right)^{\alpha_i}\right]$$

where U is as above and $\Sigma_i\alpha_i = 1$, $\alpha_i > 0$, all i. Let $c = \Sigma_i c_i$. Now given the assumed constant returns to scale technology, equilibrium requires relative prices of unity among all goods.[2] With these prices, consumers will select color proportions c_i/c equal to α_i for all i, and given this mix, $V(c_1,\ldots,c_n) = U(c)$. Without altering the example, one can think of all agents having the same α-weights, of agents distributed by a fixed c.d.f. $F(\alpha)$ of weights, or of each agent drawing a period-t weight α from F in a way which is unpredictable even to that agent. In each of these cases, the equilibrium output mix (per capita) is $(\bar{\alpha}_1 y_1,\ldots,\bar{\alpha}_n y_n)$ each period, where $\bar{\alpha}_i = \int \alpha_i \, dF(\alpha)$. I imagine this sort of elaboration is what we always have in mind when we work with aggregative models.

Next, imagine each agent as consisting of a two-person household, one of whom spends each day shopping (call that person the *shopper*) and the other of whom works at the production of a single color (call that person the *worker*). Production and sale occur at spatially distinct stores. Each day, the worker goes to work at the same store, while the shopper moves from store to store purchasing the mix dictated by the current drawing of α. Equilibrium dictates that the value of the worker's labor y should equal the total expenditures by the shopper over all n (at least) stores.

[2]This remark is technically premature (since equilibrium has yet to be defined) and perhaps substantively questionable as well. This scenario depends on prices being set in a spatially decentralized manner, as opposed to in a single, centralized auction, so that it may not be clear how a constant-returns technology is manifested in the structure of equilibrium prices. In the present paper, the discussion will be confined to stationary examples in which one can easily imagine a constant relative price structure arising from custom. In a situation in which market equilibrium were subject to shocks, it would, I think, be necessary to treat this issue with more care.

What will assure that this equilibrium is, in fact, executed? What, for example, prevents a shopper from collecting $2y$ in various goods in the course of a day? To get an idea of the importance of this question, let us suppose that each store keeps an exact record of each shopper's purchases and continuously informs all other stores throughout the day as to how many credits (it is almost impossible even to discuss this matter without using language suggesting securities) have been used up. Then for each shopper, each of the first $n-1$ stops necessitates $n-1$ messages, or $(n-1)^2$ per household per day. Let the workday be 8 hours, and let each message require 6 seconds of a worker's time to send. Then with 101 stores, this information transmission activity utilizes $(100)^2 \cdot 6/(60)^2 = 16\frac{2}{3}$ hours, or more than twice national product!

This issue could be pursued further by spelling out in more detail a technology for information storage, transmission, and processing and the available methods for enforcing against fraud, after the fact. An easier route is suggested by the observation that the adoption of paper currency can reduce these costs essentially to zero. Let each shopper, at the beginning of a period, be issued claims to y units of consumption. Proceeding from store to store, these claims are exhausted and redistributed to workers at the end of each day. This system (except for resources used to print currency and prevent counterfeiting) economizes perfectly on informational costs. Note that nothing has been said as to how this monetary solution to the information problem might come into being, nor is it at all clear how an individual agent, or a collection of agents, could act so as to bring this system into existence. The monetary solution involves a social convention, with the property that if (for some reason) everyone else adopts it, then it is in one's own interest to adopt it as well.

A formal definition of a monetary equilibrium with a constant money supply M which embodies this convention is developed by means of the optimal value function $v(m)$, interpreted as the value of the objective function (1) for a consumer who begins the current period with nominal balances m and behaves optimally. This function v must satisfy

$$(2) \qquad v(m) = \max_{c, m' \geq 0} \{U(c) + \beta v(m')\}$$

subject to

$$(3) \qquad m' = m - pc + py$$

$$(4) \qquad m \geq pc.$$

Here p is the constant equilibrium price level, c is current goods consumption, and m' is end-of-period balances. Equation (3) is the standard budget constraint, and (4) is the cash-in-advance constraint discussed above. Then in terms of v, equilibrium is defined as follows.[3]

[3]An alternative to this definition would be to define an equilibrium as an element of a space of infinite sequences $\{c_t, p_t, m_t\}$ of consumptions, prices, and money demands, satisfying feasibility, utility maximization, and market clearing. In this alternative setup, the equilibrium specified below (a constant sequence) is the only one, but this must (and can) be argued using a transversality condition. The stationarity built into the definition used here will prove convenient in the section following. Whether it rules out any behavior of economic interest is not known, though my own opinion is that, in the present context, it does not.

DEFINITION. *An equilibrium in the certainty economy is a number $p \geq 0$ and a continuous bounded function $v: R^+ \to R$ such that*

1. *Given p, v satisfies (2)–(4).*
2. *$(c, m') = (y, M)$ attains $v(M)$.*

That is, consumers behave optimally (condition 1) and money demand equals money supply (condition 2).

Enough has been said already to make it clear that the unique equilibrium on this definition involves $p = M/y$ and $v(M) = u(y)/1-\beta$. That is, each household spends all of its current money balances M on goods each period, replenishing these holdings with the worker's end-of-period pay. Since this example is a special case of the one analyzed in the next section, a formal substantiation of this claim is omitted.

3. An Economy With Individual Uncertainty

In this section, the technology and trading arrangements will be assumed the same as in section 2, but individual preferences will be taken to be subject to uncertainty, unpredictable even to the household itself. (Think of an unanticipated medical need or the unexpected discovery of an item of a particularly attractive color.) Formally, let the shock to preferences be a drawing, independent over time and over persons at a point in time, of a random variable θ from the fixed c.d.f. $F(\theta)$. Take F to be strictly increasing on the interval $I = [\underline{\theta}, \bar{\theta}] \subset R$ with $F(\underline{\theta}) = 0$ and $F(\bar{\theta}) = 1$. Then with a continuum of agents, there is no aggregative uncertainty: the state of the economy will not change from period to period.

Let preferences be given by

$$(5) \qquad E\left\{\sum_{t=0}^{\infty} \beta^t\, U(c_t, \theta_t)\right\}$$

where $0 < \beta < 1$, $U: R^+ \times I \to R$ is bounded, twice differentiable, with $U_c > 0$, $U_\theta > 0$, $U_{cc} < 0$, and $U_{c\theta} > 0$. Require also that for all $c \geq y$

$$(6) \qquad \lim_{\theta \to \bar{\theta}} U_c(c, \theta) = \infty$$

or that consumption may be arbitrarily urgent.[4] At the time the tth period decision is taken, regard θ_t as known, so that the expectation in (5) is taken with respect to the distribution of $(\theta_1, \theta_2, \ldots)$, with θ_0 given.

As in the preceding section, I will study an economy with the constant money supply M and seek an equilibrium in which the price level is constant at p. The situation of any *individual,* however, cannot be expected to settle down, since individuals are continually shocked by new drawings of θ. I will first develop the problem faced by a representative trader, then discuss what is meant by market clearing in this context, and then summarize these in a formal definition of equilibrium. With this accomplished, I will turn to the analytical issues involved in constructing and characterizing the equilibrium.

The budget constraints facing an agent are as in the preceding section, but

[4]Condition (6) is used only in the proof of Lemma 1, section 4, where it is clear from the context that it could be replaced, with appropriate modification in the argument, with a much weaker condition.

in this case it is convenient to let m denote an individual's *real* balances (nominal balances divided by the constant price level p). Let $v(m, \theta)$ be the optimum value function for a consumer who begins the current period with real balances m, draws an urgency to consume θ, and behaves optimally. Then that person's current period decision problem is

$$(7) \qquad v(m, \theta) = \max_{c, m' \geqslant 0} \left\{ U(c, \theta) + \beta \int_I v(m', \theta')\, dF(\theta') \right\}$$

subject to

$$(8) \qquad c + m' \leqslant m + y$$

$$(9) \qquad c \leqslant m.$$

The opportunity set defined by (8) and (9) is as drawn in Figure 1 (for given m and y). If the derived preference function for c and m', $U(c, \theta) + \int v(m', \theta')\, dF(\theta')$, has indifference curves of the usual shape, then the household will either locate at a tangency point to the line given when (8) holds with equality, spending less than its initial balances, or it will spend all it has, choosing $c = m$ and $m' = y$. Assuming this problem has a solution, denote the individual demand functions for goods and end-of-period balances by $c = c(m, \theta)$ and $m' = g(m, \theta)$. This individual decision problem will receive more detailed attention in the next section.

In *market* equilibrium in this economy, it must be true that the per capita demand for real balances (averaged over agents) equals per capita balances supplied M/p at the given nominal quantity supplied M and the assumed constant equilibrium price level p. To calculate per capita end-of-period demand one needs to know the distribution of agents by beginning-of-period balances, $\Psi(m)$, say. Given Ψ, per capita demand is

$$\int\int g(m, \theta)\, d\Psi(m)\, dF(\theta)$$

Figure 1

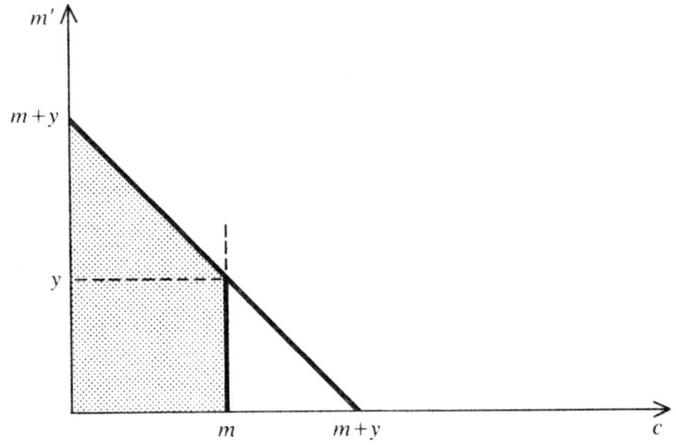

so the equilibrium condition is

$$\int\int g(m, \theta)\, d\Psi(m)\, dF(\theta) = \frac{M}{p} \cdot \tag{10}$$

In general, the p-value satisfying (10) will depend on the distribution $\Psi(m)$ of real balances over persons. In order, then, for consumers' expectations that p be constant over time to be rational (or correct) we require also that $\Psi(m)$ replicate itself over time, or that it be a stationary distribution for the stochastic difference equation

$$m_{t+1} = g(m_t, \theta_t).$$

This requirement is just that Ψ solve[5]

$$\Psi(m') = \int\int_{A(m')} d\Psi(m)\, dF(\theta) \tag{11}$$

where $A(m')$ is the region of the (m, θ) plane defined by

$$A(m') = \{(m, \theta): m \geqslant 0, \theta \in I, g(m, \theta) \leqslant m'\}. \tag{12}$$

The foregoing considerations can be summarized in the following.

DEFINITION. *An equilibrium in the economy with individual uncertainty is a number $p > 0$, a continuous bounded function $v: R^+ \times I \to R$, a pair of continuous functions $c, g: R^+ \times I \to R^+$ and a c.d.f. $\Psi: R^+ \to [0, 1]$ such that*

1. *$v(m, \theta)$ solves (7).*
2. *(c, g) solves the maximum problem (7) for each (m, θ).*
3. *g, Ψ, and p satisfy (10).*
4. *g and Ψ satisfy (11).*

4. Construction of the Equilibrium

Equilibrium was defined as four unknown functions together with a positive number. This simultaneous system may be solved sequentially, first by finding a function v which satisfies condition 1, then finding the policy functions c and g satisfying condition 2, then finding the c.d.f. Ψ satisfying condition 4, and finally finding the price p which satisfies condition 3.

The relevant facts about the value function $v(m, \theta)$ are given in

PROPOSITION 1. *There is exactly one continuous bounded function $v(m, \theta)$ satisfying (7). This solution v is strictly increasing and strictly concave with respect to m.*

Proof. The proof is standard (see, for example, Lucas 1978b), involving the following formulation and facts. Let L be the Banach space of continuous bounded functions $u: R^+ \times I \to R$, normed by

$$\| u \| = \sup_{m, \theta} |u(m, \theta)|.$$

[5]Notice that if (11) holds, (10) is equivalent to

$$\int\int m\, d\Psi(m)\, dF(\theta) = \frac{M}{P} \cdot$$

Define T as the operator on L such that (7) reads $v = Tv$. Using Berge 1963, p. 116, $T: L \to L$. Using Blackwell 1965, thm. 5, T is a contraction, so that $Tv = v$ has a unique solution $v^* \in L$ and $\| T^n u - v^* \| \to 0$ as $n \to \infty$ for all $u \in L$.

It is easy to verify that T takes nondecreasing, concave functions of m into strictly increasing, strictly concave functions of m. It follows that $v^* = \lim_{n\to\infty} T^n \cdot 0$ is nondecreasing and concave, and then, since $v^* = Tv^*$, that these properties hold strictly.

PROPOSITION 2. *There exist unique, continuous functions $c(m, \theta)$, $g(m, \theta)$: $R^+ \times I \to R^+$ such that $c = c(m, \theta)$ and $m' = g(m, \theta)$ attain the right-hand side of (7) for each (m, θ).*

Proof. The maximum problem (7) involves maximizing a continuous strictly concave function over a compact convex set. Hence $c(m, \theta)$, $g(m, \theta)$ are uniquely defined. Their continuity follows from Berge 1963, p. 116.

PROPOSITION 3. *The solution v to (7) is continuously differentiable with respect to m, for each fixed θ, and, if $c(m, \theta) > 0$,*

$$v_m(m, \theta) = U_c\left[c(m, \theta), \theta\right]. \tag{13}$$

Proof. In the interior of the region of the (m, θ) plane on which (9) is not binding, the proof follows that in Lucas 1978b, prop. 2. In the interior of the region on which (9) is binding,

$$v(m, \theta) = U(m, \theta) + \beta \int v(y, \theta')\, dF(\theta')$$

and (13) follows since $c(m, \theta) \equiv m$ in this region. Since the one-sided derivatives agree on the boundary of these two regions, the result follows.

Now the function $g(m, \theta)$ and the c.d.f. F of θ together define a Markov process

$$m_{t+1} = g(m_t, \theta_t) \tag{14}$$

with state space R^+. That is, given an initial distribution of persons by cash balances $\Psi_0(m)$, say, where $\Psi_0(m)$ is the fraction of consumers beginning period 0 with initial balances less than or equal to m, the distribution $F(\theta)$ and the difference equation (14) together determine the sequence of distributions $\Psi_1(m)$, $\Psi_2(m)$, ... which prevail at times 1, 2, ... Our interest will be in the limiting behavior of this sequence.

The behavior of this sequence of distributions can be studied by examining the characteristics of the transition probabilities of the process defined by (14) and F. For $m \geq 0$ and any measurable $A \subseteq R^+$, these are given by

$$P(m, A) = \int_{B(m)} dF(\theta)$$

where

$$B(m) = \left\{\theta \in I : g(m, \theta) \in A\right\}.$$

Then if m is the set of probability measures μ on R^+, define $S: \mathsf{m} \to \mathsf{m}$ by

$$(S\mu)(A) = \int_0^\infty P(m, A)\, \mu(dm).$$

Then if $\Psi_0(m) = \int_0^m \mu_o\,(du)$ is the initial distribution mentioned above, the tth term in the sequence is

$$\Psi_t(m) = \int_0^m (S^t\mu_o)\,(du).$$

A solution μ^* to $S\mu = \mu$ corresponds to a solution $\Psi^*(m) = \int_0^m \mu^*(du)$ to (11): a stationary distribution of agents by real balances. The process (14) will be studied here via S using results from Doob 1953, pp. 190–218,[6] and the implications of the maximum problem (7).

The first-order condition for the maximum problem (7) when (9) is ignored and (8) is used to eliminate the variable c is, in view of Proposition 3,

$$U_c(m + y - m', \theta) = \beta \int v_m(m', \theta')\,dF(\theta'). \tag{15}$$

It then follows from the strict concavity of U and v in their first arguments that the m' value, call it $\tilde{g}(m, \theta)$, satisfying (15) is increasing in m and decreasing in θ. Then, clearly, the money demand function $g(m, \theta) = \max[y, \tilde{g}(m, \theta)]$ so that $g(m, \theta)$ is as drawn in Figure 2, for θ fixed. The ergodic set for the

Figure 2

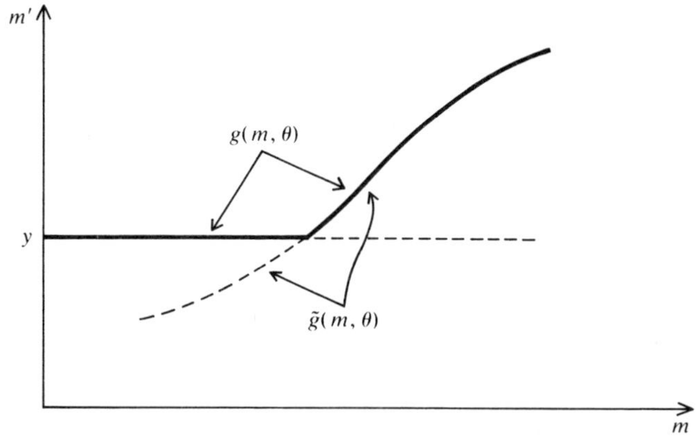

process (14) is included in $[y, \infty)$, since $g(m, \theta) \geq y$ for all (m, θ). An upper bound on m can be obtained from examination of

$$U_c(y, \underline{\theta}) = \beta \int v_m(m, \theta')\,dF(\theta') \tag{16}$$

which is the form (15) takes if $(c, m') = (y, m)$ is optimal at $(m, \underline{\theta})$, where $\underline{\theta}$ is the lower bound on θ. The right-hand side of (16) is a decreasing function of m. Since $v(m, \theta)$ is, for θ fixed, an increasing, concave, bounded, and differentiable function of m, we have

$$v(0, \theta) \leq v(m, \theta) + v_m(m, \theta)\,(-m)$$

[6] A very useful recent treatment of the same issues is given in Futia undated.

or

$$0 \leqslant m\, v_m(m, \theta) \leqslant v(m, \theta) - v(0, \theta) \leqslant B - v(0, \theta)$$

where B is a bound for v. Hence $v_m(m, \theta) \to 0$ as $m \to \infty$. It follows that (16) is solved for a unique $m = \overline{m} \geqslant y$ if

$$\beta \int v_m(y, \theta')\, dF(\theta) \geqslant U_c(y, \underline{\theta})$$

and has no solution otherwise. In the latter case, the ergodic set for the process (14) is just $E = \{y\}$. In the case where $\overline{m} > y$ satisfies (16), $g(\overline{m}, \underline{\theta}) = \overline{m}$, so that initial balances are just maintained. For $\theta > \underline{\theta}$, $g(\overline{m}, \theta) < \overline{m}$, and also for $m > \overline{m}$, $g(m, \theta) < m$, for all θ. Thus the ergodic set of the process (14) is $E = [y, \overline{m}]$. There are no cyclically moving subsets.

The next result verifies that the Doeblin condition (Doob 1953, cond. D, p. 192) holds on $[y, \overline{m}] = E$.

LEMMA 1. *There is a finite measure λ on E and an $\epsilon > 0$ such that $\lambda(A) \leqslant \epsilon$ implies $P(m, A) \leqslant 1 - \epsilon$, for all $m \in E$.*

Proof. For the case $\overline{m} = y$ the result is trivial. For the case $\overline{m} > y$, assign measure $\lambda_o \in (0, 1)$ to the point y and let $\lambda([m_1, m_2]) = (1-\lambda_o)(m_2 - m_1)/(\overline{m} - y)$ for $y < m_1 \leqslant m_2 \leqslant \overline{m}$, so that $\lambda(E) = 1$. Now using (15), $g(m, \theta) = y$ whenever

$$U_c(m, \theta) > \beta \int v_m(y, \theta')\, dF(\theta')$$

so that

$$P(m, \{y\}) = Pr\{U_c(m, \theta) > \beta \int v_m(y, \theta')\, dF(\theta')\}.$$

Then for $m \in E$,

$$P(m, \{y\}) \geqslant Pr\{U_c(\overline{m}, \theta) > \beta \int v_m(y, \theta')\, dF(\theta')\}.$$

By condition (6) $\theta^o < \overline{\theta}$ can be chosen such that $\theta \geqslant \theta^o$ implies $U_c(\overline{m}, \theta) > \beta \int U_c(y, \theta')\, dF(\theta')$, so that if $Pr\{\theta^o \leqslant \theta \leqslant \overline{\theta}\} = b$,

$$P(m, \{y\}) \geqslant b.$$

Choose $\epsilon > 0$ with $\epsilon < \lambda_o$ and $\epsilon < b$. Then $\lambda(A) \leqslant \epsilon$ implies $y \notin A$ so that for all m,

$$P(m, A) \leqslant 1 - P(m, \{y\}) \leqslant 1 - b \leqslant 1 - \epsilon.$$

This proves Lemma 1.

It then follows from Doob 1953, p. 214, that

PROPOSITION 4. *Given g as in Proposition 2, there is exactly one solution Ψ to (11) (or solution μ to $S\mu = \mu$), and $\Psi(m) = 0$ for $m < y$, $\Psi(y) > 0$, and $\Psi(\overline{m}) = 1$.*

The final step in establishing the existence of a unique equilibrium is taken by observing that (10) can be solved, given M, for a unique, positive price p.

5. Discussion of the Equilibrium

In constructing the equilibrium distribution of persons by real balance holdings, $\Psi(m)$, we began with an arbitrary distribution $\Psi_0(m)$ and then studied the limit of the sequence of distributions $\Psi_t(m)$ (that is, measures $S^t\mu_0$). This was merely a technical device for arriving at a solution Ψ to (11), but the sequence $\Psi_t(m)$ has an economic interpretation. It is the sequence of distributions which would prevail, in an economy starting at Ψ_0, if all agents believed that the current price level will prevail into the next period (that the nominal yield on money is always zero). In fact, if $\Psi_0 \neq \Psi$, prices will not be constant, so that these consumer beliefs will be confirmed only in the limit. In the vocabulary of growth theory, this equilibrium is a stationary point of an economy with static expectations, where the distributions Ψ_t play the role of capital. This equilibrium is not a golden rule (a stationary state with discount factor $\beta = 1$). In contrast to optimal growth paths, however, only the stationary state can be interpreted as an equilibrium: along any approach path, agents taking prices as given can increase their utility. This seems to me to mirror exactly Friedman's statement, in a very similar context, that while "it is easy to see what the final position [following a change in M] will be...it is much harder to say anything about the transition" (Friedman 1969, p. 6).

The shape of the equilibrium distribution of real balances is shown in Figure 3. There is a mass point at the institutional minimum holding y, and then a smooth distribution on $(y, \overline{m}]$. The existence of a mass point clearly follows from the economics of the situation: if individuals did not occasionally spend all available cash (return to y), they would be holding too much money. Money is an inventory, held against a particular contingency, and one never has an optimal inventory bounded away from zero. There is, however, no presumption that the lower bound y is visited frequently or, which comes to the same thing, that a large fraction of consumers will be at $m = y$ at any point in time.

The determinants of the demand for money, or of velocity, in this model are a mix of institutional and economic factors. Clearly, the length of a "day" will affect the equilibrium; indeed, there are economists to whom a constraint of the form $pc \leq M$ (in units, $\$/t \leq \$$) must appear unthinkable. As long as one remembers not to vary the length of a "day" in midargument, this raises no problems, however. Moreover, the rate at which the earth rotates does have important economic implications, and there is nothing to be gained in insisting on an economic explanation for this phenomenon.

The economic factors affecting money demand are preferences U, the discount factor β, the volatility F of the shocks θ and income y. Thus the amount of risk and people's attitude toward it (U and F) will affect money demand, as is appropriate in a model stressing the precautionary motive; so too will the rate of time preference. One's intuition as to the direction of effect of changes in these forces is fairly strong, but rigorous verification is somewhat complicated. The next section, a treatment of the income effect on real balance demand, illustrates a useful method for answering questions of this type and also addresses a question of substantive interest.

6. Engel Curves for Real Balances

The relationship of the demand for real balances to the level of real income has received a great deal of attention, both theoretically and empirically.

Figure 3

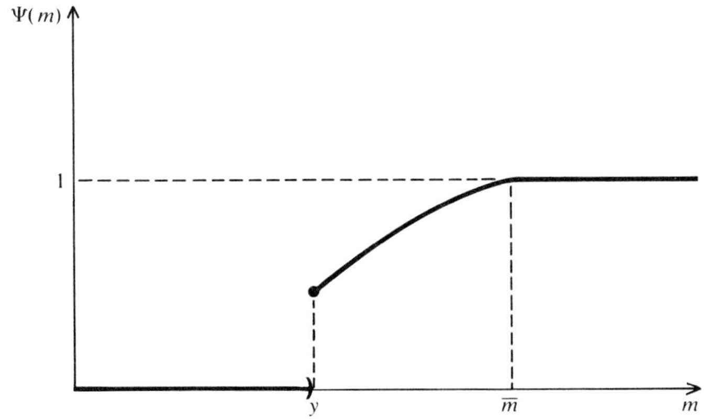

Early inventory-theoretic treatments suggested an income elasticity less than unity, a prediction which has never found any empirical confirmation. Friedman's early empirical work (1959) led to estimated income elasticities of around 1.8, which he rationalized in terms of conventional consumer demand theory by concluding that real balances, as a consumer durable, are a "luxury" good. I think it is now recognized that any empirically estimated Engel curve can be rationalized theoretically as well as any other, so that the issue is purely an empirical one. The model studied in this paper does not suggest modifications to this open conclusion, but it can be utilized to isolate the contributions of the several determinants of the income elasticity of money demand somewhat more satisfactorily than can be done with theories at the level of individual behavior only.

Real output (per capita productivity) was taken as a constant in sections 2–4. This assumption will be maintained here for each individual agent, but it will be assumed that each agent's constant income y is taken from a distribution $\Lambda(y \mid \bar{y})$ where $\bar{y}$ is mean income:

$$\bar{y} \equiv \int y \, \Lambda \left(dy \mid \bar{y}\right).$$

One may then consider the *individual* Engel curve, describing the way average real balances vary with y for given $\bar{y}$, and the *market* Engel curve, describing the way average balances vary across economies with different average income levels $\bar{y}$.

In these seemingly more complex economies, individuals continue to solve (7). Denote the resulting value and policy functions, constructed exactly as in section 4, by $v(m, \theta, y)$, $c(m, \theta, y)$, $g(m, \theta, y)$. Similarly, (11) and (12) continue to define the stationary distribution of real balances, conditioned on y, as constructed in section 4. Call this c.d.f. $\Psi \left(m \mid y\right)$. This is the fraction of time an agent with income y will hold balances less than or equal to m, independent of the average income $\bar{y}$ in society. The individual Engel curve is then

$$h(y) = \int_{y}^{\bar{m}(y)} m \, d\Psi(m \mid y). \tag{17}$$

The market Engel curve requires averaging over $\Lambda(y \mid \bar{y})$. It is

$$k(\bar{y}) = \int_0^\infty \int_y^{\overline{m}(y)} m \, d\Psi(m \mid y) d\Lambda(y \mid \bar{y}) = \int_0^\infty h(y) \, d\Lambda(y \mid \bar{y}). \tag{18}$$

Market equilibrium (price level determination) is obtained by replacing (10) with

$$k(\bar{y}) = \frac{M}{P}. \tag{19}$$

I shall turn, then, to methods for learning about the function $h(y)$, with the reader forewarned by the introduction to this section that sharp predictions are not likely to be forthcoming.

The function $h(y)$, evaluated at a particular y-value, is the mean value of the function $f(m) \equiv m$ with respect to the stationary distribution $\Psi(m \mid y)$. This function is continuous and therefore bounded on the interval $[y, \overline{m}(y)]$. I shall utilize well-known facts about mean values of continuous bounded functions with respect to stationary distributions. First,

LEMMA 2. *If $\mu^* = S\mu^*$ and for all measurable $A \subseteq R^+$*

$$\lim_{t \to \infty} (S^t \mu_o)(A) = \mu^*(A)$$

independent of μ_o, then for all continuous bounded f_0

$$\lim_{t \to \infty} \int_0^\infty f_0(m) (S^t \mu_o)(dm) = \int_0^\infty f_0(m) \mu^*(dm). \tag{20}$$

Proof. See Feller 1966, p. 243.

Second, using (14), one notices that

$$\int_0^\infty f_0(m) (S^{t+1} \mu_o)(dm) = \int_0^\infty \int_I f_0[g(m, \theta)] dF(\theta) (S^t \mu_o)(dm) \tag{21}$$

since both sides of (21) express the mean value of $f_0(m_{t+1})$ given the initial distribution μ_o. Then if the sequence $\{f_t\}$ is defined recursively from f_0 by

$$f_{t+1}(m) = \int_I f_t[g(m, \theta)] \, dF(\theta) \tag{22}$$

repeated application of (21) gives (compare Feller 1966, p. 266)

$$\int_0^\infty f_t(m) \mu_o(dm) = \int_0^\infty f_0(m) (S^t \mu_o)(dm), t = 0, 1, 2, \ldots . \tag{23}$$

Thus (20) may be replaced by

$$\lim_{t \to \infty} \int_0^\infty f_t(m) \mu_o(dm) = \int_0^\infty f_0(m) \mu^*(dm). \tag{24}$$

Moreover, since the choice of μ_o was arbitrary, $\{f_t\}$ must converge (almost everywhere) to a constant function, so that (24) [or (20)] can be replaced by

$$(25) \qquad \lim_{t\to\infty} f_t(m) = \int_0^\infty f_0(m)\mu^*(dm) \text{ for all } m \geq 0.$$

We know from Proposition 4, section 4, that the hypotheses of Lemma 2 are satisfied for each fixed y. Then Lemma 2 with (20) replaced by (25) provides an inductive method for verifying statements about mean values of functions of m with respect to the stationary distribution.

Returning to the particular function $f_0(m) \equiv m$ of interest here, we have

LEMMA 3. *Suppose $g(m, \theta, y)$ is a nondecreasing function of m and y. Then $h(y)$ as defined in (17) is a nondecreasing function of y.*

Proof. The proof is an induction on the sequence $\{f_t\}$ defined by (22) and $f_0(m) \equiv m$. Clearly $f_0(m) = m$ is nondecreasing in m and y. Then if f_t has these properties, so does f_{t+1}, from (22) and the hypotheses on $g(m, \theta, y)$. The result then follows from Lemma 2, the fact that (20) implies (25), and (25).

To verify the hypotheses of Lemma 3, we need to go back to the maximum problem (7). In section 4 (compare Figure 2) we found that $g(m, \theta, y)$ is nondecreasing in m. In the (m, θ) region on which $g(m, \theta, y) = y$, g is clearly increasing in y. From (15), one can see that this is also true when $g(m, \theta, y) > y$. This proves, applying Lemma 3,

PROPOSITION 5. *$h(y)$ is a nondecreasing function of y. From (18), it also follows that if increases in mean income $\bar{y}$ shift the entire distribution $\Lambda(y|\bar{y})$ to the right, then $k(\bar{y})$ is also an increasing function.*

It has been established, then, that both the individual and market Engel curves for real balances are upward-sloping (really, only that they are never downward-sloping) or that real balances are a normal good. The methods used to establish this fact make it fairly clear, I think, that no sharper predictions on the magnitude of the slope of this curve will be obtained without much stronger restrictions on preferences (on U and F). Put backwards, any empirically found slope would be consistent with the theory.

Since the model of this paper is inventory-theoretic, one might wonder why the scale economies which played such a prominent role in earlier theory do not seem to arise here. One way to answer this is by suggesting a modification of the model which would, or might, reintroduce them. In section 2, I suggested that the cash-in-advance constraint facing households be motivated as imposed on a household in which one member spends a day spending the cash earned by the other member on the preceding day. No provision was made for the shopper to make visits during a day to the store of the worker, picking up currency earned there in the first hour, the second hour, and so on. That is, I have taken the payments period to be institutionally rather than economically determined. Were this convention relaxed, it might be the case that increases in y would induce the number of intraday currency reorders to rise, so that real balances demanded would rise less than proportionally with income y. This modification would introduce no new possibilities for the shape of $h(y)$ into the theory. It is possible, though not a conjecture I would expend much effort to verify, that it would rule out some $h(y)$ possibilities. The cross-section results obtained by Meltzer (1963) suggest that this role of scale economies may safely be abstracted from.

7. Concluding Comments

One of many issues not touched upon above is that of the economic *efficiency* of the monetary equilibrium found in sections 3 and 4. Clearly, the equilibrium in the economy with certainty (section 2) is efficient.[7] With individual uncertainty introduced, even to define efficiency in a satisfactory way is a problem of some complexity. If one thinks of each individual's current θ as observable to all, a marginal condition expressing the idea of from each according to ability, to each according to need can be derived. Presumably, however, one is interested in the case in which agents observe their own θ, but not anyone else's, in which case issues of incentive compatibility of allocative arrangements become central.

Without exploring this difficult matter further one can, I think, see that on any efficiency criterion which takes these issues into account, the monetary equilibrium of sections 3 and 4 will not be efficient. In any period, there will be some households in a run of low θ's, with large real balances accumulated but no particular urgency to spend them. There will be others in a run of high θ's, with balances of y and a high marginal utility of current consumption. Here, then, are two sides to a nonexistent credit market on which some would gladly lend at positive interest rather than the zero yield provided by currency and others would gladly pay this premium to consume today at the expense of future consumption.

Can this gap be filled by a government-engineered deflation, in which currency is withdrawn from the system via lump-sum taxes and a positive real yield thereby created? Clearly not, though by some efficiency criteria this policy may be utility-increasing. The problem here is not one involving the attractiveness of currency on average, but one of permitting the benefits of gains from trade between differently situated agents.

The introduction of a credit market into this economy would, with impatient agents ($\beta < 1$), be associated with a positive interest rate and hence with real balance holdings at the institutionally fixed minimum level (as in section 2). (With arbitrarily short periods, this would imply arbitrarily high, or infinite, velocity.) With the introduction of some real cost associated with dealing in a credit market (say, the time involved for one's credit worthiness to be established), one can imagine a model in which currency demand is governed by a mechanism such as that studied above coexisting with a credit mechanism for larger transactions. The analysis of such a hybrid system must be left for future research.

In the present model, as in more complex elaborations which one may imagine, there is a clear sense in which money is a second-rate asset. It serves a role and commands resources only insofar as it enables the economy to economize on some sort of record keeping or other transaction cost. At best, then, money is viewed as a means of approximating some idealized real resource allocation. This feature may be contrasted with the role of money in the intergenerational models introduced by Samuelson (1958). There, money converts an economy which is allocating resources inefficiently into an efficient one. It does not provide a cheap approximation to an idealized and

[7]The assumption in section 2 that no disutility is attached to labor supply is crucial to this conclusion. See Locay and Palmon 1978, where in a context very similar to that of this paper, but with disutility attached to labor, it is shown that a Friedmanlike deflationary policy is required for the monetary allocation to be efficient. An earlier, more general treatment of this efficiency question is given in Grandmont and Younes 1972.

efficient real allocation which one can at least imagine being achieved in a decentralized, nonmonetary way; it is the only device short of centralized planning by which an efficient real allocation may be attained.

This theoretical second-rateness of money seems to me a virtue of models in which its use is motivated by a cash-in-advance constraint and therefore a reason for attempting to pursue the analysis of models of this type more deeply. In the first place, money (or currency, certainly) really is a second-rate asset: if any of us were to have free overnight access to Federal funds, we would take advantage of it. In the second place, this view of money as an aid in approximately attaining real general equilibrium is consistent with the way economists use real general equilibrium or relative price theory. When we apply theories of barter economies to problems in, say, public finance or labor economics, it is not our intent to obtain results applicable only to primitive or prehistoric societies. We apply this body of theory to money-using economies such as our own because we believe that for many problems the fact that money is used in attaining equilibrium can be abstracted from, or that the theoretical barter economy is a tractable, idealized model which approximates well (is well-approximated by) the actual, monetary economy. If this practice is sound, then we want monetary theories which rationalize it or at least which do not radically conflict with it.

Discussion by Leonid Hurwicz

1. Opening Observations

The author of the first paper, Martin Shubik, just whispered to me that, to some extent, he was proceeding in his comments on the assumption that his discussant (myself) may have been the only person who had read his paper. Possibly that was one of the more realistic assumptions made here today.

I think I should start out with the obvious warning that I am very much an outsider in this group. I have never focused on problems of monetary theory, and my comments should be viewed in that light. I will probably be more general than others have been.

Listening to the discussions about the metaphysical nature of fiat money, I was reminded of an essay from the late thirties by D. H. Robertson which was published, I think, in one of the English bank periodicals. It was written in the form of a dialogue between Socrates and an economist. Socrates was trying to understand fiat money—what it means and why it works. And he apparently had read the inscription on the British pound note. It said that the bearer of this note would be paid on demand one pound sterling. And Socrates asked, "What is this thing that one would get in exchange for a pound note?" And the economist said, "Well, it is another piece of paper just like this one." Doesn't this capture the paradox of fiat money we are all trying to explain with the help of elaborate mathematics?

Another part of the story is, I think, also relevant. Socrates and the economist had gotten to the end of their conversation where Socrates, by his usual method of questioning, had demonstrated that the economist did not have the first notion what money is or whether it makes any sense. Nevertheless, at the very end Socrates asked, "Well, how does this system work?" And the economist's parting reply was, "Very well, thank you." That may have been overly optimistic, but it seems to capture the flavor of a good part of our subject.

Another thing that struck me while listening yesterday to the debate concerning fiat money is how much more emotion people put into it compared with discussions I am more familiar with, such as those of general equilibrium. My naive interpretation of this contrast was that this is what happens as soon as the word *money* is mentioned. Somebody else pointed out that it shows either that money is not neutral or that people are not neutral about money. But what I really think is that it shows something more serious, namely, that there is a very close connection between one's abstract philosophical model and one's policy recommendation about something very immediate and concrete, for instance, whether next week the Federal Reserve should be buying or selling bonds. The closeness of this connection disturbs me. For while I feel there has been tremendous scientific progress in this field—as shown by the contributions presented here—I also see an enormous distance between the analytical conclusions one can draw from what I regard as toy models and any direct policy conclusions. Of course, somebody might ask whether there is available any better rationale for Federal Reserve policy decisions than these very abstract models. But here I am very fortunate in not being a monetary economist: I do not have to answer that question.

2. Two Questions to Ask About Money

Although I will be primarily focusing on Shubik's paper, for my own understanding I will have to put it in a perspective by relating it to others. There have been basically two kinds of papers presented at this conference: those which ask why there is such a thing as money (fiat money in particular) and those which ask, given that there is an institution of money, how the system works.

The Shubik paper is obviously in the second category, and he introduces money by fiat, his own fiat in this case. He starts with a definition which says that money is a good that can be exchanged against any other commodity (there could be one or two or almost any number except $n-1$, if I remember correctly), and from there on he has in this paper (as well as in some other papers) certain rules, which are in the nature of rules of the game. For instance, in the simplest kind of economies, you have to pay "cash on the barrelhead." So there is an extra constraint, one in addition to the usual budget constraint that we have in ordinary equilibrium models. Of course, it is very natural to ask why it is that Shubik has this kind of a restriction in this model. The explanation that Shubik gives is that if you are going to be rigorous about it, you have to be precise about defining the rules of the game. In other words, it should be possible to get a bunch of undergraduates together and give them those rules, and they should then be able to play this game. It should not run off the board, so to speak.

Now it is true that rules must be precise. But that does not imply that the rules have to be as highly determinate as in this paper. Let me give just one very trivial example. In Shubik's paper there are very precise conditions as to who makes the first move, who makes the second move, and so forth. In some respects, that is essential for this model because the author has to have the fiat money created on the first day of creation so that the rest of the game can be played. But there are aspects of the game that could be left up to the players and not made into rules, for instance, which player will put down the first card. Then, in order to complete the model, you might introduce some other elements, perhaps random moves determining who goes first. What I am saying is that the degree of determinism in the rules is not a methodological necessity, but rather a matter of analytical convenience, a device that makes it easier to work things out.

The question is whether a theory so constructed is sufficiently robust. What if it should turn out that having specified one of those details, such as the sequence of moves, you have injected something into the solution that otherwise would not have come in? It is customary for all of us who construct such models both to make simplifying assumptions, because that makes our job easier, and also to assure the audience that it does not really matter, that things would work out in roughly the same way without those assumptions. I think we are all often guilty of that. But in this particular case, being a consumer, I am entitled to be skeptical of these assurances — only mildly skeptical, though, because many of these assumptions probably are harmless. Still, it shows how much more work there is to be done.

Now, there is a point which is related to the two-part structure of this field (the two parts being, first, explaining why there is money and, second, explaining how things work, given that this money is subject to certain rules). If you are going to make certain assumptions in the first part of your work about the nature of the economy which has generated the phenomenon of money, then presumably you should somehow maintain those assumptions in the second part of your work, so that you are sure that the explanation of how money works once it exists is not inconsistent with the explanation of what permitted the institution of money to develop in the first place. Here again, we have received verbal assurance from various people in this group that the assumptions made are not going to cause any trouble. But when I look at the actual models, I do not see that there is a rigorous check on this. If we are to have a division of labor between the two parts of the field, such checks are indispensable. Ultimately, I think, it is essential to have a unified theory that embraces both parts.

3. Explaining Why Money Exists

Just one more remark about explaining how the institution of money, or fiat money, has come into existence or why it exists. There are two possible ways of thinking about that type of explanation. One is to study the history of money, going back at least to ancient times in Babylon and Asia Minor and to the goldsmiths of London and perhaps to a few places in between, and ask, Why did money come into use in these particular times and places? Taking into account the historical background, why did fiat money (as distinct from commodity money) come into existence? Thus, one could construct an *evolutionary* theory of money. Alternatively, we have an approach that does not pretend to be a potential explanation of this historical evolution. Instead, it is an *endogenous* theory of money which is somewhat static rather than evolutionary in character, and it implies a positive equilibrium level of money. What makes a theory endogenous is that you do not introduce deus ex machina rules which force people to use money, but rather you introduce elements into the situation which would make them want to use money.

Here what has struck me, and I would hope that we shall go somewhat beyond it, is the inclination toward a kind of philosophical monism, a tendency to develop a certain amount of religion that only one aspect is important while other aspects or functions are not. In this respect, I am rather in a camp with Jim Tobin and others. I am impressed by the traditional explanations involving about three or so factors of equal a priori plausibility. At the present state of knowledge, I would not know how to assess their relative importance. I could very well imagine that, for classroom purposes, we would construct different models, each of which involve only one of those aspects: store-of-value, transaction facilitation, or some other function. Each of these models by itself would perhaps be enough to explain why something like what we call money has come into existence. But then, of course, before we come to policymaking, and even earlier than that, when we come to some kind of systematic empirical testing, we would have to allow for all of these different functions of money in order to see how to relate the various features of the model to reality.

I also believe (and this, too, may be related to some things that Tobin said) that there are phenomena which we observe in the context of money which logically do not at all have to go together with money. One example of this is the credit that Shubik refers to. He starts out introducing some sort of economy in which there is just commodity money, like gold or salt. And then he says, Well, but there really is not enough of this commodity money. The reason there is not enough is that in this model there is the (Shubik) rule which says that you must pay in that commodity or you cannot buy things. You are not permitted, in effect, to barter your initial endowments. As Shubik tells the story, when you enter the trading room you have to surrender to the referee, or somebody like that, all of your initial commodity endowments other than the money commodity. In real life you might be able to barter, but his rule does not permit it. Well, I do not know whether to think that there really was this kind of phase in the history of the development of these institutions, which I doubt, or that this difficulty shows the inadequacy of this kind of model. But then Shubik says, Well, if this kind of problem develops, if there is not enough of the commodity money, credit will enter. Okay, that is one way to remedy the deficiency of this particular model. But when you think about the problem of credit as such, you can very well think of credit in a barter multiperiod economy. If people have to wait until after harvest before they can have something to eat, it is very likely they will be lent resources by somebody else. In the work of Böhm-Bawerk, and undoubtedly earlier authors, you will find many such examples. So I do not see a priori that there is a very close relationship between the phenomenon of credit and the phenomenon of money. If you are in a monetary economy, then, of course, there will be a monetary aspect, an important monetary aspect, to credit. And I think there are other examples of putting more of a burden on the monetary aspects of things than perhaps would be justified from a more general point of view.

Now let me give an example of a model that probably has much in common with Lucas'. But I must admit that I only got to see a small part of Lucas' paper, and very recently, so I apologize for any overlap. In any case, my story is not an attempt at originality. Rather, it illustrates how one can go about constructing endogenous theories without bringing in the issue of overlapping generations.

Suppose that you want to explain why, in a certain economy, a commodity money developed. And let us say that this commodity is salt. (According to Webster, the word *salary* comes from the word *salt,* so it served to some extent as commodity money.) First you postulate, for instance, that somehow the society has increased either in size or economic complexity, so the problem of the so-called double coincidence has become more severe. (I do not know why it is called a *double* coincidence; I think *coincidence* is good enough.) The probability of coincidence of wants has diminished, and that creates a need for some alternative device. If I want to sell something, and I cannot get for it what I really want, then in a model with uncertainty, since I have to take something else, I would rather take something that is not the idiosyncratic desire of just one single person in this huge society, but rather something that almost everybody uses from time to time and is likely to take off my hands later. Let us say salt turns out to be this kind of thing. In a stochastic model with time (just the transaction time, not generational time), we might find that as the economy grows the probability that people will accept salt in exchange for whatever they are selling will increase. Then it will also turn out that perhaps you would find it desirable to hold inventories of salt a little higher than would be needed just for tomorrow's soft-boiled eggs. And so you would develop a liquidity theory.

Is there anything very strange about this model? I think it is very much in the spirit of what Hicks wrote in his paper on money in the 1930s, and it seems a perfectly reasonable theory of a pure exchange economy with only an uncertainty of encounters and without overlapping generations. Of course, I have only told it in words, but it is very easy to set it to mathematical modeling music.

I mention this example only to show that, for me at least, there is no philosophical necessity for a stress on the intergenerational aspect of money. Of course, that does not mean that the intergenerational aspect is unimportant. But the example does show that the fiat phenomenon (the fact that salt will somehow acquire a value in the market that is higher than if its only use were for soft-boiled eggs) can already be present in an economy without an intergenerational structure. Admittedly, my example is not one of pure fiat money, but only of commodity money with a fiat aspect.

To get pure fiat money, it is often assumed that nothing else is durable, so that in a multigeneration world money is the only transmissible store of value. I, however, do not see a compelling necessity for making money the unique intergenerational bridge. The fact is that we do have durable goods of one sort or another, and again, there is no reason to go in a monistic direction. I think one can say that there are these other stores of value, whether land or capital or whatever, but that for certain purposes they are not adequate—for example, because of the lack of liquidity properties. Therefore, fiat money is needed in this situation as well.

4. Explaining How Money Works

Now let me go back to the more technical issues of constructing these models as games. I have already commented that one has to question very seriously the imposition of rules that are artificial and might be distorting. I think that to the greatest extent possible one should impose only those rules that are absolutely required by the logic of the problem. But I am very sympathetic with Shubik's effort to make sure that these rules are explicit enough so that one can test whether in fact the game is feasible. And here I would like to make a brief digression to some work dealing with the feasibility of game-theoretic models, work that has been going on recently which may have some lessons for our subject.

Various game-theoretic models have been constructed for pure exchange models, with the objective of setting up rules of the game so that the solution would turn out to be the competitive (Walrasian) solution. Those of us who have gone through the usual microeconomics education would think that this had been accomplished a long time ago. Isn't that what the whole story of the Walrasian auctioneer is about? Well, some people (especially Frank Hahn) have insisted that you usually do not have an auctioneer. Okay, so there is a problem: can you set up a game-theoretic market model without having an auctioneer, just with actual flesh and blood agents, and still yielding the competitive outcome?

A few years ago, David Schmeidler, a few other people, and I started constructing such models. When you try to do that, it is natural to use as motive power to push the players toward equilibrium something in the nature of excess demand. The problem is, what does it mean to have excess demand in a formal game model? Well, one way that this works out is that you are really permitting interim infeasible allocations. That obviously is very dangerous. What if there is a police raid, and the game is interrupted in the middle, before equilibrium has been reached? How are they going to pay off? So it is highly desirable to have a model in which the mathematics guarantees feasibility at every step, not only at equilibrium.

Schmeidler and others have proceeded to take care of the problem essentially by devising a balanced game. By *balanced* I simply mean that things add up properly: the sum of net trades is zero—not only at equilibrium but also away from equilibrium. But balance is only one of the two feasibility requirements. The other is what we call *individual feasibility,* which means that, for example, you rule out negative holdings because (in models without credit) negative holdings lack a sensible physical interpretation.

So the question arose whether it is possible to devise a game model which would be individually feasible as well as balanced and still yield a Walrasian outcome. Let me stress here that we had, in this work, one less constraint than some other model builders because we were not claiming to be constructing a positive theory model, only a normative one. In other words, we were not asking whether our model mirrors a real market, but rather an easier question: can we just set up rules of the game which would produce competitive market results?

Let me, then, state a problem currently being studied by Maskin, Postlewaite, and me. It is to set up rules of a game which (at all times, not merely at equilibrium) are balanced and individually feasible and produce competitive market results at equilibrium. It turns out from an example constructed by Postlewaite, and rather to our surprise, that if you insist on both feasibility conditions, it is not possible in general to set up a game which would give ordinary Walrasian outcomes. (It is possible if you have the kind of technical assumptions that rule out boundary solutions. You could do it, for example, if you have Cobb-Douglas utility functions, but not in general, when boundary solutions are possible.)

I point this out because it shows that there are serious difficulties in fitting together the ideas that would be admissible in the context of a genuine game model and the ideas that we bring in from what people refer to as general equilibrium theory but what is really the Walrasian static theory (which is, of course, a much narrower concept). And for this reason, although I may not like every one of the devices Shubik has employed, I very much applaud his insistence on checking on the feasibility aspect.[1] What I am saying is this: if you believe that the game model is the appropriate one, and if you insist on the formal feasibility aspect of it, even aside from whether the model is realistic, you must expect some very serious problems in modeling competitive markets. Whether this means that we should expect the economy to be other than as the usual competitive Walrasian model tells us it is, or whether it means that our modeling techniques are faulty is still an open question.

One aspect of solutions of noncooperative games may deserve some additional attention. We know from the elementary two-person zero-sum examples in von Neumann and Morgenstern that there may exist no pure (that is,

[1]In fact, it was a paper by Shapley and Shubik dealing with commodity money, where they did not get optimality although they had the feasibility very much under control, that stimulated me to go into this particular line of research.

nonrandomized) strategy Nash equilibrium. Consider, then, a two-person game in which both players' (unique) equilibrium strategies are mixed (randomized). Here the probability distribution (the mix) of each player's strategies is fixed (at the optimal mix), but the actual (pure) strategies used will vary from one play to another. By the definition of *Nash equilibrium,* any alternative mix would not raise (and might lower) the mathematical expectation of utility for a given agent given the (probabilistic) behavior of the other.

Let us think of one player as the monetary authority and the other as the public. Assuming that the game has a unique Nash equilibrium, one may define the problem of finding the optimal policy for the authority as simply that of finding the strategy mix maximizing its expected utility when the public plays its Nash strategy mix.

Thus, if the public's behavior is consistent with the Nash hypothesis, the authority can assure itself of attaining the value of the game (its expected utility at the Nash equilibrium) by playing its appropriate mixed strategy.[2] The point is that the public cannot defeat this strategy even if the authority's policy mix is revealed in advance. I shall not try to judge whether this has a bearing on the recent debates concerning the ineffectiveness of policies in an environment of rational expectations. (See Hurwicz 1951.[3])

Returning to controversial issues in game modeling, let me say that I am also very sympathetic with Shubik's approach to noncooperative games. In fact, I have just used the same approach, namely, that of Nash equilibrium. But we know that this concept of equilibrium has been subjected to many criticisms. It would be, I believe, a little dangerous to identify the general notion of a noncooperative game equilibrium with a particular notion that Nash proposed. Just to mention one example (and again I am not talking about empirical merit but philosophically), an alternative notion of a noncooperative game is where everybody is maximizing the minimum possible payoff (see Hurwicz 1953).[4] Perhaps the reality is that we want neither Nash nor "maximin" equilibria, but something else. We should not get too committed to any one of these game concepts at present.

What makes me think of that in particular is another aspect of Shubik's work. He notes that he is confining himself to relatively simple strategies. In his model, essentially what happens is that first everybody makes a bid on how much money they would like to get from the central bank on this first day of creation, and then they tell the trading posts how many dollars they would spend on that commodity. Ultimately they will be told how many units they will get at what price. Well, the particular aspect of simplification here is the absence of *sequential* strategies; they are all *one-move* strategies. Yet when we talk about games (say, chess), especially in extensive form, we think of a strategy as something more than a move, namely, a rule prescribing what move to make given the information concerning the preceding moves. (In fact, the term *strategy* was introduced to mean something more than a move.) In Shubik's model, however, the move and the strategy are essentially the same

[2]Interestingly enough, the Treasury Department recently decided to follow such a mixed strategy by not announcing in advance the timing of future gold sales. A Treasury official indicated that one objective was to deter speculation. (See *Minneapolis Star,* October 17, 1979, p. 3.)

[3]Author names and years refer to the works listed at the end of this book.

[4]Recently such "maximin" equilibria have been studied by William Thomson of the University of Minnesota and Eric Maskin at M.I.T.

thing: the game is almost a one-move game.

It would be natural to think of more complex behavior. The strategy could very well be that I will do such and such on the first move, and then, depending on what the other players do, I will go to the left or to the right, and so on. Going further in that direction, you get into the theory of "supergames" which have the unpleasant feature that there is an overabundance of possible equilibria. But what is the conclusion from this unpleasantness? Should we ignore the fact that people do think a couple of moves ahead? Or should we conclude that we are not using the right concept of equilibrium? I think such questions should loom rather large on our agenda.

Shubik indicated in a comment that he is basically a believer in infinite horizons, but that in fact he works with finite ones. That is true of many people because it is mathematically convenient. To compensate for the horizon truncation, Shubik uses a certain device, the surrender value of capital goods at the end of the creation. (In his world there is not only a first day of creation but also a day of judgement, when everything gets cashed in.) He feels that this device yields solutions in a finite-horizon world which correspond to stationary solutions for infinite horizons. Whether this is the case is very worth pursuing, and I would hope that it works out that way; but I think that at the moment this is just a heuristic conjecture. Furthermore, it is not out of the question that one could approach this problem of infinite horizons directly (without truncation), as has been done in other fields of allocation theory through infinite-dimensional linear spaces. Perhaps somehow these two kinds of approaches could be brought together.

Let me go back for a moment to an aspect of evolutionary theories on which I think I have quite a bit in common with the suggestions or hints that Tobin gave us yesterday. I am quite impressed by some of the research (by Schelling and Ullman-Margalit) on how social conventions develop. An example is an attempt to explain why, in a given country, people always drive on one side of the road. If you imagine that people choose randomly which side of the road to drive on, you can see why there might be some evolutionary tensions developing. Ullman-Margalit examined the Nash equilibria in a game of this kind, and the basic research question there is (from a short-run static point of view) whether it might turn out that perhaps the right conventions will not develop. In that case, there might be sufficient mortality, so that kind of society would not have a very high probability of survival as compared with others. Thus, if you added to the game-theoretic models a Darwinian evolutionary component, you could imagine a theory of how social conventions come into existence. I think it would be very worthwhile to look at money phenomena, fiat money in particular, from that point of view. We would then have an analytical theory helpful in explaining historical processes and not merely the final asymptotic outcome. And so, just as Shubik was referring to mathematical institutional economics, this would be mathematical historical economics. (You can see that there is quite a bit of imperialism on the part of mathematical economists.)

5. Normative Implications

I have one other comment, related to the normative versus positive aspects. In general, the presentations that we have had here have been in the spirit of positive science, in the sense that people try to explain existing monetary institutions and phenomena. They try to explain the essential features of monetary institutions as they exist. It is true there is a normative aspect, for instance, in Wallace's model, having to do with appropriate open market policies. But as far as the institutions are concerned, they are treated in a positive rather than normative way.

I happen to be interested in the design of economic institutions. Therefore, I would regard as a real test of these theories, not just to check whether they fit all the wiggles in, say, the historical interest rate curves, but to see to what extent they could, coming from the analytical side, result in the invention of some new institutional structures which might turn out to be of value to people who really run the system. It is my impression that most economic institutional innovations have been due not to an economist but to a lawyer, a practical banker, or perhaps a politician. I would like to reverse this to some extent. To illustrate: imagine us economists around 1880 setting up a model with enough free parameters for institutional arrangements so that when we solve it for the *institutional optimum* it turns out that we have invented the Federal Reserve System. That is what I mean by an analytical approach to the design. Of course, we are still very far away from being able to do this. But it would be interesting to see to what extent the models we have seen have in them enough leeway so that one could examine the comparative performance of alternative institutional frameworks.

6. A Final Note

Finally, let me say that the game framework has very considerable generality, because it permits one to study virtually all situations in which everybody is trying to optimize in some way. Thus the game-theoretic approach is much more general than the particular Nash or von Neumann and Morgenstern models we so often use. But even generalized game models are too specialized because they tend to ignore aspects of the economic process where informational decentralization is particularly important. An analysis of such informational issues would by far exceed the appropriate scope for my discussion. Let me, therefore, only note that Lucas' concluding comment concerning the parameters θ in his model (where agents observe their own θ but not anyone else's) is an example of dispersion of information, with significant implications for the efficiency of resource allocation.

Discussion by Milton Harris*

1. Introduction

Robert E. Lucas' paper formulates (as do the papers by Wallace and Cass, Okuno, and Zilcha in this symposium) a model in which a role for money is endogenous and explicit. The reason for developing such models stems essentially from the argument, exposited in Lucas 1976,[1] that one cannot hope to analyze the effects of policy changes using a model in which one assumes that certain behavioral relationships (for example, demand for money) are exogenous when, in fact, these relationships vary with the policy adopted. It follows that, to analyze monetary policies, one must postulate a model in which the use of and demand for money arises endogenously and explicitly from the postulated preferences of the agents (over real goods), the information structure, and the available technology of production and exchange, that is, from the basic underlying data of the economy which can be expected to remain stable in the face of changing monetary policy. I agree that the use of such models is essential for examining the effects of monetary policy and applaud the efforts of Lucas, Wallace, Cass, and others in this direction.

2. Lucas' Model

Lucas derives a simple model with an endogenous role for money, using, in essence, the following assumptions:

- There are two classes of people, those with positive marginal product in producing goods and those with zero marginal product in producing goods but positive marginal product in trading (or shopping). One cannot produce and trade at the same time. Thus it will be optimal for agents to pair off into households (or firms) consisting of one producer-storekeeper and one shopper.
- There is no economy-wide simultaneous trading.
- Future consumption is discounted.

To simplify the analysis it is also assumed that only one type of physical good can be produced (marbles), but the good can be produced in various colors. Preferences are such that agents want to consume the colors in certain fixed

*I am indebted to my colleagues Scott Richard, Robert Hodrick, and Allan Meltzer for helpful discussions. Remaining errors and snide remarks are my own.

[1]Author names and years refer to the works listed at the end of this book.

proportions. Technology is such that a given producer can produce marbles of only one color at an exogenously determined rate. Production requires only labor input, and there is no utility for leisure. Marbles are perfectly perishable.

It follows from these assumptions that the most efficient contract for effecting exchanges is for each household to be endowed with a certain amount of some perfectly divisible object called money (pieces of paper or credits in an account), and then all exchanges are of the following form: one agent agrees to hand over to the other agent one marble of her or his own color in exchange for each p units of money (p, the price level, is independent of color). Given that all exchanges are of this form, the shopper will return to the store periodically to consume any accumulated marbles and pick up any accumulated money. The period length (that is, length of time between returns to the store) will be independent of the money supply. The latter will be fixed exogenously at the beginning of time and not changed thereafter.

The object of the analysis is to determine the price level, p, as a function of the money supply, M.

Lucas also analyzes a model in which future preferences of consumers are uncertain. In this model, the object is to determine the steady-state distribution of real balances across consumers and the steady-state price level as a function of the fixed supply of nominal balances. The explicit dynamical formulation of these models which follows from the above assumptions is particularly simple and elegant. The main mathematical condition which generates a role for money is a simple Clower-type cash-in-advance constraint (see Clower 1967). In both models, Lucas shows that a competitive equilibrium allocation and price level exist in which the classical, quantity-theory propositions hold (velocity is constant and the price level is proportional to the quantity of nominal balances).

3. Critique

The models appear to have two major shortcomings from the point of view of policy analysis. First, the money supply is fixed once and for all at the beginning of time. Thus the models as presently formulated are useless for any practical analysis of policies concerning the evolution of the money supply over time. That is, one can analyze only once-and-for-all changes in the quantity of money. Second, the models exclude all assets other than money. In particular, there can be no analysis of open market operations. Moreover, it is not clear that Lucas' results would continue to hold in an economy with private credit as well as money.[2] It is clear that Lucas regards this paper as a first step which will form a basis for the addition of the aforementioned elements.

It is a fairly straightforward exercise to superimpose on Lucas' certainty model a stochastic law of motion (or policy rule) for the evolution of the money supply.[3] I have done this for the following formulation:

[2]Wilson (1978b) provides a model very similar to Lucas' certainty model. Wilson's model includes an explicit labor supply decision and private credit. The government may purchase and sell bonds issued by consumers. Wilson is not much concerned in his paper with the analysis of monetary policy; however, he does point out that the model is amenable to such analyses.

[3]A stochastic policy rule might reflect the assumption that the monetary authority cannot completely control the money supply but can determine some aspects of its distribution. As a special case, one can easily analyze an environment in which the monetary authority does have complete control simply by making the random variable in the policy rule degenerate.

$$M_{t+1} = (1 + \pi_{t+1})M_t$$

where $\{\pi_t\}$ is a sequence of independent and identically distributed random variables with support in $(-1, \infty)$ and M_t is per capita nominal balances in period t. Assume that each consumer receives a transfer at the end of period t equal to $\pi_{t+1} M_t$ (independent of the consumer's holdings of money in period t) and must decide on a level of consumption in period t before the realization of π_{t+1}. In this model, equilibrium would be defined as a pricing function $P(M_t, \pi_t)$ which defines the price level in period t as a function of the per capita stock of money in period t and the rate of increase in this stock since last period such that all output is demanded and per capita demand for money in period t is M_t for each t. It can be shown that in this model the classical quantity theory results [that is, $P(M_t, \pi_t) = M_t/y$ where y is output per capita per period] hold in equilibrium if and only if the money supply does not decline too rapidly, that is, if and only if

$$E_\pi (1 + \pi)^{-1} \leqslant 1/\beta$$

where β is the common discount factor of all agents.

The problem with this analysis is that it is no longer clear that once we allow a growing money supply the period length will be independent of the monetary policy. In particular, it may be optimal for the shopper to return to the store to pick up accumulated cash balances more often (that is, to shorten the period length) the faster is the rate of growth of prices.[4] (Lucas argues that the period length may appropriately be regarded as exogenous, mumbling something about the rate of rotation of the earth. This seems to have about as much to do with the period length as the value of Planck's constant or Avogadro's number. Lucas' argument that the period length is exogenous is correct for his model, which has a fixed equilibrium price level. The rate of rotation of the earth notwithstanding, the argument is inappropriate if the price level may grow at different rates depending on the specific monetary policy.)

4. Conclusion

The final judgment on the efficacy of the modeling approach espoused by Lucas in this paper will have to await more elaborate versions which are capable of addressing more interesting policy issues and which provide some strong positive implications on which they can be tested. Whether Lucas' approach will prove to be more tractable or fruitful than, say, the overlapping generations models embraced by Wallace and others also remains to be seen. As mentioned above, however, it is essential, if we are accurately to predict the effects of various monetary policies, to formulate models in which the demand for money arises endogenously from assumptions on the primitive taste-technology-information data of the economy.

[4] I believe this criticism also applies to the model of Wilson (1978b).

Discussion by Frank Hahn

1. A Different Approach

The discussions we have been having yesterday and today have been much more general than I expected them to be. I thought we would look at specific models and at specific questions and see whether there are any specific answers we can have. Instead, we spent a good deal of time on what I would like to call *understanding theories*. That is to say, you want some sort of model which allows you to understand the institution of money, for instance. And that is done in rather a historical way.

Some of those things I was going to say this afternoon already came up this morning, so I will be very brief about them. I think that there are legitimate questions you can ask yourself, such as, How does money ever come to be used? How do financial institutions become what they are? But I don't believe that even that is the best understanding strategy. And it is quite dangerous.

The way I would like to proceed is slightly different. That is to start off with all the monetary institutions and ask, What would have to be the case if these institutions are to survive? Now that is not the same question of how something comes to be what it is; it is a question of how something remains what it is. And that's different. For instance, you might ask yourself, Given our monetary institutions, are there any coalitions which could form to bypass the monetary system altogether and improve themselves? That would be a sort of Nash idea one might have. It is quite a different kind of question than starting with a barter world with $n(n-1)$ / 2 trading posts and saying, Why is it that someone would do something to invent money?

I have been often pleasantly taken with the American hopefulness. It seems to be that there is a great deal of history people write in which they say the world goes from one situation to a Pareto superior situation, then on to another Pareto superior situation. It is reminiscent of Candide that somehow or other if something has a benefit to all of us it will happen. Now I have almost exactly the opposite view. That is, history illustrates how often it is the case that something that is to the benefit of everyone together doesn't happen. And my question is much rather, Why doesn't it happen? For instance, why don't all party coalitions form? They don't form because of the cost of coalition formation—they have to find each other, and you might even add Marxist social consciousness to that. I find it much more interesting to wonder why there is a failure in our societies for Pareto-improving moves to be made rather than to assume, well, if something is Pareto improving, then surely sooner or later it will come to pass.

2. Specialization, Infinity, and Pareto Efficiency

There are three other points I want to make on this very general level before I come to something we are more interested in.

One is that it is quite interesting how rarely one sees the discussions of the use of money making the point which was made by Adam Smith and which somehow the Arrow-Debreu paradigm stops us from making: that the extent of the market governs the division of labor; there are increasing returns, if you like. But the function of money, in allowing specialization, in allowing a really fine division of labor, is obviously something one ought to look into. Of course one has to postulate a double coincidence before people can specialize in something and to have the division of labor carried very far. But the reason this question is very rarely asked is that in most of our models the division of labor is not a great thing because we always have diminishing returns anyway. We don't have models with increasing returns to specialization, and that is why it gets neglected. But I think, compared with bringing traders together, the function of money in allowing specialized productions is of greater importance.

Also on this level of generality, there is the problem of infinity. My own view is that it is a pseudoproblem. The idea is that if you take a finite horizon the world comes to an end, and if money had no value then, then it can't have value in the period before that, and it can't have value before that, and so on. And you are in trouble because you said you were going to look at a world which is always in rational expectations equilibrium. Well, for some purposes I find these rational expectations equilibria extremely interesting. They have sufficient intellectual meat in them to make us want to work with them. But they are not necessary to account for the positive value of money. The Grandmont-Younes-Laroque way of simply saying there is some finite probability people attach to money having a positive exchange value in the future is all you need for money to have a positive exchange value today. That seems to me pretty good and very convincing. And I don't know why we have to worry about the infinite-horizon problem. It is a serious problem; I am quite happy to worry about it as a sort of intellectual game problem. But to say we don't understand money because we haven't quite settled the infinite-horizon thing, I think, is not real.

My last point at this level of generality is one which, I think, is more important to make in America than perhaps in other places: it is the tremendous attraction Pareto efficiency has for theorists. One produces a simple model, and one then asks oneself, Will the equilibria of that be Pareto efficient in some way? Yet even with quite modest complications of models, Pareto efficiency already goes out of the window. I mean, I know of no model with a stock exchange (other than the Diamond model and even that is already restricted Pareto efficiency) in which you can say that the economy is going to be Pareto efficient in equilibrium. Indeed, when you have a share market it is not at all clear what the criterion function for the managers of firms should be. And on top of that, you have the missing market problems, you have any number of reasons why any allocation you see in the world is not going to be Pareto efficient.

Now it is true that it is quite interesting to take a very simple model and just ask, In this model what will the world look like? and try to isolate particular effects. But this leads people to say, This shows that monetary institutions can or can't sustain a Pareto optimum. That is a slightly pompous attitude, considering that it is only in a very stripped-down version of the world that we ought to be looking for Pareto efficiency.

Indeed, I think one of the most interesting research problems for us is to get alternative notions of efficiency which are not the Pareto efficiency kind but which one could call *institutional efficiency* problems. I mean, for instance, the work by Grossman and Hart on social Nash optima and production social Nash optima. There are any number of versions of the world we can look at in defining Pareto efficiency. In particular, it seems to me that if we say one social arrangement is Pareto inefficient, then we ought to be able to say that someone could do something about it. If there is no way to do anything about it, then it is not interesting to say it is Pareto inefficient. That is because we have to define it relative to the movements we can make in the particular state we are interested in. And that leads to quite different notions of efficiency—richer ones, but also less satisfactory ones. We lose some of these beautiful theorems which we all know about.

3. Non-Walrasian, Bootstrap Equilibria

I have now come to what I consider a much more interesting question which I haven't heard discussed at all at this conference. If you look at the current work on rational expectations or at Lucas' model or at any of this kind of literature, you find that the dominant equilibrium notion, the particular description of the economy, is Walrasian. Now the Walrasian equilibrium isn't by any means the only equilibrium notion we can have. I don't mean we ought to look at models with rigid prices, but we ought to look at models of sequences of markets in which in each particular sequence prices may be nonclearing. There may be, for instance, involuntary accumulation of inventories or rationing or some combination of these. The question now is whether the sequence of markets always has to approach a Walrasian long-run or stationary, rational expectations equilibrium or could it get stuck somewhere quite differently; could it go to some other point.

There is every prospect that a sequence of short-period equilibria in which agents receive both price and quantity signals may get stuck at an equilibrium which is not a Walrasian equilibrium at all. Now I am not saying stuck forever because I don't know what's going to happen forever. But I am saying stuck for a long time. And if you take that view, then money and monetary policy take on quite different aspects; matters become more interesting.

You see, one of the things I have always found very hard to understand is the following syllogism: A Walrasian equilibrium is homogeneous of degree zero in the money stock and prices and, let us add, expected prices. Therefore, an increase in the quantity of money will lead to an equiproportionate increase in prices. That seems to be a complete nonsequitur. The fact that an equilibrium is homogeneous in that way doesn't tell you where the economy will move if you inject more money. In order to get the sentence to make sense you have to add that the Walrasian equilibrium is unique; that the Walrasian equilibrium is the only equilibrium you are going to look at; and that you are going to say that the economy pretty smartly goes from one equilibrium to another, that it very quickly finds itself in equilibrium again. I think all of these things are extremely dubious, and I was hoping, actually, that this conference would be discussing some of these aspects rather than the meta-questions of why we have money at all, what the peasants did when they were bargaining women for cows, what the world looked like then.

The point about much of the irritation I personally find with some of the literature on money is that the most important premise on which it is built, namely, that the Walrasian equilibrium is a paradigm we should look at, is never discussed—it is taken for granted.

Now in a discussion between Keynesian economics and, let us say, new monetarism, you have got to somehow get the debate up to the point where it is discussable. Keynes, as you know, was a very careless writer, very sloppy. I think the *General Theory* contains nothing which we would recognize as a proof of any proposition. Nonetheless, Keynes had a certain vision of the economy, a vision I share, and I think it is very relevant to monetary theory. It is, roughly speaking, that an economy can have *bootstrap equilibria*. That is to say, there are equilibria which are perfectly rational for each of the agents, which nonetheless are very bad equilibria, and which can be actually changed through either monetary or fiscal policy. Now obviously this is not the time to start this discussion, but what I want to say is that if you are going to challenge the Keynesian view you must also show that there is no coherent and empirically persuasive account of non-Walrasian equilibrium.

My view is that the troubles which have arisen recently, but have been around all the time, is that Keynes and the Keynesians were totally ignorant of value theory. They had no micro theory worth having. I don't think Keynes even understood it. But if one is going to discuss anything that looks like Keynesian economics, then I am pretty certain one will have to look at small economies in which agents are sufficiently large to have some quasi-monopoly power. I cannot for the life of me see why it would be taboo to look at such economies. We look casually around, and General Motors doesn't look very small, and trade unions don't look very small—there are large agents around. And when there are large agents around, then the Walrasian model isn't so helpful. The question now is, How can we describe an equilibrium of a world in which there are these large agents? If we started with that, I am pretty sure that we could finish (this is conjecture, of course) with bootstrap equilibria. By that I mean a world which is what it is because each individual, in looking at the optimum reactions, say, Nash-like ones, assumes that the other agents are going to continue doing what they are, and the other agents' policy makes each particular individual's action rational. Now if there are bootstrap equilibria like that, and that is an open question, then the problems of policy become quite different.

In recent years Malinvaud and others in France have tried to formalize models of this kind, but they go to the other extreme, from having prices very flexible to having prices absolutely rigid. At the moment, however, there are others in this country and elsewhere studying hybrid models in which one looks at price changes and price adjustments as well as these quantity constrained equilibria. My impression is, to put it at its weakest, that there are being fashioned equilibrium notions which have as much claim to our attention as the Walrasian ones. And if that for now is to be granted, then the idea of money becomes quite different. The whole question of whether or not even anticipating monetary policy correctly would mean that monetary policy would have no effects is very much at risk. And indeed, one would now like to discuss and construct rational expectations equilibria in which both prices and quantity distributions enter into the rational theories of agents. It would be surprising if in such a world Keynesian propositions found no support.

Now I would have very much enjoyed it if we had had some debate on this issue because the moment one says that the equilibrium notion is Walrasian all opponents have to go quietly. By this I mean that a rational expectations–Walrasian equilibrium has the properties which are claimed for it. But it is an equilibrium which carries very little conviction—not only because of the rational expectations part, which is perhaps the least damnable, but also because in this world there is no description of how the world could ever have become what it is. Why is the world in rational expectations equilibrium? Some answer, We only understand equilibrium. I think that is a play on words. The economies we study out of Walrasian equilibrium may be in a different kind of equilibrium. It seems a logical mistake to assert that everything that is not a Walrasian equilibrium is a disequilibrium. There are an enormous number of interesting and important equilibrium notions which we ought to explore.

4. A Note on Trading Uncertainty

There is only one other thing I wanted to say, and I shall finish on that. It is that we had very little talk yesterday or today about the liquidity of assets. In recent years Krepps and Goldman have been studying the question of how far the holding of money gives flexibility. One of the things about flexibility and money is that you may face trading uncertainties (not price uncertainties) which a Walrasian model completely rules out. By *trading uncertainty* I mean whether or not you will be able to trade what you want to trade at the going price. Now it is clear that trading uncertainties exist and that you may want to insure yourself against some of them. Indeed, trading uncertainties may give you a ranking of assets by liquidity. In any case, a formal theory of liquidity is still lacking, and yet it seems quite important for monetary theory. There is clearly room here for some interesting non-Walrasian work.

2 Post-Conference Contributions

The Optimum Quantity of Money

Truman Bewley

1. Introduction

My purpose is to show that underlying what seems to be Milton Friedman's vision of reality there is a rigorous model of competitive equilibrium which can serve as an alternative to the Arrow-Debreu model. More precisely, a careful analysis of Friedman's (1969, pp. 1–50)† paper, "The Optimum Quantity of Money," leads naturally to a model in which an equilibrium is a stationary sequence of temporary equilibria and is also Pareto optimal. It is Pareto optimal even though there is no forward trading and there are no markets for contingent claim contracts.

I do not know whether Friedman would agree with my analysis, nor do I claim that he should agree. My aim is to synthesize his ideas and my own.

In "The Optimum Quantity of Money," Friedman argues that an economy cannot be economically efficient if any consumer economizes on cash balances. Consumers should be constrained by their average flow of income, but not by immediate shortages of cash. Wasteful economizing of cash would be avoided if money earned a real rate of interest equal to consumers' rate of time preference. The quantity of money which would be held by society in this situation is called the *optimum quantity of money*.

In explaining his ideas, Friedman uses a simple model, which he calls "a hypothetical simple society." This is a stationary society with a constant population and with given tastes and resources. Consumers buy and sell services. Money is the only durable object which may be exchanged. There is no borrowing and lending. The nominal stock of money is fixed. Consumers are subject to random shocks. The shocks are such that "mean values do not (change)." I interpret this last assumption as meaning that the shocks form a stationary stochastic process.

I define a mathematically precise version of Friedman's model. I assume that the model is of an exchange economy, with no production, although Friedman is not clear on this point. The most important specification I make is that consumers live forever. Here, I follow Friedman. He says that it is "simplest to regard the members of this society as being immortal and unchangeable." However, one could also interpret his model as an intergener-

†Author names and years refer to the works listed at the end of this book.

ational model similar to Samuelson's (1958) consumption loan model. The random shocks in Friedman's model are assumed to form a Markov chain. Corresponding to each of the finitely many states of the chain, there is a Walrasian pure trade economy. Each consumer has an endowment and a concave utility function which is a function of the state. The endowments are not storable, but must be traded and consumed in the period in which they appear. Each consumer acts so as to maximize the expected value of the discounted infinite sum of her or his utilities from consumption. Consumers are assumed to have rational expectations in that they know the true probability distribution of future prices and of their own utility functions and endowments. Money has price one in every period. It is not needed to pay for purchases and does not enter anyone's utility function. It is useful to consumers only because it allows them to spend more than they earn sometimes. The only intertemporal aspect of the model is that consumers must decide each period how much money to save or dissave.

The assumption that consumers live forever involves a delicate question of interpretation. What is involved is the interpretation of the time scale and of the nature of the random events. My model is designed to represent what one would see approximately in a grander model if one looked at how consumers reacted to everyday fluctuations over a short period of time. I think of random events as small events which tend to average out after a year or so. Periods are days, and a day two years hence is nearly infinitely far away. The infinite horizon should not be taken literally. It is simply a way to look at the consumer's life as a process rather than in totality.

My point of view seems to be roughly consistent with Friedman's. He specifically assumes that physical resources and the "state of the arts" are fixed. These assumptions would not be appropriate if he visualized a period of time spanning from five to ten years, say. However, my point of view is not entirely consistent with what Friedman says. For he asserts that one "reason for holding money is as a reserve for future emergencies." Emergencies are hardly the everyday events I have in mind. I do not find it appropriate to assume that ordinary consumers could ever hold sufficient assets to be able to handle major emergencies, even if money did pay interest. Most people are simply not that rich. The best they can do is buy insurance against specific catastrophies. I also part company with Friedman in not making money necessary for transactions. Friedman states that in his model the two motives for holding money are self-insurance and to circumvent the double coincidence of wants needed for barter. However, introducing transaction costs, limited information about trading possibilities, and so on, would only complicate my model. It would not change the conclusions.

I now return to what I do. I define a *monetary equilibrium* to be an infinite sequence of random temporary equilibria such that the price of money is always one and such that all prices are uniformly bounded away from zero and infinity. By assuming that prices are bounded, I exclude the inflationary equilibria which apparently may occur in almost any model with an infinite horizon and rational expectations. (See, for example, Gale 1973, p. 24, and Calvo 1978.)

The sequence of random price vectors in a monetary equilibrium do not necessarily obey a stationary probability law. This fact is a weakness of the concept of monetary equilibrium. For it makes little sense to assume rational expectations if the probability distributions involved are not stationary. (Observation does not reveal the distribution law of a nonstationary distribution.) I suspect that in a wide class of cases there exist no stationary monetary equilibria. I hope to turn to this question in a later paper.

I make two strong assumptions about endowments and utility functions, which guarantee that consumers need money in order to compensate for fluctuations in their incomes and needs. I then prove that there exists a monetary equilibrium provided that the interest earned on money is less than every consumer's rate of time preference. I also prove that in this case a monetary equilibrium need not be Pareto optimal. More precisely, if each consumer always consumes something, then the equilibrium is not Pareto optimal. This is in accord with Friedman's argument. All consumers economize on money balances to some extent, since their rate of time preference exceeds the rate of interest. Since consumers economize, the equilibrium cannot be Pareto optimal.

Consumers would not economize on money balances if the rate of interest equaled their rate of time preference. They would accumulate money balances until they were fully self-insured. For self-insurance would be costless, since the trade-off between present and future expenditure would be the same when measured in terms of money or utility. So following Friedman, I assume that all consumers have the same rate of time preference and that money earns interest at this rate. I prove that in this case there exists no monetary equilibrium, for almost every choice of consumers' random endowments. (*Almost every* means for all endowments except those belonging to a set of Lebesque measure zero.) In proving this result, I make a special assumption which guarantees that the underlying stochastic fluctuation is sufficiently random. The idea of the proof is that a monetary equilibrium can exist only if the pattern of net expenditures of each consumer is periodic and not random. Periodicity can be destroyed by small perturbations in endowments. (Such periodicity is illustrated by the example given in section 13.)

If the pattern of net expenditures of some consumers were not periodic, they would need an infinite quantity of money in order to insure themselves completely. For they would have to protect themselves against an arbitrarily long run of bad luck. In short, I prove that almost surely the optimum quantity of money is infinite.

I express the infiniteness of the optimum quantity of money in another way. I show that for almost every choice of consumers' endowments the following is true. The real stock of money in a monetary equilibrium may be made arbitrarily large by paying interest on money at a rate which is sufficiently close to the common rate of time preference.

One might interpret these results as a criticism of Friedman's notion of an optimum quantity of money: I make his model precise and reduce the idea to an absurdity. However, this would not be a valid interpretation of my work. It seems fair to say that Friedman's primary interest was in economic policy. From a practical point of view, the idea that the optimum quantity of money is infinite is perhaps just silly. This idea becomes important only when one tries to use a precise model of general equilibrium in order to express Friedman's ideas.

It might seem that the infiniteness of the optimum quantity of money is simply an artifact of my model. It is, of course, a consequence of the bizarre assumption that consumers never die. However, the theoretical problem cannot be resolved by assuming that consumers do die. For if consumers do die, the optimum rate of interest may not lead to a Pareto optimal allocation. Imagine, for the moment, a version of my model with mortal consumers. Suppose that each consumer lives many periods and is replaced at death by a new consumer. Suppose also that there is no inheritance and that consumers know when they are going to die. Then, consumers would spend all their money during their last period of life. Also toward the end of their life, they would tend to decumulate money. As a result, they might at some point be caught without enough cash. Such illiquidity would cause economic inefficiency. Clearly, no matter what the rate of interest, there would exist a monetary equilibrium and the real quantity of money would be finite. Hence, given a social welfare function, there would exist an optimum real rate of interest. However, there is no reason to believe that this rate of interest would equal the common rate of time preference. Monetary equilibrium with an optimum rate of interest would not necessarily give rise to a Pareto optimal allocation. I do not pursue this line of thought in this paper.

I return now to the idea that the optimum quantity of money is infinite in the model of this paper. I interpret the infiniteness of the optimum quantity of money as expressing the idea that the optimum quantity of money in a more realistic model would be so large that consumers would rarely be constrained in their day-to-day lives by lack of cash. That is, they would be able to insure themselves effectively against small fluctuations.

In the theory of the consumer, self-insurance is expressed as constancy of the marginal utility of money. It stays constant over time, even as prices and current needs and income fluctuate. I call this assumption the *permanent income hypothesis*. This is a notion I have explained before, using a model of a single consumer (see Bewley 1977d). Here I express the idea in a general equilibrium framework and relate it to Friedman's ideas on the optimum quantity of money.

Ideally, I would like to have proved that if the rate of interest paid on money were sufficiently close to the common rate of time preference, then in a monetary equilibrium each consumer's marginal utility of money would be nearly constant. Unfortunately, I could not prove this, and it may not be true. If a monetary equilibrium is not stationary, one can say little about marginal utilities of money. As I have said, it is not clear whether stationary monetary equilibria exist.

The permanent income hypothesis leads naturally to a new version of equilibrium theory. In this theory, each consumer's demand function is defined by the assumption that the marginal utility of money is constant. Consumers simply spend money on each good until the utility gained from consuming the quantity bought with the last dollar equals the fixed marginal utility of money. Their budget constraint is that their long-run average expenditures per period not exceed their long-run average income per period. These long-run averages are computed using the true distribution of future prices, for consumers are assumed to know this distribution. Consumers adjust their marginal utility of money so as to bring their average expenditures into line with their average income.

Assume that each consumer's demand is defined in this fashion. I define a *stationary equilibrium* to be a stationary distribution of prices such that aggregate excess demand is always zero. I prove that in the model of this paper a stationary equilibrium exists and is Pareto optimal. (I have discussed stationary equilibrium in three unpublished papers: Bewley 1977a, b, c.)

Stationary equilibrium is a way of describing the world when the quantity of money is optimal. This might seem confusing, for money plays no role in stationary equilibrium. But since the optimum quantity of money is infinite, it cannot play a role. In fact, the absence of money is an advantage from my point of view, for I seek a simple model of general equilibrium.

The fact that money disappears from the model expresses Hahn's (1971a) criticism of Friedman's theory of the optimum quantity of money. Hahn expresses his main criticism this way: "The necessary conditions for Pareto-efficiency in a world of uncertainty with inter-temporal choice will in general be fulfilled by a market economy only if money plays no role." Hahn elaborates this point in three other papers (see Hahn 1971b, 1973a, b). An allocation is Pareto optimal only if it can be generated by equilibrium in Arrow-Debreu markets for forward and contingent claims. But in such an equilibrium, money plays no role. Hence, money is "inessential" in any system which generates Pareto optimal allocations.

In order to reconcile Hahn's and Friedman's ideas, one may think of Friedman's optimum quantity of money as optimal only in some asymptotic or approximate sense. One can think of money as present but nearly irrelevant from the point of view of equilibrium theory. Since cash rarely constrains consumers, it may be ignored.

This point of view also helps to reconcile Hahn's views with those of Starrett (1973). Starrett argued that Pareto inefficiency arises in Hahn's model of equilibrium with transaction costs only because of the lack of an intertemporal unit of account. Starrett is careful to point out that this unit of account would not be real money. In his model, consumers have unlimited ability to borrow and lend the unit of account. The only restriction is that debt be repaid in the last period of life. The point of my work is that in a model much like Hahn's, real money resembles Starrett's intertemporal unit of account asymptotically as the rate of interest approaches the common rate of time preference.

The concept of stationary equilibrium involves many notions that are commonly associated with modern politically conservative economic thinking. Not only is stationary equilibrium related to Friedman's optimum quantity of money and to his permanent income hypothesis, but it is based on the idea of rational expectations. I view stationary equilibrium as expressing rigorously the conservative vision of Walrasian equilibrium.

The notion of stationary equilibrium can serve as an alternative to the Arrow-Debreu model. By an alternative, I mean that each model is appropriate in certain settings. (The Arrow-Debreu model is defined in Arrow 1964 and in Debreu 1959, chapter 7.) Stationary equilibrium has the obvious advantage that trading takes place all the time, not exclusively in some ethereal initial period. However, in my opinion, stationary equilibrium can be thought of as applying only in short-run contexts where random shocks are never severe. If the context is not the short run, then stationarity does not make sense. The world changes over long periods of time. If random shocks are severe, then external insurance is needed. External insurance is formalized by contingent claim contracts.

The notion of stationary equilibrium is intriguing, in spite of its limitations. For instance, it provides a partial solution to a problem posed by Arrow (1974). The problem is to explain why we do not in reality observe complete markets for contingent claims. I intend to develop this point in a later paper.

Turning to another matter, I give a new solution in this paper to a problem posed by Hahn (1965). The problem is how to prove the existence of a competitive equilibrium in which money has a positive price. My monetary equilibrium is such an equilibrium. The device I use to give money value is the infinite horizon (together with the need for insurance). This is, of course, an artificial device, though perhaps more elegant than others that have appeared in the literature.

I wish to emphasize that I do not view this existence result as in any way explaining why money exists, nor as providing a basis for monetary theory. The existence result is simply a convenient way to describe precisely an aspect of reality which interests me here. Much of what is monetary about money is excluded from my model.

The following three sections contain formal definitions, assumptions, and statements of results. In section 5, I attempt to relate my work to the vast literature on the optimal quantity of money and on the link between general equilibrium and monetary theory. The body of the paper gives formal proofs. The basic idea of the proof that the optimum quantity of money is infinite may be found in Schechtman 1976. The last section contains an example.

2. Definitions, Notation, and the Model

2.1. *Notation*

R^L denotes L-dimensional Euclidean space. Let x and y belong to R^L. The expression $x \geqq y$ means $x_k \geqq y_k$, for all k; $x > y$ means $x \geqq y$ and $x \neq y$; $x >> y$ means $x_k > y_k$, for all k. R^L_+ denotes $\{x \in R^L \mid x \geqq 0\}$, and int R^L_+ denotes $\{x \in R^L \mid x >> 0\}$.

Let $f: U \to (-\infty, \infty)$ be twice differentiable, where U is an open subset of R^L. $Df(x)$ denotes the vector of first derivatives of f at x. $D^2f(x)$ denotes the matrix of second-order partial derivatives at x.

Prob $[A \mid B]$ denotes the conditional probability of A given B, where A and B are formulas describing events. Prob $[A]$ denotes the probability of A. $E(x \mid B)$ denotes the expectation of the random variable x given the event B. Ex denotes the expectation of the random variable x.

2.2. *The Underlying Stochastic Process*

Exogenous fluctuations are governed by a stochastic process $\{s_n\}_{n=-\infty}^{\infty}$. The random variables s_n take their values in a set A. A is called the set of states of the *environment*. I assume that $\{s_n\}$ is a Markov chain. That is, $\{s_n\}$ is a Markov process with stationary probabilities, and A is a finite set. If a and b belong to A, then P_{ab} denotes the transition probability, Prob $[s_{n+1} = b \mid s_n = a]$, for any n. Similarly, $P^{(k)}_{ab} =$ Prob $[s_{n+k} = b \mid s_n = a]$, for $k \geqq 1$. I also assume that $\{s_n\}$ is ergodic with no transient states. That is, there is a positive integer n such that $P^{(n)}_{ab} > 0$, for all a and b.

Since $\{s_n\}$ is ergodic, there exists a unique stationary probability distribution on A, $(\pi_a)_{a\in A}$. π satisfies $\pi_b = \Sigma_{a\in A}\, \pi_a P_{ab}$, for all $b \in A$. Since $\{s_n\}$ has no transient states, $\pi_a > 0$ for all $a \in A$.

I will always assume that s_1 is distributed according to π. That is, the probability distribution of $(s_1, s_2, \ldots)$ is determined by the unique stationary distribution for the process $\{s_n\}$.

A *history* for the process $\{s_n\}$ from time n to time $n + m$ is a finite sequence $a_n, a_{n+1}, \ldots, a_{n+m}$ such that $a_k \in A$, for all k, and Prob $[s_n = a_n, \ldots,$

$s_{n+m} = a_{n+m}] > 0$. Histories will be denoted by $a_n, \ldots, a_{n+m}$. A *history following* a_n is a finite sequence $a_{n+1}, \ldots, a_{n+m}$ such that $a_n, a_{n+1}, \ldots, a_{n+m}$ forms a history.

2.3. *The Economy*

The economy is a pure trade economy with no production. Initial endowments and utility functions fluctuate in response to fluctuations in s_n.

There are L commodities and I consumers, where L and I are positive integers. The *endowment* of consumer i is determined by $\omega_i : A \rightarrow R^L_+$, for $i = 1, \ldots, I$. $\omega_i\ (s_n)$ is the endowment vector of the consumer in period n. The *utility function* of consumer i is $u_i : R^L_+ \times A \rightarrow (-\infty, \infty)$. Consumer i's utility function at time n is $u_i\ (\cdot, s_n) : R^L_+ \rightarrow (-\infty, \infty)$. I assume that for all i, $u_i\ (\cdot, a)$ is everywhere twice differentiable. Also, $Du_i\ (x,a) >> 0$ and $D^2U_i\ (x,a)$ is negative definite, for all x. In other words, $u_i\ (\cdot, a)$ is differentiably strictly monotone and strictly concave.

A *consumption plan* for a consumer is of the form $x = [x_n\ (a_i,\ldots,a_n)]$, where $n = 1,2,\ldots$ and $a_1,\ldots,a_n$ varies over histories and where each $x_n\ (a_1,\ldots, a_n)$ belongs to R^L_+. The consumer's consumption bundle at time n is $x_n\ (s_1,\ldots, s_n)$.

Consumer i discounts utility at the rate δ_i, where $0 < \delta_i \leqq 1$. The consumer's *rate of time preference* is $\delta_i^{-1} - 1$.

The expected value of the utility to consumer i of a consumption plan x is $U_i\ (x) = E\ \{\Sigma_{n=0}^{\infty}\ \delta_i^{n-1}\ u_i\ [x_n\ (s_1, \ldots, s_n), s_n]\}$, where E denotes the expected value operator. $U_i\ (x)$ is well defined as long as $\delta_i < 1$ and the $x_n\ (s_1, \ldots, s_n)$ are uniformly bounded.

An *allocation* is a set of consumption plans $(x_i) = (x_1, \ldots, x_I)$, where x_i is the consumption plan of consumer i. The allocation is said to be *feasible* if $\Sigma_{i=1}^{I}\ [x_{in}\ (a_1, \ldots, a_n) - \omega_i\ (a_n)] = 0$, for all n and all histories $a_1, \ldots, a_n$.

If $\delta_i < 1$, for all i, then a feasible allocation (x_i) is said to be *Pareto optimal* if there exists no other feasible allocation $(\bar{x}_i)$ such that $U_i\ (\bar{x}_i) \geqq U_i\ (x_i)$, for all i and $U_i\ (\bar{x}_i) > U_i\ (x_i)$, for some i. This definition makes no sense if $\delta_i = 1$, for some i. Suppose that $\delta_i = 1$, for all i. Then the feasible allocation (x_i) is said to be Pareto optimal if there exists no feasible allocation $(\bar{x}_i)$ such that

$$(1) \qquad E\left\{\sum_{n=1}^{N} u_i\ [\bar{x}_{in}\ (s_1, \ldots, s_n), s_n]\right\} \geqq E\left\{\sum_{n=1}^{N} u_i\ [x_{in}\ (s_1, \ldots, s_n), s_n]\right\}$$

for all i and N; with inequality for some i and N.

2.4. *Monetary Equilibrium*

A *price system* is of the form $p = [p_n\ (a_1, \ldots, a_n)]$, where the $p_n\ (a_1, \ldots, a_n)$ belong to R^L_+. The price vector at time n is $p_n\ (a_1, \ldots, a_n)$.

Let $r \geqq 0$ denote the nominal interest rate paid on money. Interest payments are financed by a lump-sum tax. Let τ_i be the tax payments paid by consumer i each period. $M_{in}\ (p, x; a_1, \ldots, a_n)$ denotes the *money holdings* of consumer i at the end of period n, given the price system p, the consumption program x, and the history $a_1, \ldots, a_n$. $M_{in}\ (p, x; a_1, \ldots, a_n)$ is defined inductively as follows.

$$(2) \qquad \begin{aligned} &M_{i0}\ (p,x) \equiv M_{i0} \text{ is given, and} \\ &M_{in}\ (p,x; a_1, \ldots, a_n) = (1 + r)\ M_{i,n-1}\ (p,x; a_1, \ldots, a_{n-1}) \\ &\qquad + p_n\ (a_1, \ldots, a_n) \cdot [\omega_i\ (a_n) - x_{in}\ (a_1, \ldots, a_n)] - \tau_i \end{aligned}$$

for all $n \geqq 1$ and for all histories $a_1, \ldots, a_n$.

I will assume that $\Sigma_{i=1} M_{i0} = 1$. In order to assure that the nominal supply of money never changes, I assume that $\Sigma_{i=1}^{I} \tau_i = r$.

The *budget set* of consumer i, given a price system p, is $\beta_i(p) = \{x \mid x$ is a consumption program such that $M_{in}(p,x; a_1, \ldots, a_n) \geqq 0$, for all n and for all histories $a_1, \ldots, a_n\}$.

In order to guarantee that $\beta_i(p)$ be nonempty, I assume that $\tau_i = rM_{i0}$, for all i. If τ_i exceeded rM_{i0}, the consumer might have no way to avoid being driven to bankruptcy by tax payments.

If $\delta_i < 1$, then consumer i's maximization problem is the following:

$$\max\left(E\left\{\sum_{n=1}^{\infty} \delta_i^{n-1} u_i\,[x_n(s_1, \ldots, s_n), s_n]\right\}\,\middle|\, x \in \beta_i(p)\right). \tag{3}$$

$\xi_i(p)$ denotes the solution to this problem, if it exists. $\xi_i(p)$ does indeed exist, provided that the components of p are uniformly bounded away from zero and infinity. It is not necessary to prove this fact for the purposes of this paper. The strict concavity of the functions $u_i(\cdot, a)$ guarantees that the solution of (3) is unique.

If $\delta_i = 1$, then (3) makes no sense. However, one may still obtain a plausible definition of $\xi_i(p)$, though $\xi_i(p)$ is no longer necessarily unique. I will return to this matter in a subsection below.

A *monetary equilibrium* is a vector $[p, (x_i)]$, where p is a price system, (x_i) is an allocation, and both satisfy the following conditions:

(4) (x_i) is a feasible allocation.

(5) The components of $p_n(a_1, \ldots, a_n)$ are uniformly bounded away from zero and infinity as n and $a_1, \ldots, a_n$ vary.

(6) $x_i \in \xi_i(p)$, for all i.

Remark. Given a monetary equilibrium $[p,(x_i)]$ with positive interest rate r, it is possible to define an equivalent deflationary equilibrium $[\bar{p}, (x_i)]$ with no interest payments. One simply deflates the taxes and prices at rate r. $\bar{p}$ is defined by $\bar{p}_n(a_1, \ldots, a_n) = (1+r)^{-n+1} p_n(a_1, \ldots, a_n)$. The tax payments of consumer i in period n are $\bar{\tau}_{in} = (1+r)^{-n+1}\tau_i$. The consumer's holdings of money at the beginning of period n turn out to be $\overline{M}_{in}(\bar{p},x_i; s_1, \ldots, s_n) = (1+r)^{-n+1} M_{in}(p,x_i; s_1, \ldots, s_n)$.

2.5. *Marginal Utilities of Money When* $\delta_i < 1$

There are marginal utilities of money associated with any monetary equilibrium $[p, (x_i)]$, provided that $r \leqq \delta_i^{-1} - 1$. I will always assume that $r \leqq \delta_i^{-1} - 1$. The marginal utilities of money are simply the multipliers associated with the consumers' budget constraints. The marginal utility of money of consumer i is an infinite vector $\lambda_i = [\lambda_{in}(a_1, \ldots, a_n)]$, where each $\lambda_{in}(a_1, \ldots, a_n)$ is a positive number. The marginal utility of money must be distinguished from the marginal utility of expenditure. The vector of marginal utilities of expenditure associated with x_i and p is always denoted by $\alpha_i = [\alpha_{in}(a_1, \ldots, a_n)]$, where again each $\alpha_{in}(a_1, \ldots, a_n)$ is a positive number. $\alpha_{in}(a_1, \ldots, a_n)$ is defined as follows:

(7) $\alpha_{in}(a_1, \dots, a_n)$ is the smallest number t such that

$$\frac{\partial u_i[x_{in}(a_1, \dots, a_n), a_n]}{\partial z_k} \leqq t\, p_{nk}(a_1, \dots, a_n)$$

for all k; with equality if $x_{ink}(a_1, \dots, a_n) > 0$.

In this formula, $\partial u_i(x,a) / \partial z_k$ denotes the partial derivative of $u_i(x,a)$ with respect to the kth component of x.

λ_i and α_i satisfy the following conditions. These apply for all i, n, and $a_1, \dots, a_n$.

(8) $$\lambda_{in}(a_1, \dots, a_n) = \max\{\alpha_{in}(a_1, \dots, a_n), \delta_i(1+r)E[\lambda_{i,n+1}(a_1, \dots, a_n, s_{n+1}) \mid s_n = a_n]\}.$$

(9) $$\lambda_{in}(a_1, \dots, a_n) > \delta_i(1+r)E[\lambda_{i,n+1}(a_1, \dots, a_n, s_{n+1}) \mid s_n = a_n]$$

only if $M_{in}(p, x_i; a_1, \dots, a_n) = 0$.

(10) $\lambda_{in}(a_1, \dots, a_n) > \alpha_{in}(a_1, \dots, a_n)$ only if $x_{in}(a_1, \dots, a_n) = 0$.

The marginal utilities of money are uniformly bounded above and away from zero. Before stating this fact, I define some key bounds.

(11) Let $\bar{\omega} \in R^L_+$ be such that $\Sigma^I_{i=1}\omega_i(a) \ll \bar{\omega}$, for all $a \in A$. There exist $\underline{q}$ and $\bar{q}$ such that $0 \ll \underline{q} \ll Du_i(x,a) \ll \bar{q}$, for all $a \in A$ and for all $x \in R^L_+$ such that $x \leqq \bar{\omega}$.

The existence of $\underline{q}$ and $\bar{q}$ follows from the strict monotonicity of the functions $u_i(\cdot, a)$ and from the continuity of their derivatives. By (5), there exist vectors $\underline{p}$ and $\bar{p}$ in R^L_+ such that $0 \ll \underline{p} \leqq p_n(a_1, \dots, a_n) \leqq \bar{p}$, for all n and $a_1, \dots, a_n$. The bounds on the marginal utilities of money are as follows:

(12) $$\min_k \bar{p}_k^{-1}\underline{q}_k \leqq \lambda_{in}(a_1, \dots, a_n) \leqq \max_k \underline{p}_k^{-1}\bar{q}_k, \text{ for all } i, n, \text{ and } a_1, \dots, a_n.$$

I now sketch the proof that if $\delta_i < 1$, then marginal utilities of money exist and satisfy (8)–(10) and (12). I here use the methods of Schechtman 1976 or of my own paper (Bewley 1977d). Let $\lambda^N_i = [\lambda^N_{in}(a_1, \dots, a_n)]$ be the vector of marginal utilities of money associated with the solution of the problem

$$\max\left(E\left\{\sum_{n=1}^{N} \delta_i^{n-1} u_i[x_n(s_1, \dots, s_n), s_n]\right\} \;\middle|\; x \in \beta_i(p)\right)$$

This problem clearly has a solution, and the λ^N_i satisfy (8)–(10) and (12). It is not hard to show that the numbers $\lambda^N_{in}(a_1, \dots, a_n)$ are nondecreasing in N. (See Schechtman 1976, p. 224, Theorem 1.7, or Bewley 1977d, p. 270, Lemma 5.1.) The $\lambda^N_{in}(a_1, \dots, a_n)$ are uniformly bounded above. This follows from the following facts: $r \leqq \delta_i^{-1} - 1$; prices are uniformly bounded away from zero and bounded above (5); and utility functions are concave and have continuous finite derivatives. $\lambda_{in}(a_1, \ldots, a_n)$ is simply $\lim_{N\to\infty} \lambda_{in}^N(a_1, \ldots, a_n)$. Passage to the limit in (8)–(10) and (12) proves that λ_i satisfies the same conditions.

2.6. *Demand When* $\delta_i = 1$

I now turn to the question of the definition of demand when $\delta_i = 1$ (and $r = 0$). A program x belongs to $\xi_i(p)$ if $x \in \beta_i(p)$ and if there exists a vector of marginal utilities of money, $\lambda_i = [\lambda_{in}(a_1, \ldots, a_n)]$, such that x, λ_i, and p satisfy (8)–(10), with $\delta_i(1+r) = 1$, and also satisfy (13) and (14) below.

(13) There exists $\overline{M} > 0$ such that $M_{in}(p,x; a_1, \ldots, a_n) \leqq \overline{M}$, for all n and $a_1, \ldots, a_n$.

(14) There exist positive numbers $\underline{\lambda}$ and $\overline{\lambda}$ such that $\underline{\lambda} \leqq \lambda_{in}(a_1, \ldots, a_n) \leqq \overline{\lambda}$, for all n and $a_1, \ldots, a_n$.

Programs in $\xi_i(p)$ are optimal in a long-run average sense. In fact, if $\bar{x} = [\bar{x}_n(a_1, \ldots, a_n)] \in \xi_i(p)$, then $\bar{x}$ solves the problem

$$\text{(15)} \qquad \max\left(\liminf_{N\to\infty} N^{-1} E\left\{\sum_{n=1}^{N} u_i[x_n(s_1, \ldots, s_n), s_n]\right\} \,\middle|\, x_i \in \beta_i(p)\right).$$

First observe that

$$\max\left(\liminf_{N\to\infty} N^{-1} E\left\{\sum_{n=1}^{N} u_i[x_n(s_1, \ldots, s_n), s_n]\right\} \,\middle|\, x_i \in \beta_i(p)\right)$$

$$\leqq \liminf_{N\to\infty} N^{-1} \max\left(E\left\{\sum_{n=1}^{N} u_i[x_n(s_1, \ldots, s_n), s_n]\right\} \,\middle|\, x_i \in \beta_i(p)\right).$$

It follows that it is sufficient to prove that there is a constant B such that

$$\text{(16)} \qquad \max\left(E\left\{\sum_{n=1}^{N} u_i[x_n(s_1, \ldots, s_n), s_n]\right\} \,\middle|\, x_i \in \beta_i(p)\right)$$

$$\leqq E\left\{\sum_{n=1}^{N} u_i[\bar{x}_n(s_1, \ldots, s_n), s_n]\right\} + B, \text{ for all } N.$$

I now prove (16). Let λ_i be the vector of marginal utilities of money associated with $\bar{x}$. Clearly, $\bar{x}$ solves the problem

$$\max\Bigg(E\Bigg\{\sum_{n=1}^{N} u_i[x_n(s_1, \ldots, s_n), s_n]$$

$$+ \lambda_{iN}(s_1, \ldots, s_N)\, M_{iN}(p,x; s_1, \ldots, s_N)\Bigg\} \,\Bigg|\, x \in \beta_i(p)\Bigg).$$

For this is a finite dimensional maximization problem with a concave objective function. Hence, it is sufficient to satisfy the first-order conditions. But these conditions are given by (8)–(10).

By (13) and (14), $E[\lambda_{iN}(s_1, \ldots, s_N) M_{iN}(p,x; s_1, \ldots s_N)] \leqq \overline{\lambda}\,\overline{M}$. It follows that

(16) is true with $B = \overline{\lambda}\,\overline{M}$. This completes the proof that $\bar{x}$ solves (15).

2.7. *Stationary Equilibrium*

Stationary equilibrium is the concept of equilibrium appropriate when the rate of interest equals the common rate of time preference. It is defined as follows.

A *stationary consumption plan* is a function $x : A \rightarrow R^L_+$. A *stationary allocation* is of the form $(x_i) = (x_1, \ldots, x_I)$, where x_i is a stationary consumption plan. The bundle allocated to consumer i in period n is $x_i(s_n)$. The allocation (x_i) is *feasible* if $\Sigma^I_{i=1} [x_i(a) - \omega_i(a)] = 0$, for all $a \in A$.

To every stationary consumption plan x, there corresponds the infinite consumption program $\hat{x} = \hat{x}_n(a_1, \ldots, a_n)$, defined by $\hat{x}_n(a_1, \ldots, a_n) = x(a_n)$. A feasible stationary allocation (x_i) is said to be *Pareto optimal* if the corresponding allocation $(\hat{x}_i)$ is Pareto optimal.

Remark. One can also conceive of stationary consumption plans and prices which would be functions of the infinite history $(\ldots, a_{n-1}, a_n)$ and not just of the current state a_n. A stationary monetary equilibrium, if it existed, would be stationary in this sense, for the history would determine the current distribution of money balances.

A *stationary price system with deflation rate* r is of the form (p,r), where $r \geqslant 0$ is the deflation rate and $p : A \rightarrow R^L_+$ is such that $p(a) > 0$, for all a. The interpretation is that the price vector at time n is $(1+r)^{-n+1}p(s_n)$.

Given $p : A \rightarrow R^L_+$, the *stationary budget set* of consumer i is $\beta_i(p) = \{x : A \rightarrow R^L_+ \mid \Sigma_{a \in A}\ \pi_a\, p(a) \cdot [x(a) - \omega(a)] \leqq 0\}$, where π is the stationary distribution on A.

The *stationary expected utility* of consumer i is $U_i(x) = \Sigma_{a \in A}\ \pi_a u[x(a), a]$, where x is a stationary consumption program.

The *stationary demand* for consumer i, given a stationary price system (p,r), is the unique stationary consumption plan $\xi_i(p)$ which solves the problem $\max\{U_i(x) \mid x \in \beta_i(p)\}$.

If the deflation rate equals the consumer's rate of time preference, then $\xi_i(p)$ describes an infinite consumption program which is optimal given a long-run budget constraint. To be precise, suppose that the deflation rate r is positive. Then the infinite consumption program $\hat{\xi}_i(p)$ corresponding to $\xi_i(p)$ solves the problem

$$\max\left(E\left\{\sum_{n=1}^{\infty}(1+r)^{-n+1}u_i[x_n(s_1, \ldots, s_n), s_n]\right\}\right|$$

$$x \text{ is an infinite consumption program which satisfies}$$

$$\left. E\left\{\sum_{n=1}^{\infty}(1+r)^{-n+1}p(s_n) \cdot [x_n(s_1, \ldots, s_n) - \omega_i(s_n)]\right\} \leqq 0\right).$$

Now suppose that there is no deflation. Then $\xi_i(p)$ solves the problem

$$\max\left(\liminf_{N \rightarrow \infty} N^{-1}E\left\{\sum_{n=1}^{N}u_i[x_n(s_1, \ldots, s_n), s_n]\right\}\right|$$

$$x \text{ is an infinite consumption program which satisfies}$$

$$\left. \liminf_{N \rightarrow \infty} N^{-1}E\left\{\sum_{n=1}^{N}p(s_n) \cdot [x_n(s_1, \ldots, s_n) - \omega_i(s_n)]\right\} \leqq 0\right).$$

I may now define stationary equilibrium. A *stationary equilibrium with deflation rate* r is a vector $[p,r,(x_i)]$, where (p,r) is a stationary price system with deflation rate r, (x_i) is a feasible stationary allocation, and $x_i = \xi_i(p)$, for all i. The rate of deflation r plays no role in the conditions defining a stationary equilibrium. It becomes important only when one interprets the equilibrium.

One may think of consumers in a stationary equilibrium as keeping the marginal utility of money constant. The marginal utility of money of consumer i is the Lagrange multiplier associated with the constraint $\Sigma_{a\in A} \pi_a p(a)\cdot x(a) \leqq \Sigma_{a\in A} \pi_a p(a)\cdot \omega(a)$. It is, of course, simply a positive number, λ_i. Together with p, λ_i determines consumer i's demand. That is, if $\xi_i(p) = [x_i(a)]_{a\in A}$, then for each a, $x_i(a)$ is determined by the following set of inequalities:

$$\frac{\partial u_i[x_i(a),a]}{\partial z_k} \leqq \lambda_i p_k(a), \text{ for all } k; \text{ with equality if } x_{ik}(a) > 0.$$

3. Assumptions

Here I collect the assumptions I use. Many have already been mentioned in the previous section.

ASSUMPTION 1. *$\{s_n\}$ is a stationary Markov chain.*

The realization of the random variables s_n belongs to the finite set A.

ASSUMPTION 2. *$\{s_n\}$ is ergodic and has no transient states.*

$\pi = (\pi_a)_{a\in A}$ denotes the unique stationary distribution of $\{s_n\}$. $\pi_a > 0$, for all $a \in A$.

$\omega_i : A \to R_+^L$ describes the initial endowment of consumer i. I make use of the following conditions on the ω_i.

ASSUMPTION 3. *For every i, $\omega_i(a) \neq 0$, for some $a \in A$.*

ASSUMPTION 4. *For every $a \in A$, $\Sigma_{i=1}^I \omega_i(a) \geqq I(1,\ldots,1)$.*

The validity of this assumption depends on the choice of the units of commodities. In more general terms, I have simply assumed that $\Sigma_{i=1}^I \omega_i(a) >> 0$, for all a.

$u_i : R_+^L \times A \to (-\infty,\infty)$ is the utility function of consumer i. I make the following regularity assumptions about the u_i.

ASSUMPTION 5. *For all i and a, $u_i(\cdot,a)$ is everywhere twice continuously differentiable.*

ASSUMPTION 6. *For every i and a and for every $x \in R_+^L$, $D^2u_i(x,a)$ is negative definite and $Du_i(x,a) >> 0$.*

The next assumption has to do with initial money balances and the tax system.

ASSUMPTION 7. *$\Sigma_{i=1}^I M_{i0} = 1$, and for all i, $M_{i0} > 0$ and $\tau_i = r M_{i0}$, where r is the interest rate on money.*

The next two assumptions guarantee that a monetary equilibrium exists. They are very strong. The γ appearing in these assumptions is some small positive constant.

ASSUMPTION 8. *For every $a \in A$, Prob $[\omega_{ik}(s_2) \leqq \gamma$, for $k = 1,\ldots,L \mid s_1 = a] > 0$, where $0 < \gamma < 1$.*

Let $\underline{q}$ and $\bar{q}$ be as in (11).

ASSUMPTION 9. *There exists* $Q \in R^L$ *such that* $Q >> 0$ *and the following are true. For all i and a,* $Du_i(x,a) >> Q$, *whenever x is such that* $x_k \leqq \gamma \underline{q}_k^{-1} \sum_{j=1}^{k} \bar{q}_j$, *for all k. Also, for every k, a, and i,* $\partial u_i(x,a)/\partial x_k << Q_k$, *if* $x \in R_+^L$ *is such that* $x \leqq (1,\ldots,1)$ *and* $x_k = 1$.

The validity of this assumption depends, of course, on the choice of scale for the utility functions.

The next assumption expresses the idea that the Markov process $\{s_n\}$ is sufficiently random.

ASSUMPTION 10. *There exists a state* $a \in A$ *for which there are at least three distinct histories which begin and end with a. Each of these histories contains a state which is distinct from a and does not appear in either of the other two histories.*

4. Theorems

In all the following theorems, I assume that Assumptions 1–7 apply. Assumptions 8 and 9 are used only in Theorems 1 and 4. Assumption 10 is used only in Theorems 3 and 4.

THEOREM 1. *Assume that Assumptions 8 and 9 apply. If* $\delta_i < (1+r)^{-1}$, *for all i, then there exists a monetary equilibrium provided that* $\min_i \delta_i$ *is sufficiently large.*

THEOREM 2. *Suppose that* $\delta_i < (1+r)^{-1}$, *for all i. Let* $[p,(x_i)]$ *be a monetary equilibrium such that* $x_{in}(a_1,\ldots,a_n) \neq 0$, *for all i, n, and* $a_1,\ldots,a_n$. *Then the allocation* (x_i) *is not Pareto optimal.*

In the following theorem, Ω denotes the space $\{(\omega_1,\ldots,\omega_I) \mid \omega_i : A \rightarrow \text{int } R_+^L, \text{ for all } i\}$. If $\omega = (\omega_i) \in \Omega$, then $\mathcal{E}(\omega)$ denotes the economy with utility functions $u_1,\ldots,u_I$ and with initial endowment functions $\omega_1,\ldots,\omega_I$. Notice that Ω may be viewed as a subset of $R^{L|A|}$, where $|A|$ is the number of points in A. The statement *for almost every* $\omega \in \Omega$ means for all ω except for ω belonging to a subset of Ω of Lebesque measure zero.

Recall that P_{ab} denotes the trânsition probability from a to b in A.

THEOREM 3. *Assume that* $I \geqq 2$ *and that Assumption 10 applies. If* $\delta_i = (1+r)^{-1}$, *for all i, then* $\mathcal{E}(\omega)$ *has no monetary equilibrium, for almost every* $\omega \in \Omega$.

THEOREM 4. *Assume that* $I \geqq 2$ *and that Assumptions 8–10 apply. Assume also that* $\delta_i = (1+r)^{-1}$, *for all i, where* $r > 0$. *Then for almost every* $\omega \in \Omega$ *the following is true. Let* r_k *be such that* $0 \leqq r_k < r$, *where* $k = 1,2,\ldots$. *For each k, let* $[p^k,(x_i^k)]$ *be a monetary equilibrium for* $\mathcal{E}(\omega)$ *with interest rate* r_k. *If* $\lim_{k\rightarrow\infty} r_k = r$, *then* $\lim_{k\rightarrow\infty} p_n^k(a_1,\ldots,a_n) = 0$, *uniformly with respect to n and* $a_1,\ldots,a_n$.

THEOREM 5. *If* $\delta_i = \delta \leqq 1$, *for all i, then there exists a stationary equilibrium with deflation rate* $\delta^{-1}-1$. *Such an equilibrium is Pareto optimal.*

An example given in section 13 illustrates the need for the special assumption in Theorem 2 and for Assumption 10 in Theorems 3 and 4.

5. Review of the Literature

I review briefly the literature on the optimal quantity of money and on the relation of monetary theory to equilibrium theory. Not all of this literature is directly related to my own work. However, my own work falls in this general area. Since the literature is large and confusingly diverse, it seems worthwhile to review it. I first deal with the literature on the optimum quantity of money.

It seems to be impossible to attribute the idea of the optimum quantity of money to any one author. It must have been in the air for some time. In a paper of 1953 (pp. 251–62), Friedman discussed the fact that inflation leads consumers to economize unnecessarily on cash balances. This idea was formalized by Bailey in a paper appearing in 1956. In the same year the idea was empirically tested by Cagan. In a paper of 1963 (p. 535), Samuelson mentioned the idea that the real rate of interest on money should be positive, at least in idealized models. In a paper of 1963 (p. 113), Harry Johnson remarked that money should earn the same real rate of interest as other assets. Samuelson developed his idea somewhat in two papers of 1968 and 1969. Tobin discussed the same idea in a paper published in 1968 (p. 846). Both Samuelson and Tobin argued that from the point of view of efficiency, economic agents should be saturated with money balances; hence, money should bear a real rate of return high enough to remove all incentive to economize on it. This idea was discussed at length by Friedman in "The Optimum Quantity of Money," which appeared in 1969 (pp. 1–50).

There was a long debate about whether money should bear interest in reality. Friedman (1969) advanced this idea. Harry Johnson (1970), Tsiang (1969), Clower (1968, 1970), and Phelps (1972, pp. 201–220; 1973) made important contributions to the debate. Johnson was mainly concerned about substitution between money and interest-bearing assets. Since money does not bear interest, consumers economize on it in order to buy other assets. Tsiang expressed the view that if money bore interest at a rate equal to the general rate of return on capital, then it would tend to displace all other assets. Clower's main point was that one cannot make practical recommendations about monetary policy in terms of models which do not capture those aspects of reality which make money useful. Phelps related the question of the optimal level of inflation (or deflation) to the theory of optimal taxation. He pointed out that inflation is a form of tax, so that there is a trade-off between deadweight losses caused by inflation and those caused by other taxes.

The issues raised by Johnson and Tsiang cannot be discussed in terms of my model, since money is the only asset in my model. Nor can I discuss the theory of optimal taxation, for I permit lump-sum taxes. My model is, of course, open to Clower's criticism. There are no transaction costs, no information problems, and so on which could explain why money exists. But I do not make practical recommendations either.

I note in passing that in *Inflation Policy and Unemployment Theory* Phelps mentioned the idea that consumers would have an insatiable demand for liquidity if the real rate of interest equaled the rate of time preference (see Phelps 1972, pp. 181–82). This is, of course, one of the main ideas of this paper.

The theory of the optimal quantity of money is related to the literature on the optimal rate of growth of the money supply from the point of view of growth theory. This is a vast literature. See, for example, Johnson 1967, Levhari and Patinkin 1968, Marty 1968, Sidrauski 1967, and Tobin 1956, 1965. This literature is surveyed in Stein 1970. One of the main preoccupations of the literature is the effect of the real rate of interest on saving and investment. Most of the discussion is in terms of Keynesian and Solow growth models.

A revival of this literature was initiated recently by Brock (1974, 1975). He formulates the problem in terms of a mathematically rigorous, infinite-horizon growth model. In it, all consumers are identical and live forever. Utility is additively separable with respect to time. There is no uncertainty. Consumers have perfect foresight and maximize the discounted infinite sum of present and future utilities. The utility of each period depends on consumption, leisure, and real balances.

Brock's model of a single consumer is similar to my own, except that Brock puts money directly in the utility function. (In my model, uncertainty and the heterogeneity of consumers are what give money value.) The questions Brock asks are different from my own and also from those posed in the earlier literature on growth and money. His primary concern is with uniqueness of the perfect-foresight equilibrium. He also studies the response of the model to anticipated future changes in the nominal supply of money. He discusses the optimal quantity of money and proves that it is infinite if the marginal utility of money is not eventually zero. (The marginal utility of money in Brock's model is measured directly by the utility function.)

Calvo (1979) studies the uniqueness of equilibrium in models similar to that of Brock. Calvo allows money to appear in the production function.

I now turn to the enormous literature on models which describe in detail how and why people use money and why it is socially useful to do so.

The early papers of Baumol (1952) and Tobin (1956) use an inventory-theoretic model to explain why people hold money rather than interest-bearing assets. Money is the sole means of payment, and each purchase or sale of an interest-bearing asset involves a fixed transaction cost.

Clower and Howitt (1978) analyze an inventory-theoretic model of consumer behavior in a model with both transaction costs and inventories of goods. They find that because of delicate questions of timing, average cash balances can depend in a discontinuous way on the parameters of the consumer's problem.

Feige and Parkin (1971), Niehans (1975), and Perlman (1971) also introduce commodity inventories into the story told by Baumol and Tobin. They discuss the optimal quantity of money in a semiformal general equilibrium framework. That is, they give general equilibrium interpretations of the first-order conditions of consumer equilibrium, but they do not prove that equilibria exist. The work of Feige and Parkin and of Perlman has led to some controversy. See Feige, Parkin, Avery, and Stones 1973, Perlman 1973, and Russell 1974.

The model of consumer behavior most closely related to my own is that of Foley and Hellwig (1975). In their model, as in mine, money is needed only for self-insurance. Consumers live forever and maximize the expected value of a discounted infinite stream of utilities. Utility in each period depends on consumption and leisure. Consumers fluctuate between being employed and being involuntarily unemployed. They use money to compensate for the resulting fluctuations in income. The model is of partial equilibrium in that it is a model of a single consumer. Foley and Hellwig demonstrate that the probability distribution of money holdings converges to a long-run stationary distribution.

There is a large literature which analyzes in detail the role of money in transactions. Authors in this area try to show why exchange involving money is simpler and cheaper than barter. They also look for the essential difference between money and other goods. Works in this area include Brunner and Meltzer 1971, Niehans 1969, 1971, Ostroy 1973, Ostroy and Starr 1974, Saving 1971, and Starr 1972.

The papers just referred to explain why individuals would find money convenient if others were willing to accept it. They also explain why money is socially useful. But they do not describe a rigorous model in which it would be completely rational for every individual to accept and use money. The problem is that if one thinks in terms of a finite-horizon model, money would have no value in the last period. By backward induction, it would have no value in any period. In order to bypass this problem, one must think of equilibrium as an ongoing process, as I do in this paper. Shubik does so as well in his game-theoretic approach to monetary theory. (See, for instance, his paper in this volume.) Robert Jones (1976) treats equilibrium as an ongoing process in a model which includes costs of finding a trading partner. His equilibria may be interpreted as Nash equilibria. He also describes a process which leads in an evolutionary way to the adoption of a medium of exchange.

Samuelson's 1958 consumption loan model is another example of a model of an ongoing process in which money has value. This model has been much studied. See, for instance, Gale 1973, Grandmont and Laroque 1973, and the papers in this volume by Cass, Okuno, and Zilcha and Wallace.

There have been many rigorous, finite-horizon general equilibrium models in which money is given value by imposing somewhat artificial terminal conditions. These works include Hahn 1973b, Heller 1974, Heller and Starr 1976, Kurz 1974b, Sontheimer 1972, and Starr 1974. All of these papers, except that of Starr, include transaction costs. Kurz's model allows barter and monetary trade to occur simultaneously with distinct transaction costs.

Another approach to giving money value is simply to assume that consumers believe it will have value in the terminal period. That is, the value of money is a consequence of consumer expectations. This is the approach taken by Grandmont (1974). Drandrakis (1966) seems to have had the same approach in mind in his early work on temporary equilibrium theory. Grandmont proves the existence of a temporary equilibrium with a positive price for money in a two-period model in which consumers believe that the real value of money in the second period is bounded away from zero. These beliefs are not necessarily rational. In my model, money also has value only because consumers believe it will be valuable in the future. Because I use an infinite horizon, I am able to prove that these beliefs are rational.

Yet another way to obtain equilibrium with a positive price for money is to use the Clower constraint in an infinite-horizon model with rational expectations. The Clower constraint is the requirement that goods can be exchanged only for money. It was proposed by Clower in 1967. The Clower constraint serves to make money useful. The infinite horizon does away with the problem of the value of money in the terminal period. Grandmont and Younes (1972, 1973), Hool (1976), Lucas (this volume), and Wilson (1978b) all take this approach. Grandmont and Younes prove the existence of a stationary monetary equilibrium and analyze the optimal quantity of money. Hool solves a difficulty met by Grandmont and Younes. Wilson analyzes in detail the nature of the equilibria in his model.

The Clower constraint has a curious interpretation. In monetary models which specify transaction costs, it is usually automatic that goods can be exchanged only for money (or for other goods). This is so in the papers of Hahn (1973b), Heller (1974), Heller and Starr (1976), and Kurz (1974b). However, in models which do not specify transactions, the Clower constraint must be interpreted as a payments lag. It takes one period for money to pass from buyer to seller.

The recent paper of Müller and Schweizer (1978) uses the temporary equilibrium approach of Grandmont (1974). But their model includes transaction costs and constraints related to those of Clower.

My work is closely related to the literature on temporary equilibrium. Both monetary and stationary equilibria, as I define them, are forms of temporary equilibrium. Unlike many models of temporary equilibrium, my models have rational expectations. The literature on temporary equilibrium has been surveyed by Grandmont (1977).

6. Lemmas

The lemmas of this section express relations between the marginal utility of expenditure and equilibrium prices. I assume throughout that Assumptions 1–10 apply.

Let $\mathcal{E}(a)$, for $a \in A$, be the pure trade economy corresponding to state $a \in A$. That is, $\mathcal{E}(a)$ has I consumers and L commodities. The utility function of the ith consumer is $u_i(\cdot, a) : R^L_+ \to (-\infty, \infty)$. That consumer's initial endowment is $\omega_i(a) \in R^L_+$.

An *equilibrium with transfer payments for* $\mathcal{E}(a)$ is of the form $[q, (y_i)]$, where $q \in R^L_+$ is the price vector and (y_i) is a feasible allocation for $\mathcal{E}(a)$. These must satisfy $q > 0$ and $u_i(y_i, a) = \max\{u_i(y, a) \mid y \in R^L_+ \text{ and } q \cdot y \leqq q \cdot y_i\}$, for all i. The transfer payment of consumer i is $q \cdot [\omega_i(a) - y_i]$. Clearly, if every consumer's transfer payment is zero, then the equilibrium is in fact a Walrasian equilibrium in the usual sense.

The marginal utility of expenditure of consumer i associated with $[q, (y_i)]$ is defined to be the Lagrange multiplier, α_i, associated with the problem $\max\{u_i(y, a) \mid y \in R^L_+ \text{ and } q \cdot y \leqq q \cdot y_i\}$. That is,

(17) α_i is the smallest number t such that $\dfrac{\partial u_i(y_i, a)}{\partial x_k} \leqq t\, q_k$ for all k; with equality if $y_{ik} > 0$.

Throughout this section, $\underline{q}$ and $\overline{q}$ are as in (11).

LEMMA 1. *$(\max_i \alpha_i^{-1})\, \underline{q} << q << (\max_i \alpha_i^{-1})\, \overline{q}$, whenever $[q, (y_i)]$ is an equilibrium with transfer payments for $\mathcal{E}(a)$, for some $a \in A$, and where (α_i) is the vector of marginal utilities of expenditure associated with $[q, (y_i)]$.*

Proof. If $[q, (y_i)]$ is an equilibrium with transfer payments for $\mathcal{E}(a)$, then $0 \leqslant y_i \leqslant \overline{\omega}$, so that $\underline{q} << Du_i(y_i, a) << \overline{q}$, for all i.

By the definition of α_j, $\alpha_j q \geqq Du_j(y_j, a)$, so that $q >> (\max_i \alpha_i^{-1})\, \underline{q}$. This proves the first inequality.

$\Sigma_{i=1}^I y_i = \Sigma_{i=1}^I \omega_i(a) >> 0$, so that for each $k = 1, \ldots, L$, $y_{ik} > 0$, for some i. (Here I have used Assumption 4.) For this i, $\partial u_i(y_i, a) / \partial x_k = \alpha_i q_k$, so that $q_k < \alpha_i^{-1} \overline{q}_k$. This proves the second inequality.

Q.E.D.

LEMMA 2. *Let $[q, (y_i)]$ be an equilibrium with transfer payments for $\mathcal{E}(a)$, for some a, and let (α_i) be the vector of associated marginal utilities of expenditure. Then $\max_i \alpha_i < b \min_i \alpha_i$, where $b = \max_k \underline{q}_k^{-1} \bar{q}_k$.*

Proof. It follows from the definition of α_i that for each i, $\partial u_i(y_i, a) / \partial x_k = \alpha_i q_k$, for some k. But $\bar{q}_k > \partial u_i(y_i, a) / \partial x_k$. Also, by the previous lemma, $q_k > (\min_j \alpha_j)^{-1} \underline{q}_k$. Putting these inequalities together, I obtain $\bar{q}_k > \alpha_i (\min_j \alpha_j)^{-1} \underline{q}_k$. It follows that $\alpha_i < \underline{q}_k^{-1} \bar{q}_k \min_j \alpha_j \leqq b(\min_j \alpha_j)$.

Q.E.D.

An *equilibrium for $\mathcal{E}(a)$ with transfer payments and marginal utilities of money* is defined to be $[q, (y_i), (\lambda_i)]$, where $[q, (y_i)]$ is an equilibrium with transfer payments for $\mathcal{E}(a)$ and where $\lambda_i \geqq \alpha_i$, for all i, with equality if $y_i > 0$. Here (α_i) is the vector of marginal utilities of expenditure associated with $[q, (y_i)]$.

LEMMA 3. *Let $[q, (y_i), (\lambda_i)]$ be an equilibrium for $\mathcal{E}(a)$ with transfer payments and marginal utilities of money, where $a \in A$. Then $(\max_i \lambda_i^{-1}) \underline{q} << q << b(\max_i \lambda_i^{-1}) \bar{q}$, where b is as in Lemma 2.*

Proof. The first inequality follows trivially from Lemma 1, since $\lambda_i \geqq \alpha_i$, for all i.

In order to prove the second inequality, let i be such that $\alpha_i = \min_j \alpha_j$. By Lemma 1, $q << \alpha_i^{-1} \bar{q}$. By Assumption 4, there exists j such that $y_j > 0$. Then, $\lambda_j = \alpha_j$, and by Lemma 2, $\alpha_j \leqq b\alpha_i$. Putting these inequalities together, I obtain $q << b\lambda_j^{-1} \bar{q}$.

7. Proof of Theorem 1

The first step of the proof is to truncate the economy at the Nth period, artificially giving money utility in the Nth period. I use a standard fixed point argument to prove that the truncated economy has an equilibrium in which money has price one in every period. I then prove that the N-period equilibrium prices are uniformly bounded away from zero and infinity. This fact allows me to apply a Cantor diagonal argument in order to obtain a monetary equilibrium in the limit as N goes to infinity. The hard part of the proof is the demonstration that N-period equilibrium prices are bounded above and bounded away from zero. Prices are bounded above because money is needed for self-insurance and because high prices make the real stock of money low. Prices are bounded away from zero because there is a limit to the level of real balances that consumers will hold. This limit exists because the interest rate is less than consumers' rates of time preference.

7.1. *The Finite-Horizon Economy*

I truncate the economy at period N. In the truncated economy, it is sufficient to deal with N-period price systems and programs. These specify prices and consumption bundles in the first N periods only. An N-period allocation (x_i) is feasible if $\sum_{i=1}^{I} [x_{in}(a_1, \ldots, a_n) - \omega_i(a_n)] = 0$, for all histories $a_1, \ldots, a_n$ and for all n such that $1 \leqq n \leqq N$.

Given an N-period price system p, $\xi_i^N(p)$ denotes the unique N-period program which solves the following maximization problem:

$$(18) \qquad \max\left(E\left\{ \sum_{n=1}^{N} \delta_i^{n-1} u_i[x_n(s_1, \ldots, s_n), s_n] + \delta_i^{N-1} M_{iN}(p, x; s_1, \ldots, s_N) \right\} \right|$$

x is an N-period consumption program and $M_{in}(p, x; a_1, \ldots, a_n) \geqq 0$, for all histories $a_1, \ldots, a_n$ and for $1 \leqq n \leqq N\Big)$.

Notice that money is given utility in the last period.

An N-period monetary equilibrium is of the form $[p, (x_i)]$, where p is an N-period price system and each x_i is an N-period program. These must satisfy the following conditions.

(19) $\quad x_i = \xi_i^N(p)$, for all i.

(20) $\quad (x_i)$ is a feasible allocation.

(21) $\quad p_n(a_1, \ldots, a_n) > 0$, for all histories $a_1, \ldots, a_n$ and for all n such that $1 \leqq n \leqq N$.

LEMMA 4. *For each $N \geqq 1$, there exists an N-period monetary equilibrium.*

Proof. For the purposes of this proof, I allow money to have a different price in every period. Component $L + 1$ of the vector of prices in any one period corresponds to the price of money. Price vectors vary over $\Delta = \Pi_{n=1}^N \Pi_{a_1, \ldots, a_n} \Delta^L$, where $\Delta^L = \{q \in R_+^{L+1} \mid \Sigma_{i=1}^{L+1} q_i = 1\}$. If $q \in \Delta$, I write $q = [q_n(a_1, \ldots, a_n)]$.

I now add a vector $\vec{\epsilon} = (\epsilon, \ldots, \epsilon)$ to the initial endowment of each consumer in every state of the world, where $\epsilon > 0$. That is, I assume that the initial endowment of consumer i in state a is $\omega_i(a) + \vec{\epsilon}$, for all i and a. I also give each consumer ϵ units of money in each period. Later, I will let ϵ go to zero.

The plan of consumer i is denoted by (x_i, M_i), where $x_i = [x_{in}(a_1, \ldots, a_n)]$ and $M_i = [M_{in}(a_1, \ldots, a_n)]$.

I truncate the consumption sets as follows. Let $\bar{\omega} \in R_+^L$ be such that $\Sigma_{i=1}^L \omega_i(a) + \vec{\epsilon} << \bar{\omega}$, for all $a \in A$. I forbid each consumer to demand more than $\bar{\omega}_j$ units of good j, for all j, and to hold more than two units of money. In precise terms, I truncate consumer i's budget set to be the following compact set, given $q \in \Delta$.

$$\beta_i^T(q, \epsilon) = \{(x_i, M_i) \mid 0 \leqq x_{in}(a_1, \ldots, a_n) \leqq \bar{\omega}, 0 \leqq M_{in}(a_1, \ldots, a_n) \leqq 2$$

$$\text{and } q_n(a_1, \ldots, a_n) \cdot [x_{in}(a_1, \ldots, a_n), M_{in}(a_1, \ldots, a_n)]$$

$$\leqq q_n(a_1, \ldots, a_n) \cdot [\omega_i(a_n) + \vec{\epsilon}, (1+r) M_{i,n-1}(a_1, \ldots, a_{n-1}) + \epsilon - \tau_i],$$

$$\text{for all histories } a_1, \ldots, a_n \text{ and for } n = 1, \ldots, N\}.$$

It follows from Assumption 7 that $\beta_i^T(q, \epsilon)$ is nonempty.

I let $\xi_i^T(q)$ be the set of solutions to the problem

$$\max\Big(E\Big\{ \sum_{n=1}^N \delta_i^{n-1} u_i[x_{in}(s_1, \ldots, s_n), s_n] + \delta_i^{N-1} M_{iN}(s_1, \ldots, s_N)\Big\} \Big| \; (x_i, M_i) \in \beta_i^T(q, \epsilon)\Big).$$

Since a consumer begins every period with a positive amount of every good, including money, it follows that $\xi_i^T(q)$ is a continuous function of q.

The monotonicity of u_i implies that

$$\begin{aligned}(22) \qquad & \text{if } \xi_i^T(q) = (x_i, M_i), \\ & \text{then } q_n(a_1, \ldots, a_n) \cdot [x_{in}(a_1, \ldots, a_n), M_{in}(a_1, \ldots, a_n)] \\ & = q_n(a_1, \ldots, a_n) \cdot [\omega_i(a_n) + \vec{\epsilon}, (1+r) M_{i,n-1}(a_1, \ldots, a_{n-1}) + \epsilon - \tau_i], \\ & \text{for all } i, n, \text{ and } a_1, \ldots, a_n.\end{aligned}$$

I define the aggregate excess demand function, $Z(q)$, as follows. Let $q \in \Delta$, and let $\xi_i^T(q) = (x_i, M_i)$, for each i. Then $Z(q) = [Z_n(q; a_1, \ldots, a_n)]$, where $Z_n(q; a_1, \ldots, a_n) = \{\Sigma_{i=1}^I [x_{in}(a_1, \ldots, a_n) - \omega_i(a_n) - \vec{\epsilon}, M_{in}(a_1, \ldots, a_n) - (1+r) M_{i,n-1}(a_1, \ldots, a_{n-1}) - \epsilon + \tau_i]\}$.

(22) implies that

$$q_n(a_1, \ldots, a_n) \cdot Z_n(q; a_1, \ldots, a_n) = 0,$$

$$\text{for } q \in \Delta \text{ and for all } n \text{ and } a_1, \ldots, a_n.$$

This is the version of Walras' law appropriate for the price space Δ. Hence, by a slight extension of the standard fixed point argument, there is $q \in \Delta$ such that $Z(q) \leqq 0$. Let $\xi_i^T(q) = (x_i, M_i)$, for $i=1, \ldots, I$. (The standard fixed point argument may be found in Debreu 1959, p. 82, or in Arrow and Hahn 1971, p. 28. My proof is much like that in Hahn 1971b.) I call $[q, (x_i), (M_i)]$ an ϵ-modified equilibrium.

I now let ϵ_k, $k = 1, 2,$ be a sequence of positive numbers converging to zero. For each k, let $[q^k, (x_i^k), (M_i^k)]$ be an ϵ_k-modified equilibrium. By passing to a subsequence, I may assume that $\lim_{k\to\infty} [q^k, (x_i^k), (M_i^k)] = [q, (x_i), (M_i)]$. I will show that $q >> 0$. Let $p = [p_n(a_1, \ldots, a_n)]$ be defined by

$$(23) \qquad p_n(a_1, \ldots, a_n) = q_{n,L+1}^{-1}(a_1, \ldots, a_n) \\ [q_{n1}(a_1, \ldots, a_n), \ldots, q_{nL}(a_1, \ldots, a_n)].$$

It will be seen that $[p, (x_i)]$ is an N-period monetary equilibrium.

Before proving that $q >> 0$, I collect some facts.

First,

$$\begin{aligned}(24) \qquad & \sum_{i=1}^{I} [x_{in}(a_1, \ldots, a_n) - \omega_i(a_n)] \leqq 0 \text{ and} \\ & \sum_{i=1}^{I} [M_{in}(a_1, \ldots, a_n) - (1+r) M_{i,n-1}(a_1, \ldots, a_{n-1}) + \tau_i] \leqq 0, \\ & \text{for all } n \text{ and } a_1, \ldots, a_n\end{aligned}$$

It follows from (24) that $\Sigma_{i=1}^I M_{in}(a_1, \ldots, a_n) \leqq 1$, for all n and $a_1, \ldots, a_n$. It is easy to see that $\Sigma_{i=1}^I M_{in}^k(a_1, \ldots, a_n) \geqq 1$, for all k, n, and $a_1, \ldots, a_n$. Hence, $\Sigma_{i=1}^I M_{in}(a_1, \ldots, a_n) \geqq 1$. In conclusion,

$$(25) \qquad \sum_{i=1}^{I} M_{in}(a_1, \ldots, a_n) = 1, \text{ for all } n \text{ and } a_1, \ldots, a_n.$$

Next I observe that

$$(26) \qquad q_n(a_1, \ldots, a_n) \cdot \left\{ \sum_{i=1}^{N} [x_{in}(a_1, \ldots, a_n) - \omega_i(a_n)], \right.$$

$$\left. \sum_{i=1}^{I} [M_{in}(a_1, \ldots, a_n) - (1+r) M_{i,n-1}(a_1, \ldots, a_{n-1}) + \tau_i] \right\} \leqq 0,$$

for all n and $a_1, \ldots, a_n$.

I now prove that $q_n(a_1, \ldots, a_n) >> 0$, for all n and $a_1, \ldots, a_n$. The proof is by backwards induction n.

Let $n = N$, and fix $a_1, \ldots, a_N$. I first show that $q_{N,L+1}(a_1, \ldots, a_N) > 0$. Suppose that $q_{N,L+1}(a_1, \ldots, a_n) = 0$. Then $q_{Nk}(a_1, \ldots, a_N) > 0$, for some $k \leqq L$. There is some i such that $\omega_{ik}(a_N) > 0$ (by Assumption 4). Then $q_N(a_1, \ldots, a_N) \cdot [\omega_i(a_N), (1+r) M_{i,N-1}(a_1, \ldots, a_{N-1}) - \tau_i] > 0$. It follows easily that

$$(27) \qquad [x_{iN}(a_1, \ldots, a_N), M_{iN}(a_1, \ldots, a_N)] \text{ solves the problem}$$

$$\max[u_i(x, a_N) + M \mid q_N(a_1, \ldots, a_N) \cdot (x, M) \leqq q_N(a_1, \ldots, a_N)$$

$$\cdot [\omega_i(a_N), (1+r) M_{i,N-1}(a_1, \ldots, a_{N-1}) - \tau_i]$$

$$\text{and } 0 \leqq x \leqq \bar{\omega} \text{ and } 0 \leqq M \leqq 2].$$

Since $q_{N,L+1}(a_1, \ldots, a_N) = 0$, it follows that $M_{iN}(a_1, \ldots, a_N) = 2$. This contradicts (25). Hence, $q_{N,L+1}(a_1, \ldots, a_N) > 0$.

By (25), $M_{iN}(a_1, \ldots, a_n) > 0$, for some i. For this i, (27) is true. It follows at once from the monotonicity of u_i that if $q_{Nk}(a_1, \ldots, a_N) = 0$, then $x_{iNk}(a_1, \ldots, a_N) = \bar{\omega}_k > \Sigma_{j=1}^{I} \omega_{jk}(a_N)$. This contradicts (24). Hence, $q_N(a_1, \ldots, a_N) >> 0$.

Now suppose by induction that $q_{n+k}(a_1, \ldots, a_{n+k}) >> 0$, for all histories $a_1, \ldots, a_{n+k}$, and for $k = 1, \ldots, N-n$. It follows easily that for each i and $a_1, \ldots, a_n$, x_i solves the problem $\max \big(E\{ \Sigma_{k=1}^{N-n} \delta_i^{n+k-1} u_i [\hat{x}_{n+k}(s_1, \ldots, s_{n+k}), s_{n+k}] + \delta_i^{N-1} \hat{M}_N(s_1, \ldots, s_N) \mid s_n = a_n\} \mid (\hat{x}, \hat{M}) \in \beta_i^T(q, 0)$ and $\hat{M}_n(a_1, \ldots, a_n) = M_{in}(a_1, \ldots, a_n)\big)$. That is, x_i solves the maximization problem for periods $n+1$ and beyond. It follows that money is useful in period n, and hence, I may repeat the argument just made in order to prove that $q_n(a_1, \ldots, a_n) >> 0$, for all $a_1, \ldots, a_n$. This completes the proof that $q >> 0$.

I must now show that $[p, (x_i)]$ is an N-period monetary equilibrium, where p is defined by (23). It follows from what has been said that $x_i = \xi_i^N(p)$. The feasibility of (x_i) follows from (24), (26), and the fact that $q >> 0$. Clearly, $p >> 0$, so that $[p, (x_i)]$ satisfies conditions (19)–(21) of the definition of any N-period monetary equilibrium.

Q.E.D.

Remark. The proof of Lemma 4 made no use of Assumptions 1–3, 8, or 9. The proof applies even if the utility functions are only continuous, strictly concave, and strictly monotone.

7.2. *Boundedness From Above*

I next prove that prices in N-period monetary equilibria are uniformly bounded from above. It now becomes important to keep track of marginal utilities of money. If $[p, (x_i)]$ is an N-period equilibrium, the marginal utility of money of consumer i associated with $[p, (x_i)]$ is a vector $\lambda_i = [\lambda_{in}(a_1, \ldots, a_n)]$. Similarly, let $\alpha_i = [\alpha_{in}(a_1, \ldots, a_n)]$ be the vector of marginal utilities of expenditure of consumer i associated with $[p, (x_i)]$. $\alpha_{in}(a_1, \ldots, a_n)$ is defined by (7). λ_i satisfies (28)–(30) below, for all histories $a_1, \ldots, a_n$ and for $n = 1, \ldots, N$:

(28) $\lambda_{iN}(a_1, \ldots, a_N) = \max[\alpha_{iN}(a_1, \ldots, a_N), 1]$. If $n < N$, then

$$\lambda_{in}(a_1, \ldots, a_n) = \max\{\alpha_{in}(a_1, \ldots, a_n), \delta_i(1+r) E[\lambda_{i,n+1}(a_1, \ldots, a_n, s_{n+1}) \mid s_n = a_n]\}.$$

(29) $\lambda_{iN}(a_1, \ldots, a_N) > 1$ only if $M_{iN}(p, x_i; a_1, \ldots, a_N) = 0$. If $n < N$, then

$$\lambda_{in}(a_1, \ldots, a_n) > \delta_i(1+r) E[\lambda_{i,n+1}(a_1, \ldots, a_n, s_{n+1}) \mid s_n = a_n]$$

only if $M_{in}(p, x_i; a_1, \ldots, a_n) = 0$.

(30) For all n, $\lambda_{in}(a_1, \ldots, a_n) > \alpha_{in}(a_1, \ldots, a_n)$ only if $x_{in}(a_1, \ldots, a_n) = 0$.

This subsection is devoted to the proof of the following.

LEMMA 5. *There exist $\bar{p} \in R^L_+$, $\underline{\lambda} > 0$, and $\underline{\delta}$ such that $0 < \underline{\delta} < (1+r)^{-1}$ and the following are true. Let $[p, (x_i)]$ be any N-period monetary equilibrium, and let (λ_i) be the associated vector of marginal utilities of money. If $\delta_i \geqq \underline{\delta}$, for all i, then $p_n(a_1, \ldots, a_n) \leqq \bar{p}$ and $\lambda_{in}(a_1, \ldots, a_n) \geqq \underline{\lambda}$, for all i, all n, and all histories $a_1, \ldots, a_n$.*

In order to prove this lemma, I need some preliminary lemmas, which exploit Assumptions 4 and 9. The economies $\mathcal{E}(a)$ appearing in the next lemma were defined at the beginning of section 6. γ is as in Assumptions 8 and 9.

LEMMA 6. *Let $[q, (y_i)]$ be a Walrasian equilibrium for $\mathcal{E}(a)$, for any $a \in A$, and let (α_i) be the associated vector of marginal utilities of expenditure, defined by (17). If i and a are such that $\omega_{ik}(a) \leqq \gamma$, for all k, then $\alpha_i > \max\{\alpha_j \mid j$ is such that $q \cdot y_j \geqq \sum_{k=1}^L q_k\}$.*

Remark. There exists j such that $q \cdot y_j > \sum_{k=1}^L q_k$, for by Assumption 4, $q \cdot \sum_{j=1}^I y_j \geqq q \cdot \sum_{i=1}^I \omega_i(a) \geqq I \sum_{k=1}^L q_k$.

In order to prove the above lemma, I make use of the following fact.

(31) For each i and a, $u_i(x, a) \geqq u_i[(1, \ldots, 1), a]$ implies that $\partial u_i(x, a) / \partial x_k < Q_k$, for some k such that $x_k > 0$. Here, $Q = (Q_1, \ldots, Q_k)$ is as in Assumption 9.

This fact follows from Assumption 9 and from the concavity of $u_i(x, a)$.

Proof of Lemma 6. By assumption, $\omega_{ik}(a) \leqq \gamma$, for all k. It follows that $\underline{q}_k y_{ik} \leqq (\min_j \alpha_j) q_k y_{ik} \leqq (\min_j \alpha_j) q \cdot y_i = (\min_j \alpha_j) q \cdot \omega_i(a) \leqq \bar{q} \cdot \omega_i(a) \leqq \gamma \sum_{m=1}^L \bar{q}_m$, for all k. Here, I have made use of Lemma 1. In summary, $y_{ik} \leqq \gamma \underline{q}_k^{-1} \sum_{m=1}^L \bar{q}_m$, for all k. Therefore, by Assumption 9,

$$(32) \qquad \frac{\partial u_i\,(y_i, a)}{\partial x_k} > Q_k, \text{ for all } k.$$

Let j be such that $q \cdot y_j \geqq \Sigma_{m=1}^{L} q_m = q \cdot (1,\ldots,1)$. Then $u_j\,(y_j, a) \geqq u_j\,[(1,\ldots,1), a]$, so that by (31)

$$(33) \qquad Q_k > \frac{\partial u_j\,(y_j, a)}{\partial x_k}, \text{ for some } k \text{ such that } y_{jk} > 0.$$

By the definition of α_i and α_j [see (17)],

$$(34) \qquad \alpha_i\, q_k \geqq \frac{\partial u_i\,(y_i, a)}{\partial x_k} \text{ and } \frac{\partial u_j\,(y_j, a)}{\partial x_k} = \alpha_j\, q_k,$$

where k is as in (33).

Putting (32)–(34) together, it follows that $\alpha_i > \alpha_j$. This proves the lemma.

Q.E.D.

The next lemma says that Lemma 6 holds uniformly.

LEMMA 7. *There exists $\epsilon > 0$ such that the following is true. Let $[q,(y_i)]$ be any equilibrium with transfer payments for $\mathcal{E}\,(a)$, where $a \in A$. Let (α_i) be the vector of associated marginal utilities of expenditure. Suppose that $\mid q \cdot [y_i - \omega_i(a)] \mid \leqq \epsilon\, max_j\, \alpha_j^{-1}$, for all i. Then $\alpha_i \geqq (1+\epsilon)\, max\{\alpha_j \mid j$ is such that $q \cdot y_j \geqq \Sigma_{k=1}^{L} q_k\}$, for any i such that $\omega_{ik}(a) \leqq \gamma$, for all k.*

Proof. If ϵ did not exist, then for some $a \in A$, there would exist a sequence $[q^k, (y_i^k)]$, $k = 1, 2, \ldots,$ of equilibria with transfer payments for $\mathcal{E}\,(a)$, such that

$$(35) \qquad \mid q^k \cdot [\omega_i(a) - y_i^k] \mid \; \leqq k^{-1} \max_j(\alpha_j^k)^{-1}, \text{ for all } i, \text{ and}$$

$$(36) \qquad \alpha_i^k < (1+k^{-1})\alpha_j, \text{ where } q^k \cdot y_j^k \geqq \sum_{n=1}^{L} q_n^k \text{ and } \omega_{ik}(a) \leqq \gamma, \text{ for all } k.$$

Here, (α_i^k) is the vector of marginal utilities of expenditure associated with $[q^k, (y_i^k)]$.

I now apply a compactness argument. Without loss of generality, I may assume that $\min_j \alpha_j^k = 1$, for I may replace q^k by $(\min_j \alpha_j^k) q^k$. Since $\min_j \alpha_j^k = 1$, Lemma 1 implies that $\underline{q} << q^k << \overline{q}$, for all k. The set of feasible allocations for $\mathcal{E}\,(a)$ is compact. Hence, I may choose a convergent subsequence of equilibria. The limit $[q,(y_i)]$ is an equilibrium for $\mathcal{E}\,(a)$ with transfer payments. The corresponding subsequence of (α_i^k) converges to (α_i), where (α_i) is the vector of marginal utilities of expenditure associated with $[q,(y_i)]$. Passing to the limit in (35), I obtain $q \cdot [\omega_i(a) - y_i] = 0$, so that $[q,(y_i)]$ is a Walrasian equilibrium for $\mathcal{E}\,(a)$. Passing to the limit in (36), I obtain $\alpha_i \leqq \alpha_j$, where $q \cdot y_j \geqq \Sigma_{n=1}^{L} q_n$ and $\omega_{ik} \leqq \gamma$, for all k. This contradicts Lemma 6.

Q.E.D.

Proof of Lemma 5. It is sufficient to prove that there exist $\underline{\delta}$ and $\underline{\lambda}$ as in the lemma. For by Lemma 3, I may let $\overline{p} = b\underline{\lambda}^{-1}\overline{q}$.

Let $\underline{\delta} = (1+\epsilon^2)^{-1}(1+r)^{-1}$, and let $\underline{\lambda} = \epsilon(1+\epsilon)^{-1}$, where $\epsilon > 0$ is so small that it satisfies the conditions of Lemma 7 and

(37) $\epsilon \leqq \min\{P_{ab} \mid a,b \in A \text{ and } P_{ab} > 0\}$.

(P_{ab} is the probability of transition from a to b.)

I now prove that $\underline{\delta}$ and $\underline{\lambda}$ satisfy the conditions of Lemma 5. Assume that $(1+r) > \delta_i \geqq \underline{\lambda}$, for all i. I must prove the following.

(38) $\lambda_{in}(a_1, \ldots, a_n) \geqq \underline{\lambda}$, for all i, for all histories $a_1, \ldots, a_n$ and for $n = 1, \ldots, N$.

I prove (38) by backwards induction on n. Clearly, (38) is true for $n = N$, for $\lambda_{iN}(a_1, \ldots, a_N) \geqq 1 > \underline{\lambda}$.

Suppose that (38) is true for $n+1$. First I claim that

(39) for any history $a_1, \ldots, a_{n+1}$, $\lambda_{i,n+1}(a_1, \ldots, a_{n+1}) \geqq (1+\epsilon)\underline{\lambda}$, whenever $\omega_{ik}(a_{n+1}) \leqq \gamma$, for all k.

For suppose that $\omega_{ik}(a_{n+1}) \leqq \gamma$, for all k, and that $\lambda_{i,n+1}(a_1, \ldots, a_{n+1}) < (1+\epsilon)\underline{\lambda}$. Without loss of generality, I may assume that $i = 1$.

Observe that $\{p_{n+1}(a_1, \ldots, a_{n+1}), [x_{i,n+1}(a_1, \ldots, a_{n+1})]\}$ forms an equilibrium with transfer payments for $\mathcal{E}(a_n)$. These transfer payments are made with money. Since there is only one unit of money in the economy, $| p_{n+1}(a_1, \ldots, a_{n+1})\cdot[x_{i,n+1}(a_1, \ldots, a_{n+1}) - \omega_i(a_{n+1})| \leqq 1 = \epsilon[(1+\epsilon)\underline{\lambda}]^{-1} < \epsilon[\lambda_{1,n+1}(a_1, \ldots, a_{n+1})]^{-1}$. Now by (28), $\lambda_{i,n+1}(a_1, \ldots, a_{n+1}) \geqq \alpha_{i,n+1}(a_1, \ldots, a_{n+1})$, for all i, so that $| p_{n+1}(a_1, \ldots, a_{n+1})\cdot[x_{i,n+1}(a_1, \ldots, a_{n+1}) - \omega_i(a_{n+1})] | \leqq \epsilon \max_i[\alpha_{i,n+1}(a_1, \ldots, a_{n+1})]^{-1}$. Therefore, by Lemma 7,

$$\alpha_{1,n+1}(a_1, \ldots, a_{n+1}) \geqq (1+\epsilon)\alpha_{i,n+1}(a_1, \ldots, a_{n+1}),$$

where i is such that

$$p_{n+1}(a_1, \ldots, a_{n+1})\cdot x_{i,n+1}(a_1, \ldots, a_{n+1}) \geqq \sum_{k=1}^{L} p_{n+1,k}(a_1, \ldots, a_n) > 0.$$

Since $x_{i,n+1}(a_1, \ldots, a_{n+1}) > 0$, $\alpha_{i,n+1}(a_1, \ldots, a_{n+1}) = \lambda_{i,n+1}(a_1, \ldots, a_{n+1})$. Therefore, $\lambda_{1,n+1}(a_1, \ldots, a_{n+1}) \geqq \alpha_{1,n+1}(a_1, \ldots, a_{n+1}) \geqq (1+\epsilon)\lambda_{i,n+1}(a_1, \ldots, a_{n+1}) \geqq (1+\epsilon)\underline{\lambda}$, where the last inequality follows from the induction hypothesis. This contradicts the hypothesis about $\lambda_{1,n+1}(a_1, \ldots, a_{n+1})$ and so proves (39).

I now prove that $\lambda_{in}(a_1, \ldots, a_n) \geqq \underline{\lambda}$, for all i and $a_1, \ldots, a_n$. By Assumption 8 and by condition (37) on ϵ, $\text{Prob}[\omega_{ik}(s_{n+1}) \leqq \gamma, \text{ for all } k \mid s_n = a_n] \geqq \epsilon$. Therefore, by the induction hypothesis and by (28) and (39), $\lambda_{in}(a_1, \ldots, a_n) \geqq \delta_i(1+r)E[\lambda_{i,n+1}(a_1, \ldots, a_n, s_{n+1}) \mid s_n = a_n] > \underline{\delta}(1+r)[(1-\epsilon)\underline{\lambda} + \epsilon(1+\epsilon)\underline{\lambda}] = \underline{\lambda}$. This completes the induction step in the proof of (38) and hence proves the lemma.

Q.E.D.

7.3. *Boundedness From Below*

The next lemma asserts that prices in N-period monetary equilibrium are uniformly bounded away from zero.

LEMMA 8. *If* $\delta_i < (1+r)^{-1}$, *for all i, then there exist* $\underline{p} \in R_+^L$ *and* $\overline{\lambda} > 0$ *such that* $\underline{p} >> 0$ *and the following are true. If* $[p,(x_i)]$ *is an N-period monetary equi-*

librium and (λ_i) *is the associated vector of marginal utilities of money, then* $p_n(a_1, \ldots, a_n) \geqq \underline{p}$ *and* $\lambda_{in}(a_1, \ldots, a_n) \leqq \bar{\lambda}$, *for all histories* $a_1, \ldots, a_n$ *and for all* n.

Proof. It is sufficient to find $\bar{\lambda}$ as in the lemma, for by Lemma 3, I may let $\underline{p} = \bar{\lambda}^{-1}\underline{q}$.

I prove the lemma only for the case $r > 0$, since the proof for the case $r = 0$ is similar and slightly easier. Let

$$\bar{\lambda} = b + b^2(\bar{q} \cdot \bar{\omega}\left[\sum_{k=1}^{K}(1+r)^{k-1}\right]r(\max_i \tau_i^{-1}) \tag{40}$$

where $b = \max_k \underline{q}_k^{-1}\bar{q}_k$ and $\bar{\omega}$, $\underline{q}$, and $\bar{q}$ are as in (11). Here K is a positive integer such that

$$\min_i[\delta_i(1+r)]^{-K}b^{-1} > 1. \tag{41}$$

Notice that by Assumption 7, $\tau_i > 0$, for all i, so that $\bar{\lambda} < \infty$.

It is sufficient to prove the following:

(42) $\lambda_{in}(a_1, \ldots, a_n) \leqq \bar{\lambda}$, for all i, for all histories $a_1, \ldots, a_n$ and for $n = 1, \ldots, N$.

I prove (42) by backwards induction on n. First, (42) is true if $n = N$. To see that this is so, fix $a_1, \ldots, a_N$ and let i be such that $M_{iN}(p, x_i; a_1, \ldots, a_N) > 0$. Then by (29), $\lambda_{iN}(a_1, \ldots, a_N) = 1$. Also, $\alpha_{iN}(a_1, \ldots, a_N) \leqq \lambda_{iN}(a_1, \ldots, a_N) = 1$. Hence, by Lemma 2, $\alpha_{jN}(a_1, \ldots, a_N) \leqq b$, for all j. But then by (28), $\lambda_{jN}(a_1, \ldots, a_N) \leqq \max(b, 1) = b$, for all j. Finally, by (40), $b \leqq \bar{\lambda}$. This proves (42) for $n = N$.

Suppose by induction that (42) is true for $n+1, \ldots, N$ and that for some i and $a_1, \ldots, a_n$, $\lambda_{in}(a_1, \ldots, a_n) > \bar{\lambda}$. Without loss of generality, I may assume that $i = 1$, so that

$$\lambda_{1n}(a_1, \ldots, a_n) > \bar{\lambda}. \tag{43}$$

I will prove that (43) implies the following.

(44) There exist i and a history $a_{n+1}, \ldots, a_{n+T}$ following a_n such that $\lambda_{i,n+t}(a_1, \ldots, a_{n+t}) \geqq [\delta_i(1+r)^{-t}b^{-1}\bar{\lambda}$ and $M_{i,n+t}(p, x_i; a_1, \ldots, a_{n+t}) \geqq r^{-1}\tau_i - \bar{\lambda}^{-1}b^2(\bar{q} \cdot \bar{\omega})[\sum_{k=1}^{t}(1+r)^{k-1}]$, for $t = 0, \ldots, T$, where $T = \min(K, N-n)$.

(44) leads to a contradiction. First suppose that $T = N - n$. Then (40) and (44) imply that $M_{iN}(p, x_i; a_1, \ldots, a_N) > 0$. But then $\lambda_{iN}(a_1, \ldots, a_N) = 1$. However, by (40) and (44), $\lambda_{iN}(a_1, \ldots, a_N) \geqq [\delta_i(1+r)]^{n-N}b^{-1}\bar{\lambda} \geqq b^{-1}\bar{\lambda} > 1$, which is a contradiction.

Suppose that $T = K$. Then (41) and (44) imply that $\lambda_{i,n+K}(a_1, \ldots, a_{n+K}) \geqq [\delta_i(1+r)]^{-K}b^{-1}\,\bar{\lambda} > \bar{\lambda}$, which contradicts the induction hypothesis. This proves that (44) leads to a contradiction and hence that (43) is impossible. Hence, the induction step in the proof of (42) will be completed once (44) is proved.

I now prove (44). Let i be such that $rM_{i,n}(p, x_i; a_1, \ldots, a_n) \geqq \tau_i$, where a_1,

$\ldots, a_n$ are as in (43). Such an i exists by Assumption 7.

I first show that $\lambda_{in}(a_1, \ldots, a_n) \geqq b^{-1}\bar{\lambda}$. Observe that $\bar{\lambda} < \lambda_{1n}(a_1, \ldots, a_n) = \max\{\alpha_{1n}(a_1, \ldots, a_n), \delta_1(1+r)E[\lambda_{1,n+1}(a_1, \ldots, a_n, s_{n+1}) \mid s_n = a_n]\} \leqq \max[\alpha_{1n}(a_1, \ldots, a_n), \delta_1(1+r)\bar{\lambda}] = \alpha_{1n}(a_1, \ldots, a_n)$. The second inequality follows from the induction hypothesis on n [regarding (42)]. Hence, by Lemma 2, $\lambda_{in}(a_1, \ldots, a_n) \geqq \alpha_{in}(a_1, \ldots, a_n) \geqq b^{-1}\alpha_{1n}(a_1, \ldots, a_n) > b^{-1}\bar{\lambda}$. I have now proved that i exists such that the inequalities of (44) are satisfied for $t = 0$.

I now prove by induction on t that $a_{n+1}, \ldots, a_{n+T}$ exist as in (44). Suppose that the conditions of (44) are satisfied for t no larger than some nonnegative integer; call it t again. I may suppose that $t < T$. Then, $M_{i,n+t}(p, x_i; a_1, \ldots, a_{n+t}) \geqq r^{-1}\tau_i - \bar{\lambda}^{-1}b^2(\bar{q}\cdot\bar{\omega})\,[\Sigma_{k=1}^{t}(1+r)^{k-1}] > 0$. The last inequality follows from (40). Hence, by (29), $\lambda_{i,n+t}(a_1, \ldots, a_{n+t}) = \delta_i(1+r)E[\lambda_{i,n+t+1}(a_1, \ldots, a_{n+t}, s_{n+t+1}) \mid s_{n+t} = a_{n+t}]$, so that for some a_{n+t+1}, $\lambda_{i,n+t+1}(a_1, \ldots, a_{n+t+1}) \geqq [\delta_i(1+r)]^{-1}\lambda_{i,n+t}(a_1, \ldots, a_{n+t}) \geqq [\delta_i(1+r)]^{-(t+1)}b^{-1}\bar{\lambda}$. The last inequality follows from the induction hypothesis on t.

I now show that $M_{i,n+t+1}(p, x_i; a_1, \ldots, a_{n+t+1}) \geqq r^{-1}\tau_i - \bar{\lambda}^{-1}b^2(q\cdot\bar{\omega})\,[\Sigma_{k=1}^{t+1}(1+r)^{k-1}]$. If $\alpha_{i,n+t+1}(a_1, \ldots, a_{n+t+1}) < \lambda_{i,n+t+1}(a_1, \ldots, a_{n+t+1})$, then by (30) $x_{i,n+t+1}(a_1, \ldots, a_{n+t+1}) = 0$, so that $M_{i,n+t+1}(p, x_i; a_1, \ldots, a_{n+t+1}) \geqq (1+r)M_{i,n+t}(p, x_i; a_1, \ldots, a_{n+t}) - \tau_i \geqq (1+r)\,\{r^{-1}\tau_i - \bar{\lambda}^{-1}b^2\,(q\cdot\bar{\omega})\,[\Sigma_{k=1}^{t}(1+r)^{k-1}]\} - \tau_i \geqq r^{-1}\tau_i - \bar{\lambda}^{-1}b^2(q\cdot\bar{\omega})\,[\Sigma_{k=1}^{t+1}(1+r)^{k-1}]$. The third inequality follows from the induction hypothesis on t.

Suppose now that $\alpha_{i,n+t+1}(a_1, \ldots, a_{n+t+1}) = \lambda_{i,n+t+1}(a_1, \ldots, a_{n+t+1})$. Then by the choice of a_{n+t+1}, $\alpha_{i,n+t+1}(a_1, \ldots, a_{n+t+1}) > b^{-1}\bar{\lambda}$. It follows from Lemma 2 that $\min_j \alpha_{j,n+t+1}(a_1, \ldots, a_{n+t+1}) > b^{-2}\bar{\lambda}$, so that by Lemma 1, $p_{n+t+1}(a_1, \ldots, a_{n+t+1}) \leqq b^2\bar{\lambda}^{-1}\bar{q}$. Hence, $p_{n+t+1}(a_1, \ldots, a_{n+t})\cdot x_{i,n+t+1}(a_1, \ldots, a_{n+t+1}) \leqq b^2\bar{\lambda}^{-1}\,(\bar{q}\cdot\bar{\omega})$. It follows that $M_{i,n+t+2}(p, x_i; a_1, \ldots, a_{n+t+1}) \geqq (1+r)M_{i,n+t+1}(p, x_i; a_1, \ldots, a_{n+t+1}) - \tau_i - b^2\bar{\lambda}^{-1}(\bar{q}\cdot\bar{\omega}) \geqq (1+r)[r^{-1}\tau_i - \bar{\lambda}^{-1}b^2(\bar{q}\cdot\bar{\omega})\,\Sigma_{k=1}^{t}(1+r)^{k-1}] - \tau_i - b^2\bar{\lambda}^{-1}(\bar{q}\cdot\bar{\omega}) = r^{-1}\tau_i - \bar{\lambda}^{-1}\,b^2(\bar{q}\cdot\bar{\omega})\,\Sigma_{k=1}^{t+1}(1+r)^{k-1}$.

This completes the proof that the two inequalities of (44) are satisfied for $t+1$ and so completes the induction step in the proof of (44).

This completes the proof of Lemma 8.

7.4. *Passage to the Limit*

I now apply a Cantor diagonal argument to the N-period equilibria in order to obtain a monetary equilibrium in the limit.

Let $\underline{\delta}$ be as in Lemma 5 and suppose that $\underline{\delta} < \delta_i < (1+r)^{-1}$, for all i. For each positive integer N, let $[p^N, (x_i^N)]$ be an N-period monetary equilibrium, and let (λ_i^N) be the vector of associated marginal utilities of money. By Lemmas 5 and 8, $\underline{p} \leqq p_n^N(a_1, \ldots, a_n) \leqq \bar{p}$ and $\underline{\lambda} \leqq \lambda_{in}^N(a_1, \ldots, a_n) \leqq \bar{\lambda}$, for all i, n, N, and $a_1, \ldots, a_n$. Similarly, $0 \leqq x_{in}^N(a_1, \ldots, a_n) \leqq \bar{\omega}$, for all i, n, N, and $a_1, \ldots, a_n$. Hence, the components of the vectors $[p^N, (x_i^N)]$ and (λ_i^N) are uniformly bounded. There are countably many of these components. There exists a subsequence of N such that one of those components converges. There exists a subsequence of this subsequence such that another component converges. Continuing in this way, I choose a sequence of subsequences, one for each component. Taking the kth member of the kth subsequence, I obtain a subsequence of N such that all components converge. Let $p = [p_n(a_1, \ldots, a_n)]$, $x_i = [x_{in}(a_1, \ldots, a_n)]$, and $\lambda_i = [\lambda_{in}(a_1, \ldots, a_n)]$ be the limits of this Cantor subsequence. I claim that $[p, (x_i)]$ is a monetary equilibrium with associated marginal utilities of money (λ_i).

Clearly, $\underline{p} \leqq p_n(a_1, \ldots, a_n) \leqq \bar{p}$, for all n and $a_1, \ldots, a_n$. Hence, condition

(5) of the definition of a monetary equilibrium is satisfied.

Since $\Sigma_{i=1}^{I}[x_{in}^{N}(a_1, \ldots, a_n) - \omega_i(a_n)] = 0$, the same is true in the limit, and so (x_i) is a feasible allocation. This is condition (4) of the definition of equilibrium.

I now show that $x_i \in \xi_i(p)$, for all i, and so verify the last condition, (6).

First, $M_{i,n}(p^N, x_i^N; a_1, \ldots, a_n) = (1+r)M_{i,n-1}(p^N, x_i^N; a_1, \ldots, a_{n-1}) - \tau_i + p_n^N(a_1, \ldots, a_n)\cdot[\omega_i(a_n) - x_{in}^N(a_1, \ldots, a_n)] \geqq 0$, for all N. Passing to the limit in these expressions and using the fact that M_{i0} is given, I obtain that $M_{in}(p, x_i; a_1, \ldots, a_n) \geqq 0$, for all i, n, and $a_1, \ldots, a_n$. Hence, x_i satisfies the constraints of the consumer maximization problem (3).

I now prove that $[p,(x_i)]$ and (λ_i) satisfy conditions (8)–(10), (13), and (14). First, it should be clear that $M_{in}(p,x_i;a_1,\ldots,a_n) \leqq \Sigma_{j=1}^{I} M_{jn}(p,x_j;a_1,\ldots,a_n) = 1$, for all i, n, and $a_1,\ldots,a_n$. This is condition (13). Condition (14) follows by passage to the limit in the inequalities $\underline{\lambda} \leqq \lambda_{in}^N(a_1,\ldots,a_n) \leqq \overline{\lambda}$. It remains to verify conditions (8)–(10). Let (α_i^N) be the vector of marginal utilities of expenditure associated with the N-period monetary equilibrium $[p^N, (x_i^N)]$. The convergence of the subsequence of $[p^N,(x_i^N)]$ implies that the corresponding subsequence of (α_i^N) converges to (α_i), where (α_i) is the vector of marginal utilities of expenditure associated with $[p,(x_i)]$. [The (α_i) are defined by (7).] $[p^N, (x_i^N)]$, (λ_i^N), and (α_i^N) together satisfy (28)–(30). Passage to the limit in these inequalities gives (8)–(10).

It now follows by definition that $x_i \in \xi_i(p)$ when $\delta_i = 1$. I must now show $x_i = \xi_i(p)$ when $\delta_i < 1$. If $x_i \neq \xi_i(p)$, then there exists $\bar{x} \in \beta_i(p)$ such that $E\{\Sigma_{n=1}^{\infty} \delta_i^{n-1} u_i[\bar{x}_n(s_1,\ldots,s_n),s_n]\} > E\{\Sigma_{n=1}^{\infty} \delta_i^{n-1} u_i[x_{in}(s_1,\ldots,s_n),s_n]\} + \epsilon$, where $\epsilon > 0$. Choose N such that $\delta_i^{N-1} < (2\overline{\lambda})^{-1}\epsilon$ and $E\{\Sigma_{n=N+1}^{\infty} \delta_i^{n-1} \mid u_i[\bar{x}_n(s_1,\ldots,s_n), s_n] \mid\} < \epsilon/4$ and $E\{\Sigma_{n=n+1}^{\infty} \delta_i^{n-1} \mid u_i[x_{in}(s_1,\ldots,s_n),s_n] \mid \} < \epsilon/4$. (It is easy to see that these series converge.) x_i solves the problem

$$(45) \qquad \max\left(E\left\{\sum_{n=1}^{N} \delta_i^{n-1}u_i[x_n(s_1,\ldots,s_n),s_n] + \delta_i^{N-1}\lambda_{iN}(s_1,\ldots,s_n)M_{in}(p,x_i;s_1,\ldots,s_n)\right\}\middle|\; x \in \beta_i(p)\right)$$

since p, x_i, and λ_i satisfy (8)–(10). However, $E\{\Sigma_{n=1}^{N} \delta_i^{n-1}u_i[\bar{x}_n(s_1,\ldots,s_n),s_n] + \delta_i^{N-1}\lambda_{iN}(s_1,\ldots,s_N)M_{iN}(p,\bar{x};s_1,\ldots,s_n)\} \geqq E\{\Sigma_{n=1}^{\infty} \delta_i^{n-1}u_i[\bar{x}_n(s_1,\ldots,s_n),s_n]\} - \epsilon/4 > E\{\Sigma_{n=1}^{\infty} \delta_i^{n-1}u_i[x_n(s_1,\ldots,s_n),s_n]\} + 3\,\epsilon/4 > E\{\Sigma_{n=1}^{N} \delta_i^{n-1}u_i[x_n(s_1,\ldots,s_n),s_n] + \delta_i^{N-1}\lambda_{iN}(s_1,\ldots,s_n) M_{iN}(p,x_i;s_1,\ldots,s_N)\}$. The last inequality follows from the fact that $E[\delta_i^{N-1}\lambda_{iN}(s_1,\ldots,s_N) M_{iN}(p,x_i; s_1,\ldots,s_N)] < \delta_i^{N-1}\overline{\lambda} < \epsilon/2$. Hence, I have contradicted the fact that x_i solves the problem (45). This proves that $x_i = \xi_i(p)$.

I have now completed the verification of condition (6) and so have proved Theorem 1.

Q.E.D.

8. Proof of Theorem 2

First I observe that

$$(46) \qquad \lambda_{in}(a_1, \ldots, a_n) = \alpha_{in}(a_1, \ldots, a_n), \text{ for all } i,\ n, \text{ and } a_1, \ldots, a_n$$

where (α_i) is the vector of marginal utilities of expenditure associated with the monetary equilibrium $[p, (x_i)]$. (46) follows from (8), (10), and the assumption that $x_{in}(a_1, \ldots, a_n) \neq 0$, for all i, n, and $a_1, \ldots, a_n$.

Next I observe that if the allocation (x_i) is Pareto optimal, then

$$\lambda_{in}(a_1, \ldots, a_n) = \delta_i (1+r) E[\lambda_{i,n+1}(a_1, \ldots, a_n, s_{n+1}) \mid s_n = a_n], \tag{47}$$

for all i, n, and $a_1, \ldots, a_n$

where (λ_i) is the vector of marginal utilities of money associated with the monetary equilibrium $[p, (x_i)]$.

By (8), the left-hand side of (47) is at least as great as the right-hand side. Suppose that for some i, n, and $a_1, \ldots, a_n$, $\lambda_{in}(a_1, \ldots, a_n) > \delta_i (1+r) E[\lambda_{i,n+1}(a_1, \ldots, a_n, s_{n+1}) \mid s_n = a_n]$. Then by (9), $M_{in}(a_1, \ldots, a_n) = 0$, so that for some $j \neq i$, $M_{jn}(a_1, \ldots, a_n) > 0$. Again by (9), $\lambda_{jn}(a_1, \ldots, a_n) = \delta_j (1+r) E[\lambda_{j,n+1}(a_1, \ldots, a_n, s_{n+1}) \mid s_n = a_n]$. Now I use (46) and find that $\alpha_{in}(a_1, \ldots, a_n) > \delta_i (1+r) E[\alpha_{i,n+1}(a_1, \ldots, a_n, s_{n+1}) \mid s_n = a_n]$ and $\alpha_{jn}(a_1, \ldots, a_n) = \delta_j (1+r) E[\alpha_{j,n+1}(a_1, \ldots, a_n, s_{n+1}) \mid s_n = a_n]$. A standard argument now shows that a Pareto improvement could be made. Roughly speaking, consumer i should spend ϵ units of money more in period n (and when history $a_1, \ldots, a_n$ occurs), where $\epsilon > 0$ is very small. And consumer i should spend $(1 + r)\,\epsilon$ units less in the next period. Consumer j should spend ϵ less units of money in period n and $(1 + r)\,\epsilon$ more in the following period. Thus, I have contradicted the assumption that (x_i) is Pareto optimal. This proves (47).

It follows from (47) that for each n and each history $a_1, \ldots, a_n$ there exists a_{n+1} following a_n such that $\lambda_{1,n+1}(a_1, \ldots, a_{n+1}) \geqq [\delta_1 (1 + r)]^{-1} \lambda_{1n}(a_1, \ldots, a_n)$. Hence, there exists an infinite sequence $a_1, a_2, \ldots$, such that $\lambda_{1n}(a_1, \ldots, a_n) \geqq [\delta_1 (1 + r)]^{-n+1} \lambda_{11}(a_1) > 0$. Since $\delta_1 (1 + r) < 1$, it follows that $\lim_{n\to\infty} \lambda_{1n}(a_1, \ldots, a_n) = \infty$. This contradicts (12), so that (x_i) cannot be Pareto optimal.

Q.E.D.

9. A Lemma

In this section I prove a lemma which is in turn used in the next section to prove Theorem 3. The statement of this lemma involves the concept of *stationary equilibrium with transfer payments*. Such an equilibrium is of the form $[p, (x_i)]$, where p is a stationary price system and (x_i) is a stationary allocation. Each x_i must solve the problem

$$\max\left\{ \sum_{a\in A} \pi_a u_i[y(a), a] \;\middle|\; y : A \to R_+^L \text{ and } \sum_{a\in A} \pi_a p(a)\cdot[y(a) - x_i(a)] \leqq 0 \right\} \tag{48}$$

where (π_a) is the stationary distribution on A. The transfer payment of consumer i is $\Sigma_{a\in A} \pi_a p(a)\cdot[\omega_i(a) - x_i(a)]$.

Given a stationary equilibrium with transfer payments $[p, (x_i)]$, money holdings are defined as before. That is, $M_{in}(p, x_i; a_1, \ldots, a_n) = (1 + r) M_{i,n-1}(p, x_i; a_1, \ldots, a_{n-1}) + p(a_n)\cdot[\omega_i(a_n) - x_i(a_n)] - \tau_i$. I now allow the initial holdings, M_{i0}, to be arbitrary, though I continue to assume that $\Sigma_{i=1}^I M_{i0} = 1$ and $\Sigma_{I=1}^I \tau_i = r$.

LEMMA 9. *For almost every $\omega \in \Omega$, the following is true. Let $[p, (x_i)]$ be any stationary equilibrium for $\mathcal{E}(\omega)$ with transfer payments. Then for any distribution of initial money balances and for any $a_1 \in A$, $M_{in}(p, x_i; a_1, \ldots, a_n) <$*

0, for some i and some history $a_2, \ldots, a_n$ following a_1.

The proof of this lemma involves the marginal utilities of money associated with a stationary equilibrium $[p, (x_i)]$. These are the Lagrange multipliers associated with the constrained maximization problems (48). The marginal utility of money of consumer i is a number λ_i.

Stationary equilibrium with transfer payments may be thought of as a function of the associated marginal utilities of money. This fact is expressed by the following lemma, which I do not prove here. Its proof is contained in Bewley 1977c.

LEMMA 10. *To each $(\lambda_i) >> 0$, there corresponds a unique stationary equilibrium with transfer payments such that (λ_i) is the corresponding vector of marginal utilities of money.*

The proof of Lemma 9 depends on the fact that the relation between stationary equilibrium and marginal utilities of money is nearly differentiable.

In order to express this fact, I drop $a \in A$ from the notation, for the moment. Let $u_i : R^L_+ \rightarrow (-\infty, \infty)$ satisfy Assumptions 5 and 6, for $i = 1, \ldots, I$. Given $\lambda > 0$ and $p \in R^L_+$ such that $p >> 0$, $X_i(p, \lambda)$ denotes the unique vector in R^L_+ which satisfies the following (if such a vector exists):

$$(49) \qquad \frac{\partial u_i [X_i(p, \lambda)]}{\partial z_k} \leqq \lambda p_k, \text{ for } k = 1, \ldots, L; \text{ with equality if } X_{ik}(p, \lambda) > 0.$$

$X_i(p, \lambda)$ is consumer i's demand as a function of prices and her or his marginal utility of money. $X_i(p, \lambda)$ may not be defined if some price is too low relative to λ. I let $G = \{(p, \Lambda) \in \text{int } R^L_+ \times \text{int } R^I_+ \mid X_i(p, \Lambda_i) \text{ is defined for all } i\}$. It is easy to see that G is an open set and that each of the functions X_i is continuous on G.

Now let $\omega \in R^L_+$ be such that $\omega >> 0$. Think of ω as the total initial endowment of the economy. Given $\Lambda = (\Lambda_1, \ldots, \Lambda_I) \in \text{int } R^I_+$, $P(\Lambda)$ denotes the unique vector $p \in \text{int } R^L_+$ such that $\Sigma^I_{i=1} X_i(p, \Lambda_i) = \omega$. $P(\Lambda)$ is a market-clearing price vector, given the demand functions $X_i(p, \lambda)$. Clearly, $P(\Lambda) >> 0$. I prove in Bewley 1977c that P is a continuous function.

Observe that $P(\Lambda)$ is homogeneous of degree minus one with respect to Λ. That is, $P(t\Lambda) = t^{-1} P(\Lambda)$, for all $t > 0$. Hence, I may restrict Λ to int $\Delta^{I-1} = \{\Lambda \in \text{int } R^I_+ \mid \Sigma^I_{i=1} \Lambda_i = 1\}$.

LEMMA 11. *int Δ^{I-1} is the union of finitely many sets, closed in int Δ^{I-1}, on each of which the function $P(\Lambda)$ is continuously differentiable. Similarly, G is the union of finitely many sets, closed in G, on each of which all of the functions $X_i(p, \Lambda_i)$ are continuously differentiable.*

Proof of Lemma 11. First I deal with the functions $X_i(p, \Lambda_i)$.

Let $\mathcal{S}$ be the set of all subsets of $\{1,\ldots,L\}$. For each $S \in \mathcal{S}$, let

$$C_{Si} = \left\{ (p, \lambda) \in G \;\middle|\; \frac{\partial u_i [X_i(p, \lambda)]}{\partial z_k} = \lambda p_k, \text{ for } k \in S, \right.$$
$$\left. \text{and } X_{ik}(p, \lambda) = 0, \text{ for } k \notin S \right\}.$$

Clearly, C_{Si} is closed in G and $G = \cup \{C_{Si} \mid S \in \mathcal{S}\}$. I show that X_i is continuously differentiable on each set C_{Si}.

Let $X_{Si}(p, \lambda)$ be the function defined by

$$(50) \qquad \frac{\partial u_i\,[X_{Si}(p, \lambda)]}{\partial z_k} = \lambda p_k, \text{ if } k \in S$$

$$X_{Sik}(p, \lambda) = 0, \text{ if } k \notin S.$$

Clearly, if $(p, \lambda) \in C_{Si}$, then $X_{Si}(p, \lambda)$ is well defined and equals $X_i(p, \lambda)$.

Recall that a function defined on a closed set $C \subset R^n$ is said to be differentiable if it has a differentiable extension $\hat{f}$ defined on an open neighborhood of C. Hence, I must show that X_{Si} has a continuously differentiable extension to an open neighborhood of C_{Si}.

Since $u_i : R^L_+ \to (-\infty, \infty)$ is continuously differentiable, it has a continuously differentiable extension $\hat{u}_i : V \to (-\infty, \infty)$, where V is an open neighborhood of R^L_+.

I now apply the implicit function theorem to the equation (50) with $\hat{u}_i$ substituted for u_i. By the implicit function theorem, X_{Si} is defined and differentiable on an open neighborhood of C_{Si} if the matrix of partial derivatives of the left-hand side of (50) with respect to the components of X_{Si} is invertible, these partial derivatives being evaluated at an arbitrary point $X_{Si}(p, \lambda)$ for $(p, \lambda) \in C_{Si}$. This matrix of partial derivatives is given here, where I have assumed that $S = \{1,\ldots,K\}$. u_i appears in the matrix rather than $\hat{u}_i$, for the derivatives are evaluated at a point in the domain of u_i.

$$(51) \qquad \begin{pmatrix}
\dfrac{\partial^2 u_i}{\partial z_1 \partial z_1} & \cdots & \dfrac{\partial^2 u_i}{\partial z_K \partial z_1} & \dfrac{\partial^2 u_i}{\partial z_{K+1} \partial z_1} & \cdots & \cdots & \dfrac{\partial^2 u_i}{\partial z_L \partial z_1} \\
\vdots & & \vdots & \vdots & & & \vdots \\
\dfrac{\partial^2 u_i}{\partial z_K \partial z_1} & \cdots & \dfrac{\partial^2 u_i}{\partial z_K \partial z_K} & \dfrac{\partial^2 u_i}{\partial z_{K+1} \partial z_K} & \cdots & \cdots & \dfrac{\partial^2 u_i}{\partial z_L \partial z_K} \\
0 & \cdots & 0 & 1 & 0 & \cdots & 0 \\
\vdots & & \vdots & 0 & 1 & \ddots & \vdots \\
\vdots & & \vdots & \vdots & \ddots & 1 & 0 \\
0 & \cdots & 0 & 0 & \cdots & 0 & 1
\end{pmatrix}$$

This matrix is invertible. For by Assumption 6 the matrix $D^2 u_i(x) = (\partial^2 u_i / \partial z_k\, \partial z_m)$ is negative definite. Hence, the submatrix in the upper left-hand corner of (51) is negative definite and so is invertible. It follows at once that the whole matrix is invertible. This completes the proof that X_i is differentiable on C_{Si}. Since the matrix (51) depends continuously on the components of X_{Si}, it follows that X_i is continuously differentiable on C_{Si}.

I now turn to the function $P(\Lambda)$. Let $\mathcal{S}^I = \{(S_1, \ldots, S_I) \mid S_i \in \mathcal{S}, \text{ for all } i\}$. If $S \in \mathcal{S}^I$, let $C_S = \{\Lambda \in \text{int } \Delta^{I-1} \mid [P(\Lambda), \Lambda_i] \in C_{S_i i}, \text{ for all } i\}$. Since P is a continuous function, C_S is closed in int Δ^{I-1}. Clearly, int $\Delta^{I-1} = \cup \{C_S \mid S \in \mathcal{S}^I\}$.

Now let $S \in \mathcal{S}^I$ be such that C_S is not empty. Recall that $P(\Lambda)$ satisfies the equation $\Sigma_{i=1}^I X_i [P(\Lambda), \Lambda_i] = \omega >> 0$. Essentially, what I do is to apply the implicit function theorem to this equation. In order to do so, I let $f_S(p, \Lambda) = \Sigma_{i=1}^I X_{S_i i}(p, \Lambda_i)$, where $X_{S_i i}$ is defined by (50) and S_i is the ith component of S. Let E be the matrix of partial derivatives of $f(p, \Lambda)$ with respect to the components of p, these derivatives being evaluated at $[P(\Lambda), \Lambda]$. I must show that E is invertible.

Let $D_p X_{S_i i} [P(\Lambda), \Lambda_i]$ denote the matrix of partial derivatives of the function $X_{S_i i}(p, \lambda)$ with respect to the components of p, these derivatives being evaluated at $(p, \lambda) = [P(\Lambda), \Lambda_i]$. It is easy to see that $D_p X_{S_i i} [P(\Lambda), \Lambda_i]$ is of the form $\Lambda_i E_i$, where E_i is defined as follows. Let $D^2_{S_i} u_i \{X_{S_i i} [P(\Lambda), \Lambda_i]\}$ be the $| S_i | \times | S_i |$ matrix of second-order partial derivatives of u_i with respect to variables with indices in S_i. This matrix is negative definite. If k and m belong to S_i, then the $(k, m)^{\text{th}}$ entry of E_i is that entry of the inverse of $D^2_{S_i} u_i \{X_{S_i i} [P(\Lambda), \Lambda_i]\}$ which corresponds to k^{th} and m^{th} commodities. The rest of the entries of E_i are zero.

Let $\Lambda \in C_S$. For each $k = 1, \ldots, L$, $X_{ik} [P(\Lambda), \Lambda_i] > 0$, for some i. This statement follows from the fact that $\Sigma_{i=1}^I X_i [P(\Lambda), \Lambda_i] = \omega >> 0$. Therefore, for each k, the kth row of E_i is nonzero, for some i. Hence, since the Λ_i are all positive, every row and column of $E = \Sigma_{i=1}^I \Lambda_i E_i$ is nonzero. It now follows from the nature of the matrices E_i that E is negative definite. Hence, E is nonsingular, as was to be proved.

Q.E.D.

For each $a \in A$, let $X_i(p, \lambda, a)$ be defined from $u_i(\cdot, a)$ by (49). Similarly, if $\Lambda \in \text{int } R^I_+$ and $\omega \in \text{int } R^L_+$, let $P(\Lambda, \omega, a)$ be the unique vector $p \in \text{int } R^L_+$ such that $\Sigma_{i=1}^I X_i(p, \Lambda, a) = \omega$. For each a and ω, Lemma 11 applies to the functions $X_i(p, \lambda, a)$ and $P(\Lambda, \omega, a)$. Also, it is easy to see that $P(\Lambda, \omega, a)$ is a continuous function of ω. (In fact, P is just as differentiable with respect to ω as it is with respect to Λ.)

I now turn to the proof of Lemma 9. Throughout the proof, if $\omega \in \Omega$, then $\omega^T = [\omega^T(a)]_{a \in A}$ is defined by $\omega^T(a) = \Sigma_{i=1}^I \omega_i(a)$. The total initial endowment of the economy is ω^T.

Proof of Lemma 9. I first prove the lemma for $r = 0$.

By Assumption 10, I may choose $a_1 \in A$ for which there are two histories going from a_1 to itself. Also, each of these histories contains an element which is distinct from a_1 and does not appear in the other history. For notational simplicity, I assume that these distinct elements occur just after a_1 in the histories. Let $a_1, a_2^1, \ldots, a_N^1$ and $a_1, a_2^2, \ldots, a_{N_2}^2$ be the two histories, where $a_{N_1}^1 = a_{N_2}^2 = a_1$. Then a_2^1 does not appear in $a_2^2, \ldots, a_{N_2}^2$ and a_2^2 does not appear in $a_2^1, \ldots, a_{N_1}^1$. Also, I may assume that a_2^j does not appear in $a_3^j, \ldots, a_{N_j}^j$, for $j = 1, 2$, for I may eliminate closed loops beginning with a_2^j.

Let $[p, (x_i)]$ be a stationary equilibrium with transfer payments for $\mathcal{E}(\omega)$, where $\omega \in \Omega$. Let $\Lambda = (\Lambda_i)$ be the vector of associated marginal utilities of money. Then $p(a) = P[\Lambda, \omega^T(a), a]$ and $x_i(a) = X_i\{P[\Lambda, \omega^T(a), a], \Lambda_i, a\}$, for all i and a. I now simplify the notation by writing $P[\Lambda, \omega^T(a), a]$ as $P(\Lambda,$

$\omega^T, a)$ and by writing $X_i\{P[\Lambda, \omega^T(a), a], \Lambda_i, a\}$ as $X_i(\Lambda, \omega^T, a)$.

The net expenditure of consumer i during the course of the cycle $a_2^j, \ldots, a_N^j$ is $\Sigma_{n=2}^{N_j} p(a_n^j) \cdot [x_i(a_n^j) - \omega_i(a_n^j)]$, for $j = 1, 2$. If this quantity is not zero, for $j = 1, 2$, then the money balances of some consumers must be negative at some time and for some history. For with positive probability, $a_2^j, \ldots, a_{N_j}^j$ could be repeated an arbitrarily large number of times in succession. In this case, consumer i would accumulate or lose an arbitrarily large quantity of money. In either case, someone would eventually hold a negative quantity of money. Therefore, in order that Lemma 9 be true, it is enough that

(52) for almost every $\omega \in \Omega$, $\sum_{n=2}^{N_j} p(a_n^j) \cdot [x_i(a_n^j) - \omega_i(a_n^j)] \neq 0$,

for $j = 1$ or 2 and for some i.

The equation $\Sigma_{n=2}^{N_j} p(a_n^j) \cdot [x_i(a_n^j) - \omega_i(a_n^j)] = 0$ holds if and only if $\omega_{i1}(a_2^j) = [p_1(a_2^j)]^{-1} \mid \Sigma_{n=2}^{N_j} p(a_n^j) \cdot [x_i(a_n^j) - \omega_i(a_n^j)] + p_1(a_2^j)\, \omega_{i1}(a_2^j) \mid$, where $\omega_{i1}(a)$ is the first component of $\omega_i(a)$ and $p_1(a)$ is the first component of $p(a)$. Substituting the appropriate functions of Λ and ω^T, I obtain

(53)
$$\omega_{i1}(a_2^j) = [P_1(\Lambda, \omega^T, a_2^j)]^{-1} \left| \sum_{n=2}^{N_j} P(\Lambda, \omega^T, a_n^j) \cdot [X(\Lambda, \omega, a_n^j) - \omega_i(a_n^j)] + P_1(\Lambda, \omega^T, a_2^j)\, \omega_{i1}(a_2^j) \right|.$$

Notice that the right-hand side of (53) does not depend on either $\omega_{i1}(a_2^1)$ or $\omega_{i1}(a_2^2)$, provided that $\Sigma_{i=1}^{I} \omega_{i1}(a_2^j)$ is held constant. Here I use the assumption that for each j, a_2^j does not appear in $a_3^j, \ldots, a_{N_j}^j$ and does not appear in $a_2^k, \ldots, a_{N_k}^k$, for $k \neq j$. I now parameterize ω by $(\omega_\alpha, \omega_\beta)$, where ω_α is the vector $[\omega_{11}(a_2^1), \ldots, \omega_{I-1,1}(a_2^1), \omega_{11}(a_2^2), \ldots, \omega_{I-1,1}(a_2^2)]$ and ω_β is the vector

$$\left\{ \left[\sum_{i=1}^{I} \omega_{i1}(a_2^j) \right]_{j=1,2}, [\omega_{ik}(a_2^j)]_{i=1,\ldots,I;\, k=2,\ldots,L;\, j=1,2}, [\omega_i(a)]_{i=1,\ldots,I;\, a \neq a_2^1, a_2^2} \right\}.$$

Clearly, $(\omega_\alpha, \omega_\beta)$ is simply a coordinate system for Ω.

The right-hand side of (53) depends only on Λ and ω_β. Denote this right-hand side by $f_{ji}(\Lambda, \omega_\beta)$, where $j = 1, 2$ and $i = 1, \ldots, I$. (52) may now be rewritten as

(54) for almost every $\omega \in \Omega$, $f_{ji}(\Lambda, \omega_\beta) \neq \omega_{i1}(a_2^j)$, for $j = 1$ or 2 and for some $i = 1, \ldots, I-1$.

In order that Lemma 9 be true, it is sufficient that (54) be true for every $\Lambda \in \text{int}\, R_+^I$. More precisely, it is sufficient to prove the next statement.

(55) For almost every $\omega \in \Omega$, the following is true. For every $\Lambda \in \text{int}\, R_+^I$, $f_{ji}(\Lambda, \omega_\beta) \neq \omega_{i1}(a_2^j)$, for $j = 1$ or 2 and for some $i = 1, \ldots, I-1$.

The functions f_{ji} are continuous, so that the set of ω in Ω for which (55) is true is measurable. It follows from the Fubini theorem that it is enough to prove (55) for ω with ω_β constant. More precisely, it is sufficient to prove the following.

(56) For each fixed $\bar{\omega}_\beta$, the following is true for almost every $\omega_\alpha = [\omega_{11}(a_2^1), \ldots, \omega_{I-1,1}(a_2^2)]$. For every $\Lambda \in \text{int } R_+^I$, $f_{ji}(\Lambda, \bar{\omega}_\beta) \neq \omega_{i1}(a_2^j)$, for $j = 1$ or 2 and for some i, $i = 1, \ldots, I-1$.

I now prove (56). Since $\bar{\omega}_\beta$ is constant, I may write $f_{ji}(\Lambda, \bar{\omega}_\beta)$ as $f_{ji}(\Lambda)$. Notice that f_{ji} is homogeneous of degree zero. That is, $f_{ji}(t\Lambda) = f_{ji}(\Lambda)$, for all $t > 0$. Hence, I may restrict Λ to int Δ^{I-1}. Consider the function F: int $\Delta^{I-1} \rightarrow R^{2I-2}$ defined by $F(\Lambda) = [f_{11}(\Lambda), \ldots, f_{1,I-1}(\Lambda), f_{21}(\Lambda), \ldots, f_{2,I-1}(\Lambda)]$. (56) is simply the assertion that almost every ω_α does not belong to the range of F. Hence, it is sufficient to prove the following.

(57) The range of F is of measure zero.

By Lemma 11, F is continuously differentiable on each of a finite number of sets closed in int Δ^{I-1}, the union of which is int Δ^{I-1}. dim $\Delta^{I-1} = I-1 < 2I-2$, since $I \geqq 2$. Therefore, the range of F is of measure zero.

This completes the proof of Lemma 9 for the case $r = 0$. I now turn to the case $r > 0$. The proof is quite similar.

I now use Assumption 10 to obtain three histories, $a_1, a_2^j, \ldots, a_{N_j}^j$, where $j = 1, 2, 3$ and $a_{N_j}^j = a$, for all j. Also for each j, a_2^j does not appear in $a_3^j, \ldots, a_{N_j}^j$ and does not appear in either sequence $a_2^k, \ldots, a_{N_k}^k$, for $k \neq j$.

Let $[p, (x_i)]$ be a stationary equilibrium. Suppose that consumer i is in state a_1 during period one and has M_i units of money at the end of the period. Suppose that consumer i then passes through the cycle $a_2^j, \ldots, a_{N_j}^j$. Then at the end of period N_j, she or he has $M_i(1+r)^{N_j-1} + \Sigma_{n=2}^{N_j}(1+r)^{N_j-n}\{p(a_n^j) \cdot [\omega_i(a_n^j) - x_i(a_n^j)] - \tau_j\}$ units of money. This sum must equal M_i, for all j, if it is to be true that no consumer ever holds negative money balances.

I now proceed as before. If $\omega \in \Omega$, then ω_α and ω_β are defined as follows.

$$\omega_\alpha = [\omega_{11}(a_2^1), \ldots, \omega_{I-1,1}(a_2^1), \omega_{11}(a_2^2), \ldots, \omega_{I-1,1}(a_2^2), \omega_{11}(a_2^3), \ldots, \omega_{I-1,1}(a_2^3)] \text{ and}$$

$$\omega_\beta = \left\{ \left[\sum_{i=1}^{I} \omega_{i1}(a_2^j) \right]_{j=1,2,3}; [\omega_{ik}(a_2^j)]_{i=1,\ldots,I;\, k=2,\ldots,L;\, j=1,2,3}; [\omega_i(a)]_{i=1,\ldots,I;\, a \neq a_2^1, a_2^2, a_2^3} \right\}.$$

$M = (M_i)$ denotes the vector of initial holdings of money, held at the end of period one in state a_1. M varies over $\Delta^{I-1} = \{M \in R_+^I \mid \Sigma_{i=1}^I M_i = 1\}$. It is sufficient to prove the next statement.

(58) For each fixed $\bar{\omega}_\beta$, the following is true, for almost every ω_α: For every $(M, \Lambda) \in \Delta^{I-1} \times \text{int } R_+^{I-1}$, $f_{ji}(M, \Lambda, \bar{\omega}_\beta) \neq \omega_{i1}(a_2^j)$, for $j = 1, 2$, or 3 and for some $i = 1, \ldots, I-1$

where $f_{ji}(M, \Lambda, \bar{\omega}_\beta) = -(1+r)^{2-N_j}[P_1(\Lambda, \omega^T, a_2^j)]^{-1}\Big(M_i\big[(1+r)^{N_j-1} - 1\big] + \Sigma_{n=2}^{N_j}(1+r)^{N_j-n}\big\{P(\Lambda, \omega^T, a_2^j) \cdot [\omega_i(a_n^j) - X_i(\Lambda, \omega^T, a_2^j)] - \tau_j - (1+r)^{N_j-2}P_1(\Lambda, \omega^T, a_2^j)\,\omega_{i1}(a_2^j)\big\}\Big)$. In this formula, ω^T is the total initial endowment determined by $\bar{\omega}_\beta$.

Now let F: $\Delta^{I-1} \times \text{int } R_+^{I-1} \rightarrow R^{3I-3}$ be defined by $F(M, \Lambda) = [f_{11}(M, \Lambda, \bar{\omega}_\beta), \ldots, f_{1,I-1}(M, \Lambda, \bar{\omega}_\beta), f_{21}(M, \Lambda, \bar{\omega}_\beta), \ldots, f_{3,I-1}(M, \Lambda, \bar{\omega}_\beta)]$. (58) is implied by the next statement.

(59) For each $\bar{\omega}_\beta$ the range of F has measure zero.

The dimension of the domain of F is $2I-2$ The dimension of its range is $3I-3$, which exceeds $2I-2$ since $I \geqq 2$. By Lemma 11, F is continuously differentiable on each of finitely many sets closed in $\Delta^{I-1} \times \text{int } R_+^{I-1}$. These facts imply (59).

This completes the proof of Lemma 9.

Q.E.D.

10. Proof of Theorem 3

Let $\omega \in \Omega$ be such that

(60) if $[p,(x_i)]$ is a stationary equilibrium for $\mathcal{E}(\omega)$ with transfer payments, then for any distribution of initial money balances and for any $a_1 \in A$, $M_{in}(p,x_i;a_1,\ldots,a_n) < 0$, for some i and some history $a_2,\ldots,a_n$ following a_1.

By Lemma 9, it is enough to prove that if $\delta_i = (1+r)^{-1}$, then $\mathcal{E}(\omega)$ has no monetary equilibrium.

The outline of the proof that $\mathcal{E}(\omega)$ has no monetary equilibrium is as follows. If $\mathcal{E}(\omega)$ had a monetary equilibrium, then the associated marginal utilities of money for each consumer would form a supermartingale. Hence, by the supermartingale convergence theorem, they would converge, so that they would eventually be nearly constant. If they were nearly constant, then some consumer would eventually exhaust her or his holdings of money. This contradiction establishes that $\mathcal{E}(\omega)$ has no monetary equilibrium. The idea that a consumer would exhaust money holdings is used to prove the following lemma.

LEMMA 12. *Let $\underline{\lambda}$ and $\bar{\lambda}$ be positive numbers and $\underline{\lambda} < \bar{\lambda}$. Then there exists a positive integer K, depending on $\underline{\lambda}$ and $\bar{\lambda}$, such that the following is true. Let $[p,(x_i)]$ be any monetary equilibrium, and let (λ_i) be the vector of associated marginal utilities of money. Suppose that $\underline{\lambda} \leqq \lambda_{in}(a_1,\ldots,a_n) \leqq \bar{\lambda}$, for all n and $a_1,\ldots,a_n$. Then for any history $a_1,\ldots,a_n$, the following must hold for some i and for some history $a_{n+1},\ldots,a_{n+k}$ following a_n, where $1 \leqq k \leqq K$: $| \lambda_{i,n+k}(a_i, \ldots,a_{n+k}) - \lambda_{in}(a_i,\ldots,a_n) | > K^{-1}$.*

Proof. Suppose that the lemma were false. Then there would exist a sequence of monetary equilibria $[p^K,(x_i^K)]$ such that for some history $a_1^K, \ldots, a_{n_K}^K$, $| \lambda_{i,n_K+k}^K(a_1^K,\ldots,a_{n_K}^K,a_{n_K+1},\ldots,a_{n_K+k}) - \lambda_{in_K}^K(a_1^K,\ldots,a_{n_K}^K) | \leqslant K^{-1}$, for all histories $a_{n_K+1},\ldots,a_{n_K+k}$ following $a_{n_K}^K$, where $1 \leqslant k \leqslant K$.

Since there are only finitely many points in A, I may assume that $a_{n_K}^K = \bar{a}_1 \in A$, for all K. I may also assume that $n_K = 1$, for all K. For I may restrict $[p^K,(x_i^K)]$ to histories following $a_1^K,\ldots,a_{n_K}^K$. That is, I may define $[\hat{p}, (\hat{x}_i)]$ by $\hat{p}_n(\bar{a}_1,a_2,\ldots,a_n) = p_{n_K+n}^K(a_1^K, \ldots, a_{n_K}^K,a_2, \ldots, a_n)$ and so on. $[\hat{p}, (\hat{x}_i)]$ is defined only for histories starting with $\bar{a}_1$, but this is sufficient for my purposes. I use $[p^K,(x_i^K)]$ again to denote $[\hat{p},(\hat{x}_i)]$. In summary, I may assume that

(61) $| \lambda_{ik}^K(\bar{a}_1,a_2,\ldots,a_k) - \lambda_{i1}^K(\bar{a}_1) | \leqq K^{-1}$, for all histories $\bar{a}_1,a_2,\ldots,a_k$ beginning with $\bar{a}_1$, where $1 \leqq k \leqq K$.

By a Cantor diagonal argument, I may obtain a subsequence of monetary equilibria—call it $[p^K,(x_i^K)]$ again—such that $[p^K,(x_i^K)]$ and (λ_i^K) all converge. The limit $[p,(x_i)]$, forms a monetary equilibrium (restricted to histories beginning with $\bar{a}_1$). In proving this fact, one proceeds as in the last section of the proof of Theorem 1. The limit marginal utilities of money (λ_i) are the marginal utilities of money corresponding to $[p,(x_i)]$. By passage to the limit in (61), I obtain that $\lambda_{in}(\bar{a}_1,a_2,\ldots,a_n) = \lambda_i(\bar{a}_1)$, for all i and for all histories $\bar{a}_1,a_2,\ldots$ beginning with $\bar{a}_1$.

By Lemma 10, there is a unique stationary equilibrium $[\hat{p},(\hat{x}_i)]$ with marginal utilities of money $[\lambda_i(\bar{a}_1)]$. Hence, $x_{in}(\bar{a}_1,a_2,\ldots,a_n) = \hat{x}_i(a_n)$ and $p_n(\bar{a}_1, a_2,\ldots,a_n) = \hat{p}(a_n)$, for all histories $\bar{a}_1,a_2,\ldots,a_n$. It now follows from (60) that $M_{in}(p,x_i;\bar{a}_1,a_2,\ldots,a_n) < 0$, for some i and some $a_2,\ldots,a_n$. This contradicts the fact that $[p,(x_i)]$ is a monetary equilibrium. This completes the proof of Lemma 12.

Q.E.D.

I may now prove Theorem 3.

Proof of Theorem 3. Let $[p,(x_i)]$ be a monetary equilibrium, and let (λ_i) be the associated marginal utilities of money. Since $\delta_i(1 + r) = 1$, (8) implies that

(62) $\lambda_{in}(a_1,\ldots,a_n) \geqq E\,[\lambda_{i,n+1}(a_1,\ldots,a_n,s_{n+1}) \mid s_n = a_n]$, for all i, n, and $a_1,\ldots,a_n$.

(62) says that the random variables $\lambda_{in}(s_1,\ldots,s_n)$ form a supermartingale. Since the $\lambda_{in}(s_1,\ldots,s_n)$ are nonnegative, I may apply the supermartingale convergence theorem (Doob 1953, p. 324). This theorem implies that the $\lambda_{in}(s_1,\ldots,s_n)$ converge almost surely. Let $\lambda_{i\infty}(s_1,s_2,\ldots)$ be the limit random variable, for $i = 1,\ldots,I$.

By (12) or (14), the components of the λ_i are bounded away from zero and infinity, so that I may apply Lemma 12. Let K be as in the lemma.

Since $\lim_{n\to\infty} \lambda_{in}(s_1,\ldots,s_n) = \lambda_{i\infty}(s_1,s_2,\ldots)$ almost surely, there exists N such that Prob $[\,|\lambda_{in}(s_1,\ldots,s_n) - \lambda_{i\infty}(s_1,s_2,\ldots)| \geqq (2K)^{-1}$, for some i and some $n \geqq N] < \epsilon^K$, where $\epsilon = \min\{P_{ab} \mid a,b \in A,\ P_{ab} > 0\}$ and the P_{ab} are the transition probabilities of the Markov chain $\{s_n\}$. It follows that there exists a history $a_1,\ldots,a_N$ such that Prob $[\,|\lambda_{in}(a_1,\ldots,a_N,s_{N+1},\ldots,s_n) - \lambda_{iN}(a_1,\ldots,a_n)| \geqq K^{-1}$, for some $n > N \mid s_N = a_N] < \epsilon^K$. But for any history $a_{N+1},\ldots,a_n$ following a_N with $n \leqq N + K$, Prob $[(s_{N+1},\ldots,s_n) = (a_{N+1},\ldots,a_n) \mid s_N = a_N] \geqq \epsilon^K$. Therefore, $|\lambda_{in}(a_1,\ldots,a_N,a_{N+1},\ldots,a_n) - \lambda_{iN}(a_1,\ldots,a_N)| < K^{-1}$, for all n such that $N < n \leqq N + K$ and for all $a_{N+1},\ldots,a_n$ following a_N. This statement contradicts Lemma 12. This completes the proof of Theorem 3.

Q.E.D.

11. Proof of Theorem 4

The rough idea of the argument is as follows. If the price systems p^k did not converge to zero, then the sequence $[p^k,(x_i^k)]$ would have a limit point $[p,(x_i)]$ which would be much like a monetary equilibrium with interest rate equal to $\delta^{-1} - 1$. An argument similar to the proof of Theorem 3 shows that no such limit equilibrium exists, almost surely.

There is a snag in this argument. Prices in a monetary equilibrium are uniformly bounded away from zero, and they need not be so in $[p,(x_i)]$. However, prices in $[p,(x_i)]$ are bounded above, and this fact makes it possible to imitate the proof of Theorem 3.

The limit equilibrium $[p,(x_i)]$ is what I call a pseudomonetary equilibrium.

A *pseudomonetary equilibrium* is a vector $[p,(x_i),(\lambda_i)]$. $p = [p_n(a_1,\ldots,a_n)]$ is a price system. (x_i) is an allocation in the usual sense. λ_i is a vector of marginal utilities of money, as before, except that I allow some or all of the numbers $\lambda_{in}(a_1, \ldots, a_n)$ to be infinite. $[p,(x_i),(\lambda_i)]$ must satisfy the following conditions.

(63) (x_i) is a feasible allocation.

(64) For some $\underline{\lambda} > 0$, $\lambda_{in}(a_1, \ldots, a_n) \geqq \underline{\lambda}$, for all i, n, and $a_1, \ldots, a_n$.

For all i, n, and $a_1, \ldots, a_n$,

(65) $$\lambda_{in}(a_1,\ldots,a_n) = \max \{\alpha_{in}(a_1,\ldots,a_n), E[\lambda_{i,n+1}(a_1,\ldots,a_n,s_{n+1}) \mid s_n = a_n]\}$$

(66) $$\lambda_{in}(a_1,\ldots,a_n) > E[\lambda_{i,n+1}(a_1,\ldots,a_n,s_{n+1}) \mid s_n = a_n]$$ only if $M_{i,n+1}(a_1, \ldots, a_n) = 0$

(67) $$\lambda_{in}(a_1,\ldots,a_n) > \alpha_{in}(a_1,\ldots,a_n) \text{ only if } x_{in}(a_1,\ldots,a_n) = 0$$

(68) $$M_{in}(p,x_i;a_1,\ldots,a_n) \geqq 0 \text{ and } \sum_{i=1}^{I} M_{in}(p,x_i;a_1,\ldots,a_n) = 1.$$

Notice that (64) and Lemma 3 imply that $p_n(a_1,\ldots,a_n) \leqq b\,\underline{\lambda}^{-1}\,\bar{q}$, for all n and $a_1,\ldots,a_n$. Also, if $\lambda_{in}(a_1,\ldots,a_n) < \infty$ for some i, then by Lemma 3, $p_n(a_1, \ldots,a_n) \gg 0$. If $p_n(a_1,\ldots,a_n) > 0$ and $\lambda_{in}(a_1,\ldots,a_n) = \infty$, then $x_{in}(a_1,\ldots,a_n) = 0$.

I say that a pseudomonetary equilibrium is nontrivial if $\lambda_{in}(a_1,\ldots,a_n) < \infty$, for some i, n, and $a_1,\ldots,a_n$.

In order to show that nontrivial pseudomonetary equilibria do not exist almost surely, I introduce the concept of pseudostationary equilibrium with transfer payments.

A *pseudostationary equilibrium with transfer payments* is a vector $[p,(x_i),(\lambda_i)]$, where p and the x_i are functions from A to R^L_+ and each λ_i belongs to $(0,\infty]$. Notice that the λ_i may be infinite. $[p,(x_i),(\lambda_i)]$ must satisfy the following conditions.

(69) (x_i) is a feasible stationary allocation.

(70) For all i and a, $$\frac{\partial u_i[x_i(a),a]}{\partial z_k} \leqq \lambda_i p_k(a), \text{ for } k = 1,\ldots,L;$$ with equality if $x_{ik}(a) > 0$.

I say that a pseudostationary equilibrium with transfer payments, $[p,(x_i),(\lambda_i)]$, is nontrivial if $\lambda_i < \infty$, for some i. Then $p(a) \gg 0$, for all i. If $[p,(x_i),(\lambda_i)]$ is nontrivial and $\lambda_i = \infty$, then $x_i(a) = 0$, for all a.

The lemma before simply says that Lemma 9 applies to pseudostationary equilibrium.

LEMMA 13. *For almost every* $\omega \in \Omega$, *the following is true. Let* $[p,(x_i),(\lambda_i)]$ *be any nontrivial pseudostationary equilibrium for* $\mathcal{E}(\omega)$ *with transfer payments. Then for any distribution of initial money balances and for any* $a_1 \in A$, $M_{in}(p,x_i;a_1,\ldots,a_n) < 0$, *for some i and some history* $a_2,\ldots,a_n$ *following* a_1.

Proof. The proof of this lemma differs from that of Lemma 9 only in detail. Since there are only finitely many subsets of $\{1,\ldots,I\}$, one may fix the subset of consumers for whom $\lambda_i = \infty$. Those consumers consume nothing. The rest of the argument is as in section 9.

Lemma 14 below is the analogue of Lemma 12.

(71) Let $\omega \in \Omega$ be such that if $[p,(x_i),(\lambda_i)]$ is a nontrivial pseudostationary equilibrium for $\mathcal{E}(\omega)$ with transfer payments, then for any distribution of initial money balances and for any $a_1 \in A$, $M_{in}(p,x_i;a_1,\ldots,a_n) < 0$, for some i and some history $a_2,\ldots,a_n$ following a_1.

LEMMA 14. *Let* $\underline{\lambda}$ *and* $\overline{\lambda}$ *be positive numbers such that* $0 < \underline{\lambda} < \overline{\lambda}$. *Then there exists a positive integer K, depending on* $\underline{\lambda}$ *and* $\overline{\lambda}$, *such that the following is true. Let* $[p,(x_i)]$ *be any pseudomonetary equilibrium for* $\mathcal{E}(\omega)$, *and let* (λ_i) *be the vector of associated marginal utilities of money. Suppose that* $\lambda_{in}(a_1,\ldots,a_n) \geqslant \underline{\lambda}$, *for all i, n, and* $a_1,\ldots,a_n$. *Let* $a_1,\ldots,a_n$ *be any history, and suppose that* $\lambda_{in}(a_1,\ldots,a_n) \leqq \overline{\lambda}$, *for some i. Then* $|\lambda_{i,n+k}(a_1,\ldots,a_{n+k}) - \lambda_{in}(a_1,\ldots,a_n)| > K^{-1}$, *for some i such that* $\lambda_{in}(a_1,\ldots,a_n) < \infty$ *and for some history* $a_{n+1},\ldots,a_{n+k}$ *following* a_n, *where* $1 \leqq k \leqq K$.

Proof. This lemma follows from (71) just as Lemma 12 followed from (60).

I need one more lemma which guarantees that prices in the equilibria $[p^k, (x_i^k)]$ are uniformly bounded from above.

LEMMA 15. *Let* $\delta_i = \delta < 1$, *for all i. There exist* $\overline{p} \in R_+^L > 0$ *and* $\underline{r} > 0$ *with* $0 < \underline{r} < \delta^{-1} - 1$ *such that the following are true. Let* $[p,(x_i)]$ *be any monetary equilibrium with interest rate r, and let* (λ_i) *be the vector of associated marginal utilities of money. If* $\underline{r} \leqslant r < \delta^{-1} - 1$, *then* $p_n(a_1,\ldots,a_n) \leqq \overline{p}$ *and* $\lambda_{in}(a_1,\ldots,a_n) \geqq \underline{\lambda}$, *for all i, all n, and all histories* $a_1,\ldots,a_n$.

Proof. It is sufficient to prove that $\underline{\lambda}$ and $\underline{r}$ exist as in the lemma. For by Lemma 3, I may let $\overline{p} = b\underline{\lambda}^{-1}\overline{q}$.

Let $\epsilon > 0$ be as in the proof of Lemma 5, and let $\underline{\lambda} = \epsilon(1+\epsilon)^{-1}$ and $\underline{r} = \delta^{-1}(1+\epsilon^2)^{-1}(1+2^{-1}\epsilon^2) - 1$. By choosing ϵ sufficiently small I may assure that $\underline{r} > 0$. Clearly, $\underline{r} < \delta^{-1} - 1$. Note that $\underline{\lambda}$ is as in Lemma 5.

Suppose that $\underline{r} \leqq r < \delta^{-1} - 1$, and let $[p,(x_i)]$ be a monetary equilibrium with interest rate r. Also, let (λ_i) be the vector of marginal utilities of money associated with $[p,(x_i)]$. By (12) or (14) there exists $\lambda > 0$ such that $\lambda_{in}(a_1,\ldots,a_n) \geqq \lambda$, for all i, n, and $a_1,\ldots,a_n$. Suppose that $\lambda < \underline{\lambda}$. I will show that

(72) $\lambda_{in}(a_1,\ldots,a_n) \geqq \lambda(1+2^{-1}\epsilon)^k$, for all i, n, and $a_1,\ldots,a_n$ and for all positive integers k such that $\lambda(1+2^{-1}\epsilon^2)^{k-1} < \underline{\lambda}$.

Clearly, (72) implies the lemma. For let k be such that $(1+2^{-1}\epsilon^2)^{k-1}\lambda < \underline{\lambda}$ and $(1+2^{-1}\epsilon^2)^k \lambda \geqq \underline{\lambda}$. By (72) $\lambda_{in}(a_1,\ldots,a_n) \geqq (1+2^{-1}\epsilon^2)^k \lambda \geqq \underline{\lambda}$, for all i, n, and $a_1,\ldots,a_n$, as is to be proved.

I prove (72) by induction on k. (72) is true for $k = 0$, by the definition of λ. Suppose that k is such that $\lambda(1+2^{-1}\epsilon^2)^k < \underline{\lambda}$, and assume by induction that

$\lambda_{in}(a_1,\ldots,a_n) \geqq \lambda(1 + 2^{-1}\epsilon^2)^k$, for all i, n, and $a_1,\ldots,a_n$. The proof of (39) proves that $\lambda_{in}(a_1,\ldots,a_n) \geqq (1+\epsilon)(1+2^{-1}\epsilon^2)^k\lambda$, if $\omega_{ik}(a_n) \leqq \delta$, for all k. But then, as in the proof of Lemma 5, $\lambda_{in}(a_1,\ldots,a_n) \geqq \delta(1+\underline{r})[(1-\epsilon)+\epsilon(1+\epsilon)](1+2^{-1}\epsilon^2)^k\lambda = \lambda(1+2^{-1}\epsilon^2)^{k+1}$. This completes the induction step in the proof of (72) and hence proves the lemma.

Q.E.D.

I now turn to the proof of Theorem 4.

Proof of Theorem 4. By Lemma 13, I may assume that (71) applies to $\mathcal{E}(\omega)$. Let $[p^k,(x_i^k)]$ be a sequence of monetary equilibria for $\mathcal{E}(\omega)$, the kth having interest rate r_k. By Lemma 3, it is sufficient to show that

(73) if $[p^k,(x_i^k)]$ is as in the theorem, then $\lim_{k\to\infty}\lambda_{in}^k(a_1,\ldots,a_n) = \infty$ uniformly

where (λ_i^k) is the vector of marginal utilities of money associated with $[p^k,(x_i^k)]$.

Suppose that (73) were false. Then there would exist a subsequence of $[p^k,(x_i^k)]$—call it $[p^k,(x_i^k)]$ again—with the following property. There is $\overline{\lambda} < \infty$ such that for each k, $\lambda_{i_k n_k}^k(a_1^k,\ldots,a_{n_k}^k) \leqq \overline{\lambda}$, for some i_k and $a_1^k,\ldots,a_{n_k}^k$. Since there are finitely many indices i and a, I may assume that $i_k = i$ and $a_{n_k}^k = \overline{a}_1$, for all k. Also, $[p^k,(x_i^k)]$ forms an equilibrium when restricted to histories following $a_1^k,\ldots,a_{n_k}^k$. Therefore, I may assume that $n_k = 1$, for all k. In summary, I may assume that for some i and $\overline{a}_1$, $\lambda_{i1}^k(\overline{a}_1) \leqq \overline{\lambda}$, for all k. Without loss of generality, I may assume that $i = 1$, so that $\lambda_{11}^k(\overline{a}_1) \leqq \overline{\lambda}$, for all k.

By a Cantor diagonal argument, I can prove that there exists a subsequence of $[p^k,(x_i^k)]$ such that $p_n^k(\overline{a}_1,a_2,\ldots,a_n)$, $x_{in}^k(\overline{a}_1,a_2,\ldots,a_n)$, and $\lambda_{in}^k(\overline{a}_1,a_2,\ldots,a_n)$ all converge for all i, all n, and all histories $a_2,\ldots,a_n$ following $\overline{a}_1$. Let $[p,(x_i)]$ and (λ_i) denote the vectors of limits. It is easy to see that $[p(x_i),(\lambda_i)]$ is a pseudomonetary equilibrium, except that it is defined only for histories beginning with $\overline{a}_1$. (64) follows from Lemma 15. (65) and (66) follow from the fact that $\lim_{k\to\infty}(1+r_k)\,\delta = 1$.

I now show that I may assume the following.

(74) For every i, either $\lambda_{in}(\overline{a}_1,a_2,\ldots,a_n) = \infty$, for all $n \geqq 1$ and for all histories $\overline{a}_1,a_2,\ldots,a_n$, or $\lambda_{in}(\overline{a}_1,a_2,\ldots,a_n) < \infty$, for all $n \geqq 1$ and for all histories $\overline{a}_1,a_2,\ldots,a_n$.

Clearly, (65) implies that the following is true.

(75) If $\lambda_{i1}(\overline{a}_1) < \infty$, then $\lambda_{in}(\overline{a}_1,a_2,\ldots,a_n) < \infty$, for all i, n, and $a_2,\ldots,a_n$.

I now proceed by induction on i. Since $\lambda_{11}(\overline{a}_1) \leqq \overline{\lambda} < \infty$, (75) implies that (74) is true for $i = 1$. Suppose by induction that (74) is true for $i = 1,\ldots,j-1 < I$. If $\lambda_{j1}(\overline{a}_1) < \infty$, then (75) implies that (74) is true for j. If $\lambda_{jn}(\overline{a}_1,a_2,\ldots,a_n) = \infty$, for all n and $\overline{a}_1,a_2,\ldots,a_n$, then (74) is true for j. Suppose that $\lambda_{j1}(\overline{a}_1) = \infty$ and that $\lambda_{jn}(\overline{a}_1,a_2,\ldots,a_n) < \infty$, for some n and $a_2,\ldots,a_n$. Then $[p,(x_i),(\lambda_i)]$ forms a pseudomonetary equilibrium when restricted to histories beginning with $(\overline{a}_1,a_2,\ldots,a_n)$. Hence, I may relabel a_n as $\overline{a}_1$, and I have that (74) is true for $i = 1,\ldots,j$. This completes the induction step, and so I may assume that (74) is satisfied.

Now I proceed more or less as in the proof of Theorem 3. Let $J = \{i=1,\ldots,I \mid \lambda_{i1}(\bar{a}_1) < \infty\}$. By assumption, $1 \in J$. For all $i \in J$, the random variables $\lambda_{in}(\bar{a}_1,s_2,\ldots,s_n)$ form a supermartingale. Hence, they converge almost surely.

Now let K be as in Lemma 14, where the $\underline{\lambda}$ in Lemma 14 is the same as the $\underline{\lambda}$ in Lemma 15. Let the $\bar{\lambda}$ of Lemma 14 be such that $\bar{\lambda} > 2\,\lambda_1(\bar{a}_1)$. Finally, let $\underline{\eta} = \min\{P_{ab} \mid P_{ab} > 0, a,b \in A\}$.

Since the random variables $\lambda_{in}(\bar{a}_1,s_2,\ldots,s_n)$ converge almost surely, there exists N such that Prob $[\,|\lambda_{in}(\bar{a}_1,s_2,\ldots,s_N,s_{N+1},\ldots,s_n) - \lambda_{iN}(\bar{a}_1,s_2,\ldots,s_N)\,| > K^{-1}$, for some $i \in J$ and for some $n > N \mid s_1 = \bar{a}_1] < 2^{-1}\eta^K$. Next, observe that Prob $[\lambda_{1N}(\bar{a}_1,s_2,\ldots,s_N) \leqq \bar{\lambda} \mid s_1 = \bar{a}_1] \geqq \frac{1}{2}$, since $\bar{\lambda} > 2\lambda_1(\bar{a}_1)$ and the random variables $\lambda_{1n}(s_1,s_2,\ldots,s_n)$ form a nonnegative supermartingale. These two inequalities imply that there exist $a_2,\ldots,a_N$ with the property that $\lambda_{1N}(\bar{a}_1, a_2,\ldots,a_N) \leqq \bar{\lambda}$ and Prob $[\,|\lambda_{in}(\bar{a}_1,a_2,\ldots,a_N, s_{N+1},\ldots,s_n) - \lambda_{iN}(\bar{a}_1,a_2,\ldots,a_N)\,| > K^{-1}$, for some $i \in J$ and some $n > N \mid s_N = a_N] < \eta^K$. Hence, by the choice of η, $|\,\lambda_{in}(\bar{a}_1,a_2,\ldots,a_N,a_{N+1},\ldots,a_n) - \lambda_{in}(\bar{a}_1,a_2,\ldots,a_N)\,| \leqq K^{-1}$, for all $i \in J$ and for all $a_{N+1},\ldots,a_n$ following a_N such that $N \leqq n \leqq N+K$. This contradicts Lemma 14. This completes the proof of Theorem 4.

Q.E.D.

12. Proof of Theorem 5

What follows is largely a reinterpretation of the argument given by Arrow (1964) in his pioneering paper.

I first prove that a stationary equilibrium exists. In order to do so, I define a pure trade economy $\mathcal{E}$ which represents, roughly speaking, a cross section of the economy at one moment in time. The commodity space of $\mathcal{E}$ is $R^{L|A|}$, where $|A|$ is the number of points in A. I write $x \in R^{L|A|}$ as $x = [x(a)]_{a\in A}$, where $x(a) \in R^L$. The initial endowment of the ith consumer is $\omega_i = [\omega_i(a)]_{a\in A}$, $i = 1,\ldots,I$. The utility function of the ith consumer is $\Sigma_{a\in A}\,\pi_a u_i[x_i(a),a]$, where (π_a) is the stationary distribution on A.

By Debreu 1959, p. 83, $\mathcal{E}$ has an equilibrium, $[p,(x_i)]$. By the strict monotonicity of the function $u_i(\cdot\,,a)$, $p(a) >> 0$, for all a. Let $\bar{p} = [\bar{p}(a)]$, where $\bar{p}(a) = \pi_a^{-1}p(a)$. $\bar{p}(a)$ is well defined, since $\pi_a > 0$, for all a (see Assumption 2). I claim that $[\bar{p}, \delta^{-1} - 1,(x_i)]$ is a stationary equilibrium with deflation rate $\delta^{-1} - 1$. First, $\Sigma_{a\in A}\,\pi_a\bar{p}(a)\cdot x(a) = \Sigma_{a\in A}\,p(a)\cdot x(a) = p\cdot x$, for all $x \in R^{L|A|}$. Hence, the fact that $[p,(x_i)]$ is an Arrow-Debreu equilibrium implies that for each i, x_i solves the problem

$$(76)\qquad \max\left\{\sum_{a\in A}\pi_a u_i(x,a) \;\middle|\; x \in R_+^{L|A|} \text{ and } \sum_{a\in A}\pi_a\bar{p}(a)\cdot[x(a) - \omega_i(a)] \leqq 0\right\}.$$

Clearly, $\bar{p}$ is a stationary price system and (x_i) is a feasible stationary allocation. Hence, $[\bar{p}, \delta^{-1} - 1,(x_i)]$ is a stationary equilibrium with deflation rate $\delta^{-1} - 1$.

Suppose that $\delta = 1$ and that $[p, 0, (x_i)]$ is a stationary equilibrium with deflation rate zero. I prove that (x_i) is Pareto optimal. Let $\lambda_i > 0$ be the Lagrange multiplier associated with the maximization problem (76). Recall that the consumption program $\hat{x}_i$ is defined by $\hat{x}_{in}(a_1,\ldots,a_n) = x_i(a_n)$, for all i, n, and $a_1,\ldots,a_n$. I must show that $(\hat{x}_i)$ is Pareto optimal in the sense of (1). $(\hat{x}_i)$ solves the first-order conditions of the social maximization problem

$$(77) \qquad \max\left(\sum_{i=1}^{I} \lambda_i^{-1} E\left\{ \sum_{n=1}^{N} u_i\,[y_{in}(s_1,\ldots,s_n), s_n]\right\} \middle| \; (y_i) \text{ is a feasible allocation}\right)$$

for all values of N. For by the definition of λ_i,

$$(78) \qquad \frac{\partial u_i\,[x_i(a_n), a_n]}{\partial z_k} \leqq \lambda_i\, p_k(a_n), \text{ for all } k, i, n, \text{ and } a_n; \quad \text{with equality if } x_{ik}(a_n) > 0.$$

(78) gives the first-order conditions for a solution to (77). Since the objective function of (77) is concave, it is sufficient to satisfy the first-order conditions. Hence, $(\hat{x}_i)$ solves (77). This proves that (x_i) is Pareto optimal.

Suppose now that $\delta < 1$ and that $[p, \delta^{-1} - 1, (x_i)]$ is a stationary equilibrium (with deflation rate $\delta^{-1} - 1$). The proof that (x_i) is Pareto optimal is exactly as in the previous paragraph, except that (77) and (78) become the two formulas below:

$$\max\left(\sum_{i=1}^{I} \lambda_i^{-1} E\left\{ \sum_{n=1}^{\infty} \delta^{n-1} u_i\,[y_{in}(s_1,\ldots,s_n), s_n]\right\} \middle| \; (y_i) \text{ is a feasible allocation}\right).$$

$$\delta^{n-1} \frac{\partial u_i\,[x_i(a_n), a_n]}{\partial z_k} \leqq \lambda_i\, \delta^{n-1} p_k(a_n), \text{ for all } k, i, n, \text{ and } a_n; \quad \text{with equality if } x_{ik}(a_n) > 0.$$

13. An Example

The following example illustrates why special assumptions are needed in Theorems 2, 3, and 4. In the example, the Markov chain $\{s_n\}$ is cyclic and has two states. There are two consumers. One consumer has a relatively high preference for consumption in one state, and the other consumer prefers consumption in the other state. Therefore, there is a Pareto optimal allocation in which each consumer consumes the entire endowment of both consumers when the preferred state occurs. I call this allocation the *alternating allocation*. I assume that no interest is paid on money.

At first I assume that the consumers' rates of time preference are positive and show that the alternating Pareto optimal allocation is the allocation of a monetary equilibrium. Thus, Theorem 2 does not hold, and the example justifies the assumption made in Theorem 2 that each consumer always consumes something.

I next assume that each consumer's rate of time preference is equal to the interest rate, which is zero. In this case, the alternating Pareto optimal allocation is still that of a monetary equilibrium, so that the optimum quantity of money is finite. This is so even if the endowment functions are allowed to vary over an open set. Hence, Theorems 3 and 4 do not hold, and the example shows the need for Assumption 10 in these theorems.

I now describe the example. $A = \{a, b\}$. The transition probabilities are defined by $P_{aa} = P_{bb} = 0$ and $P_{ab} = P_{ba} = 1$. Thus, the stochastic process $\{s_n\}$

alternates between a and b. The process starts at time 1 in state a with probability 1/2 and in state b with probability 1/2. There are two consumers and one good. The endowments are defined by $\omega_1(a) = \omega_1(b) = \omega_2(a) = \omega_2(b) = 1$. The utility functions are defined as follows: $u_1(x, a) = u_2(x, b) = 12 \log(1+x)$, where x is the quantity consumed of the good; $u_1(x, b) = u_2(x, a) = 3 \log(1+x)$. The initial holdings of money are $M_{10} = M_{20} = 1/2$. Money earns no interest. That is, $r = 0$.

Suppose that $1/2 < \delta_i < 1$, for $i = 1,2$. I claim the following is a monetary equilibrium. The price system p is defined by $p_1(a) = p_1(b) = 1/2$ and $p_n(a_1, \ldots, a_n) = 1$, for all $n > 1$ and for all $a_1, \ldots, a_n$. The allocation (x_1, x_2) is defined as follows. For all n and $a_1, \ldots, a_n$,

$$x_{1n}(a_1, \ldots, a_n) = \begin{cases} 2, \text{ if } a_n = a \\ 0, \text{ if } a_n = b \end{cases}$$

$$x_{2n}(a_1, \ldots, a_n) = \begin{cases} 0, \text{ if } a_n = a \\ 2, \text{ if } a_n = b. \end{cases}$$

It should be clear for $n \geqq 1$ that

$$M_{1n}(a_1, \ldots, a_n) = \begin{cases} 0, \text{ if } a_n = a \\ 1, \text{ if } a_n = b \end{cases}$$

$$M_{2n}(a_1, \ldots, a_n) = \begin{cases} 1, \text{ if } a_n = a \\ 0, \text{ if } a_n = b. \end{cases}$$

In order to verify that the above is an equilibrium, it is enough to verify that each consumer satisfies the first-order conditions for her or his optimization problem. Since the consumers are symmetric, I need only deal with consumer 1. It is easy to see that this consumer's marginal utility of expenditure, $\alpha_1 = [\alpha_{1n}(a_1, \ldots, a_n)]$, is as follows: $\alpha_{11}(a) = 8$. $\alpha_{11}(b) = 2$. If $n > 1$, then

$$\alpha_{1n}(a_1, \ldots, a_n) = \begin{cases} 4, \text{ if } a_n = a \\ 1, \text{ if } a_n = b. \end{cases}$$

It follows easily that consumer 1's marginal utility of money is as follows: $\lambda_{11}(a) = 8$. $\lambda_{11}(b) = 4\delta_1$. If $n > 1$, then

$$\lambda_{1n}(a_1, \ldots, a_n) = \begin{cases} 4, \text{ if } a_n = a \\ 4\delta_1, \text{ if } a_n = b. \end{cases}$$

Finally,

$$E[\lambda_{1,n+1}(a_1, \ldots, a_n, s_{n+1}) \mid a_n = a] = \begin{cases} 4\delta_1, \text{ if } a_n = a \\ 4, \text{ if } a_n = b. \end{cases}$$

It is easy to see that α_1 and λ_1 satisfy conditions (8)–(10). For instance, $\lambda_{11}(a) = 8 > 4\delta^2 = \delta_1 E[\lambda_{12}(a_1, s_2) \mid a_1 = a]$, and $M_{11}(a) = 0$. Also, $\alpha_{11}(b) = 2 < 4\delta_1 = \lambda_{11}(b)$ and $x_{11}(b) = 0$.

It should be clear that the allocation (x_1, x_2) is Pareto optimal, even though the rate of interest is less than the rate of time preference. Hence, some special condition is needed in Theorem 2.

Now suppose that $\delta_1 = \delta_2 = 1$. Let the initial endowments satisfy the condition $3/4 < \omega_i(c) < 5/4$, for $c = a,b$ and $i = 1,2$. Let the endowment of money and the utility functions be as before. I claim that $[p, (x_1, x_2)]$ is a monetary equilibrium where $[p, (x_1, x_2)]$ is defined as follows: $p_1(a) = [2\omega_2(a)]^{-1}$. $p_1(b) = [2\omega_1(b)]^{-1}$. If $n > 1$,

$$p_n(a_1, \ldots, a_n) = \begin{cases} [\omega_2(a)]^{-1}, \text{ if } a_n = a \\ [\omega_1(b)]^{-1}, \text{ if } a_n = b \end{cases}$$

$$x_{1n}(a_1, \ldots, a_n) = \begin{cases} \omega_1(a_n) + \omega_2(a_n), \text{ if } a_n = a \\ 0, \text{ if } a_n = b \end{cases}$$

$$x_{2n}(a_1, \ldots, a_n) = \begin{cases} 0, \text{ if } a_n = a \\ \omega_1(a_n) + \omega_2(a_n), \text{ if } a_n = b. \end{cases}$$

It is easy to verify that this allocation is Pareto optimal in the sense of (1). Hence, Theorems 3 and 4 do not apply.

Some Remarks on Monetary Policy in an Overlapping Generations Model

W. A. Brock and J. A. Scheinkman*

1. Introduction

It is the purpose of this paper to show that certain results (derived from rational expectations monetary models where real balance services enter the utility function directly)—such as that an increase in the *mean* of the rate of growth of the money supply induces a welfare loss and an increase in the *variance* of the rate of growth of the money supply may cause an increase in welfare—are not dependent upon the Friedman-Patinkin-Samuelson device of inserting real balances into the utility function.

More specifically, we set up an overlapping generations model in which money balances are the only way of carrying wealth from periods of high endowment to periods of low endowment. Our setup is like that of Samuelson (1958),[1] Cass and Yaari (1966b), Gale (1973), Lucas (1972), and Cass, Okuno, and Zilcha (this volume). In particular, we use the Cass-Okuno-Zilcha discussion of rational expectations equilibria with a positive price of money and the Gale analysis of Gale's "Samuelson case." However, no one except Lucas (1972) has addressed the question of whether an increase in the mean rate of growth in the money supply would cause a welfare loss in an overlapping generations model. In Lucas, though, monetary transfers during the period were proportional to the individual's beginning-of-period balances, so Lucas' agents suffered no capital losses on money due to inflation. Furthermore, although Eden (1975) studied the case of random money supply and obtained the result that an increase in the variance of the rate of growth of money could increase equilibrium welfare, no one has studied such a question in a model without real balances in the utility function. We take up both issues here.

Section 2 sets up the model and studies rational expectations equilibria

*For extremely useful comments on this work, we thank David Cass, Robert Lucas, Don Roper, Charles Wilson, Edward Sieper, the Economics Seminar at the University of California, Berkeley, and the participants of the Australian National University Economics Seminar and the 1977 MSSB Conference at Dartmouth, New Hampshire. This research was supported by NSF Grant 74-19692. None of the above are responsible for errors or shortcomings contained herein.

[1]Author names and years refer to the works listed at the end of this book.

when the money supply grows at a constant nonrandom rate σ. It is shown that an increase in the rate of growth of the money supply leads to welfare loss. Other properties of equilibria are explored as well.

In section 3 uncertainty in the rate of growth of the money supply is introduced. It is shown that if there is no uncertainty in tastes and endowments then there is an equivalent deterministic monetary policy in the sense that the same stationary real balance equilibrium is generated by that policy as was generated by the random policy.

Section 4 contains a study of equilibria when real balances converge to 0 as $t \to \infty$ and a discussion of the economic meaning of such equilibria.

Section 5 contains a summary and conclusion.

Before we begin we want to acknowledge that we have borrowed ideas from Cass and Shell's notes (undated), Okuno and Zilcha 1977, and Wallace 1977.

Finally, we would like to acknowledge the intellectual influence of Black (1974) upon us in stressing the importance of the nonuniqueness problem discussed in section 4 for monetary policy. Calvo (1978, 1979) has written two interesting papers on related topics.

2. The Model

The model presented here is a simple overlapping generations model. Each consumer lives two periods. There is no population growth, and there is only one consumption good. Consumers born in period t are called *young* at t and *old* at $t + 1$. They each receive endowments of w_y in period t and $w_o < w_y$ in period $t + 1$. Furthermore, in period $t + 1$ they receive a monetary transfer h_{t+1}. The consumption good is perishable, but consumers may carry money from t to $t + 1$. Their utility function is given by $u[c_y(t)] + \delta u[c_o(t)]$. Formally, each consumer solves

$$\text{maximize } u[c_y(t)] + \delta u[c_o(t+1)] \tag{1}$$

subject to

$$p_t c_y(t) + m_y(t) = p_t w_y$$

$$p_{t+1} c_o(t+1) = m_y(t) + h_{t+1} + p_{t+1} w_o$$

where $c_y(t)$ is consumption of a young person at t, $c_o(t + 1)$ is consumption of an old person at $t + 1$, and $m_y(t)$ is money demand by young people at t. If u is strongly concave [that is, $u''(x) < 0$] and $u'(0) = +\infty$, a sufficient condition for a solution to (1) is given by

$$\frac{u'[c_y(t)]}{u'[c_o(t+1)]} = \frac{p_t}{p_{t+1}} \delta \tag{2}$$

and

$$c_y < w_y .$$

Now we are ready to define a monetary equilibrium for a money supply sequence

$$\{m_t^s\}_{t=0}^{\infty}.$$

DEFINITION. *A sequence* $\{p_t\}_{t=0}^{\infty}, p_t > 0, t = 0,1,\ldots$ *is a monetary equilibrium if*

(a) *For all* $t, c_y(t) + c_o(t) = w_o + w_y = \overline{w}$.
(b) $m_t^s = m_y(t), t=0,1,2,\ldots$.

Note that (b) is just the requirement that money supply be equal to money demand in every period since old people demand no money. We are now ready to prove an easy but basic result for the case of certainty.

PROPOSITION 1. *If* $h_t \equiv m_t^s - m_{t-1}^s \equiv \sigma m_{t-1}^s, \sigma > -1$, *and if* c_y *and* c_o *are positive numbers such that* $u'(c_y) = \delta u'(c_o)/(1 + \sigma)$, $c_y + c_o = \overline{w}$, *and if* $0 < c_o - w_o$, *then* $p_{t+1} \equiv (1 + \sigma)p_t$, $p_0 \equiv m_0^s/(c_o - w_o)$ *forms an equilibrium sequence.*

Proof. We will show that $\{p_t\}_{t=1}^{\infty}$, and $c_y(t) \equiv c_y, t = 0, 1, \ldots, c_o(t) \equiv c_o, t = 0, 1,\ldots$ satisfy (2) and the definition of a monetary equilibrium. On the one hand, it is obvious from the definition of $\{p_t\}$ that (2) is satisfied. On the other hand, we must show that market clearing obtains. It is enough to show that the money market clears. Now

$$m_y(0) = p_0(w_y - c_y) = p_0(c_o - w_o) = m_0^s.$$

Hence (b) holds for $t = 0$. Suppose now that (b) holds for $t \leqq \tau - 1$. Then

$$p_0 = \frac{m_0^s}{(c_o - w_o)}$$

and therefore

$$p_\tau = \frac{m_0^s (1 + \sigma)^\tau}{(c_o - w_o)} \equiv \frac{m_\tau^s}{(c_o - w_o)}.$$

From the budget constraint of the young consumer and the construction of $\{p_t\}$ we have

$$m_y(\tau) = p_\tau(w_y - c_y) = p_\tau(c_o - w_o) = m_\tau^s.$$

This ends the proof.

Before going on we warn the reader that has not looked at Gale 1973 or the conference papers of Cass-Okuno-Zilcha and Wallace that there is a continuum of perfect foresight equilibria. The stationary equilibrium of Proposition 1 is just one of these. We defer study of the others until section 4.

It may be helpful to develop a graphical depiction of equilibria before doing any more analysis. For the case $h_t = 0, t = 1,2,\ldots$, follow the Cass-Okuno-Zilcha (COZ) paper and recognize that the solution $[c_y(t), c_o(t + 1)]$ of the consumer's problem lies on the offer curve. Then depict the dynamics of a perfect foresight equilibrium as do COZ.[2] Unfortunately this neat depic-

[2]David Cass pointed out to us that if we work with real transfers y^{th} directly then to each sequence of real transfers $y_1, y_2, \ldots$, in particular the stationary sequence $\bar{y}$, we may draw an offer curve through the point $(w_y, w_o + y_t)$. If we do this for the stationary case $(w_y, w_o + \bar{y})$, we may trivially adopt COZ's technique to depict the equilibrium dynamics graphically and hence apply their analysis directly to our stationary σ-equilibria. This is so because the young's demand

tion of the equilibrium dynamics is not as useful when $h_t \neq 0$ since the offer curve at each date depends upon $\{h_t\}$.

We can, however, depict the stationary σ-equilibria graphically. Given a utility function $U(c_y,c_o)$ consider the income consumption curve—call it ICC(σ)—generated by the problem

$$\text{maximize } U(c_y,c_o)$$

subject to

$$c_y + (1+\sigma)c_o = I$$

as I varies. Stationary σ-equilibria are contained in the set of points $E(\sigma)$ where the ICC(σ) intersects the economy's production possibility frontier

$$\text{PPF} = \{(c_y,c_o) \mid c_y + c_o = w_y + w_o \equiv \overline{w}\}.$$

A point $[\bar{c}_y(\sigma),\bar{c}_o(\sigma)] \in E(\sigma)$ is indeed a σ-equilibrium if positive real balances are carried at $[\bar{c}_y(\sigma),\bar{c}_o(\sigma)]$. In order to check for positive real balances, just check that the elderly are spending more than w_o, or what is the same thing, that the young are spending less than w_y. Graphically speaking, points in $E(\sigma)$ that lie to the left of (w_y,w_o) on the PPF are σ-equilibria.

Such a graphical apparatus may be used with profit in constructing examples. We shall rely on COZ to aid us in briefly expositing some examples.

The first example is one where the barter equilibrium is Pareto optimal, but $\sigma < 0$ may be chosen so that the resulting stationary monetary equilibrium is Pareto optimal. This shows that the "existence proposition" (as COZ call it) in Samuelson's basic model does not obtain when $\sigma \neq 0$. To construct the example, set $(w_y,w_o) \equiv (\hat{c}_y,\hat{c}_o)$ and follow Proposition 2(b) below. In other words, choose $\sigma < 0$ and check that the ICC(σ) cuts the PPF left of $(\hat{c}_y,\hat{c}_o)$ in the normal case. Show this by noting that the ICC(0) cuts the PPF exactly at $(\hat{c}_y,\hat{c}_o)$ and by noticing that c_o is cheaper than c_y when $\sigma < 0$.

The first example is what COZ call a "coexistence example." We did not need heterogeneity of tastes, as did COZ, but we did need $\sigma \neq 0$ in order to create such an example.

Turn now to a second example.

In order to create what COZ call a "nonoptimality example," choose (w_y,w_o) so that it is not Pareto optimal. Anywhere to the right of $(\hat{c}_y,\hat{c}_o)$ on the PPF will do. Now choose $\sigma > 0$ so that the ICC(σ) cuts the PPF to the right of $(\hat{c}_y,\hat{c}_o)$ but to the left of (w_y,w_o). By Proposition 2(a) such a σ-equilibrium is not Pareto optimal.

It is important to recognize that in the COZ examples $\sigma = 0$. The counterexamples that they present are more fundamental in the sense that gov-

$[c_y(t),c_o(t+1)]$ lies on the offer curve through $(w_y,w_o+\bar{y})$. Equilibrium $[c_y(t),c_o(t)]$ must satisfy $c_y(t) + c_o(t) = w_y + w_o$.

In order to depict an equilibrium path graphically, start at a point $[c_y(0),c_o(0)]$ on the

$$\text{PPF} \equiv \{(c_y,c_o) \mid c_y + c_o \equiv w_y + w_o \equiv \overline{w}\}.$$

Find a point $[c_y(0),c_o(1)]$ on the offer curve through $(w_y,w_o+\bar{y})$. Now find a point $[c_y(1),c_o(1)]$ on the PPF. Continue in this manner. Therefore the minor adaptation of the COZ analysis that was suggested above applies directly to the stationary σ-equilibria.

ernment is not doing anything to distort the terms of trade between present and future in their examples.

We feel, however, that the case $\sigma \neq 0$ drives home the point that the mere act itself of introducing a social mechanism such as money that allows finitely lived people in a world of perishable goods to store value has little to do with efficiency per se even when preferences are very well behaved. Take note that we are not saying that there is no way that government can manage the money supply that will improve efficiency. COZ do not tell us that there is no way to steer their nonoptimality example to a Pareto optimum by a well chosen monetary policy. It would be interesting to ask what conditions on preferences and endowments guarantee the existence of some monetary policy that will lead to a Pareto optimum equilibrium.

Let us get back to analysis. For fixed δ, what happens when σ varies?

Since

$$U_y(c_y,c_o) = \frac{1}{(1+\sigma)} U_o(c_y,c_o)$$

$$c_y + c_o = \overline{w}$$

$$c_y + (1+\sigma)c_o = I,$$

for the case $U(c_y,c_o) \equiv u(c_y) + \delta u(c_o)$ we have

$$\frac{\partial c_y}{\partial \sigma} = -\left[u''(c_y) + \frac{\delta u''(\overline{w} - c_y)}{(1+\sigma)}\right]^{-1} \delta u'(\overline{w} - c_y) \frac{1}{(1+\sigma)^2} > 0$$

and therefore

$$\frac{\partial c_y}{\partial \sigma} > 0.$$

But notice that this is valid only for $c_y < w_y$. (By Proposition 1 the requirement that $c_y < w_y$ is needed for equilibrium, namely, $c_o > w_o$, obtains.) Thus a higher rate of monetary expansion induces a higher consumption when young.

What can be said about Pareto optimality? We can prove this:

PROPOSITION 2.

(a) *For $\sigma > 0$, if a time stationary equilibrium exists, then it is Pareto inefficient.*

(b) *For $\sigma \leqq 0$, if a time stationary equilibrium exists, it is Pareto optimum.*

Proof.

(a) Let $\hat{c}_y$, $\hat{c}_o$ be defined by

$$\hat{c}_y + \hat{c}_o = \overline{w}$$

and

$$u'(\hat{c}_y) = \delta u'(\hat{c}_o).$$

Call $(\hat{c}_y,\hat{c}_o)$ the *global Pareto optimum*. Then, if $\bar{c}_o(\sigma)$ and $\bar{c}_y(\sigma)$ denote the consumption bundles in the competitive equilibrium associated with $\sigma \neq 0$ we know that $\bar{c}_y(\sigma) > \hat{c}_y$ and $\bar{c}_o(\sigma) < \hat{c}_o$. We show that the allocation $(\hat{c}_o,\hat{c}_y)$ Pareto dominates $[\bar{c}_o(\sigma),\bar{c}_y(\sigma)]$. Clearly the old consumer at time zero is better off. Also

$$u(\hat{c}_y) + \delta u(\hat{c}_o) > u[\bar{c}_y(\sigma)] + \delta u[\bar{c}_o(\sigma)]$$

since $\hat{c}_y,\hat{c}_o$ solve the problem

$$\text{maximize } u(c_y) + \delta u(c_o)$$

subject to

$$c_y + c_o = \overline{w}$$

and

$$\bar{c}_y(\sigma),\bar{c}_o(\sigma) \text{ satisfy } \bar{c}_y(\sigma) + \bar{c}_o(\sigma) = \overline{w}.$$

This ends the proof of part (a).

(b) Now consider the case $\sigma \leqq 0$. The proof is by contradiction. Suppose we may make some individual better off without making anyone else worse off. Then we must give that person more in old age. This is so because if we give her or him more in youth we must take it away from the old one who is still alive. Hence we may suppose without loss of generality that it is the first person who is made better off by the proposed reallocation. Hence there exists a feasible allocation $\{c_y(t), c_o(t)\}_{t=0}^{\infty}$ with

$$u[c_y(t)] + \delta u[c_o(t+1)] \geqq u[\bar{c}_y(\sigma)] + \delta u[\bar{c}_o(\sigma)] \text{ for } t = 0,1,2,\ldots$$

and

$$c_o(0) > \bar{c}_o(\sigma).$$

Now since u is strictly concave,

$$u[c_y(0)] - u[\bar{c}_y(\sigma)] < u'[\bar{c}_y(\sigma)]\,[c_y(0) - \bar{c}_y(\sigma)]$$

$$= u'[\bar{c}_y(\sigma)][\bar{c}_o(\sigma) - c_o(0)].$$

Since the proposed reallocation Pareto dominates $[\bar{c}_y(\sigma),\bar{c}_o(\sigma)]$, u is concave, and $c_y(0) + c_o(0) \leqq \overline{w}$, we must have

$$\delta u[c_o(1)] - \delta u[\bar{c}_o(\sigma)] \geqq u[\bar{c}_y(\sigma)] - u[c_y(0)]$$

$$\geqq u'[\bar{c}_y(\sigma)][\bar{c}_y(\sigma) - c_y(0)]$$

$$\geqq u'[\bar{c}_y(\sigma)][c_o(0) - \bar{c}_o(\sigma)].$$

The chain of inequalities derived above gives us

(3) $$\delta u[c_o(1)] - \delta u[\bar{c}_o(\sigma)] > u'[\bar{c}_y(\sigma)][c_o(0) - \bar{c}_o(\sigma)] > 0.$$

Again, the concavity of u gives us

(4) $$\delta u[c_o(1)] - \delta u[\bar{c}_o(\sigma)] \leqq \delta u'[\bar{c}_o(\sigma)][c_o(1) - \bar{c}_o(\sigma)].$$

From (3) and (4) together we get

$$\frac{c_o(1) - \bar{c}_o(\sigma)}{c_o(0) - \bar{c}_o(\sigma)} > \frac{u'[\bar{c}_y(\sigma)]}{\delta u'[\bar{c}_o(\sigma)]} = \frac{1}{(1 + \sigma)}.$$

If $\sigma < 0$, then replacing 0 by 1 and 1 by 2 in the above reasoning, continuing in the above manner we eventually obtain

$$c_o(t) - \bar{c}_o(\sigma) > \left(\frac{1}{1 + \sigma}\right)^t [c_o(0) - \bar{c}_o(\sigma)] > \overline{w} - \bar{c}_o(\sigma)$$

for t large enough which is a contradiction to $c_o(t) \leqq \overline{w}$.

For the case $\sigma = 0$, it may be possible that

$$\lim_{t \to \infty} [c_o(t) - \bar{c}_o(0)] \equiv \gamma < \overline{w} - \bar{c}_o(\sigma).$$

In such a case we must have

$$\lim_{t \to \infty} [\bar{c}_y(0) - c_y(t)] = \gamma.$$

But note that $\bar{c}_y(0) \equiv \hat{c}_y, \bar{c}_o(0) \equiv \hat{c}_o$. The strong concavity of u guarantees us that for a t sufficiently large

$$u[c_y(t)] + \delta u[c_o(t)] < u(\hat{c}_y) + \delta u(\hat{c}_o)$$

since $\hat{c}_y, \hat{c}_o$ solve

$$\text{maximize } u(c_y) + \delta u(c_o)$$

subject to

$$c_y + c_o = \overline{w}.$$

This is a contradiction to the hypothesis that $\{c_y(t), c_o(t)\}$ Pareto dominates $(\hat{c}_y, \hat{c}_o)$.

Q.E.D.

Notice that our results concerning Pareto optimality differ from those of Lucas (1972). The reason is that Lucas assumed that transfers were proportional to the money holdings of the consumer. In our model transfers are given exogenously; hence, for higher rates of expansion of the money supply the individual tries to economize in real money balances and so consumes more when young. More to the point, $\sigma \neq 0$ imposes a wedge between the marginal rate of substitution (MRS) and the marginal rate of transformation which is unity along the PPF.

Existence of a stationary equilibrium with a positive price for money requires that the MRS evaluated at the initial endowment point be less than $1/(1+\sigma)$. When $w_o > 0$, if the factor of monetary expansion, $1 + \sigma$, becomes too large, there will exist no pair c_y, c_o with $u'(c_y) = \delta u'(c_o)/(1+\sigma)$, $c_y + c_o = \overline{w}$, *and* $c_o > w_o$. Hence in such a case no stationary monetary equilibrium will exist. We can, however, prove the following result:

PROPOSITION 3. *For a given* $\overline{w}$ *suppose* $w_y > \hat{c}_y$ *and consequently* $w_o < \hat{c}_o$. *Then there exists* $\epsilon > 0$ *such that for each* $\sigma \leqq \epsilon$, *there exists* $p_o(\sigma)$ *such that the sequence* $p_t(\sigma)$ *with* $p_{t+1}(\sigma) = (1 + \sigma)p_t(\sigma)$, $t = 0,1,\ldots$ *form an equilibrium.*

Proof. By assumption $u'(w_y) < \delta u'(w_o)$ and hence $u'(w_y) < \delta u'(w_o)/(1+\sigma)$ for any $\sigma < \epsilon$ for some $\epsilon > 0$. Consequently we may find $c_y(\sigma)$ and $c_o(\sigma)$ such that $c_y(\sigma) + c_o(\sigma) = \overline{w}$ and $u'[c_y(\sigma)] = \delta u'[c_o(\sigma)]/(1+\sigma)$ with $c_y(\sigma) > w_y$ and hence $c_o(\sigma) < w_o$. The result follows from Proposition 1.

The reader should notice that when the rate of deflation is high enough *every generation but the* 0th *one is made worse off than at its initial endowment.* It may seem strange that the introduction of money makes one enter into transactions that lower utility. One should not forget, however, that in a deflation $h_t < 0$. Hence the deflation is equivalent to a tax on old people (except, of course, the first generation of old people).

If one would consider a model as the one considered here but with t ranging from $-\infty$ to ∞, then it is obvious that $\sigma = 0$ would yield the unique Pareto optimum stationary equilibrium. This is because in such a case there will be no 0th generation being made better off by the increase in the real value of their money holdings caused by the expected deflation.

Turn now to the case of uncertainty.

3. The Money Supply Is Random

The purpose of this section is to formulate a notion of rational expectations equilibrium in the overlapping generations setup introduced in section 2 for the case when the money supply is *random*. After doing this we will demonstrate that for a given variance of the rate of growth of the money supply there is a deterministic growth rate that gives the same real allocation in equilibrium. This follows from observing that the price level is proportional to the quantity of money in a stationary rational expectations equilibrium. Hence it turns out that when the variance of the money supply increases the variance of the price level increases, and this in turn may increase the average real rate of return on cash over any interval of time due to the convexity of the function $f(p) \equiv 1/p$. Given that money provides the only means of carrying wealth forward from youth to old age in this model, it seems plausible that people will be made better off if the average real rate of return on this asset is increased.

Let us get into the details.

The real side of the model is the same as that in section 2. The only difference is that given $\tilde{m}_t^s$ at each $t + 1$ the transfer is given by

$$\tilde{h}_{t+1} \equiv (\tilde{A} - 1)\tilde{m}_t^s \equiv \tilde{\sigma}\tilde{m}_t^s \tag{5}$$

where $\tilde{A}$ is a random variable. For example, we will put

$$(6) \qquad \tilde{A} = \begin{Bmatrix} A + \lambda, \text{ probability } 1/2 \\ A - \lambda, \text{ probability } 1/2 \end{Bmatrix}$$

where A is constant and study what happens to equilibrium values when λ increases.

At each time t the young solve

$$(7) \qquad \text{maximize } u[\tilde{c}_y(t)] + \delta E_t u[\tilde{c}_o(t+1)]$$

subject to

$$(8) \qquad \tilde{p}_t \tilde{c}_y(t) + \tilde{m}_y(t) = \tilde{p}_t w_y$$

$$(9) \qquad \tilde{p}_{t+1}\tilde{c}_o(t+1) = \tilde{m}_y(t) + \tilde{h}_{t+1} + \tilde{p}_{t+1} w_o$$

$$= \tilde{m}_y(t) + (\tilde{A} - 1)\tilde{m}_t^s + \tilde{p}_{t+1} w_o .$$

Here E_t denotes the mathematical expectation conditional on information available at t. Also, variables with tildes are random.

The old consume at t according to

$$(10) \qquad \tilde{p}_t \tilde{c}_o(t) = \tilde{m}_y(t-1) + \tilde{h}_t + \tilde{p}_t w_o .$$

We may now define a rational expectations equilibrium.

DEFINITION. *Given the random process* $\{\tilde{m}_t^s\}_{t=0}^{\infty}$, *a sequence of random variables* $\{p_0, \tilde{p}_1, \tilde{p}_2, \ldots\}$ *is a rational expectations equilibrium (R.E.) if money demand equals money supply and goods demand equals goods supply for almost every realization of* $\{\tilde{m}_t^s\}_{t=0}^{\infty}$. *That is, for almost all realizations of* $\{\tilde{m}_t\}_{t=0}^{\infty}$ *we have*

$$(11) \qquad \tilde{c}_y(t) + \tilde{c}_o(t) = w_o + w_y = \overline{w}, \quad t = 0,1,2,\ldots$$

$$(12) \qquad \tilde{m}_t^s = \tilde{m}_y(t), \quad t = 0,1,2,\ldots.$$

The definition just says that people know the probability distribution of the money supply process and the price level process and that their expectations are confirmed.

Time 0 is special since we must specify the initial stock of money as the holdings of the old that are living at time 0. That is,

$$(13) \qquad m_0^s = m_o(0)$$

and

$$(14) \qquad p_0 c_o(0) = m_o(0) + p_0 w_o = m_0^s + p_0 w_o .$$

Hence, as in the certainty case, we are assuming that

$$(15) \qquad p_0 = m_0^s / [c_o(0) - w_o].$$

As in the certainty case we will choose $c_o(0)$ and define p_0 via (14) in order to create an equilibrium candidate that is stationary in the real variables.

In order to solve for an R.E., let us derive the first-order necessary conditions for an optimum of $(\tilde{P})$ given $\{\tilde{p}_t\}$. From (8) and (9) we get

$$u\,[c_y(t)] + \delta E_t u\,[c_o(t+1)] \tag{16}$$

$$= u\,[w_y - \tilde{m}_y(t)/\tilde{p}_t] + \delta E_t u\left\{[\tilde{m}_y(t) + (\tilde{A} - 1)m_t^s]/\tilde{p}_{t+1} + w_o\right\}.$$

Differentiate both sides of (16) with respect to $\tilde{m}_y(t)$ to get

$$-u'\,[c_y(t)](1/\tilde{p}_t) + \delta E_t\{u'\,[c_o(t+1)]\,(1/\tilde{p}_{t+1})\} \leqq 0 \;\; [=0, \text{ if } \tilde{m}_y(t) > 0]. \tag{17}$$

Now in an R.E. it is necessary that

$$\tilde{m}_t^s = \tilde{m}_y(t), \;\; t = 0, 1, 2, \ldots \tag{18}$$

$$m_0^s \equiv m_o(0).$$

Put (17) in real balance form, and use (18) to get

$$-u'\,[c_y(t)]\,\tilde{x}_t + \delta E_t\{u'\,[c_o(t+1)]\,[\tilde{m}_y(t)\,/\tilde{p}_{t+1}]\} \tag{19}$$

$$= -u'\,[c_y\,(t)]\,\tilde{x}_t$$

$$+\, \delta E_t\{u'\,[c_o\,(t+1)]\,[\tilde{m}_y(t+1)\,/\tilde{p}_{t+1}]\,[\tilde{m}_y(t)\,/\tilde{m}_y\,(t+1)]\}$$

$$= -u'\,[c_y\,(t)]\,\tilde{x}_t + \delta E_t\{u'\,[c_o\,(t+1)]\,(\tilde{x}_{t+1})\,[\tilde{m}_s(t)\,/\tilde{m}_s(t+1)]\} \leqq 0.$$

Here

$$\tilde{x}_t \equiv \tilde{m}_y(t)\,/\tilde{p}_t. \tag{20}$$

In order to find a solution to the R.E. equations we will try for an R.E. of the form

$$\tilde{c}_o(t) = \bar{c}_o,\;\; \tilde{c}_y(t) = \bar{c}_y,\;\; \tilde{x}_t = \bar{x} > 0,\;\; \tilde{p}_t = \tilde{m}_s(t)/\bar{x} \tag{21}$$

where all barred quantities are constant and nonrandom.

From (19) and (21), if $\bar{x} > 0$, we must have

$$-u'(\bar{c}_y) + \delta u'(\bar{c}_o)\,E_t\{\tilde{m}_s(t)\,/\tilde{m}_s(t+1)\} = 0. \tag{22}$$

But

$$E_t\{\tilde{m}_s(t)\,/\tilde{m}_s(t+1)\} = E_t\{1/\tilde{A}\} = 1/2\{[1/(A+\lambda)] + [1/(A-\lambda)]\}. \tag{23}$$

Notice that the right-hand side of (23) increases as λ increases for $0 \leqq \lambda < A$. Let

$$\bar{R} \equiv E_t\{1/\tilde{A}\}. \tag{24}$$

Can we find $(\bar{c}_y, \bar{c}_o)$ such that

$$(25)\qquad u'(\bar{c}_y) = \delta \bar{R}\, u'(\bar{c}_o)$$

$$(26)\qquad \bar{c}_y + \bar{c}_o = \bar{w} \equiv w_y + w_o?$$

Examine Figure 1.

Figure 1

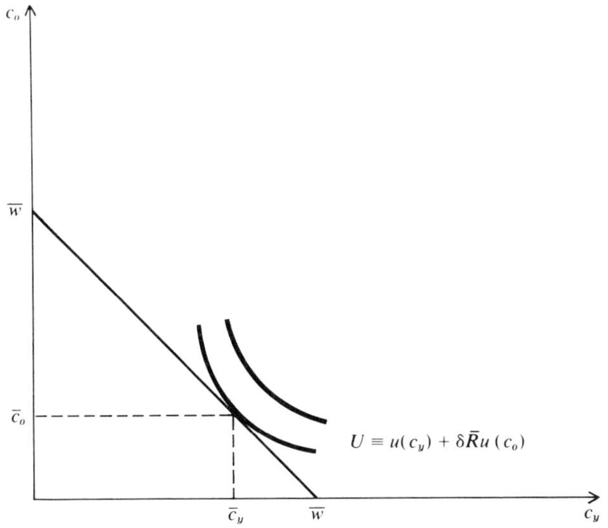

Obviously the point of tangency in Figure 1 solves (25) and (26). Now define p_0 by

$$(27)\qquad p_0\bar{c}_o = m_0^s + p_0 w_o$$

that is,

$$(28)\qquad p_0 = m_0^s/(\bar{c}_o - w_o).$$

Define $\bar{x}$ by

$$(29)\qquad m_0^s/p_0 = \bar{x} = \bar{c}_o - w_o.$$

Put

$$(30)\qquad \tilde{p}_1 = \tilde{m}_1^s/\bar{x},\ \tilde{p}_2 = \tilde{m}_2^s/\bar{x}, \ldots.$$

We may sum up the above into

THEOREM 1. *If (25) and (26) have a solution* $\bar{c}_y > 0$, $\bar{c}_o > 0$, *and* $\bar{c}_o - w_o > 0$, *then* $\bar{x} = \bar{c}_o - w_o$, $p_0 = m_0^s/(\bar{c}_o - w_o)$, $\tilde{p}_t = \tilde{m}_t^s/\bar{x}$, $t = 1, 2, \ldots$ *is an R.E.*

Proof. This follows immediately by the construction of the R.E. welfare economics.

It is interesting to explore what values of (A, δ_o, λ) lead to a Pareto improvement over $(A_o, \delta_o, \lambda_o)$. To examine this question notice that the young achieve the highest utility when $(\bar{c}_y, \bar{c}_o)$ solves

$$\text{(31)} \qquad \text{maximize } u(c_y) + \delta u(c_o)$$

$$\text{subject to } c_y + c_o = \overline{w} \equiv w_y + w_o.$$

This is so because steady state utility for people born at 0, 1, 2, . . . is highest for solutions of (31).

However, the utility of old people living at $t = 0$ may not be the highest possible at $c_o = \bar{c}_o$.

We will show that there exist initial conditions $(A_o, \delta_o, \lambda_o)$ such that increasing the variance of the money supply will make everyone better off in R.E. For let $A_o > 1$, $\lambda_o = 0$. Then

$$\delta_o \bar{R} = \delta_o / A_o < \delta_o.$$

Let

$$c_y\,(A_o, \delta_o, \lambda_o), \quad c_o\,(A_o, \delta_o, \lambda_o)$$

denote the solution of (25) and (26). Now let λ_o increase to a value $\bar{\lambda}_o$ such that

$$1/2\delta \left\{ \frac{1}{A_o - \lambda_o} + \frac{1}{A_o + \bar{\lambda}_o} \right\} = \delta_o.$$

Obviously the utility of the people born at 0, 1, 2, ... is increased by this move since

$$\delta_o \bar{R} = \delta_o$$

after the increase in λ_o to $\bar{\lambda}_o$.

What about the utility of the old people at time 0? Their consumption rises since

$$c_o(A_o, \delta_o, \lambda_o)$$

increases in λ for $A_o > 1$, $\lambda_o = 0$. Hence the elderly living at 0 are better off as well.

What are the economics behind this apparently paradoxical result? Since $A_o > 1$, inflation is going on at the rate $A_o - 1$ when $\lambda = 0$. Money is the only way for the young to carry wealth from the period of high endowment to the period of low endowment. Recall that $w_y > w_o$. But when $A_o > 1$, money is depreciating at the rate $A_o - 1$. So the young consume more in their youth than is optimal, for they would like to consume to maximize $u(c_y) + \delta u(c_o)$ subject to $c_y + c_o = \overline{w}$.

But now let $\lambda > 0$. The real rate[3] of return on cash balances increases due to the convexity of $f(p) = 1/p$. Hence money depreciates less, and the young are made better off in lifetime utility terms since they save more for their old age even though on the average inflation is proceeding at the rate $A_o - 1$.

Turn to the old at time 0. Only the elderly receive fiat money transfers in this model. The money held by the elderly at time 0 is worth more to the young living at time 0 after λ increases. Hence the young are willing to pay more in terms of the consumption goods to the old at time 0 in order to obtain their money. Hence the old at 0 are better off.

For what positions $Z_o \equiv (A_o, \delta_o, \lambda_o)$ is it possible to find $Z = (A, \delta_o, \lambda)$ such that everyone is better off in the R.E. $[c_y(Z), c_o(Z)]$? The lifetime utility of young people living at $t = 0,1,2,\ldots$ is increased whenever $\bar{R}$ is made closer to unity. This is so because lifetime utility is maximized at the choice of (c_y, c_o) that solves

$$\text{maximize } u(c_y) + \delta u(c_o)$$

subject to

$$c_y + c_o = \overline{w}$$

that is (provided that $c_y > 0$, $c_o > 0$),

$$u'(c_y) = \delta u'(c_o), \quad c_y + c_o = \overline{w}. \tag{32}$$

But in R.E. we have

$$u'(c_y) = \delta \bar{R}\, u'(c_o), \quad c_y + c_o = \overline{w}. \tag{33}$$

Hence driving $\bar{R}$ nearer to unity leads to an increase in lifetime utility for young people living at $t = 0, 1, 2, \ldots$.

[3]This result is similar to the result that the real rate of return on bonds may increase when the variance of the rate of inflation increases. In order to see the latter, let

(a) $Q_{t+1} = (1 + r)Q_t$

(b) $P_{t+1} = (1 + \pi)P_t$

describe the nominal rate of return on bonds and the evolution of the price level, respectively. Here r and π are the nominal rate of return on bonds and the (random) rate of inflation, respectively. Then the expected real rate of return on bonds in $t+1$ given t is given by

(c) $E_t\{[Q_{t+1}/P_{t+1} - Q_t/P_t]/(Q_t/P_t)\} = E_t\{(1 + r)/(1 + \pi) - 1\}$.

Now for simplicity consider the random variable

$$\pi \begin{cases} = \bar{\pi} + \lambda, \text{ probability } 1/2 \\ = \bar{\pi} - \lambda, \text{ probability } 1/2. \end{cases}$$

An increase in λ corresponds to an increase in the variance of π about its mean $\bar{\pi}$. It is trivial to check that an increase in π will increase the right-hand side of (c). Hence, in this case, an increase in the variance of the rate of inflation will increase the real rate of return on bonds. This type of result is general for symmetric distribution functions.

What about the old living at $t = 0$? It is easy to see that an increase in $\bar{R}$ leads to an increase in c_o. Totally differentiate both sides of (33) with respect to $\bar{R}$ in order to prove this result. Hence any increase in R_o when $R_o < 1$ is Pareto superior. If $R_o \geqq 1$, further increases benefit the aged at $t = 0$ but harm everyone else.[4]

R_o may be increased by decreasing A or by increasing λ. Hence when $R_o < 1$ we see that increasing the variance of the rate of growth of the money supply or decreasing the mean of the rate of growth of the money supply leads to a welfare improvement for everyone.

It is worth pointing out how the graphical apparatus used to illuminate Propositions 1 and 2 may be used to study the case of uncertainty. Notice that

$$\bar{R} \equiv E_t\{\tilde{m}_s(t) / \tilde{m}_s(t + 1)\}$$

plays the role of $1/(1 + \sigma)$ in Propositions 1 and 2. Hence, define $\bar{\sigma}$ by

$$\frac{1}{1 + \bar{\sigma}} \equiv \bar{R}.$$

Call $\bar{\sigma}$ the equivalent deterministic growth rate. Then look at the intersection of the ICC($\bar{\sigma}$) and the PPF as in section 2. This intersection is the R.E. studied earlier in section 3. Increasing the variance of $\tilde{A}$ amounts to decreasing $\bar{\sigma}$, so it is not surprising that welfare is increased if $\bar{\sigma} > 0$. In fact, as pointed out to us by Don Roper of the University of Utah, it might be more natural to view $\bar{\sigma}$ as a measure of the mean rate of growth of the money supply.

It is natural to look for the analogue of Friedman's optimum quantity of money in this model for the case $\lambda = 0$. A Pareto optimum is located at $R_o = 1$:

$$R_o \equiv 1/A_o \equiv 1. \tag{34}$$

Hence constant money supply is Pareto optimum. This is the same as Friedman's case, since he manages the money supply so that the real rate of return on it is zero. His case corresponds to $R_o \equiv 1$ in our model. Because people discount the utility of their progeny, Friedman needs to contract the money supply at the rate of time preference in order to force the real rate of return on it to be zero. However, all policies $A_o \leqq 1$ are Pareto optimal in our model. The reader is referred to Brock 1974 for an explicitly formulated version of Friedman's model.

[4]It is fruitful to think of $R - 1$ as a measure of distortion introduced by monetary policy. This is so because $R = 1$ is optimal in the sense that steady-state utility and hence equilibrium utility is maximal for all generations except the elderly living at time 0.

If one asks the question as has been suggested by Hurwicz — What monetary policy R will optimize equilibrium utility for all generations beginning at $T = -\infty$ and ending at $t = +\infty$? — then the answer is to put $R = 1$.

The $R = 1$ policy is attractive since a move to it from any policy $R \neq 1$ will help an infinitude of generations and harm at most the elderly living at time 0. Out of all the Pareto optima $R \geqq 1$, the $R = 1$ policy appears especially attractive since it maximizes capitalized steady-state utility.

One should not make too much of the result that an increase in variance of the money supply may increase welfare. There is no real uncertainty in our model. That is, real balances are deterministic. The result merely says that for a given random rate of growth of the money supply there is an equivalent deterministic monetary policy that yields the same value of $\bar{R}$. We are not advocating that the Fed start flipping coins in order to figure out what to do next.

4. Other Equilibria

It was Gale (1973) who first showed in the nonstochastic case with constant money stock that besides the stationary equilibrium studied above there exists in general a continuum of equilibria. This result still persists in our model. The treatment that follows borrows from Gale's treatment of what he calls the "Samuelson case," and we wish to thank Charles Wilson of the University of Wisconsin for pointing out to us the relevance of Gale's work to our problem.

Turn back to the beginning of section 3. Let us write equation (19) in real balance form in order to study expeditiously all the R.E. equilibria with $\tilde{p}_t > 0$, $t = 0,1,2,\ldots$ that are *not random* in real balances, that is,

$$(35) \qquad -u'(w_y - x_t)\,x_t + \delta E_t\,\{u'(w_o + x_{t+1})\,(x_{t+1})\,[m_s(t)\,/\,m_s(t+1)]\} \leqq 0 \quad (= 0 \text{ if } x_t > 0).$$

Notice that we did not put a tilde on x_t, x_{t+1} since we are restricting ourselves to the study of the selections of (35) that are nonrandom. Now

$$(36) \qquad E_t\,\{\tilde{m}_s(t)\,/\,\tilde{m}_s(t+1)\} = E_t\,\{1/\tilde{A}\} \equiv \bar{R}.$$

Hence (35) becomes

$$(37) \qquad -u'(w_y - x_t)\,x_t + \delta\bar{R}u'(w_o + x_{t+1})\,x_{t+1} \leqq 0 \quad (= 0 \text{ if } x_t > 0).$$

Let us restrict attention to those solutions of (37) where $x_t > 0$, $t = 0,1,2,\ldots$. A sufficient condition for $x_t > 0$, $t = 0,1,2,\ldots$ will be given shortly. Hence

$$(38) \qquad u'(w_y - x_t)\,x_t \equiv A(x_t) = \delta\bar{R}u'(w_o + x_{t+1})\,x_{t+1} \equiv B(x_{t+1}).$$

We will argue below that under reasonable assumptions on u Figure 2 tells the story. Figure 2 is intended to capture the following basic properties:

(a) $A(0) = B(0) = 0$.
(b) B may not decrease for $x > \bar{x}$.
(c) A is always increasing.
(d) $A'(0) < B'(0)$.
(e) There is just one $\bar{x} > 0$ such that $A(\bar{x}) = B(\bar{x})$; that is, $A(x) < B(x)$ for $x \in (0,\bar{x})$.

If $w_y > 0$ and $w_o > 0$, then (a) obviously holds. Property (b) will be assumed throughout. To prove (c), calculate

$$(39) \qquad A'(x) = -u''(w_y - x)\,x + xu'(w_y - x) > 0, \quad \text{for } x > 0$$

Figure 2

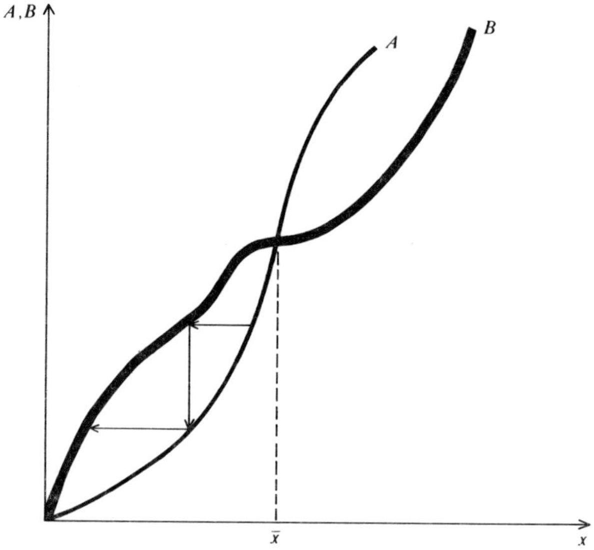

since

$$u'' \leqq 0,\ \ u' > 0,\ \ x > 0.$$

Turn now to (d). From (39) we obtain

(40) $A'(0) = 0$, provided $w_y > 0$.

Calculate $B'(0)$. We have

(41) $B'(x) = \delta R u'(w_o + x) + \delta R u''(w_o + x)x,\ \ B'(0) = \delta R u'(w_o) > 0.$

Hence (d) holds.

Let us examine (e). Here for $x > 0$

(42) $A(x) = B(x)$

if

(43) $u'(w_y - x) = \delta R u'(w_o + x).$

The left-hand side of this is increasing while the right is decreasing. Hence the assumption that $u'(w_y) < \bar{R}u'(w_o)$ is sufficient for (e). This assumption will be maintained throughout.

The following theorem obtains.

THEOREM 2. *Let the difference equation $A(x_t) = B(x_{t+1})$ satisfy properties (a)–(e). Then (i) $x_t \searrow 0$, $t \to \infty$ or (ii) $x_t = \bar{x}$, $t = 0,1,2,\ldots$ or (iii) $x_t \nearrow \infty$, $t \to \infty$, for any solution $\{x_t\}$.*

Proof. This is obvious from Figure 2. Here $x_t \searrow 0$ means that the sequence x_t decreases to 0, $t \to \infty$. Analogously $x_t \nearrow \infty$, $t \to \infty$.

Remark. Notice that the function $B(\cdot)$ is not required to be nondecreasing on $[0, \bar{x}]$ and that $A(x_t) = B(x_{t+1})$ may be satisfied for more than one x_{t+1} for each x_t.

We have proven above that (c), (d), and (e) must hold in the class of models we are considering and that (a) holds when $w_y > 0$ and $w_o > 0$. The following lemma will be useful in verifying condition (b).

LEMMA. *If for $y > 0$, $[-u'(y)] / [u''(y)\, y] \geqslant 1$ (that is, the coefficient of relative risk aversion is $\geqslant 1$), then $B'(x) > 0$ for $x > 0$.*

Proof. $[-u'(y)] / [u''(y)\, y] \geqslant 1$ implies $u''(w_o + x)(w_o + x) + u'(w_o + x) > 0$ for any $x > 0$. Now since $u''(w_o + x)\, w_o < 0$, we must have $u''(w_o + x)\, x + u'(w_o + x) > 0$. The result follows from (41).

Q.E.D.

Solutions $\{x_t\}$ such that $x_t \to \infty$ as $t \to \infty$ cannot be R.E.'s, since from the budget constraint $x_t \leqslant w_y$ must hold. All other solutions are equilibria, however.

THEOREM 3. *Let $\{x_t\}_{t=0}^{\infty}$ be any solution of $A(x_t) = B(x_{t+1})$ with $x_t \leqslant w_y$ for $t \geqslant 0$. Let $\tilde{p}_t = \tilde{m}_t^s / x_t$, $t = 0,1,2,\ldots$.* Then the stochastic process $\{\tilde{p}_t\}_{t=0}^{\infty}$ *is an R.E. price level sequence.*

Proof. Just check that $\{\tilde{p}_t\}$ satisfies the definition of an R.E.

Notice that $x_t \to 0$, $t \to \infty$ implies that people are ultimately driven to the consumption of their endowments. Such an equilibrium is not Pareto optimal because there exists a reallocation that makes some generations better off while making no other generation worse off. To construct such an allocation, simply wait until a time T_o when $x(T_o)$ is near zero and give some of the young person's endowment to the old living at T_o. Do this for all $t \geqq T_o$. It is trivial to see that this proposed reallocation is a Pareto improvement because at T_o, for example, the young who are harmed at T_o are given enough more (in their old age) by the young at $T_o + 1$ so that on the whole they are better off.

Notice that in such a case the welfare implications of a change in the rate of expansion of the money supply is no longer obvious, since one has to know which equilibria the economy will go to. Two solutions to this problem are possible. One is to introduce a weaker ordering requiring only the existence of better equilibria, and in this case the results of section 4 will hold. Another is to try to get rid of the nonstationary equilibria. This can be accomplished either by making an alternative assumption to (a) or by changing the specification of the model.

We first study the case in which the following condition holds besides (b)–(e).

(a′) $B(0) > 0,\ \ A(0) = 0.$

The picture is now as in Figure 3. As before, if $x_0 < \bar{x}$ then $x_{t+1} < x_t$. But now $B(x) > \epsilon$ for all $x \geqslant 0$ for some $\epsilon > 0$. And $\lim_{x \to 0} A(x) = 0$. Hence eventually

Figure 3

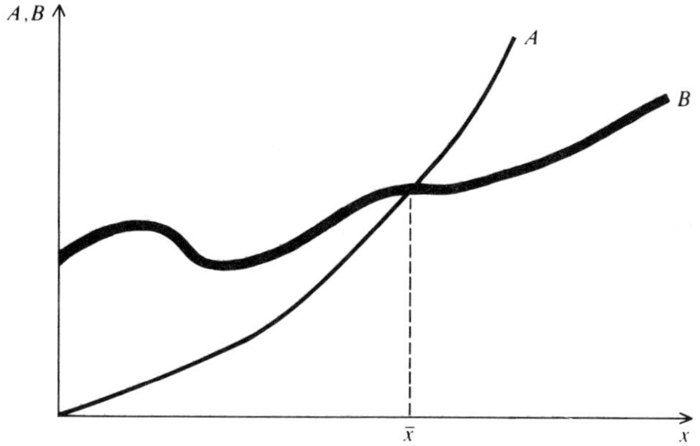

solutions with $x_0 < \bar{x}$ cannot be continued. Hence we have proven

THEOREM 4. *Under (a′) and (b)–(e), the stationary equilibrium is the unique R.E. which is nonrandom in real balances.*

An obvious example in which (a′) holds is given by $u(y) = \log y$ and $w_y > 0$, $w_o = 0$. In this case (b) also holds, as can be verified by using the lemma. Since (c), (d), and (e) are general properties in our model, Theorem 4 will be true in such a case.

We now return to the case where (a) holds instead of (a′). What is the economic meaning of equilibria when $x_t \to 0$, $t \to \infty$, and should we take such equilibria seriously or do they just reflect a specification of the model that is too loose for sound economics? As the model stands, it is silent about which of the multitude of equilibria the economy will follow for a given money supply process $\{\tilde{m}_t^s\}_{t=0}^{\infty}$. Notice also that the price level grows faster than the money supply along equilibria such that $x_t \to 0$, $t \to \infty$. We shall henceforth call such equilibria *hyperinflationary*.

The economic story is as follows. Suppose people expect a hyperinflationary path of the price level and act on such expectations. They will be fulfilled! Hence people by the very act of forming expectations on the nominal price level can have an impact on the evolution of real balances and drive themselves into a hyperinflation. Furthermore, only one of the infinitude of equilibria is not hyperinflationary.[5]

[5]It is perhaps appropriate at this point to quote from an Australian journalist, P. P. McGuinness (1977), who is describing to his readers what he calls a "recent innovation in monetarist thinking," namely, "rational expectations":

> For example, it has been suggested that attitudes to government deficit financing will have a major influence on whether it is inflationary or not. If people believe that the financing of the deficit must be inflationary, then they will act in such a way that that belief will be validated.

McGuinness comes very close here to describing a situation where beliefs themselves, independent of the underlying money supply process, determine the equilibrium path of the price level, and that is exactly the situation described by Theorem 3.

We are not sure whether to attach much economic significance to such equilibria for reasons that are outside the model. For example, with an additively separable utility function, if any change is made in the specification of the model that requires the holding of at least $\epsilon > 0$ real balances no matter how small ϵ is, then only one of the equilibria remains: $x_t = \bar{x}$, $t = 0,1,2,\ldots$. This is so because looking at Figure 2 we see that there will be a first time where the demand for real balances by the young which is greater than or equal to ϵ will be smaller than the supply by the old.

What changes in the specification of the model will lead to the holding of at least $\epsilon > 0$ worth of real balances for all t? A time-honored one is to require each generation while young to set aside ϵ units of purchasing power which is paid out in taxes to the government during that youth. This money is then returned to the young in a lump sum at the beginning of their old age. This social security system in effect requires the young to carry ϵ units of real balances. Notice that ϵ may be chosen arbitrarily provided it is less than the difference between w_y and the consumption of the young at the stationary equilibrium. Hence, for example, in our model an *arbitrarily small amount of social security coupled with a monetary policy that makes $\bar{R} = 1$ leads to a Pareto optimum*. Generating a demand for fiat money by requiring it to be used for payment of taxes is a common device in the theoretical money literature. But Edward Sieper of the Australian National University reminded us of Gale's "business cycle" which is depicted in Figure 3b of COZ. So a device that rules out equilibria where real balances go to zero is not enough to rule out equilibria that cycle, for instance. Furthermore, after looking at COZ we are convinced that one can construct just about any type of equilibrium.

Another device is to introduce a transaction technology into the model that leads to an indirect utility function that would lead to the demand for at least $\epsilon > 0$ units of real balances in order to facilitate transactions. It seems reasonable to conjecture that there exists a Becker-Lancaster activity analysis model of the household that would lead to the retention of some positive number $\epsilon > 0$ units of real balances for a given future bounded interval of rates of change of the price level.[6]

[6]The requirement that there exist a bounded interval that contains the rate of price level changes against which the economy is posited to retain real cash balances of at least $\epsilon > 0$ is important. Obviously no such $\epsilon > 0$ will exist in any reasonable economic model of the demand for money if the rate of change of the price level is unbounded.

Let us examine the nonrandom case.

Is p_{t+1}/p_t associated with $x_t \to 0$, $t \to \infty$, $A(x_t) = B(x_{t+1})$ bounded? Let $m_t^s = (1 + \sigma)^t m_0^s$, $m_0^s > 0$. Then

$$x_{t+1}/x_t = (1 + \sigma)\,(p_t/p_{t+1})$$

so that

$$p_{t+1}/p_t = (1 + \sigma)\,(x_t/x_{t+1}).$$

Now

$$u'(w_y - x_t)x_t = \delta R u'(w_o + x_{t+1})x_{t+1}$$

so that

$$x_t/x_{t+1} = \delta R u'(w_o + x_{t+1})/u'(w_y - x_t) \simeq \delta R u'\,(w_o)/u'(w_y)$$

More devices of introducing a minimal demand for cash balances for rates of change of the price level contained in a given bounded interval may be generated by the imaginative economist. Notice that the $x_t \searrow 0$ equilibria depicted in Figure 2 have bounded rates of change of the associated price level. This line of thought is pursued in Scheinkman's discussion in this volume.

5. Some Remarks on the Meaning of All This

In this paper we set up an overlapping generations model of a monetary economy that followed Samuelson 1958 and used it to study, for example, the robustness of some results that had been previously derived from models with real balances in the utility function. The device of putting real balances into the utility function has been controversial since the services of money are not explicitly modeled in such a formulation.

We found that, roughly speaking, perfectly anticipated inflations lead to welfare losses in such a model. In particular, let

$$R = E(1/\tilde{A})$$

where $A = 1 + \tilde{\sigma}$, $\tilde{\sigma}$ equals the random rate of growth of the money supply, and E equals the mathematical expectation of the random variable $1/\tilde{A}$. Then if $R_o < 1$, any change that leads to an increase in R_o leads to an increase in welfare for all generations. If $R_o \geqq 1$, an increase in R_o leads to an increase in the welfare of the elderly living at $t = 0$ but a fall in the welfare of all other generations.

These results follow from the assumptions that the indifference curve of the young at the endowment point cuts the PPF from below (that is, the marginal rate of substitution is less than one) and that money is the only means of transferring wealth from youth to old age.

It is natural to ask if these results are themselves robust to minor alterations of the model. Clearly if a capital good (which may be just inventories of consumption goods) is introduced that pays a return greater than that on cash balances (which is negative in an inflation), then the demand for money may disappear; with an alternative, more efficient store of value, no equilibrium with a positive price of money may exist. But if one introduces transaction costs for getting in and out of capital, then the demand for money with associated positive equilibrium price for money is likely to reappear if such transaction costs are large enough, and our results on the inflation tax, for example, are likely to obtain.

If the indifference curve of the young cuts the PPF from above at the endowment point, then there will be difficulties with existence of equilibrium with a positive price of money, since the young will want to borrow but the old will want to consume rather than lend. This observation leads us naturally to the question of whether overlapping generations models are a good foundation for monetary theory.

Erecting a monetary theory on the formulation of an overlapping generations model with the time span of a generation covering some twenty-five

for x_t, x_{t+1} near zero. Hence the growth factor p_{t+1}/p_t converges to the finite number

$$(1 + \sigma)\delta R u'(w_o)/u'(w_y) = \delta u'(w_o)/u'(w_y)$$

as $t \to \infty$. And hence the rate of growth of the price level is bounded along equilibria $x_t \to 0$, $t \to \infty$. The random case is similar.

years will strike the reader as bizarre indeed. We defend studying such a model because it allows us to gain insights into what is likely to happen in a more complicated model where a "generation" is one or two weeks, an individual lives for from five to six thousand "generations," and people carry money in order to consume in weeks they don't receive a paycheck and because it is too costly to move in and out of higher yielding capital goods every few weeks.

Now in such a model, for every individual who receives a large money endowment and a small real endowment at the beginning of "generation" t there must be another individual whose net money endowment is low and whose whole real endowment is high at the beginning of "generation" t, so that gains from trade are possible, and thus the aggregate stock of money has a chance of being held, in equilibrium, by the economy as a whole. Furthermore, the endowment (or wage) pattern (for each individual) of real goods and money must alternate in order to give individuals an incentive to carry money forward. Are such conditions satisfied well enough in the real world so that Gale's "Samuelson case" is a good abstraction? We don't know.

It is to capture the salient features of this more complicated economy that the fictions of generation, small endowment at old age, large endowment at youth, and each old generation having an offsetting young generation were introduced. Obviously in the overlapping generations case it may be more realistic to look at the case of low endowment at youth and high endowment in the second period of life, which Gale (1973) calls the "classical case." But there is no equilibrium with positive price of money in this case unless the indifference curve of the young through (w_y, w_o) cuts the PPF from below, and this is unlikely if $w_y < w_o$. There seems to be no compelling reason to reject Gale's "classical case" just because it is inconvenient to those who want to erect monetary theory on the foundations of the overlapping generations model (OLG).

Wallace's paper in this volume makes a spirited argument that overlapping generations models are likely to be the best models of money. He argues that fiat money is intrinsically useless and inconvertible. Hence, he argues, the continuum of equilibria in the OLG reflects just the "tenuousness" of equilibrium value of an asset that is intrinsically useless.

But two papers by Charles Wilson (1978a,b) explore a model that is more in the spirit of Clower in the sense that the equilibrium value of money ultimately derives from the "Clower budget constraint" that the value of an agent's current consumption cannot exceed the value of the agent's money holdings at the beginning of the trading period. (The Lucas paper in this volume also studies a model of this type.) Wilson's papers show that a multitude of equilibria exist when agents are finite lived. This seems to capture the tenuousness that Wallace is looking for without having to go through such contortions as ruling out Gale's "classical case" or having to rule out capital goods that can be costlessly traded.

How are we as economists to view the multitude of equilibria? The OLG gives no clue as to which one the economy will converge to, if any. Are we to believe that all are equally likely? Are we to make even money bets that a constitutional amendment to hold the money supply constant in a constant population deterministic economy with zero technological change will lead to rampant inflation? Hardly.

Yet to rule out such equilibria because they do not accord well with empirical work that supports the quantity theory as a long-run proposition (see Lucas 1978a) leaves unexplained the mechanism by which the economy converges to an equilibrium where the price level is proportional to the quantity of money.

We can follow Scheinkman's reasoning in this volume that if money is essential (in a sense that he makes precise) then all candidate equilibria with real balances converging to zero are untenable.

But this argument won't take care of periodic equilibria. In long-horizon models with a small rate of time preference and near linear utility, intertemporal arbitrage will crush periodic equilibria. This suggests that in the real world the correct time metric for an OLG model to be a good model of money would allow it to admit long and/or damped cycles only. After all, if the cycle had a period of two weeks and a high amplitude it would be arbitraged down in the real world. If it had a period of ten years then matters are more problematic. Utility should display more curvature and time preference should increase as the time metric (relative to which such utility and time preference are measured) is elongated.

What about equilibria such that real balances remain bounded away from zero and infinity but display no recognizable growth pattern? Again, for reasonable preferences relative to a sensible time metric, the price level would not move much weekly, monthly, or possibly even yearly on such equilibria. What about movements over a decade? Here again the case is not so clear.

About all we can say for sure is that the complications of multiple equilibria for monetarist doctrine and monetary policy need more research.

Transaction Demand for Money and Moral Hazard

John Bryant*

1. Introduction

The only existing tractable coherent model of fiat money is Samuelson's (1958)[1] pure consumption loan model (p.c.l.m.). However, most economists (including Samuelson himself?) do not take the p.c.l.m. as a serious model of money. This paper presents a case in favor of the p.c.l.m. as a serious model of fiat money. Indeed, it is argued that any model which implies fiat money must be essentially similar to the p.c.l.m. That is to say, the p.c.l.m. parsimoniously satisfies conditions which are necessary for any model of valued fiat money. The p.c.l.m. is, then, the preferred model of fiat money and should be the source of the null hypotheses for monetary economics.

Doubtless many will not find the above parsimony argument convincing, and for good reason. To say that the p.c.l.m. satisfies the necessary conditions for a model of fiat money does not say that the p.c.l.m. captures the important attributes of fiat money as it exists in the economy. Certainly the proposition that any model which satisfies the necessary conditions for fiat money will behave in all important respects like the p.c.l.m. is a nonprovable proposition. However, the number of possible modifications and embellishments of the p.c.l.m. is limitless, and to aimlessly produce them is an unproductive exercise.

A common specific criticism of the p.c.l.m. is that it involves only the store-of-value, not the transaction, motive for money holding. This criticism has force only when coupled with the presumption that including a transaction motive substantially alters the implications of the p.c.l.m. This paper answers this particular criticism in two ways. First, it is not at all obvious that the p.c.l.m. fails to include the transaction motive. Second, two models are presented which by anyone's definition should be considered transaction models but which are modifications of the p.c.l.m. and which have the same implications for at least some important questions.

The new models presented in this paper belong to the class of "informa-

*I thank Preston Miller and Neil Wallace for valuable comments and suggestions. Errors are my responsibility alone.

[1]Author names and years refer to the works listed at the end of this book.

tion'' models of money (see Brunner and Meltzer 1971). Fiat money is used in transactions because the information costs of other means of transacting are too high. In the models presented here, borrowing and lending is the alternative means of transacting and the cost arises because of moral hazard. Moreover, it is argued that in an important sense these models exhaust the possible ''information'' models of fiat money.

Three problems which any model of valued fiat money must solve are the possible dominance of money by contracts, seigniorage, and the assignment of a terminal value to money. In the next section we describe the first problem and discuss its relation to the transaction motive of holding money. Then we turn to the p.c.l.m. and show how it solves all three problems. Finally, we describe two new models which solve the first problem in a manner different from that of the p.c.l.m.

2. Dominance by Contracts

Fiat money is money which is intrinsically worthless; it does not enter utility or production functions and is not automatically convertible into something which does. In the usual (Arrow-Debreu) exchange problem, individuals are endowed with varying quantities of several goods which they then trade to reach a Pareto optimal set of consumption bundles. The transformation from endowments into consumption bundles is assumed costless (reversible). There is said to be a complete market if all possible exchanges of goods can be made. In such complete markets there is no role for fiat money.

To introduce fiat money the market must be made incomplete; frictions must be added to the model. Certain sequences of bilateral trades are made impossible or costly, as in Shapley and Shubik 1977. In general, an object is being used as money for transaction purposes if it is used in a trade but rather than consume it the recipient trades it again. Fiat money can be introduced into these transaction models of money by making all goods which enter utility functions costly to transfer and by introducing an object, fiat money, which is not costly to transfer.

Typically, transaction costs are introduced into the technology of the physical exchange of goods, for example, the ''trading post'' models in Shapley and Shubik 1977. There are innumerable possible nonlinearities in the technology of exchange that can yield the result that all goods are not exchanged at a single geographic place and point in time. Moreover, in a model with costs of exchange (linear or otherwise) a sequence of bilateral exchanges is often more costly than a single multilateral exchange.

Such costly physical exchange of goods is not, however, necessary or sufficient for the existence of money. First, let us consider sufficiency. The individuals involved in a sequence of exchanges can sign a contract for the delivery of goods at the efficient place and time. If such contracts are costless, the transactions made feasible by them include as a subset those made feasible by money (see Brunner and Meltzer 1971, p. 785). The outcome of any set of exchanges involving money can be achieved through contracts for multilateral exchange without the use of money. Therefore, for money to have value it is necessary that such contracts be costly or infeasible. That costly physical exchange is not necessary for a fiat money equilibrium is demonstrated by the p.c.l.m. which does not involve such costs. The introduction of frictions is correct, but the crucial frictions for valued fiat money involve contracts, not the technology of the physical exchange of goods.

Money makes certain transactions feasible or less costly. If the set of possible transformations of endowments without money is binding in the direction affected by money, money has value.

The problem of dominance of money by contracts and the question of transaction versus store-of-value motives for holding money are closely related. To illustrate this we consider Hahn's (1973a) distinction between models in which money is "essential" and those in which it is "inessential." Goods can differ both in their physical attributes and in their time dimension. That is to say, two goods which are identical except in their date of production can be treated as separate goods. Naturally, goods which do not overlap in time cannot be physically exchanged one for the other. If transactions are limited to such exchanges, then money can be introduced into the market to allow transactions between goods which do not overlap in time. Hahn objects to such store-of-value models in that in them money is not "essential." That is to say, if one treats time like any other attribute and assumes that trade occurs in a single market, then the role of money disappears in such models. Hahn's objection to the store-of-value models is a special case of the observation that it is frictions in contract writing that are crucial to the existence of money. If contract writing is impossible or costly, then the inability to physically exchange goods that do not overlap in time is a constraint on the possible transformations of initial endowments, a constraint which can generate money holding. If contracts are costless, then the constraint on physical exchanges is irrelevant and money is "inessential."

3. The Pure Consumption Loan Model (p.c.l.m.)

Now let us consider a version of the Samuelson pure consumption loan model. First we show how it solves the dominance by contracts problem, and then we consider the seigniorage and terminal value problems.

Time is discrete and is a double-countable infinity of periods; time has no beginning or end. Each period, N identical individuals are born, and they live two periods. In their first period of life they are endowed with an amount K of a transferable but nonstorable consumption good, that good being the same in every period. In their second period of life they are endowed with nothing. Individuals maximize $U(C_1,C_2)$ where $U(\cdot)$ is a utility function with the usual properties, and C_1 and C_2 are the individual's consumption of the consumption good in the first and second periods of life, respectively.

In this model no trades are possible without money because *contracts* with the yet to be born are impossible. The time sequence imposed on the goods does matter in an essential way. The model can be viewed as a single market in which certain contracts, the only desirable contracts, cannot be written. There is no need to interpret the index as time, although doing so provides a good explanation of why the contracts cannot be written. If fiat money is imposed on the model, then individuals can trade first-period endowment for second-period consumption without ever contracting with the unborn, and with simple restrictions on the utility functions, for example, $U_2(C_1,0) = \infty$, there is a valued fiat money equilibrium.

One crucial element of the p.c.l.m. is the fact that all generations cannot get together and write contracts. However, the impossibility of writing contracts is not the only attribute of the p.c.l.m. which makes it a viable model of fiat money. Shell (1971) has noted that the *seigniorage* problem is central to the inefficiency of competitive equilibrium in the p.c.l.m.[2] This is a problem which must be addressed by any model of valued fiat money. Generally it is assumed that fiat money is costless to produce. Therefore, the only market solution is for fiat money to be without value. Valued fiat money is not a market solution, so it must be imposed from outside the market and the market participants must not be allowed to produce it. In the p.c.l.m. this problem is avoided by each generation being unable to produce fiat money but getting fiat money from the previous generation in exchange for goods.

There is a third problem which must be addressed by any model of fiat money. When the market closes someone must be holding the money. Therefore, that person must have been willing to make a transaction of goods for money or must have foregone a transaction of money for goods when the market was operating. Since fiat money by definition has no intrinsic value, this behavior requires explanation. In the p.c.l.m. a generation sells its money holdings for goods to the next generation next period; in other words, the market never closes. This problem we refer to as the *terminal value problem*.

Thus, the p.c.l.m. very parsimoniously handles necessary problems for a model of money: money is given an advantage over contracts (the latter are infeasible), and the seigniorage and terminal value problems are solved. One difficulty with the model is the interpretation of it as a store-of-value not a transaction model of money. We have already seen that by Hahn's definition the p.c.l.m. is not a store-of-value model. The reason the p.c.l.m. is given this store-of-value interpretation is that in the model people hold money as a means of saving for their retirement. This criticism of the p.c.l.m. does have appeal. After all, the reason many transactions are handled in money rather than by contract is not that some of the potential contractors are not yet born. And if an implication of the model is taken to be that transactions in money will only be of that sort, the model is rejected. In other words, this is an objection to the way the p.c.l.m. handles the dominance by contracts problem.

4. Two Alternative Models

To respond to this criticism we turn to some alternative "information" models of fiat money. In these models we use the method of the p.c.l.m. to solve the seigniorage and terminal value problems. That is to say, the models are overlapping generations models. However, the models solve the dominance by contracts problem in a different manner. People live many periods, and the reason that money exists is not because they cannot contract with the unborn, but because contract writing is costly or impossible.

4.1. *Model 1*

This first model is structured so that contracts are impossible, yielding a valued fiat money equilibrium. Except as noted below, the model is identical to the p.c.l.m. Suppose N individuals are born each period and live $2n$ periods. $N/2$ have endowment stream $\Omega^1_{1\times 2n} = k, k, \ldots, k$, and $N/2$ have endowment stream $\Omega^2_{1\times 2n} = K, k, K, k, \ldots, K, k$, where $K > k$. All individuals

[2] In a model with costless contracts this seigniorage problem can arise if there are a countably infinite number of individuals. There is no Nash equilibrium set of contracts in such a model. Perhaps this could be used as an explanation of why a fiat money solution is imposed by a government, but it does seem a farfetched explanation for the existence of valued fiat money.

have the identical concave utility function $W(C_{1\times 2n}) = W(C_1, \ldots, C_{2n}) = U(C_1) + \ldots + U(C_{2n})$.

To consider the possibility of contracts, we must introduce more structure. Our bankruptcy law is that no one can be reduced below k. Moreover, people are unidentifiable, except as to having made a commitment last period to give or receive goods this period. The only possible contracts are, then, one-period contracts. But there is no Nash equilibrium with one-period contracts either. For suppose there were. The optimal strategy for a deviant poor person is to offer to supply an infinite amount of goods tomorrow for goods today. If this is an equilibrium strategy, then the probability of a rich person getting a legitimate contract is zero, so the demand for contracts is zero. As another way to see this, consider a futures market. Suppose the promise of 1 unit tomorrow has price P in terms of goods today. For $P > 0$, all the poor will offer an infinite amount, so $P = 0$. We have a moral hazard explanation for the impossibility of contracts.

The stationary fiat money solution is that the $N/2$ poor consume $C^1_{1\times 2n} = k, \ldots, k$ and don't use money, and the $N/2$ rich consume $C^2_{1\times 2n} = (K+k)/2, \ldots, (K+k)/2$ and do use money. The nonmonetary equilibrium is $C^1 = \Omega^1$, $C^2 = \Omega^2$. Without moral hazard and with a futures market, the nonmonetary equilibrium is $C^1_{1\times 2n} = k, \ldots, k$ and $C^2_{1\times 2n} = (K+k)/2, \ldots, (K+k)/2$, and there is no valued fiat money equilibrium.

In this model there is valued fiat money and contracts cannot exist. We now modify the model to have borrowing and lending be costly and to allow the coexistence of valued fiat money and borrowing and lending.

4.2. *Model 2*

N individuals are born each period, they live $2n \geq 4$ periods, and all have endowment stream $\Omega_{1\times 2n} = k, K, \ldots, k, K$. Because of the way money is introduced into this market—purchase from the previous generation—there is no way money alone can yield an optimal distribution of consumption for individuals. Only by borrowing can they increase first-period consumption.

Assume that U is unbounded above. Unless it is possible to verify that individuals can make good on their promises, no contracts are possible for the same reason as in Model 1. Instead of assuming that no such verification is possible, as before, let us assume a verification technology of a particular simple and unrealistic form. For every unit of good promised tomorrow it costs v units of goods today to verify that the borrower will not be bankrupt next period. Since offering to borrow is costless, the only solution is for all borrowers to have their contracts verified. Clearly, if $v = 1$, there will be no borrowing because the equilibrium rate of interest is nonnegative (zero actually). However, there is a stationary valued money equilibrium. If $v = 0$, a futures market yields the optimal consumption stream and there is no demand for money. Is there an intermediate value of v such that borrowing and lending and valued fiat money can coexist? While the proof is rather tedious (see the Appendix), the answer is that the model can be rigged so that this is so. If v and $U(\cdot)$ satisfy

$$\frac{U'(K)}{U'[(k+K)/2]} > (1-v) > \frac{U'[(k+K)/2]}{U'(k)}$$

then there is an integer I such that if $n \geq I$, there is such an equilibrium.

Borrowing and lending and money can coexist in Model 2 because individuals are poorly endowed at birth and because people live long enough that desired lending exceeds borrowing. However, the p.c.l.m. can be similarly modified as shown in Wallace (this volume). If some individuals are endowed in their second period of life but not their first, yet aggregate endowment is still larger in the first period, borrowing and lending can coexist with money holding in the p.c.l.m. The advantage of Model 2 in this regard is only that it assumes identical endowments and has costly contracts rather than a mix of costless (within-generation) and impossible (between-generation) contracts.

We have, then, models of fiat money in which fiat money exists because individuals cannot costlessly be known to be able to meet their contractual obligations. The transactions which occur do take place through time, so it still may be objected that these are store-of-value, not transaction models. However, the important point here is that money enters not because contracts with the unborn are impossible, but because contracts with anyone are impossible or costly to police.

To make our case that these are not store-of-value models more convincing, some simple further modifications can be sketched. Suppose, for example, that individuals live n periods, not $2n$, but there are two goods in each period, goods 1 and 2. Let there be two kinds of people with endowments $\Omega^1_{2\times n} = (k,K)', (k,K)', \ldots, (k,K)'$, and $\Omega^2_{2\times n} = (K,k)', (K,k)', \ldots, (K,k)'$, respectively. Suppose further that the markets for each of the two goods must be physically separate, there is no direct exchange, one cannot be two places at once, and the markets for the two goods operate in sequence. Then as long as contracts cannot be costlessly verified across markets, money and borrowing and lending can coexist as in Model 2. In this model money is held for between-period transactions by the first group of individuals but is held for within-period transactions by the second group of individuals. Note that without the ordering of markets or some other scheme to limit velocity money dominates borrowing and lending, but money has limiting value zero. The exchange of goods today for goods tomorrow is not desirable, and the terminal value problem reappears. Or consider a model with identical individuals in a world of three goods with endowment path $\Omega_{3\times n} = (k,K,k)', (K,k,K)', (k,K,k)', \ldots, (k,K,k)'$.

Any appearance of a store-of-value nature of the demand for money in these models comes from the overlapping generations structure. One can use some other means of solving the seigniorage and terminal value problems —for example, appropriate government intervention — and have multigood models that remove even this slight appearance of a store-of-value role of money. In such multigood models it is not important to the existence of valued fiat money that markets be ordered, although the coexistence of money and borrowing and lending requires that money not dominate the latter. But efforts in this direction do seem misguided in the face of the empirical fact that all actions take place through time. Moreover, by eliminating the time dimension in the model one removes the possibility of analyzing some problems of interest, for example, the distortions of inflation.

One objection to the above models is that they do not exhaust the set of models which generate valued fiat money by assuming that income streams are not known with certainty and contracts are not enforceable. Specifically, it could be argued that moral hazard is not the explanation for the use of money, but that uncertain income streams and costly information are. This objection does not stand up under scrutiny.

Suppose the problem is not the individual making bad faith contracts but the individual having a random income stream. With complete markets and costless knowledge of the stochastic structure this would not matter; the individual would just trade contingent claims. Suppose learning about the stochastic structure is costly. If transactions are limited to bilateral exchanges, then an individual's promises would not be used for transaction purposes in a series of exchanges. But this is not relevant, for if costless contracts are available, a single multilateral exchange would be negotiated anyway. Also, with scale technologies, or interdependent production costs at a point in geographic location and time, promises are not traded for goods at a single point. But this also does not explain the need for money. Multiple exchange contracts can be negotiated with the intermediary engaged in evaluating such promises. It may be that such contracts are costly to organize, not to verify. However, organization costs can be modeled just as verification costs are.

This is not to say that uncertain endowments are not interesting in their own right. For example, in the above models there is a unique rate of return at which individuals diversify between money and loans, and at this rate the portfolio is indeterminate. With stochastic repayment there may be many rates of return consistent with diversification, each implying a unique portfolio. However, such randomness can easily be included in the p.c.l.m.

The above models in an important sense exhaust the set of "information" models of money, models in which fiat money dominates contracts because of uncertain returns, costly information, and costly organization and enforcement of contracts. Yet these models are simple modifications of the p.c.l.m., and by almost anyone's definition they involve the transaction motive. Does the inclusion of transaction motive affect the important implications of the models? It would seem not. Let us consider the major properties of the p.c.l.m. as treated by Wallace (in this volume). As the reader can easily verify, in the above models, as with the p.c.l.m., dominance in return distribution by another asset drives out fiat money; there is a nonmonetary equilibrium; there is the possibility of multiple monetary equilibria with different rates of inflation; and a costless endowment tax is Pareto superior to printing money to cover deficits. Also like the p.c.l.m., with only a change in some details the models can be included in the Lucas (1972) incomplete information model, the Kareken-Wallace (1978) country-specific fiat money model, the Bryant-Wallace (1979b) model of open market operations, or the Bryant (1978) model of depression.

5. Summary

The p.c.l.m. parsimoniously handles three problems essential to a model of fiat money. Contracts which can substitute for money are not feasible, and the seigniorage and terminal value problems are solved. The p.c.l.m. should, then, be the source of null hypotheses concerning the behavior of fiat money in the economy.

The objection that the p.c.l.m. is not a proper model of fiat money because it fails to capture the transaction motive of holding money is invalid. We have produced "information" models of fiat money, models which are unambiguously transaction models but which are modifications of the p.c.l.m. with the same important properties. Moreover, these models exhaust the possible "information" models of money, which suggests that searching for further modifications or alternative models of fiat money is not now a productive activity.

Appendix

To prove

$$\text{(A1)} \qquad \frac{U'[(K+k)/2]}{U'[k]} < (1-v) < \frac{U'[K]}{U'[(K+k)/2]}$$

implies that if individuals live long enough, valued fiat money and borrowing and lending can coexist in Model 2.

Let $\Omega_{1\times 2J} = (k, K, \ldots, k, K)$ where J is a large integer. It is easily shown that interest on loans is zero in a stationary monetary equilibrium and that the borrower pays the verification cost. Also, the individual borrows only in odd periods of life and lends or acquires money only in even periods. The individual's problem can be written as

$$\max \sum_{i=1}^{2J} U(C_i)$$

subject to

$$C_{2j+1} = k + l_{2j} + m_{2j} + (1-v)b_{2j+1} \qquad j = 0, \ldots, J-1$$

$$C_{2j+2} = K - l_{2j+2} - m_{2j+2} - b_{2j+1}$$

$$l_0 = m_0 = b_{2J} = 0$$

where l, m, and b are lending, money holding, and borrowing. Lending and money holding are perfect substitutes to the individual. The first-order necessary conditions are

$$\text{(A2)} \qquad (1-v)U'(C_j) \leqslant U'(C_{j+1}) \quad = \text{if } b_j > 0 \qquad j=1,\ldots,2J$$

$$\text{(A3)} \qquad U'(C_j) \geqslant U'(C_{j+1}) \qquad = \text{if } l_j \text{ or } m_j > 0.$$

First we prove that the left-hand side of (A1) implies there is borrowing in the first period. Suppose there is no borrowing in the first period ($C_1 = k$). Since (A3) implies that consumption is nondecreasing, and consuming K from period 2 on is not feasible, the individual must lend or hold money in period 2. Then (A3) implies $C_2 = C_3$ or $K - l_2 - m_2 = k + l_2 + m_2 + (1-v)b_3$. This implies $C_2 \geqslant (K+k)/2$. But then

$$(1-v)U'(C_1) = (1-v)U'(k) > U'[(K+k)/2] \geqslant U'(C_2)$$

by the left-hand side of (A1), which violates (A2).

Next we show that there is a first odd-numbered period in which the individual does not borrow. Suppose in odd-numbered periods up to $2j-1$ the individual does borrow. By iterative substitution of (A2) and (A3), $U'(C_{2j-1}) \leq (1-v)^{j-1}U'(C_1)$. As j becomes large, $U'(C_{2j-1}) \to 0$, but this is impossible as it implies that consumption grows without bound which clearly is nonoptimal (K is an upper bound).

Now we show that if there is no borrowing in period $2j-1$, there is no borrowing in period $2j+1$. The person who did not borrow in period $2j-1$ must lend or hold money in period $2j$. Then (A3) implies $C_{2j} = C_{2j+1}$ or $K - l_{2j} - m_{2j} = k + l_{2j} + m_{2j} + (1-v)b_{2j+1}$. This implies $C_{2j+1} \geq (1/2)[K+k]$. However, $C_{2j-2} \leq K$. This and the right-hand side of (A1) imply

$$(1-v)U'(C_{2j+1}) \leq (1-v)U'[(K+k)/2] < U'[K] \leq U'[C_{2j+2}]$$

which implies $b_{2j+1} = 0$ by (A2).

So there is a period beyond which the individual does not borrow. But lending or acquiring money in even periods continues. Therefore, if J is large enough, the individual's lending or holding money exceeds her or his borrowing. Because this is a representative individual, aggregate lending and money holding exceeds aggregate borrowing, and there is a valued fiat money equilibrium. Since all individuals borrow in their first period of existence, valued fiat money and borrowing and lending coexist.

Money in Consumption Loan Type Models: An Addendum

David Cass*

1. The Cass-Okuno-Zilcha Conjecture

In the paper by Cass, Okuno, and Zilcha in this volume, we presented several examples of consumption loan type models exhibiting the nonexistence of any competitive equilibrium which is Pareto optimal. One sort of example, involving nonmonotonicity in tastes, seemed very special (see section 5.2). Evidently it depended on having just the right combination of some consumption satiation and some boundary endowments. We conjectured that such speciality wasn't essential to the intuitive proposition being advanced, that somewhat less than total satiation might unfavorably restrict potential intertemporal market transfers — even given the institution of money, in its role as a store of value, as a common means of facilitating trade between the present and the future. Rather, we proposed as a more likely reason for such speciality the particular analytic methodology being utilized, the limitation to considering only models for which competitive equilibria could be essentially characterized as the nonnegative solutions to a first-order difference equation (and thus completely represented in terms of a two-dimensional diagram).

It turns out that while our intuition was correct, our reasoning wasn't. In fact, it is now apparent that the only operative constraint was simply our lack of sufficient ingenuity.

In the next section I sketch a robust nonoptimality example; nonexistence of Pareto optimal equilibrium persists in the presence of small perturbations in both tastes and endowments. The peculiar nature of the satiation phenomena introduced in this example entails other interesting anomalies as well. Two of these additional results are briefly discussed in the final section.

2. A Robust Nonoptimality Example

Consider the basic model described in section 2 of Cass-Okuno-Zilcha, and suppose once again that there are two consumers in every generation but the oldest, $G_0 = \{0\}$ and $G_t = \{2t-1, 2t\}$ for $t \geqq 1$, and that odd-numbered

*This note was written during my visit as a Sherman Fairchild Distinguished Scholar at the California Institute of Technology. I am very grateful to Caltech—and especially its fine group of social scientists—for providing me this excellent opportunity to conduct uninterrupted research in such a congenial environment.

consumers, $h = 2t-1$ for $t \geqq 1$, are of α-type; even-numbered, $h = 2t$ for $t \geqq 1$, of β-type. Their respective tastes and endowments are assumed to be as specified in Figure 1a. The critical general features of this specification are that both α- and β-type consumers can become satiated in second-period consumption — though at least one type can never become satiated in first-period consumption — while the α- but not the β-type consumer is relatively overburdened with second-period income. Figure 1b exploits the more specific features introduced in order to simplify exposition, especially the particular linear structure of the offer curves of both types of consumers at all except very low real rates of return. The figure makes plain that, while there

Figure 1
Nonoptimality Due to Nonmonotonicity:
An Example With Potential Satiation
in Second-Period Consumption

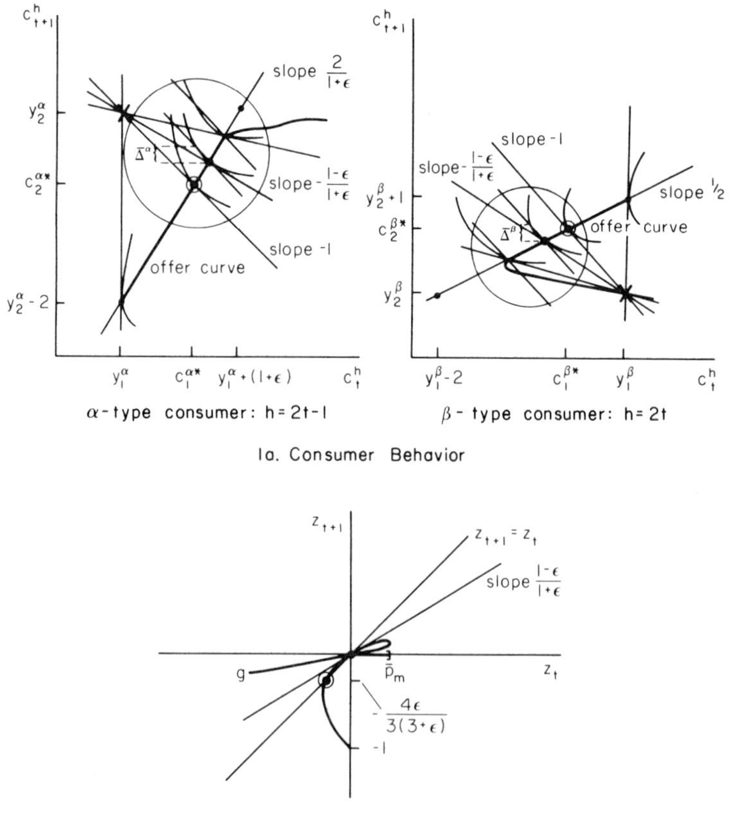

1a. Consumer Behavior

1b. Dynamical System

are a plethora of both barter and monetary equilibria in this example, nevertheless every competitive equilibrium must exhibit real rates of return which satisfy the uniform bound

$$\frac{\partial U^h(c^h)}{\partial c_t^h} \bigg/ \frac{\partial U^h(c^h)}{\partial c_{t+1}^h} = p_t/p_{t+1} = z_{t+1}/z_t \leqq (1-\epsilon)/(1+\epsilon) < 1$$

for $h = 2t-1, 2t$ and $t \geqq 1$.

Hence, it is easily seen (referring to the encircled portions of Figure 1a and appealing to the specific characteristics of the geometric construction briefly remarked in the following paragraph) that every competitive allocation is dominated by a corresponding feasible allocation which is identical except for a sequence of sufficiently small one-for-one forward transfers between only α-type consumers

$$0 < -\Delta c_t^{2t-1} = \Delta c_{t+1}^{2t-1} = \Delta c^\alpha < \bar{\Delta}^\alpha \text{ for } t \geqq 1$$

(or alternatively, only β-type consumers

$$0 < -\Delta c_t^{2t} = \Delta c_{t+1}^{2t} = \Delta c^\beta < \bar{\Delta}^\beta \text{ for } t \geqq 1).$$

That this example is legitimate and, more importantly, that its welfare significance is invariant to sufficiently small perturbations in both tastes and endowments should become self-evident from close examination of Figure 2. This figure contains directions for constructing a well-behaved utility function consistent with my specification of the α-type consumer; a similar procedure can be employed to justify my specification of the β-type consumer. Since both constructs are very closely patterned after that already analyzed at great length in Cass-Okuno-Zilcha (see Appendix section A2), I omit further elaboration here.

3. Additional Difficulties Associated With Satiation Phenomena

3.1. *Nonexistence of Competitive Equilibrium*

Figure 3 displays a technically minor modification of the preceding example which entails a substantively major conclusion. By merely shifting portions of both consumers' indifference maps so that the α-type (respectively, β-type) consumer's offer curve is considerably less (more) steeply sloped at negative real rates of return near zero, competitive equilibrium ceases to exist.

At first blush this result is somewhat surprising. All consumers' tastes and endowments continue to enjoy the same regularity properties as before. Upon closer inspection, however, the source of the difficulty is easily discovered. The peculiar second-period nature of satiation has now combined with the intrinsic one-directional nature of time in just such a manner that there is simply not enough structural interrelationship between generations to admit trade—even trade only among members of each generation—through the market mechanism. Deficiency of this sort is well-known to create difficulties for the existence of competitive equilibrium in the standard Arrow-Debreu model. [See, in particular, the illuminating seminal analysis of McKenzie (1959).†] This version of the example suggests that in the intertem-

†Author names and years refer to the works listed at the end of this book.

Figure 2
Construction of an Offer Curve Exhibiting Perverse Behavior at Extreme Relative Prices

$$\lim_{x \to \infty} -\left[\frac{\partial f}{\partial x} \middle/ \frac{\partial f}{\partial y}\right]_{\underline{f}=0} > \lim_{x \to \infty} -\left[\frac{\partial \bar{f}}{\partial x} \middle/ \frac{\partial \bar{f}}{\partial y}\right]_{\bar{f}=0} > \frac{\bar{y}-\underline{y}}{\bar{x}-\underline{x}}$$

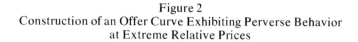

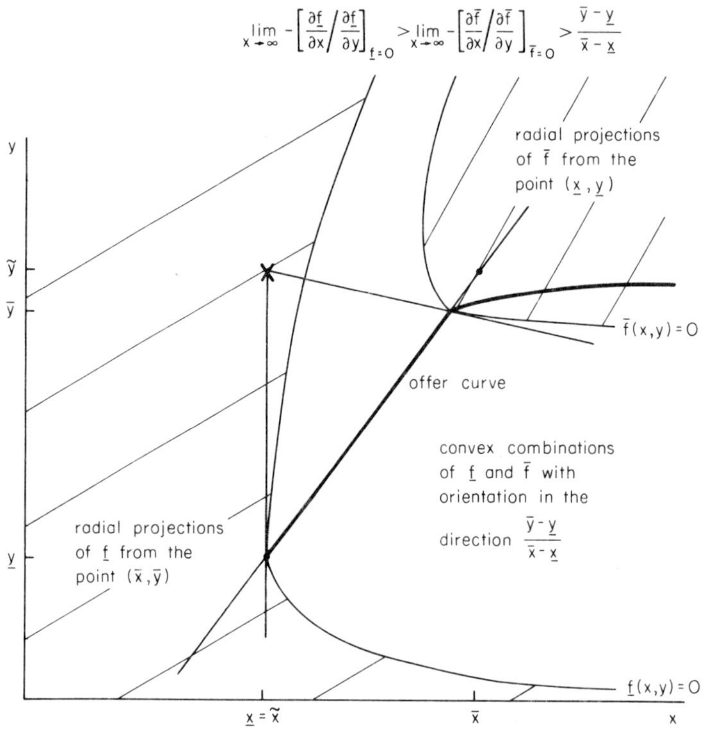

poral context these difficulties should not be peremptorily dismissed as mere curiosities. It also hints at a commonality between the circumstances giving rise to nonoptimality and those giving rise to nonexistence which should be thoroughly investigated.

3.2. Ineffectiveness of Social Security

Subject to well-known standard qualifications, the second basic theorem of welfare economics, that every Pareto optimal allocation is a competitive equilibrium (given an appropriate initial distribution of endowments), obtains in consumption loan type models. [See, in particular, the even more comprehensive analysis of McFadden, Majumdar, and Mitra (forthcoming).] In the present example (in either its original or modified form), for instance, any redistribution of endowments according to the scheme

$$y^{h\delta} = \begin{cases} y^0 - \dfrac{4\epsilon}{3(3+\epsilon)} & \text{for } h = 0 \\ c^{\alpha*} + (\delta, -\delta) & \text{for } h = 2t-1, t \geq 1 \\ c^{\beta*} + (-\delta, \delta) & \text{otherwise} \end{cases}$$

permits attaining a barter equilibrium which is Pareto optimal (supported by prices $p_t = 1$ for $t \geqq 1$ and yielding the allocation

$$c^h = \begin{cases} y^0 - \dfrac{4\epsilon}{3(3+\epsilon)} & \text{for } h = 0 \\ c^{\alpha *} & \text{for } h = 2t-1,\ t \geqq 1 \\ c^{\beta *} & \text{otherwise}). \end{cases}$$

The central message of this example, of course, is that the historical advent of money as a store of value may not be an adequate proxy for such a redistribution of endowments. Thus there remains at least partly unanswered an extremely interesting question: What are the simplest extra-market in-

Figure 3
Version of the Example With No Competitive Equilibrium
(Barter or Monetary)

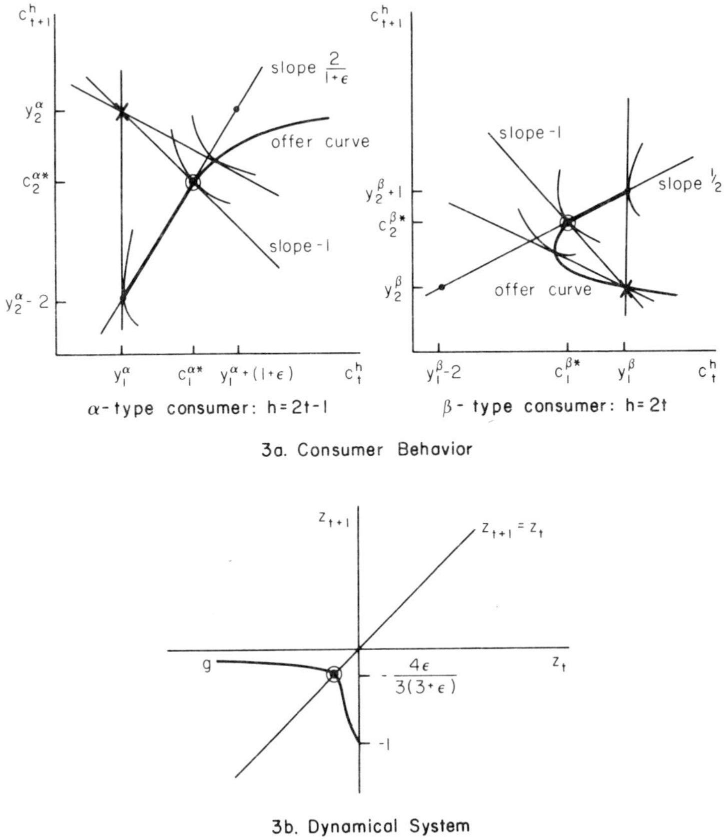

stitutional arrangements — perhaps involving some direct redistribution of endowments — which will permit attaining Pareto optimality in a wide class of intertemporal market environments?

I hazard the opinion, based primarily on extensive analysis of consumption loan type models embodying both variety of commodities and diversity of consumers, that a minimal qualification for any such arrangement will be a large degree of flexibility in confronting heterogeneity across agents.

Figure 4
Version of the Example With a Simple Social Security System Which Will Not Permit Attaining Pareto Optimality

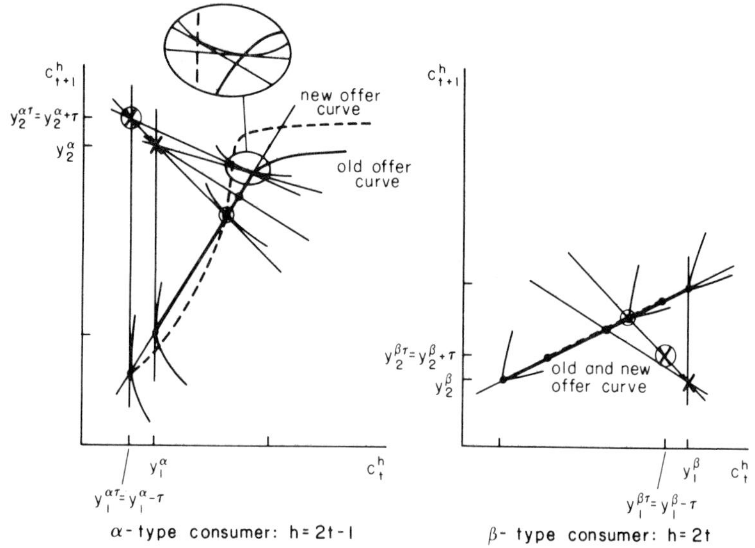

4a. Consumer Behavior

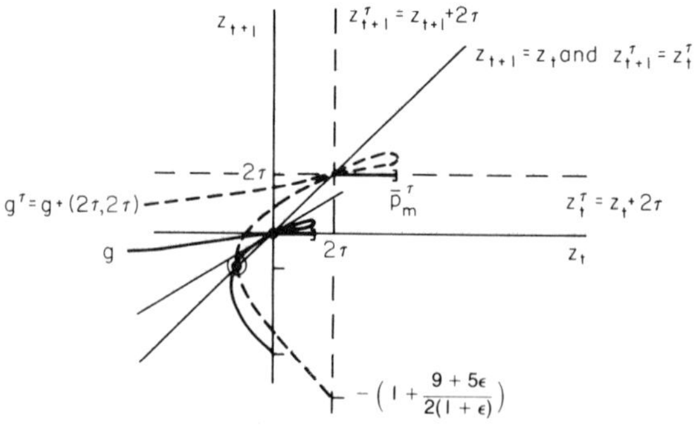

4b. Dynamical System

This view is suggestively supported (but by no means precisely or conclusively demonstrated) by considering, for instance, the scope of a perpetual per capita transfer τ from young to old — or a simple social security system — in the present example. It is a fairly straightforward matter to establish that whether or not such uniform social transfers are potent enough to permit attaining Pareto optimality through additional market transfers is problematical and ultimately depends on whether or not they conceivably admit barter equilibrium at some nonnegative real rate of return. Figure 4 presents a polar version of the example in which a simple social security system is necessarily ineffective. The figure is more or less self-explanatory once it is noted that any shift from first- to second-period income essentially results in some distorted rotation of the reflected generational offer curve (still defined relative to original endowments) around its intersection with the 45° line in the negative quadrant.

Clearly, this counterexample depends on the particular structure of the distortion displayed in Figure 4b, which in turn depends on the particular character of the behavior displayed in Figure 4a — especially the relative sensitivity of the α-type consumer (and the absolute insensitivity of the β-type consumer) to shifts from first- to second-period income. The opposite polar version of the present example, reversing these sensitivities, yields a model in which a simple social security system is potentially effective.

In Defense of a Basic Approach

David Cass and Karl Shell*

1. Fiat Money: Not Just Another Commodity

Macroeconomic control of contemporary private enterprise economies is exercised primarily through changes in the magnitude of the government's deficit (fiscal policy) and changes in the composition of the government's debt, that is, its cumulated deficits, between "fiat" money and "fiat" bonds (monetary policy). To understand macroeconomic policy, we must be able to explain how the private sector reacts to government expenditures, taxes and transfers, and money creation and extinction.

Government debt (in its various forms) can serve in a host of roles for the private sector—as a store of value, as a convenient means for transactions, as an exclusive vehicle for tax payments, and so forth. These various roles are generally closely interdependent and strongly influenced by the particular conventional and institutional arrangements in an economy. One of them, however, is crucial to all the others: *If money and bonds do not serve as a value store, then they cannot serve any other useful function.* Our current research focuses on the role of money and bonds as a store of value—not because we are necessarily persuaded that this is the most interesting aspect of the paper assets created by the government, but rather because we are firmly

*These reflections were set down several months after the Federal Reserve Bank of Minneapolis conference on "Models of Monetary Economies." Their proximate cause was the generally negative reaction by the conference participants to Neil Wallace's forthright assertion of the importance of consumption loan or overlapping generations models for understanding monetary phenomena in a private, market economy. We support Wallace's basic position. Indeed, we have for some time believed (and preached) that these models offer an intellectually attractive framework for studying many aspects of decentralized intertemporal allocation—provided, of course, that some care is taken to distinguish between fundamental or inherent features and convenient or provisional simplifications. This opportunity to articulate our position is also a natural forum for us to air our misgivings about various currently fashionable prejudices in monetary and macroeconomic theory and to present our views about various more constructive alternatives for future development.

The collaboration underlying this paper has taken place over several years, encompassing both Shell's visit as a Guggenheim Fellow at CEPREMAP during 1977–78 and Cass' visit as a Sherman Fairchild Distinguished Scholar at Caltech during 1978–79. The paper itself represents an effort to lay out the general methodological position motivating a series of specific analytical studies of overlapping generations models. It thus constitutes part of a more extensive project being underwritten by a grant to the Center for Analytic Research in Economics and the Social Sciences (at Penn) from the National Science Foundation. We are grateful to all these institutions for their support and encouragement.

convinced that this basic function must be well understood before we can begin to understand any of their more complicated functions.

Jim Tobin has taught us that, for most purposes of understanding decentralized allocation involving stores of value, there is no essential difference between paper currency, Treasury bills, and any other government issue. So as a convenience, we will refer to all forms of government debt as simply *money*.

It is obvious (and well-known) that money cannot have a positive price—that is, cannot be a store of value—in the conventional finite-horizon model in which the "end of the world" is known with certainty. The reason is simple. At the end of the last period, money is worthless. Therefore, in the next-to-last period, all individuals desire to dispose of money holdings in order to avoid capital losses. This drives the price of money to zero at the end of the next-to-last period. And so on. Individuals with foresight, not wanting to be stuck with the monetary "hot potato," thus drive the price of money to zero in each period.

Some students of money-macro may claim that it is easy to modify the classical Walrasian model to allow (even insure!) the price of money to be positive. Simply introduce money balances as arguments in utility functions or production functions, reflecting the reduced transaction costs in a monetary economy. (Never mind how we transform nominal to real when there are many commodities.) We reject this approach. Imbedding money in preferences or technologies does nothing to explain its role as a store of value. Moreover, such reduced forms are at best poor proxies for their structural counterparts. (We will have more to say about modeling transaction constraints below.) Worst of all, to the extent that this maneuver is successful, it is also likely to be misleading.

We know that money is not just another commodity. Tastes and endowments (including production possibilities) determine the relative price of apples in terms of oranges in the simple equilibrium model. But unlike ordinary Walrasian goods, the usefulness or "productivity" of money depends on its price. In particular, suppose that a barter equilibrium exists for a given market economy (with a given payments mechanism) without nominal money. Then it must be the case that, when such money is introduced into the economy, one of the new equilibria will be the old barter equilibrium with positive nominal money bearing a zero price. It could be that all households would be better off if the price of money were positive. But this does not imply that a zero price is a disequilibrium price. Trust in fiat money is only a recent development, and even today such faith is hardly universal.

2. Modeling Fiat Money: The Overlapping Generations Approach

The natural way to avoid modeling "hot-potato" money is to avoid modeling a finite-horizon economy. Individuals surely know they won't be around forever. They likely don't even expect their influence to persist much beyond their own lifetimes; that would be silly. But they do believe—or, if you prefer, act as if they believe—that contemporary economic institutions are essentially immortal. An obvious model to build on, then, is Samuelson's model of overlapping generations: Economic agents come and go, disposing of their finite wealth over their finite lifetimes, while economic society is presumed to continue without known end.

It is unfortunate that this type of model has been almost exclusively associated with narrow issues in intertemporal welfare theory. (An outstanding exception, of course, is Bob Lucas' influential contribution to the money-macro field.) We, as much as anybody, must share the blame. Perhaps it would be useful to find a less connotative label for its basic structure; while *overlapping generations* is clearly better than *consumption loan,* it too carries overly restrictive associations. Be that as it may, this basic structure has two general features which we believe are indispensable to the development of macroeconomics as an intellectually convincing discipline. While both have already been mentioned, at least indirectly, both will bear repeating for emphasis.

First, it is genuinely dynamic. In this it significantly departs from the basically atemporal character of most received doctrine: There is explicit recognition of both the inherent mortality (as well as vitality) of the actors, together with the continual (as well as unceasing) evolution of their stage.

Second, it is fundamentally disaggregative. In this it is founded in perhaps the oldest theoretical tradition in economics: There is a clear distinction between economic agents' objectives and constraints—and hence the mainsprings of their individual behavior—and the economic system's coherent resolution of their joint interaction.

Isn't this, you ask, a pretentious basis on which to justify analysis of obviously rudimentary versions of the overlapping generations model, for instance, that contained in several of the contributions to this volume? Not at all.

While it is important to distinguish the inherent underlying character of this model, it is also important to recognize the potential significance of its various provisional specializations. These would include such simplifying assumptions as that of homogeneous households (both within and across generations), two-period lifetimes, a single physical commodity, distribution without any production (or with, at most, very elementary production), complete and costless markets, and full and accurate information (concerning both the present and the future). Taken together they constitute reducing the model to its barest essential elements (within a conventional framework of maintained assumptions, to be sure). The parallel with the reduction of the classical Walrasian model to its leading special case of pure distribution of two commodities between two households is unmistakable. In both cases such reduction is perfectly acceptable for certain purposes, according to a fundamental precept: Skeletal models yield (or verify) definite counterexamples but only suggest (or illustrate) possible theorems. Perhaps most important, we are confident that, through the normal scientific process, tentative results derived from the simplest versions of the overlapping generations model—and many other questions as well—will be investigated in much more general terms. Indeed, we know that some of these more extensive analyses are already well under way.

Following the cardinal rule that simple models can best be employed to produce counterexamples, variations of the overlapping generations parable have been insightfully utilized to teach us several valuable lessons. First and foremost, of course, are the optimality counterexamples contained in Paul Samuelson's seminal analysis itself: Purely by virtue of the one-directional, open-ended nature of time, *competitive allocation may fail to be Pareto optimal.* But there are other lessons to be learned as well, with both positive and normative implications. Especially instructive are the determinacy counterexamples stemming from the introduction of money into the basic story: Purely by virtue of the enormous latitude associated with the consistency criterion that aggregate outcomes accord with individual predictions, *there is typically a plethora of potential monetary equilibria.*

Vast multiplicity of potential competitive equilibria is an inherent property of the economy with money (or, for that matter, with any marketable asset which can serve as a temporary abode for purchasing power into perpetuity). This central feature turns out to be of crucial importance to the theory and practice of macroeconomic policy.

Consider first the solution concept normally employed in the standard general equilibrium model as applied to its overlapping generations extension. Competitive equilibrium prices are consistent with market clearing and ultimately depend only on tastes, endowments, technology, the range of markets, and the actions of government (hereafter exclusively limited to *monetary policy*[1]). But money is not desirable for its own sake, only for its market value (particularly by those individuals who are endowed with it). Hence, even in a nonstochastic environment, there are typically very many potential monetary equilibria associated with each perfectly anticipated monetary policy; within some limits, very many perceptions of the possible state of the economy (or predicted paths of market prices for commodities in terms of money) are consistent with realizations of the actual state of the economy (or observed paths of market prices for commodities in terms of money). And this remains so even if one prespecifies, for instance, some initial price, or equivalently, its reciprocal, the (present value) price of money.

A dual result to the last is that for each positive price of money there are typically very many potential monetary policies consistent with market clearing—each generally associated with a different set of competitive allocations. In short, monetary policy matters very much!

Even though the resulting competitive equilibrium is largely indeterminate, we still find this conventional solution concept too restrictive for the overlapping generations model. For example, individuals might well believe that market prices follow a process (stochastic or nonstochastic) depending on some seemingly extraneous phenomenon, say, sunspot activity. Again within some limits, if individuals believe that the economy is affected by sunspot activity, then it might well be—even imposing the "rationality" requirement that expectations be fulfilled. In this sense, the future can be said to create its own uncertainty; because sunspot activity is held to be important, its level is a proper state variable, and its possible sequences of realizations must be fully accounted for in the appropriate solution concept.

The essential point is that in a truly dynamic context, even with perfect foresight and without intrinsic uncertainty, pure theory provides no obvious natural selection of the particular elements on which individuals condition their forecasts (a point made by Bob Shiller and others); the state variables of the system cannot be determined independent of individual beliefs. Further-

[1]We adopt the convention employed in the overlapping generations (and related money-macro) literature of referring to a sequence of injections of money into the economy by means of lump-sum transfers (with either algebraic sign) as a *monetary policy*. However, we are aware of the confusion this might cause, since—especially given the rudimentary treatment of possible actions of government in this context—such means of control is much closer to what is traditionally recognized as fiscal policy. We ask to be excused for this convenient, if misleading usage.

more, if in fact sunspot activity (or some less fanciful state variable, say, calendar time itself) induces undesirable fluctuations in the economy, it may be altogether fitting for the government to announce and pursue a policy of counteracting the resultant market disruption. Economic agents — including both households and government, and no matter how sophisticated—must not only assess the "fundamentals" of the economy, but also may very well have to pay attention to the "psychology" of the market.

3. Working Toward General Theorems

What about more definite results? How do or will studies of such elementary models lead to general theorems concerning dynamic, disaggregative allocation processes? These questions are still largely, though not completely, unanswered.

The contrast between the central thrust of the first part of the Wallace paper and that of the major part of the Cass-Okuno-Zilcha paper (together with its addendum) offers a nice illustration of this state of affairs. Both analyses deal with a plausible conjecture suggested by the simplest version of the overlapping generations model, namely, that given the institution of fiat money, some competitive equilibrium (possibly nonmonetary, likely monetary) must be Pareto optimal.

On the one hand, Wallace's work (as well as Brock and Scheinkman's parallel study) shows that this conjecture has a natural extension covering a particular class of active monetary policies. Specifically, Wallace considers the situation where the money supply is being increased (or decreased) at a constant rate by means of equal nominal transfers to (or taxes from) the households in each successive generation. Then, after insuring that his idealized economy is capable of attaining competitive equilibria which closely resemble steady states, he demonstrates that when the money supply is in fact not being strictly increased, some competitive equilibrium must be Pareto optimal. Throughout his analysis, Wallace maintains all of the various simplifying assumptions mentioned above.

On the other hand, Cass, Okuno, and Zilcha investigate the original conjecture itself and show that it is quite sensitive to relaxing just one of these standard provisional specializations. In particular, they demonstrate that the proposed result may not obtain when households display systematic diversity in tastes and endowments across succeeding generations—or even significant diversity within succeeding generations, provided households are also liable to substantial satiation in consumption over their life cycles.

Undoubtedly this conjectured proposition (as well as its suggested extension) is valid in some more general contexts (at least when there is neither widespread household diversity nor excessive potential satiation). A precise statement and proof of this sort of general theorem, however, remains to be seen.

In fact, at this writing, there are virtually no well-established general theorems for the overlapping generations model available in the literature. The prime reason for this paucity of substantial results is clear: Very little is known about the most basic properties of this model except in its rudest embodiments. Thus, for instance, only recently has serious work begun on uncovering the limiting conditions under which there necessarily exists *any* competitive equilibrium in the presence of many types of (finitely lived) households, many varieties of (exogenously given) commodities, and arbitrary (typically active) monetary policy. It is worthwhile to notice that this fundamental enterprise, which is currently being undertaken by Okuno and Zilcha and Balasko and Shell, relies on obvious but critical insights gained from the simplest cases—for example, their common property that if there exists some competitive equilibrium (monetary or nonmonetary), then there exists a nonmonetary equilibrium. It is also important to realize that this work is relatively straightforward compared to that of formulating and analyzing the subtle issues involved in characterizing the intrinsic structure of the set of competitive equilibria (monetary as well as nonmonetary) in the same model or its even yet broader generalizations. Research into these more profound problems seems to us an essential next step in the further refinement of the overlapping generations model. These crucial investigations are also presently being pursued by those mentioned above (as well as several others, for example, McFadden, Mitra, and Majumdar).

The question of what constitutes a general result rather than a special case is at best nebulous. This is so even for our present purposes, where we have already explicitly focused on a particular class of economic models, those displaying the inherent structural features of the overlapping generations parable. One basic reason is that the answer to this question ultimately depends on adopting and maintaining some limited reference framework, itself a specialized and idealized view of individual capacities and the context of social arrangements through which they range. Another is that, even within such a stylized purview, there is no absolute law distinguishing good from bad (or useful from useless or realistic from unrealistic or...) simplifications.

Here, as in our own work, we have already implicitly chosen a conventional neoclassical framework. This particular view, embracing a large part of modern economic theory, emphasizes individual rationality (an apt if much abused descriptive phrase) and concentrates on market exchange of private commodities by competitive agents. We are prepared to defend this position, even while conceding that there are many seemingly attractive modifications and extensions. We think it will be more rewarding, however, if instead we sketch our more eclectic views of what are, given the neoclassical orthodoxy, good and bad simplifications. The next section addresses this issue. These remarks can be taken as extended comments on each of the various simplifying assumptions listed in section 2.

4. Good and Bad Simplifications

4.1. *Diversity of Households and Commodities*

Our synopsis of the state of current research into basic aspects of the overlapping generations model suggested one of our most fundamental methodological biases. We firmly believe that a satisfactory general theory must, at a minimum, encompass some diversity among households as well as some variety among commodities. There is simply not much (except perhaps tractability) to recommend constructing an elaborate macroeconomic edifice on microeconomic foundations built without any reinforcement from the admixture of distributional effects. To put this point bluntly: A behavioral specification in terms of the first-order conditions describing rational choice by a representative household between consumption today and tomorrow is every bit as crude an approximation as one in terms of an aggregate consumption function.

We do, however, freely acknowledge that it also makes little sense to ignore the fact that there are recognizable patterns in the distribution of tastes and endowments across households; contemporary individuals are subject to many of the same formative influences, while by and large their social and economic environment itself evolves both slowly and smoothly. Our position necessarily embraces, and even positively encourages, introducing and analyzing (consistent and verifiable) regularities in aggregate behavior. Otherwise our proposed quest for a richer macroeconomics would be self-defeating.

In particular, this means that we certainly don't subscribe to the almost total agnosticism implicit in the excess demand characterizations pioneered by Hugo Sonnenschein. But then we also surely can't ignore the thrust of their central message: Diversity of households—together with what we have known for a long time, variety of commodities—will typically impose a significant constraint on our ability to derive substantial propositions concerning qualitative effects.

4.2. *Reinterpreting Periods and Commodities*

In contrast to the clearly limiting character of the postulate that representative households choose between just two (physical) commodities, it should be emphasized that certain of the simplifying assumptions that have been commonly adopted in the overlapping generations literature are by themselves not at all restrictive. In particular, when markets are perfect, a completely general model with arbitrary but finite lifetimes is formally indistinguishable from a singularly special model with at most two-period lifetimes (but with many households in each generation and many commodities in each period)—given suitable reinterpretation of both *periods* and *commodities*. Such broad latitude in interpreting what are commodities (according to physical, spatial, temporal, eventual, ... characteristics) is so familiar from the Arrow-Debreu tradition that it needs no further elaboration here, except perhaps to underline an obvious but important caveat: Reinterpretation is severely circumscribed when, for instance, markets are incomplete or information is partial (say, especially, due to the intrinsic nature of time). In any case, it is simply inappropriate to complain that existing analyses based on the overlapping generations parable necessarily involve incredibly low velocities of money, that is, holding periods of 25-year duration. (From this viewpoint, however, the existing analyses do typically involve incredibly uniform homogeneity in tastes.)

4.3. *Capital Goods as Stores of Value*

The competitive mechanism converts privately owned commodities into privately consumed goods. The standard general equilibrium literature makes clear that whether this is accomplished indirectly by production (treating technology as part of the household endowment) together with distribution or directly by distribution alone is an inessential detail. However, in models which treat time seriously, there is an important aspect of production which will need to be accounted for: Durable productive assets (land, machines, natural resources, and the like) also serve as stores of value. A first pass in understanding the role of government debt as a store of value allows us to ignore these capital goods, since the most important element common to all assets is the intrinsic difficulty in evaluating future terms of trade. Incorporation of many alternative assets into the model of overlapping generations must nonetheless be considered to have high priority on the research agenda.

Imagine macroeconomics without a description of the choice between holding real assets and government debt (and other paper assets)!

4.4. *The Costs of Trading*

The fact that trading itself requires scarce resources cannot be avoided. One of money's principal functions is to reduce these transaction costs. While a fully satisfactory microeconomic theory of money and transactions has yet to be developed, it should be clear that the analysis must be dynamic. If trading somehow took place outside time, then the problems of matching buyers and sellers and settling their complicated sets of accounts would be of little consequence. In reality, however, all trades are dynamic, since the trading process itself requires time. Even so-called spot trades involve rather sophisticated institutional arrangements because actual contracts are not conveniently signed and executed on a perfectly synchronized basis.

When longer periods of time are involved, these difficulties are compounded. Futures trading requires more detailed monitoring procedures and more careful enforcement procedures to protect against the obvious hazards of contract nonperformance. As a result, the costs associated with borrowing are typically very high for the individual without tangible assets which can be used to guarantee her/his loan. In fact, the transaction costs on unsecured borrowing are so high that, as a good first approximation, it could be assumed that all spot and futures purchases must be financed either from present money balances or from the money received from the sale of present commodity inventories.

This means that, in addition to their intertemporal (or solvency) constraints, individuals also face period-by-period (or liquidity) constraints which limit them to trades supportable by current holdings. Monetary policy, by controlling the amount, timing, and distribution of money holdings, has an effect on aggregate demand. The government's ability to influence individual liquidity constraints is an important source of the potency of its macroeconomic policies.

Liquidity constraints, representing imperfect borrowing markets, are readily incorporated into the overlapping generations model; indeed, they have already been easily incorporated into fairly robust versions of the standard general equilibrium model (with, however, limited success since that model offers no satisfactory resolution of the "hot-potato" problem). Although a fuller understanding of the detailed structure of marketing activity is clearly desirable, we believe that straightforward modeling of constraints on individual liquidity may well capture many of the essential aspects of costly trading which are critical to macroeconomic policy.

4.5. *Expectations*

At the heart of macroeconomic theory is the determination of asset prices. But assets have value today in large measure because they have (or, more precisely, are believed to have) value tomorrow. Thus asset prices must be largely based on individual expectations about the future. How are these beliefs formed, and what is the nature of the resulting competitive equilibrium?

The perfect-foresight (or, more fashionably, rational expectations) hypothesis provides a useful starting point for understanding this process. This is not because it is a realistic informational postulate; it is surely quite unrealistic. Rather, it is because the hypothesis is the exact analogue of the familiar atemporal assumption of full information and because it is consonant with the ultimate outcome of many credible models of intelligent learning behavior. As such it provides a good benchmark (at least for some normative purposes) and accords with an inherent distaste for any theory of expectations formation which does not allow for consistent adaptation (at least in some limiting sense).

As we see it, then, the perfect-foresight hypothesis is at best a positive descriptive model only in terms of representing a plausible asymptotic structure for some very complicated process by which individuals discover how the state of the economy tomorrow will depend on the state of the world tomorrow. Modeling this process itself is therefore clearly of utmost importance. Unfortunately, like the rest of the profession, we have few specific suggestions to offer at this stage of our knowledge; idle conjecture without concrete analysis does not seem especially helpful. We can, however, foresee two obvious difficulties confronting such an enterprise.

We have argued earlier that, even given the perfect-foresight hypothesis, there is no obvious natural selection of the particular features of the world on which individuals focus in predicting the future of the economy. This must be doubly true when, in addition, individuals are groping toward enlightenment —particularly since individuals are assuredly mortal[2] (so that the learning process involves a continually changing progression of individuals) while, under the circumstances, their environment is apparently inconstant (so that there is absolutely no assurance that the world tomorrow will retain essential properties of the world today). Our parents' beliefs were greatly shaped by the advent of the New Deal; our children's will be by the advent of the OPEC cartel.

This observation suggests a related difficulty, namely, that there is no a priori justification for assuming (and therefore biasing research toward establishing) that a reasonable learning process necessarily converges to anything like perfect foresight. Even when the underlying economic "fundamentals" are agreed to be stationary, evolving market "psychology" may render perceptions of their import decidedly nonstationary. Furthermore, there is no obvious reason for assuming that an individual who holds "irrational" beliefs would be better off if converted to "rational" beliefs.

Finally, we view attempts to avoid the deep problems associated with modeling expectations formation by arbitrarily restricting either the fundamental learning process or its presumed ultimate outcome—in particular, by concentrating on uniquely determined steady states—to be basically misleading, essentially investing pure technical simplification with the aura of hard economic law. In this regard, we should mention that such restriction plays a crucial part in the purported "rational expectations" proof of the quantity theory of money. Our rebuttal to this asserted claim has already been argued in section 2.

5. Concluding Comments

There are now two main schools of thought dominating macroeconomics, the *rational expectations* (RE) school and the *Keynesian econometrics* (KE)

[2]Only gods are immortal—as well as omniscient. The assumption that households effectively live forever, not at all uncommon in the literature, is itself fairly unbelievable. But that infinitely lived households also accurately foretell eternity—even taken as an idealization—clearly defies common sense. Any fully evolved learning process necessarily requires frequently repeated individual performance, and this prerequisite is simply out of the question when a shaved die is only cast once (or, who knows, an unbalanced wheel is only spun once or . . .).

school. The KE school tends to reject the results of the RE school on the grounds that the assumptions of competitive behavior, complete markets, and perfect foresight are unrealistic. According to the RE school, the KE approach is suspect because it is not derived from consistent individual maximizing behavior.

We do not join this debate; we have chosen instead to accumulate more intellectual capital. It is clear to us that more fundamental research is needed before these issues can be put in proper perspective. While each school rejects many of the assumptions as well as conclusions of the other school, from our present viewpoint it is not even necessarily evident that either group's policy recommendations follow given its philosophical and theoretical predilections.

We plan to play a part in developing a truly dynamic analysis of government debt and intertemporal allocation. To be useful, the analysis must also be fundamentally disaggregative. We have, therefore, no choice but to build our theories on the foundation of the overlapping generations model. By definition, it is the only genuinely dynamic, basically disaggregate framework available.

General Equilibrium Approaches to the Study of Monetary Economies: Comments on Recent Developments

Ross M. Starr*

1. Introduction

Several points raised in the papers and discussions of this conference have been active research topics in the general equilibrium literature of recent years. Questions treated include positivity of the price of fiat money (that is, a bounded determinate price level in a fiat money economy), the role of money in allocation over time, and the usefulness of money as a medium of exchange. I would like briefly to sketch the framework and results for some of this research.

2. Positivity of the Price of Money

A fiat money is essentially valueless in itself; hence, if not exogenously prevented, its equilibrium price may be zero (the price level in money terms may be indefinitely high). This is inevitable in a finite-horizon model where the lack of backing for the currency is expected actually to be experienced. In contrast, the infinite-horizon models of Wallace and Cass, Okuno, and Zilcha in their conference papers can admit positive price equilibria.

A few technical points are worth noting. There will typically be discontinuities in opportunity sets and resulting individual behavior in the neighborhood of the null price of money (Hahn 1965).† This arises because the economy is effectively demonetized when the price of money is zero so that monetary transactions—available at any positive price—are discontinuously unavailable at a null price. The result is that proofs of existence of equilibrium relying on continuity are not directly applicable. Further, a transaction demand for money is of little help in preventing the null price equilibrium. When the price of money is zero, money can serve no transaction function; it becomes useless in transactions, and hence the transaction demand is zero as well. Thus the null price equilibrium is sustained.

In order to prevent the existence of a null price of money equilibrium, an excess demand for money must be created whenever the price is too low. Two independent means have been developed in the literature to do this:

*I gratefully acknowledge the support of a John Simon Guggenheim Fellowship and the assistance of the Group for the Applications of Mathematics and Statistics to Economics, University of California, Berkeley.

†Author names and years refer to the works listed at the end of this book.

expectations and taxes. Money appears in temporary equilibrium models as an intertemporal asset (sometimes the sole such asset or one of the few). Demand for goods and money in the present depends in part on expectations, particularly price expectations, about the future. In order to ensure positivity of the price of money in the present, it requires only that agents always attach positive probability to positivity of its price in the future (Grandmont 1977). Money is accepted because it is expected to be accepted. A government that extracts taxes payable in money can similarly ensure positivity of its equilibrium price. Nominal taxes can be structured so that whenever the price of money is low the demand for money to pay taxes creates an excess demand for money. Thus taxes can be used to place a floor beneath the price, bounding it away from zero (Kaulla 1920, Lerner 1947, Starr 1974). Money is then accepted because the government, its issuer, accepts it.

3. Intertemporal Monetary Economies

Sequence economies, formal models quite different from the overlapping generations sort, have been used to portray the store-of-value function of money. The market is thought of as reopening at a sequence of dates, usually without the use of futures markets. The missing futures markets may be conceived of as performing, when present, two distinct functions: price formation and intertemporal reallocation of purchasing power. The former function is formally replaced simply by the assumption of perfect foresight on prices. Money and related financial institutions are developed to replace the latter.

In a sequence economy agents face a budget constraint in each period. The value of goods delivered to the market in that period must equal the value extracted. Since agents' desired time pattern of sales may not coincide with their desired stream of purchases, a difficulty arises. It could be relieved by the use of futures markets, but these are supposed to be prohibitively costly to operate or for some other reason unavailable. The result is an intertemporally inefficient allocation (Hahn 1971b, 1973b). The solution (Starrett 1973) is to introduce a financial asset that allows a costless transfer of purchasing power between periods. This asset, to be thought of as money, allows equilibria to be efficient and efficient allocations to be supported as equilibria. Though it lacks a generational structure and will typically be applied to models with finite horizon, this approach seems to give an adequate account of the intertemporal (that is, store-of-value) role of money.

4. Bilateral Trade: Money as a Medium of Exchange

Consider trade between pairs of agents in an economy at equilibrium prices. Jevons (1875) argues that the difficulty of trade in this situation is that the commodities which the suppliers of a good may wish to purchase will not typically be those which its demanders wish to supply. In the apparently unlikely event that goods are reciprocally desired (that is, suppliers of A are demanders of B, and vice versa), a "double coincidence of wants" is said to occur, and trade can proceed directly. When this is lacking, Jevons suggests the use of money as an intermediate good in exchange.

A formalization of this problem focuses on the informational requirements of trade. It can be shown that monetary trade provides an informationally decentralized means of moving in restricted time from an arbitrary initial allocation to the equilibrium allocation. Other trading procedures require either greater information and coordination among traders or significantly more time (Ostroy 1973, Ostroy and Starr 1974, Starr 1972, 1976). Thus the use of money as a medium of exchange in bilateral trade is a device for economizing on time, information, and coordination.

By *monetary trade* I mean trade in which a single good plays a distinctive asymmetric role as one side of virtually all transactions. This differs from Wallace's treatment in his conference paper; he takes the distinguishing quality of a monetary economy to be the presence of an intrinsically useless financial asset with positive equilibrium price. Nevertheless, there is a useful relationship between the concepts. In order for monetary trade successfully to take place in the models of Ostroy (1973) and Ostroy and Starr (1974), each individual's holdings of the monetary commodity should be sufficiently large to finance all of that person's desired trades. It appears unlikely that any single real commodity should have this property, but a costlessly produced financial asset with an artificially maintained positive price could certainly have it. Hence, in seeking to put into effect monetary trading procedures it is peculiarly useful to have ample fiat money on hand. Alternative approaches to bilateral trading processes include those of Feldman (1973), Jones (1976), Madden (1975), and Townsend (1978a).

Models of Money With Spatially Separated Agents

Robert M. Townsend*

1. Introduction

This paper presents three models which explain the observation that money is used in payment for commodities and barter is not prevalent. In each of these models money is intrinsically useless, inasmuch as it does not enter directly into either utility functions or production functions, and inconvertible, inasmuch as no one stands ready to convert money into anything else.[1] Moreover, money does not enter any of the models by way of legal restrictions[2] or by way of a requirement that commodities cannot be acquired without it, à la Clower 1967.[3] Rather, money is explained in the sense that the following procedure is adopted. First, the environment is specified carefully and completely—the agents of the model, their preferences and endowments, and most important, who can communicate with whom. It is then established that there exists a monetary equilibrium, that is, a competitive equilibrium in which a fixed-supply money has value.

It is widely accepted that money cannot be explained in this sense in a standard general equilibrium model. (See, for example, Hahn 1965.) In a Walrasian model, at least, money cannot facilitate exchange; the nonmonetary competitive equilibria are Pareto optimal. (Note again that a distinction is maintained here between money—fiat money, that is—and private credit.) Thus, to get money into a model something must inhibit the operation of markets.[4] Moreover, if terminal conditions are to be avoided, time must be infinite.

In the model of Samuelson 1958, some markets are precluded in an obvious

*This paper would not have been written without the benefit of many stimulating conversations on money and debt with Neil Wallace, whom I would also like to thank for innumerable contributions to the present draft. I am also much indebted to John Bryant for several very useful conversations and for an example which played a crucial role in the development of this paper, to Robert E. Lucas, Jr., for several conversations on the Cass-Yaari model, and to Thomas J. Sargent for helpful comments. I assume full responsibility for any errors. Support for this research from the Federal Reserve Bank of Minneapolis is gratefully acknowledged.

[1]The terminology here is Wallace's (see his paper in this volume).

[2]But see the concluding section for a qualification to this statement.

[3]The implications of such Clower constraints, over and above the constraints implied by the technology of exchange, are examined, however. (Author names and years refer to the works listed at the end of this book.)

[4]See Wallace's paper in this volume and the discussion in Hahn 1973a on inessential money.

way: there can be no transactions between the current young and the young of the next generation; unborn individuals cannot trade. And in versions of this overlapping generations model, there does exist a monetary equilibrium, one which improves upon the nonmonetary equilibrium. In fact, in some versions, the monetary equilibrium is itself optimal and is associated with nonbinding nonnegativity constraints on the holding of money balances. Yet one wonders whether the properties of the overlapping generations model carry over to alternative models which explain money in the above sense.

In the models of this paper, markets are precluded in another way, by spatially separating agents. Infinitely lived agents who discount future over present consumption are allocated over time into distinct markets or islands. The crucial idea here is that markets must clear on each island in every time period. There can be no communication across islands; that is, there is no central market or exchange system. Certainly this way of decentralizing an economy is not new. Lucas (1972) uses such islands to explain the movement of economic aggregates.[5] More to the point, the explicit pairing of agents is a scheme used in various recent microeconomic approaches to money, including Starr 1972, Ostroy 1973, Feldman 1973, Ostroy and Starr 1974, and Harris (forthcoming). Yet, for the most part, these approaches are not really dynamic equilibrium theories. An important exception is Harris, but he is concerned with commodity money, not outside indebtedness.

In two of the models of this paper, the turnpike model of exchange (section 2) and Lucas' version of the Cass-Yaari (1966a) model (section 4), there exists a monetary equilibrium, that is, a competitive equilibrium with valued money. So, as claimed, these models explain money. And, as in the overlapping generations construct, this monetary equilibrium improves upon the nonmonetary equilibrium (autarky). Unlike the overlapping generations model, however, the monetary equilibria in these models with spatially separated agents are nonoptimal and are associated with binding nonnegativity constraints on the holding of money balances. Thus the decentralization of spatial separation is not completely overcome with money.[6]

The argument as to why no optimal allocation can be supported as a monetary equilibrium in these models is fairly intuitive. Suppose all agents are of the same age and all discount the future at the same rate, as in the turnpike model and Lucas' version of the Cass-Yaari model. Then if an optimal allocation is to be supported, there must be a rate of deflation equal to the common discount rate. But in the absence of taxes, such a deflation is inconsistent with individual maximization, as real wealth (real money balances) would be unbounded. That no stationary monetary equilibrium can be optimal is an immediate corollary.

As Grandmont and Younes (1972, 1973) point out, this latter conclusion appears frequently in the literature (see, for example, Clower 1970, Friedman 1969, Johnson 1970, and Samuelson 1968, 1969) where the argument turns on a divergence between the positive marginal utility of real money balances and the zero marginal cost of creating them. Grandmont and Younes are critical of this literature, and they are not alone; Clower (1970), for example, argues quite

[5] A case can be made that models of money with spatially separated agents are of interest in their own right, quite apart from providing an alternative to overlapping generations.

[6] On an a priori basis this should not be a surprise; indeed, versions of the overlapping generations model have been criticized for producing optimal monetary equilibria. See Wallace's paper in this volume.

forcefully that these welfare questions must be addressed in a model which makes explicit the monetary exchange process. Grandmont and Younes do establish the aforementioned conclusion rigorously in a general equilibrium, monetary economy. Yet, as the authors note (in Grandmont and Younes 1972, p. 357), even in their model money is introduced "in a very crude way by imposing constraints on transactions." That is, in contrast to the models of this paper, theirs is not a model which explains money. In this respect, at least, this paper may be viewed as an important extension of Grandmont and Younes and of this literature.

If lump-sum taxes on money balances are permitted, then the models with spatially separated agents of this paper can also produce Friedman's (1969) conclusions on the optimal quantity of money. That is, with lump-sum taxes, optimal allocations can be supported in an interventionist monetary equilibrium in which the rate of interest on money equals the common discount rate and in which agents are satiated with money balances, that is, the nonnegativity constraints on money balances are nonbinding. (Also see Grandmont and Younes 1972 and Bewley's paper in this volume.)

Speaking rather loosely, the overlapping generations model overturns these welfare results by pairing agents of different ages and therefore different rates of discount.[7] This is argued more fully in section 3, where the turnpike model is modified to incorporate finitely lived agents and hence becomes an overlapping generations model. It is hoped that an essential feature of the overlapping generations model is revealed.

As noted above, monetary economics necessarily involves the economics of infinity. In the overlapping generations model there is an infinite number of generations, though a finite number of agents alive at any one date. In the turnpike model and in the Cass-Yaari model presented here, there is an infinite number of agents alive at any one date. This specification ensures that no private debt is traded, so that its exclusion is endogenous, that is, not imposed by the modeler. Section 5 offers some preliminary comments on private debt (inside money) in the context of a modified turnpike model, one without the contemporaneous infinity.

Finally, a caveat is in order. The intent in what follows is to understand the implications of various exchange structures for monetary equilibria. Thus, again speaking rather loosely, preferences and endowments are held fixed across models as the exchange structure is varied. To this end, maximum generality is not pursued within the context of each model. Agents are assumed throughout to have preferences and endowments of a very special form. Moreover, certain strong symmetry conditions (on the class of allocations under consideration) are imposed exogenously, without elaboration. Finally, it may be noted that the models of this paper are successful in explaining money without the introduction of uncertainty; it remains an open question as to whether these models can approximate economies in which moral hazard and bankruptcy play a crucial role.[8]

2. A Turnpike Model of Exchange

In the turnpike model each of a countably infinite number of agents is allocated

[7] Cass, Okuno, and Zilcha argue (in their paper in this volume) that the inefficiency of monetary equilibrium emerges in the overlapping generations model under alternative assumptions.

[8] See Brunner and Meltzer 1971.

into one of a countably infinite number of spatially distinct markets or islands in each period of her or his life. The exogenous allocation procedure is such that any two agents are paired at most once during their lifetimes, and, moreover, they share no common third agent as a trading partner. All agents are born at time 0, so that at any time t all agents are of the same age. Each lives forever and faces a sequence of endowments of the single consumption good of the model which alternates between 0 and 1 unit. At any time $t \geq 0$ an agent who has an endowment of 1 unit is paired with an agent who has an endowment of 0. The consumption good cannot be stored.

An economy with these characteristics is depicted in Figure 1. Each agent is imagined to be traveling on a turnpike, either east or west. The arrows indicate the direction of travel, and the spikes indicate the markets. The numbers 0 and 1 index the endowment of an agent located at the indicated position. Initially, at $t = 0$, there is one agent at each position. It should be emphasized here that no agents have control over their lifetime itineraries. Each agent moves forward one market in each period. Also, these markets are isolated one from another; there can be no transactions or communication among them at any time.

Figure 1
The Turnpike Model

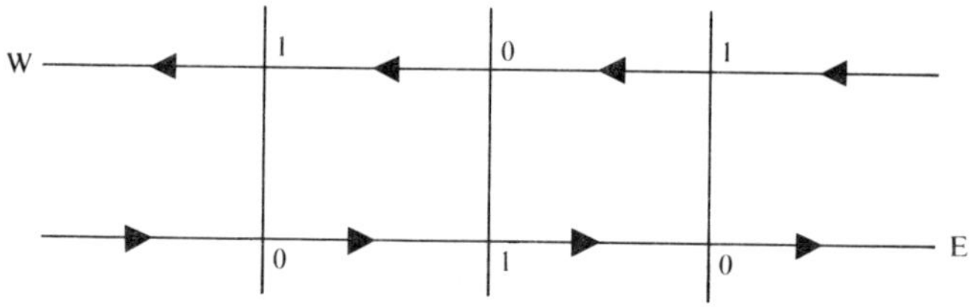

Each agent has preferences over her or his (infinite) lifetime consumption sequence $\{c_t\}_{t=0}^{\infty}$ as described by the utility function $\Sigma_{t=0}^{\infty}\beta^t U(c_t)$ where $c_t \geq 0$, $0 < \beta < 1$, and $U(\cdot)$ is strictly concave, strictly increasing, bounded, and continuously differentiable with $U'(0) = \infty$. Thus all agents have the same time separable utility function of a rather special form, and in particular, all discount future over present consumption at the same rate, β.[9]

This model displays a well-known property, the absence of double coincidence of wants. At each time t, considered in isolation, there can be no Pareto improving bilateral trade; there is only one consumption good, and more is preferred to less. One may ask, of course, whether borrowing and lending might not improve matters. Section 5 below is devoted entirely to this question in a slightly modified context, but it should be noted here that, in a sense which will be made precise, there can be no private debt in the present model. For consider an agent at time t who has 0 units of the consumption good. Such an agent might wish to issue an IOU, to be honored in better times, when the agent has 1 unit of the consumption good. Similarly, the agent's partner at time t, who has 1 unit, might be inclined to accept such an IOU. Yet the model is

[9]Recall the caveat at the end of the introduction.

constructed in such a way that the IOU can never be redeemed by the issuer; the pair will never meet again, and the purchaser of such an IOU can only pass it along to an agent "behind" the issuer. Thus, if one takes as a defining characteristic of private debt that it ultimately be redeemed by the issuer, there can be no private debt in this model.[10]

Having specified the environment for this model, the next step is to characterize Pareto optimal allocations. For this purpose a strong symmetry condition is imposed, that in any allocation, agents cannot be distinguished by their initial market position. That is, any agent who begins life with 0 units of the consumption good must be treated the same way as any other agent who begins with 0 units, independent of the initial location. All such agents are hereafter referred to as agents of *type A*. A similar restriction is placed on those who begin with 1 unit, agents of *type B*. It bears repeating here that when an allocation is termed optimal below, it is only established to be optimal in the class of symmetric allocations; there remains the possibility of a nonsymmetric allocation which is Pareto superior.

Now let c_t^i denote the number of units of consumption of an agent of type i at time t. Then an *allocation* $\{c_t^A\}_{t=0}^{\infty}, \{c_t^B\}_{t=0}^{\infty}$ is said to be *feasible* if

$$(1) \qquad c_t^A + c_t^B \leq 1, \; c_t^A \geq 0, \; c_t^B \geq 0 \qquad \text{all } t \geq 0.$$

(An allocation is said to be *interior* if consumption is strictly positive for each agent type in each time period.) It may be assumed without loss of generality in what follows that resources are fully utilized. Then to determine an interior Pareto optimal allocation, it is enough to maximize a weighted average of the utilities of the two agent types, subject to the resource constraints, as is established below. This yields

Problem 1:

$$\max_{\{c_t^A\}_{t=0}^{\infty}, \{c_t^B\}_{t=0}^{\infty}} \quad w^A\left[\sum_{t=0}^{\infty} \beta^t U(c_t^A)\right] + w^B\left[\sum_{t=0}^{\infty} \beta^t U(c_t^B)\right]$$

subject to (1) where $w^A > 0$, $w^B > 0$, $w^A + w^B = 1$. Necessary and sufficient first-order conditions for Problem 1 are

$$(2) \qquad w^i \beta^t U'(c_t^i) - \theta_t = 0, \; i = A, B \qquad t \geq 0$$

where the θ_t are positive Lagrange multipliers. Trivial manipulation of (2) yields

$$(3) \qquad \frac{U'(c_t^A)}{U'(c_\tau^A)} = \frac{U'(c_t^B)}{U'(c_\tau^B)} \qquad \text{all } t, \tau \geq 0.$$

Conditions (1) and (3) are fully equivalent with

$$(4) \qquad c_t^A = \lambda, \; c_t^B = 1 - \lambda, \; 0 < \lambda < 1 \qquad \text{all } t \geq 0.$$

[10] If there are limitations on the issue of IOUs, there can exist equilibria in which IOUs have value and are never redeemed. Such equilibria are virtually indistinguishable from equilibria with valued fiat money, as defined below.

(See Figure 2.) Thus a necessary and sufficient condition for a feasible interior allocation $\{c_t^A\}_{t=0}^{\infty}$, $\{c_t^B\}_{t=0}^{\infty}$ to be optimal is that each agent of type A receive λ units of the consumption good in each period t. That this condition is necessary for optimality follows from the obvious fact that if condition (3) is not satisfied for some periods t and τ, then there is a Pareto superior feasible allocation. That this condition is sufficient is also obvious. For suppose there exists a feasible allocation which is Pareto superior. Then it would satisfy constraint (1) and increase the value of the objective function in Problem 1, a contradiction. Hereafter, then, reference will be made to an *interior optimum* λ, in which both agents receive constant consumption.

Figure 2
Optimal Allocations in the Turnpike Model

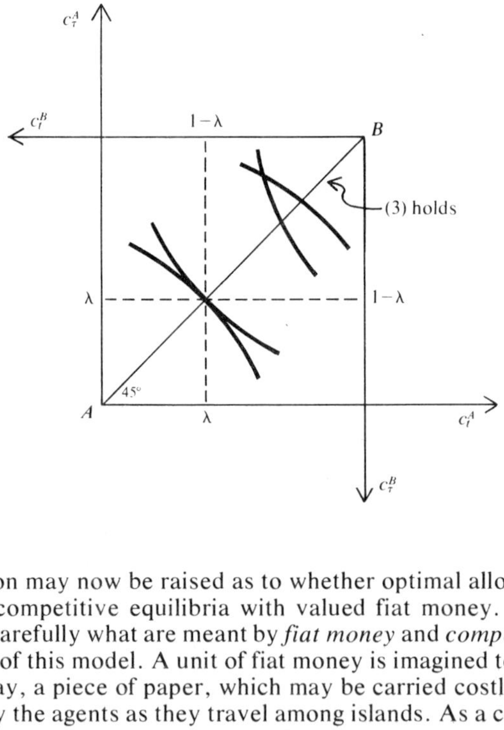

The question may now be raised as to whether optimal allocations can be supported in competitive equilibria with valued fiat money. To do so one must discuss carefully what are meant by *fiat money* and *competitive markets* in the context of this model. A unit of fiat money is imagined to be a physical commodity, say, a piece of paper, which may be carried costlessly and used in exchange by the agents as they travel among islands. As a commodity, the stock of fiat money in the possession of any trader at any time cannot be negative. On each island and at each time period there is assumed to be a competitive market in which fiat money can be exchanged for the consumption good at a specified rate. That is, agents take the price of the consumption good as given and maximize utility by choice of the amount to consume and the amount of money balances to carry over into the next period. No attempt is made here to justify the price-taking assumption or defend the competitive equilibrium notion; to the extent that the mechanism which underlies the equilibrium notion requires a large (perhaps infinite) number of agents, each agent discussed above may be taken as representative of agents in identical situations.

Consistent with the symmetry assumption, attention will be restricted to monetary equilibria in which the price of the consumption good in terms of money at any time t is the same in each market. This price is denoted p_t and is assumed to be finite and strictly positive. Also, let M_t^i denote the number of units of fiat money chosen at time $t-1$ by agent type i and carried over into period t, z_t^i denote the number of units of a lump-sum tax on money balances (or subsidy, if negative) on agent type i at the beginning of period t, and y_t^i denote the endowment of agent type i at time t. Then taking as given the sequences $\{p_t\}_{t=0}^{\infty}$, $\{z_t^i\}_{t=0}^{\infty}$ and the initial money balances M_0^i, each agent of type i is confronted with

Problem 2:

$$\max_{\{c_t^i\}_{t=0}^{\infty},\ \{M_t^i\}_{t=1}^{\infty}} \sum_{t=0}^{\infty} \beta^t U(c_t^i)$$

subject to

$$c_t^i \geqslant 0 \qquad \text{all } t \geqslant 0$$

$$M_t^i \geqslant 0 \qquad \text{all } t \geqslant 0$$

$$p_t c_t^i + M_{t+1}^i \leqslant p_t y_t^i + M_t^i - z_t^i \qquad \text{all } t \geqslant 0 \tag{5}$$

given $M_0^i \geqslant 0$, $z_0^i = 0$. Here (5) is the budget constraint which prevails in period t. With $U'(0) = \infty$, the nonnegativity constraint on consumption need not be made explicit; in contrast, the nonnegativity constraint on money balances may be binding. Assuming without loss of generality that the budget constraint (5) holds as an equality, so that in effect only $\{M_t^i\}_{t=1}^{\infty}$ need be chosen, and making the obvious substitution for the c_t^i, one obtains necessary Euler conditions for a maximum

$$-\frac{\beta^{t-1}U'(c_{t-1}^i)}{p_{t-1}} + \frac{\beta^t U'(c_t^i)}{p_t} + \theta_t^i = 0 \qquad \text{all } t \geqslant 1 \tag{6}$$

where θ_t^i is the Lagrange multiplier associated with the nonnegativity constraint on money balances, that is,

$$\theta_t^i \geqslant 0,\ \ M_t^i \geqslant 0,\ \ \theta_t^i M_t^i = 0.$$

Thus,

$$\frac{U'(c_{t-1}^i)}{\beta U'(c_t^i)} \geqslant \frac{p_{t-1}}{p_t} \qquad \text{all } t \geqslant 1 \tag{7}$$

where (7) must hold as an equality if $M_t^i > 0$ and as an inequality if and only if $\theta_t^i > 0$, that is, when the marginal utility of a unit of fiat money spent on period $t-1$ consumption exceeds the marginal utility of a unit of fiat money spent on period t consumption and there is no more fiat money to spend in period $t-1$.

A competitive equilibrium with valued fiat money may now be defined.

DEFINITION. *A monetary equilibrium is a sequence of finite positive prices* $\{p_t^*\}_{t=0}^{\infty}$ *and sequences of consumptions* $\{c_t^{i*}\}_{t=0}^{\infty}$, *money balances* $\{M_t^{i*}\}_{t=0}^{\infty}$, *and lump-sum taxes* $\{z_t^{i*}\}_{t=0}^{\infty}$ *for each agent type* $i = A, B$ *such that*

- *Maximization: the sequences* $\{c_t^{i*}\}_{t=0}^{\infty}$, $\{M_t^{i*}\}_{t=1}^{\infty}$ *solve Problem 2 relative to* $\{p_t^*\}_{t=0}^{\infty}$, $\{z_t^{i*}\}_{t=0}^{\infty}$, *and* M_0^{i*}.
- *Market clearing:* $c_t^{A*} + c_t^{B*} = 1$, *all* $t \geqslant 0$.

One may now ask whether optimal allocations can be supported in a monetary equilibria without intervention. The answer is summarized in

PROPOSITION 1. *No interior optimum* λ *can be supported in a monetary equilibrium without intervention, that is, with* $z_t^{i*} \equiv 0$ *for all* $i = A, B$.

Proof. The proof is by contradiction. Thus, suppose that the allocation $c_t^A = \lambda$, $c_t^B = 1 - \lambda$, all $t \geqslant 0$, can be supported in a monetary equilibrium without intervention. With $z_t^{i*} \equiv 0$, with $y_t^A = 0$ for t even and $y_t^B = 0$ for t odd, and with $U'(0) = \infty$, it is clear that the nonnegativity constraint on money balances cannot be binding for agent type A for choices made when t is odd or for agent type B for choices made when t is even. Thus from (7), equilibrium prices $\{p_t^*\}_{t=0}^{\infty}$ must satisfy

$$\frac{U'(\lambda)}{\beta U'(\lambda)} = \frac{p_{t-1}^*}{p_t^*} \qquad t \geqslant 2, t \text{ even}$$

$$\frac{U'(1-\lambda)}{\beta U'(1-\lambda)} = \frac{p_{t-1}^*}{p_t^*} \qquad t \geqslant 1, t \text{ odd.}$$

It follows that

$$p_t^* = \beta p_{t-1}^* \qquad \text{all } t \geqslant 1 \tag{8}$$

that is, *the rate of deflation must be* $1 - \beta$. Now consider the evolution of money balances of agent type B given the price sequence $\{p_t^*\}_{t=0}^{\infty}$ and the specified consumption sequence $c_t^B = 1 - \lambda$, all $t \geqslant 0$. Agent type B begins life with $M_0^{B*} \geqslant 0$ units of fiat money, acquires $p_0^*\lambda$ units in period 0, and spends $p_1^*(1 - \lambda)$ units in period 1. Thus

$$M_2^{B*} - M_0^{B*} = p_0^*\lambda - p_1^*(1-\lambda). \tag{9}$$

Clearly the increment to money balances from $t = 0$ to $t = 2$, the left-hand side of (9), is nonnegative if the right-hand side is nonnegative. Substituting from (8), the right-hand side is nonnegative if

$$\frac{\lambda}{1-\lambda} \geqslant \beta. \tag{10}$$

In fact, one may readily verify that the increment to money balances is nonnegative for agent type B from t to $t + 2$ for all t even, if (10) holds.

Similar calculations establish that the increment to money balances is non-negative for agent type A from t to $t + 2$ for all t odd, if

$$(11) \qquad \frac{1-\lambda}{\lambda} \geqslant \beta.$$

The left-hand sides of inequalities (10) and (11) are graphed in Figure 3 as functions of the parameter λ. As Figure 3 makes clear, with the discount rate β fixed, $0 < \beta < 1$, at least one of the relationships (10) and (11) must hold as a strict inequality for any value of λ between 0 and 1. That is, at least one agent type will be accumulating money balances over time in the above sense. But then this cannot be an equilibrium. For if (10) holds as a strict inequality, for example, agent type B could spend these excess balances at $t \geqslant 1$, t odd, and improve upon the consumption sequence $c_t^{\beta *} \equiv 1 - \lambda$. This completes the proof.

Figure 3
The Relationship Between λ and β

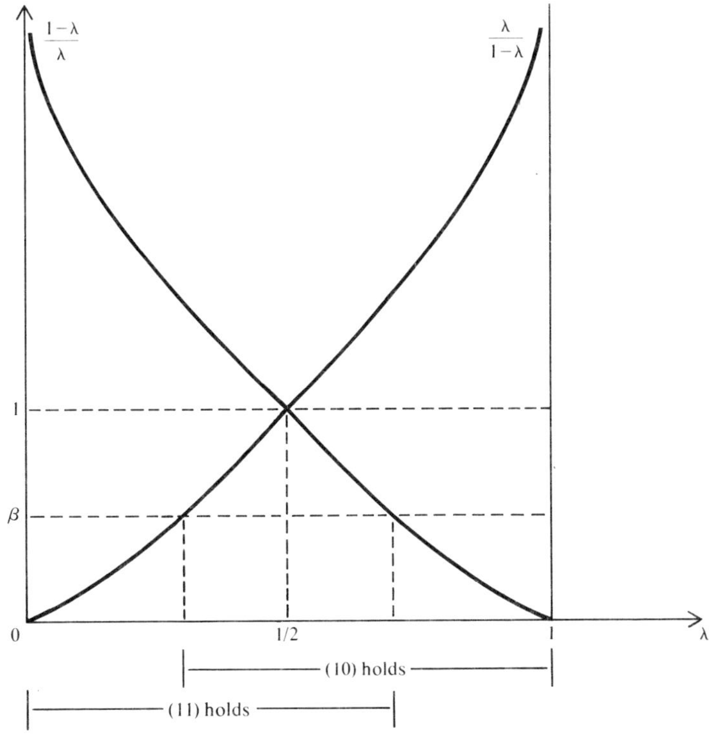

Thus, if an optimal allocation is to be attained in a monetary equilibrium, the rate of deflation must be $1 - \beta$, and, consequently, there must be some intervention by way of taxes and/or subsidies. That at least some optimal allocations can be supported in this way is established in

PROPOSITION 2. *Any interior optimum* λ *with* $\beta \leq [\lambda/(1-\lambda)]$ *and* $\beta \leq [(1-\lambda)/\lambda]$ *can be supported in a monetary equilibrium with rate of deflation* $1 - \beta$; *with* $z_t^{B*} = p_{t-1}^*[\lambda - \beta(1-\lambda)] \geq 0$ *for* $t \geq 1$, t *odd, and* $z_t^{B*} = 0$ *otherwise; and with* $z_t^{A*} = p_{t-1}^*[(1-\lambda) - \lambda\beta] \geq 0$ *for* $t \geq 2$, t *even, and* $z_t^{A*} = 0$ *otherwise.*

Proof. See the Appendix.

Given Propositions 1 and 2, one may well ask whether there exist any monetary equilibria which do not require intervention. The search for such equilibria is facilitated by the following proposition which suggests that the search can be limited to equilibria in which the nonnegativity constraints on money balances play an important role.

PROPOSITION 3. *Any monetary equilibrium with nonbinding nonnegativity constraints on money balances on each agent in each period supports an optimal allocation and hence requires some intervention.*

Proof. By hypothesis, $\theta_t^{i*} \equiv 0$. Thus from (6) it follows that

$$(12) \qquad \frac{\beta^{t-1}U'(c_{t-1}^{i*})}{\beta^t U'(c_t^{i*})} = \frac{p_{t-1}^*}{p_t^*} \qquad i = A, B \qquad \text{all } t \geq 1.$$

Manipulation of (12) yields

$$(13) \qquad \frac{\beta^t U'(c_t^{i*})}{\beta^\tau U'(c_\tau^{i*})} = \frac{p_t^*}{p_\tau^*} \qquad i = A, B \qquad \text{all } t, \tau \geq 0.$$

As (13) holds for both i,

$$(14) \qquad \frac{U'(c_t^{A*})}{U'(c_\tau^{A*})} = \frac{U'(c_t^{B*})}{U'(c_\tau^{B*})} \qquad \text{all } t, \tau \geq 0.$$

Condition (14) and the market-clearing condition of an equilibrium are sufficient for an optimum as discussed above. The conclusion of this proposition follows from Proposition 1. This completes the proof.

The search for a noninterventionist monetary equilibrium is also facilitated by the observation that, roughly speaking, a time trend to prices, say, a constant rate of deflation $1 - \beta$ as in Proposition 2, would seem to necessitate intervention in order to keep purchasing power constant. That is, one might search for an equilibrium in which prices remain constant over time, at some price $p^* > 0$. Thus it may be guessed that in a noninterventionist monetary equilibrium, each agent of type B will have 1 unit of purchasing power to be allocated over consumption in each pair of periods $(t, t + 1)$, $t \geq 0$, t even, selling the consumption good for money in period t and spending all accumulated money balances in period $t + 1$, with a binding nonnegativity constraint on money balances at $t + 1$. This will generate consumptions c^* and c^{**}, as depicted in Figure 4. Of course, each agent of type A will be doing the same thing in each pair of periods $(t + 1, t + 2)$, $t \geq 0$, t even. This discussion is summarized in

Figure 4
The Turnpike's Monetary Equilibrium

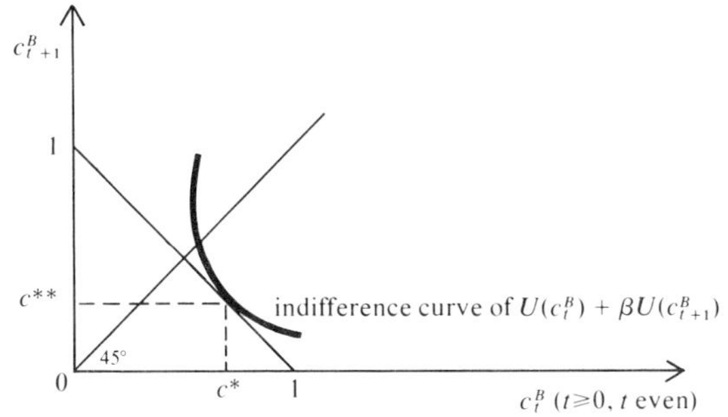

PROPOSITION 4. *There exists a noninterventionist monetary equilibrium with constant prices, with binding nonnegativity constraints on money balances in every other period, and with alternating consumption sequences. In particular for taxes and prices,*

$$z_t^{i*} \equiv 0, \;\; p_t^* \equiv p^* > 0;$$

for agent A, $M_0^{A*} = p^*c^{**}$, *and*

$$c_t^{A*} = c^{**}, \;\; M_{t+1}^{A*} = 0, \;\; \theta_{t+1}^{A*} > 0 \qquad t \geq 0, t \text{ even}$$

$$c_t^A = c^*, \;\; M_{t+1}^{A*} - p^*c^{**}, \;\; \theta_{t+1}^{A*} = 0 \qquad t \geq 1, t \text{ odd};$$

for agent B, $M_0^{B*} = 0$, *and*

$$c_t^B = c^*, \;\; M_{t+1}^{B*} = p^*c^{**}, \;\; \theta_{t+1}^{B*} = 0 \qquad t \geq 0, t \text{ even}$$

$$c_t^B = c^{**}, \;\; M_{t+1}^B = 0, \;\; \theta_{t+1}^B > 0 \qquad t \geq 1, t \text{ odd};$$

and where c^* *and* c^{**} *satisfy*

$$\frac{U'(c^*)}{\beta U'(c^{**})} = 1, \;\; c^* + c^{**} = 1.$$

The equilibrium allocation is nonoptimal but Pareto superior to autarky.
Proof. See the Appendix.

The proof of Proposition 4 utilizes the fact that for agent type A

(15) $$p_t c_t^A + p_{t+1}c_{t+1}^A = p_{t+1}y_{t+1}^A + M_t^A - M_{t+2}^A \qquad t \geq 0, t \text{ even}$$

(16) $$p_t c_t^A \leq M_t^A \qquad t \geq 0, t \text{ even}$$

where (15) is the money balance accumulation equation and (16) follows from the restriction that $M_{t+1}^A \geqslant 0$. Letting $c_t^A = c^1$, $c_{t+1}^A = c^2$, $p_t = p^1$, $p_{t+1} = p^2$, $y_{t+1}^A = y^2$, $M_t^A = M$, $M_{t+2}^A = M'$, equations (15) and (16) may be written as

$$(17) \qquad p^1c^1 + p^2c^2 = p^2y^2 + M - M'$$

$$(18) \qquad p^1c^1 \leqslant M.$$

Here, then, (17) appears as a money balance accumulation equation in a two-commodity model and (18) is a semi-Clower constraint, that the valuation of consumption of commodity one not exceed initial money balance. This formulation leads one to inquire as to the effect of a more standard Clower constraint of the form

$$(19) \qquad p^1c^1 + p^2c^2 \leqslant M$$

that the total valuation of consumption be bounded by initial money balances. Constraint (19) is not derived entirely from the technology of exchange. Imposed in addition is the requirement that agents bid in competitive markets for their own production. That is, agent type A at time $t+1$ as a producer is required to place all production y_{t+1}^A on the market and pay cash in advance for any consumption c_{t+1}^A.

Motivated by the above discussion, consider the following

DEFINITION. *A Clower-type monetary equilibrium is a sequence of finite positive prices $\{p_t^*\}_{t=0}^\infty$ and sequences of consumptions $\{c_t^{i*}\}_{t=0}^\infty$ and money balances $\{M_t^{i*}\}_{t=0}^\infty$ for each agent type i = A, B such that*

- *Maximization for type A: the sequences $\{c_t^{A*}\}_{t=0}^\infty$, $\{M_t^{A*}\}_{t=1}^\infty$ solve*

$$\max_{\{c_t^A\}_{t=0}^\infty, \{M_t^A\}_{t=1}^\infty} \sum_{\substack{t\geqslant 0 \\ t \text{ even}}} \beta^t[U(c_t^A)+\beta U(c_{t+1}^A)]$$

subject to

$$p_t^*c_t^A + p_{t+1}^*c_{t+1}^A = p_{t+1}^*y_{t+1}^A + M_t^A - M_{t+2}^A \qquad t \geqslant 0, t \text{ even}$$

$$p_t^*c_t^A + p_{t+1}^*c_{t+1}^A \leqslant M_t^A \qquad t \geqslant 0, t \text{ even}$$

$$M_{t+1}^A = M_t^A - p_t^*c_t^A \qquad t \geqslant 0, t \text{ even}$$

given $M_0^{A*} \geqslant 0$.

- *Maximization for type B: the sequences $\{c_t^{B*}\}_{t=0}^\infty$, $\{M_t^{B*}\}_{t=1}^\infty$ solve*

$$\max_{\{c_t^B\}_{t=0}^\infty, \{M_t^B\}_{t=1}^\infty} \left\{ U(c_0^B) + \sum_{\substack{t\geqslant 1 \\ t \text{ odd}}} \beta^{t-1}[\beta U(c_t^B)+\beta^2 U(c_{t+1}^B)] \right\}$$

subject to

$$p_t^*c_t^B + p_{t+1}^*c_{t+1}^B = p_{t+1}^*y_{t+1}^B + M_t^B - M_{t+2}^B \qquad t \geqslant 1, t \text{ odd}$$

$$p_t^*c_t^B + p_{t+1}^*c_{t+1}^B \leqslant M_t^B \qquad t \geqslant 1, t \text{ odd}$$

$$M_{t+1}^{B} = M_t^B - p_t^* c_t^B \qquad t \geq 1, t \text{ odd}$$

$$p_0^* c_0^B = p_0^* y_0^B + M_0^B - M_1^B$$

$$p_0^* c_0^B \leqslant M_0^B$$

given $M_0^{B*} \geqslant 0$.

- *Market clearing:* $c_t^{A*} + c_t^{B*} = 1, t \geqslant 0$.

This leads to

PROPOSITION 5. *If there exists a Clower-type monetary equilibrium with constant prices, that is, with* $p_t^* \equiv p^* > 0$, *and with a symmetric consumption sequence, that is, with* $c_{t+1}^{B*} = c_t^{A*}$ *for all* $t \geqslant 0$, *then* $c_{t+1}^{B*} = c_t^{A*} = c^*$ *and* $c_{t+1}^{A*} = c_t^{B*} = c^{**}$ *for* $t \geqslant 0$, *t even, where* c^* *and* c^{**} *are defined in Proposition 4. This allocation is nonoptimal but Pareto superior to autarky.*

Proof. The necessary conditions for a maximum include

$$\beta^t U'(c_t^{A*}) - \theta_t^A p^* - \gamma_t^A p^* = 0 \qquad t \geqslant 0, t \text{ even}$$

$$\beta^t \beta U'(c_{t+1}^{A*}) - \theta_t^A p^* - \gamma_t^A p^* = 0 \qquad t \geqslant 0, t \text{ even}$$

where $\theta_t^A > 0$ and $\gamma_t^A \geqslant 0$ are Lagrange multipliers. Thus

$$\frac{U'(c_t^{A*})}{\beta U'(c_{t+1}^{A*})} = 1 \qquad t \geqslant 0, t \text{ even.} \tag{20}$$

Similarly for agent type B

$$\frac{U'(c_t^{B*})}{\beta U'(c_{t+1}^{B*})} = 1 \qquad t \geqslant 1, t \text{ odd.} \tag{21}$$

Market clearing and the symmetry hypothesis imply

$$c_{t+1}^{B*} + c_t^{B*} = 1 \qquad \text{all } t \geqslant 0. \tag{22}$$

The unique solution to (21) and (22) is $c_t^{B*} = c^*$ and $c_{t+1}^{B*} = c^{**}$ for $t \geqslant 1$, t odd. And by the symmetry hypothesis $c_t^{A*} = c^*$, $c_{t+1}^{A*} = c^{**}$ for $t \geqslant 0$, t even. Thus by market clearing $c_0^{B*} = c^{**}$ also. It is obvious that this allocation is nonoptimal. Note also that for agent type A, for example, the consumption pair (c^*, c^{**}) dominates the endowment pair (0, 1) in periods $(t, t+1)$ for $t \geqslant 0$, t even. This completes the proof.

To be noted here is that the imposition of the full Clower constraint (19) reverses the consumption sequences from those of Proposition 4. Yet in this model the intervention implicit in the Clower constraint is not enough to attain optimal allocations.

In closing this section it may be noted that either as the discount rate goes to zero or, equivalently, as the frequency of transactions (pairings) increases, the turnpike model comes close to producing the welfare result of the overlapping generations construct, that there exists an optimal noninterventionist monetary equilibrium. To see this, note, for example, that the amount of taxation needed to support the optimal allocation $\lambda = 1/2$ goes to zero as $\beta \to 1$ (see Proposition 2). Alternatively, note that the noninterventionist monetary equilibrium consumption sequences approach the constant $\lambda = 1/2$ as $\beta \to 1$ (see Proposition 4 and Figure 4). It may well be that this welfare result holds exactly in the limit, at $\beta = 1$, if agents use the overtaking criterion to evaluate consumption paths.[11]

3. A Generalized Overlapping Generations Model

The turnpike model may be contrasted with the overlapping generations model of Samuelson (1958), which, as is well known, yields (under specified assumptions) an optimal noninterventionist monetary equilibrium. It should prove useful, then, to discover those elements which lead to the different implications of the two models. The intent of this section is to modify the turnpike model to make it more comparable to the standard overlapping generations construct. Putting this another way, the overlapping generations model is generalized; in so doing, its essential features are revealed.

The obvious modification of the turnpike model produces the model depicted in Figure 5. In effect, the turnpike model has been truncated at both ends. Here one agent is born in each period at the beginning of the eastern and western routes, and each agent lives four periods. Note that agents aged 0 and 3 periods are paired, as are agents aged 1 and 2 periods.

Figure 5
A Truncated Turnpike

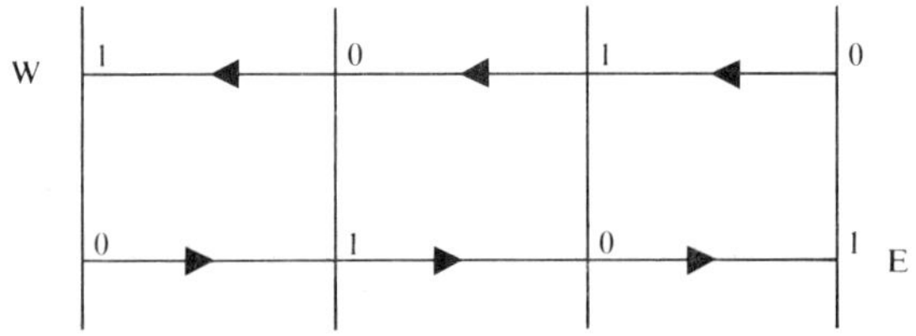

Preliminary work with this model indicated that an optimal allocation can be supported as a noninterventionist monetary equilibrium, as with the standard overlapping generations model. In such an equilibrium, prices first fall and then rise over each agent's lifetime. Moreover, the (even-aged) lifetimes of each agent can be made arbitrarily long by truncating the model further out, without altering these conclusions. But it may be noted that the age pairings in this class of models are extreme, the youngest trading with the oldest, the next-to-youngest trading with the next-to-oldest, and so on, whereas in the turnpike model one's trading partners are of the same age. Thus a more natural comparison would be to a modified model in which one's trading partners are more or less the same age. This produces the generalized overlapping generations model which is examined in the remainder of this section.

As in the turnpike model, each of a countably infinite number of agents

[11]This is left as an open question. It may be noted, however, that Grandmont and Younes (1972) do establish certain results in the limit, at $\beta = 1$, using the overtaking criterion.

faces an endowment sequence of the single nonstorable consumption good over her or his infinite lifetime which alternates between 1 and 0. Yet here all agents are not of the same age; one representative trader is born in each period t, $t \geq 0$, and begins life with an endowment of 1 unit. Each agent is again allocated into one of a countably infinite number of spatially distinct markets in each period of life, but here the allocation procedure is such that each agent is paired with an agent who is either one period older or one period younger. Figure 6 illustrates the scheme: The arrows indicate the direction of travel, and the numbers on the right of market spikes indicate the endowment of an agent whose age is indicated on the left.

Figure 6
Generalized Overlapping Generations

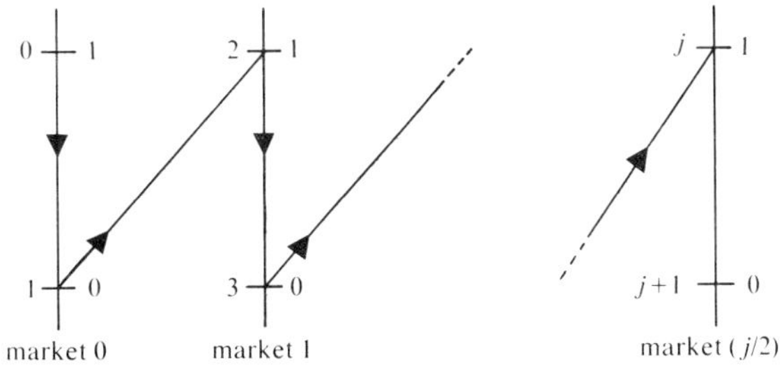

For our purpose the economy will be conceived of as beginning at time $t = 0$ but populated with agents born at times $t = -h$, $h \geq 1$. Thus at time $t = 0$, island $k = j/2, j \geq 0, j$ even, is inhabited with two (representative) agents, one born at time $-j$ with an endowment of 1 unit and one born at time $-(j+1)$ with an endowment of 0 units. At time $t = 1$, one new (representative) agent is born and enters market 0, while the other agents move forward as indicated, and so on. Note that if agents were to live two periods only, attention could be restricted to market 0 alone, an economy which is identical to the simplest two-period overlapping generations model. As will be shown, the present generalization retains the characteristics of that economy.

As in the turnpike model, there is a sense in which there can be no private debt in this model. Here, unlike in the turnpike model, agents meet each other infinitely often; an agent born at time t is paired with an agent born at time $t+1$ when the former is of age 0, 2, 4, . . . , and an agent born at time t is paired with an agent born at time $t-1$ when the former is of age 1, 3, 5, ... Yet when they meet, each of the pair has the same relative endowment position. An IOU issued by an agent of an odd age who has 0 units of the consumption good can never be redeemed by the issuer—she or he will have 0 units when the pair meets again.

To describe preferences, feasible allocations, and Pareto optimal allocations, some additional notation is needed. Thus let $\{y_j\}_{j=0}^{\infty}$ denote the endowment sequence of a typical agent over her or his lifetime, where y_j is the endowment of an agent of age j. Here, then, $y_j = 1$ for $j \geq 0, j$ even; and $y_j = 0$

for $j \geq 1, j$ odd. Let $c_j(t)$ denote the consumption of an agent born at time t who is of age $j, j \geq 0$, all t. Individual agents have the same preferences as they did in the turnpike model. That is, the objective function of an agent born at time $t \geq 0$ is $\Sigma_{j=0}^{\infty} \beta^j U[c_j(t)]$ where $0 < \beta < 1$ and $U(\cdot)$ is strictly concave, strictly increasing, bounded, and continuously differentiable with $U'(0) = \infty$. The objective function of an agent born at time $-h < 0$ is $\Sigma_{j=h}^{\infty} \beta^{j-h} U[c_j(-h)]$. An *allocation* is a consumption sequence $\{c_j(t)\}_{j=0}^{\infty}$ for each agent born at time $t \geq 0$ and a consumption sequence $\{c_j(-h)\}_{j=h}^{\infty}$ for each agent born at time $-h \leq 0$. By construction there is only 1 unit of the consumption good among the two traders of any market at any point in time. Thus an allocation is said to be *feasible* if

(23) $$c_j(t) + c_{j+1}(t-1) \leq 1 \qquad t \geq 0, j \geq 0, j \text{ even}$$

$$c_j(-h) + c_{j+1}(-h-1) \leq 1 \qquad h \geq 1, j \geq h, j \text{ even.}$$

It will be assumed in what follows, without loss of generality, that these constraints must hold as equalities.

The next step is to define Pareto optimal allocations. For this purpose, a strong symmetry condition is imposed, namely, that agents of identical ages be treated identically, even though they can be distinguished by birthdate. That is,

(24) $$c_j(t) = c_j(\tau) = c_j \geq 0, \; j \geq 0 \qquad \text{all } t, \tau.$$

Then an allocation $\{c_j\}_{j=0}^{\infty}$ is said to be *optimal* if there does not exist another allocation $\{\tilde{c}_j\}_{j=0}^{\infty}$ with the property that

(25) $$\sum_{j=h}^{\infty} \beta^{j-h} U(\tilde{c}_j) \geq \sum_{j=h}^{\infty} \beta^{j-h} U(c_j), \quad h \geq 0$$

with strict inequality for at least one such h. Note that for $h = 0$ the terms in (25) represent the utility of one agent born at time $t \geq 0$, and for $h > 0$ they represent the utility of an agent born at time $t = -h$. Thus the preferences of all agents are taken into account.

It is now claimed that the solution $\{c_j^*\}_{j=0}^{\infty}$ of the following problem is optimal in the above sense.

<u>*Problem 3:*</u>

$$\max_{\{c_j\}_{j=0}^{\infty}} \sum_{j=0}^{\infty} \beta^j U(c_j)$$

subject to

$$c_j + c_{j+1} = 1 \qquad c_j \geq 0, j \geq 0, j \text{ even.}$$

To establish the claim, note that, due to the time separable nature of the objective function and of the constraints, the unique solution to this problem is

$$c_j^* = c^*, \; c_{j+1}^* = c^{**} \qquad j \geq 0, j \text{ even}$$

where

$$\frac{U'(c^*)}{\beta U'(c^{**})} = 1, \quad c^* + c^{**} = 1.$$

Now suppose there exists a feasible allocation $\{\tilde{c}_j\}_{j=0}^{\infty}$ which Pareto dominates $\{c_j^*\}_{j=0}^{\infty}$. If an agent born at time $t \geq 0$ is to be better off under $\{\tilde{c}_j\}_{j=0}^{\infty}$, then consumption must be increased for at least one element $\tilde{c}_i$. Suppose $i \geq 0$ is even. Then feasibility requires that $\tilde{c}_{i+1}$ be decreased. But c^* and c^{**} are chosen in such a way that such changes can only make the agent born at time t worse off, that is,

$$U(\tilde{c}_i) + \beta U(\tilde{c}_{i+1}) < U(c_i^*) + \beta U(c_{i+1}^*).$$

A similar argument applies for $i \geq 0$ and odd. Hence if $\{\tilde{c}_j\}_{j=0}^{\infty}$ is to Pareto dominate $\{c_j^*\}_{j=0}^{\infty}$, it must make at least one agent born at time $-h < 0$ better off. By the above argument, an increase in utility is possible only for the relatively old person of some market at time $t = 0$, that is, only if there is an increase in the element $c_h(-h)$, $h \geq 1$, h odd. But then the representative trader born at time $t \geq 0$ must be made worse off, and, by the above argument, there can be no compensating changes elsewhere. This establishes the claim.

Unlike the procedure in the turnpike model, no attempt is made here to characterize all possible Pareto optimal allocations in the restricted class. In the simple two-period overlapping generations model, other optimal allocations in the above sense do exist. Moreover, under specified assumptions, each of these can be supported in a monetary equilibrium with deflation and lump-sum taxation. Further, there exist monetary equilibria with inflation and lump-sum subsidization which are nonoptimal. Analogues of these results could be sought here. Instead, attention will be limited to generalizing the well-known proposition mentioned at the onset of this section, that there exists a noninterventionist monetary equilibrium which supports the above described optimal allocation.

To define a monetary equilibrium, some additional notation is needed. Let p_t^k denote the price of the consumption good in market k at time t, $k \geq 0$, $t \geq 0$. Let $M_j(t)$ denote the money balances held by the agent born at time t at the beginning of period j of that agent's life, chosen at age $j-1$. As attention is restricted to noninterventionist equilibria, no notation for lump-sum taxes is needed. As before, each agent takes initial money balances and the sequence of future prices as given and maximizes utility by choice of the sequences of money balances and consumptions over her or his infinite lifetime. Thus, for an agent born at time $t \geq 0$, consider

<u>*Problem 4:*</u>

$$\max_{\{c_j(t)\}_{j=0}^{\infty},\ \{M_j(t)\}_{j=1}^{\infty}} \sum_{j=0}^{\infty} \beta^j U[c_j(t)]$$

subject to

$$c_j(t) \geq 0, \quad M_j(t) \geq 0 \qquad j \geq 0$$

(26) $$p^k_{t+j}y_j + M_j(t) = p^k_{t+j}c_j(t) + M_{j+1}(t) \qquad j \geq 0$$

given

$$M_0(t) \geq 0, \ k = \begin{cases} \dfrac{j}{2} & j \text{ even}, j \geq 0 \\ \dfrac{(j-1)}{2} & j \text{ odd}, j \geq 1. \end{cases}$$

Similarly for an agent born at time $-h < 0$, consider

Problem 5:

$$\max_{\{c_j(-h)\}_{j=h}^{\infty}, \{M_j(-h)\}_{j=h+1}^{\infty}} \sum_{j=h}^{\infty} \beta^{j-h} U[c_j(-h)]$$

subject to

$$c_j(-h) \geq 0, \ M_j(-h) \geq 0 \qquad j \geq h$$

(27) $$p^k_{j-h}y_j + M_j(-h) = p^k_{j-h}c_j(-h) + M_{j+1}(-h) \qquad j \geq h$$

given

$$M_h(-h) \geq 0, \ k = \begin{cases} \dfrac{j}{2} & j \text{ even}, j \geq h \\ \dfrac{(j-1)}{2} & j \text{ odd}, j \geq h. \end{cases}$$

One may now write out formally the following

DEFINITION. *A monetary equilibrium is a sequence of finite positive prices $\{p_t^{k*}\}_{t=0}^{\infty}$ for each market $k \geq 0$; sequences of consumptions $\{c_j^*(t)\}_{j=0}^{\infty}$ and money balances $\{M_j^*(t)\}_{j=0}^{\infty}$ for the agent born at each time $t \geq 0$; and sequences of consumptions $\{c_j^*(-h)\}_{j=h}^{\infty}$ and money balances $\{M_j^*(-h)\}_{j=h}^{\infty}$ for the agent born at each time $-h < 0$ such that*

- *Maximization for agent t: the sequences $\{c_j^*(t)\}_{j=0}^{\infty}$ and $\{M_j^*(t)\}_{j=1}^{\infty}$ solve Problem 4 given $M_0^*(t)$.*
- *Maximization for agent $-h$: the sequences $\{c_j^*(-h)\}_{j=h}^{\infty}$ and $\{M_j^*(-h)\}_{j=h+1}^{\infty}$ solve Problem 5 given $M_h^*(-h)$.*
- *Market clearing:*

$$c_j^*(t) + c_{j+1}^*(t-1) = 1 \qquad t \geq 0, j \geq 0, j \text{ even}$$

$$c_j^*(-h) + c_{j+1}^*(-h-1) = 1 \qquad h \geq 1, j \geq h, j \text{ even}.$$

To characterize one of the monetary equilibria of this model, return for a moment to Problem 4. Differentiating with respect to $M_j(t)$, familiar necessary conditions for a maximum are obtained:

$$(28) \qquad -\frac{\beta^{j-1}U'[c_{j-1}(t)]}{p^k_{t+j-1}} + \frac{\beta^j U'[c_j(t)]}{p^k_{t+j}} + \theta_j(t) = 0 \qquad j \geqslant 1$$

where $\theta_j(t)$ is the nonnegative Lagrange multiplier associated with the constraint $M_j(t) \geqslant 0$. Expression (28) yields

$$(29) \qquad \frac{U'[c_{j-1}(t)]}{\beta U'[c_j(t)]} \geqslant \frac{p^k_{t+j-1}}{p^k_{t+j}} \qquad j \geqslant 1$$

where equality prevails if $M_j(t) > 0$. As before with $U'(0) = \infty$ and $y_j = 0$ for $j \geqslant 1$, j odd, it is obvious that equality must prevail for $j \geqslant 1$, j odd, and all $t > 0$.

Now suppose the optimal allocation $c_j^* = c^*$, $c_{j+1}^* = c^{**}$, $j \geqslant 0$, j even, were to be supported in a monetary equilibrium. Then with $j = 1$ in (29) as an equality,

$$1 = \frac{U'(c^*)}{\beta U'(c^{**})} = \frac{p_t^{0*}}{p_{t+1}^{0*}} \qquad \text{all } t \geqslant 0$$

where the equality on the left follows from the construction of c^* and c^{**}. That is, the price in market 0 must remain constant over time. A similar argument yields the fact that the price of each market $k \geqslant 0$ must remain constant over time. Moreover, suppose (29) were to hold as an equality in such an equilibrium for j even as well. (That is, suppose the nonnegativity constraints on money balances were never binding.) Then with $j = 2$ in (29) as an equality,

$$\frac{1}{\beta^2} = \frac{U'(c^{**})}{\beta U'(c^*)} = \frac{p_{t+1}^{0*}}{p_{t+2}^{1*}} \qquad \text{all } t \geqslant 0$$

where again the equality on the left follows from the construction of c^* and c^{**}. That is, $p_{t+1}^{0*} > p_{t+2}^{1*}$ so that the price level would decrease as the agent born at time t moves across markets, from market 0 at time $t+1$ to market 1 at time $t+2$. Again j even and $t \geqslant 0$ were arbitrary, so this relationship would hold across any two adjacent markets for any time period t.

Thus it may be guessed that the optimal allocation c^*, c^{**} can be supported in a monetary equilibrium with constant prices over time in each market, with deflation cross-sectionally over markets, and with deflation in every other period of each agent's lifetime. Before establishing this conjecture formally, it may be instructive to answer this question: How can it be that there exists a noninterventionist monetary equilibrium in this model with deflation but without taxation? The answer, of course, is that the price level stays constant in each market. In equilibrium the relatively old person of each market passes along *all* of her or his money holdings to the relatively young person, who then does the same in the next period. That is, money itself never moves across markets, and so real balances stay constant in each market. In equilibrium, nominal money balances decline over markets with the price level; real balances stay constant over markets.

This discussion is now summarized in

PROPOSITION 6. *The optimal allocation c^*, c^{**} can be supported in a (noninterventionist) monetary equilibrium with constant prices over time in each market, with deflation rate $(1-\beta^2)$ across adjacent markets, and with nonbind-*

ing nonnegativity constraints on money balances for each agent of any age. In particular, for prices,

$$p_t^{k*} \equiv p^{k*} > 0 \qquad k \geq 0$$

$$p^{k*} = \beta^2 p^{k-1*} \qquad k \geq 1;$$

for the agent born at each time $t \geq 0$,

$$c_j^*(t) = c^*, M_{j+1}^*(t) = p^{k*}c^{**} \qquad j \geq 0, j \text{ even}$$

$$c_j^*(t) = c^{**}, M_{j+1}^*(t) = 0 \qquad j \geq 1, j \text{ odd}$$

where k is defined in Problem 4; and for the agent born at each time $-h < 0$,

$$c_j^*(-h) = c^*, M_{j+1}^*(-h) = p^{k*}c^{**} \qquad j \geq h, j \text{ even}$$

$$c_j^*(-h) = c^{**}, M_{j+1}^*(-h) = 0 \qquad j \geq h, j \text{ odd}$$

where k is defined in Problem 5.

Proof. See the Appendix.

Thus, it has been established that there exists an optimal allocation in this model which can be supported in a noninterventionist monetary equilibrium. Yet Proposition 1 asserts that this is not possible in the turnpike model. Wherein lies the difference?

To be noted is that the allocation $c_j = c^*$, $c_{j+1} = c^{**}$ for $j \geq 0$, j even, is optimal here, in this generalized overlapping generations model, but is not optimal in the turnpike model. (More specifically, the allocation $c_t^B = c^*$, $c_{t+1}^B = c^{**}$, $t \geq 0$, t even, is not optimal there, though it can be supported in a noninterventionist monetary equilibrium.) This result turns on the fact that in the overlapping generations model agents are paired at different ages. The optimal allocation takes into account that the young in each market prefer present over future consumption. Thus the age structure seems to be crucial.

4. The Lucas Version of the Cass-Yaari Model

Thus far, attention has been restricted to models which have the property that money allows the economy to achieve a Pareto superior allocation of goods over time, relative to autarky. For the individual, money plays a role in equating, at least partially, intertemporal marginal rates of substitution. This has led some to claim that money in such models serves as a store of value rather than as a medium of exchange. This section presents a third model with spatially separated agents in which money plays a role in achieving intratemporal efficiency (as well). In essence, the model is the well-known Cass-Yaari (1966a) circle, but with trader pairs and a timing of transactions as suggested by Lucas.[12]

The model consists of a countably infinite number of households and a

[12]For the most part I am reporting in this section on some results known to Lucas and his students and suggested to me by Lucas in various conversations; the interested reader is urged to consult Locay and Palmon 1978, on which this section draws heavily. The model is presented here both because it does not seem to be known generally and because it offers a natural comparison with the other two models.

countably infinite number of perishable commodities. Each (representative) household consists of a pair of agents and is imagined to be located on the real line, say, one household per integer. See Figure 7. Each household i lives forever and faces an endowment sequence of commodity i which is constant, say, 1 unit in each period $t \geq 0$. In each period t, each member of household i is capable of moving one-half the distance to one of the two adjacent integers, $(i+1)$ and $(i-1)$. Thus, in each period t, each household i is physically capable of carrying out transactions with households $(i-1)$ and $(i+1)$ in two spatially separated markets. There is no storage.

Figure 7
Lucas' Cass-Yaari Model

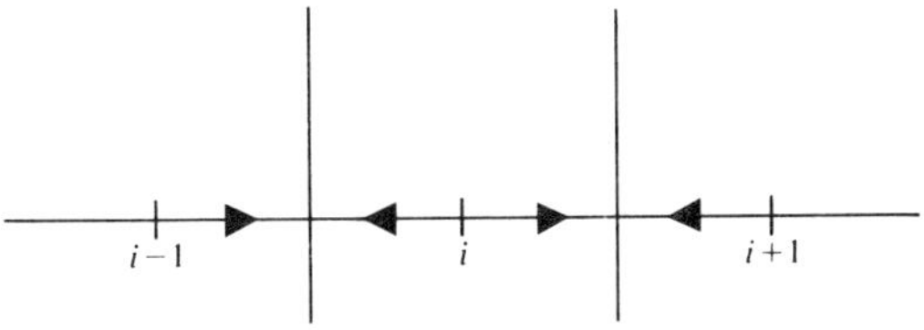

Household i cares only about commodities i and $(i+1)$ and discounts future over present consumption. Thus, letting $c_{it}(i)$ and $c_{i+1,t}(i)$ denote the number of units of consumption by household i at time t of commodities i and $(i+1)$, respectively, the preferences of household i are represented by the utility function $\Sigma_{t=0}^{\infty}\beta^t V[c_{it}(i),c_{i+1,t}(i)]$, $0 < \beta < 1$. Here also $V[\cdot,\cdot]$ is strictly concave, strictly increasing, bounded, and continuously differentiable with indifference curves which are asymptotic to the axes. (A particular functional form will be assumed for some purposes in what follows.)

As Cass and Yaari note, this model displays the absence of double coincidence of wants. At each time t each household i can trade with household $(i+1)$, but i has no commodity $(i+1)$ wants. It also should be noted that this model reverses the construction of Cass and Yaari, breaking their circle at some point and spreading it back out over the real line, with infinite extensions.[13] As in the turnpike model, this serves to eliminate the possibility of private debt. Household i may issue an IOU to household $(i+1)$ in exchange for commodity $(i+1)$, but this IOU can be returned to household i only by household $(i+1)$, and, as noted, i has no commodity $(i+1)$ wants.

The next step in the analysis is to define feasible allocations and characterize those allocations which are Pareto optimal. Without loss of generality attention is restricted to those allocations in which each household receives at most those commodities which enter its utility function. Thus an *allocation* is a sequence of consumptions $\{c_{it}(i),c_{i+1,t}(i)\}_{t=0}^{\infty}$ for each household i. An allocation is said to be *feasible* if

[13] Lucas' version of the Cass-Yaari model retains the circle.

$$(30) \qquad c_{it}(i) + c_{it}(i-1) \leqslant 1 \qquad t \geqslant 0, \text{ all integers } i$$

$$c_{it}(i) \geqslant 0, \;\; c_{it}(i-1) \geqslant 0 \qquad t \geqslant 0, \text{ all integers } i.$$

Also, without loss of generality, the resource constraint in (30) is assumed to hold as an equality. Now in order to characterize Pareto optimal allocations, a strong symmetry condition is imposed—that in any feasible allocation each household i be treated identically with respect to its own consumption, of commodity i, and other households' consumption, of commodity $(i+1)$. That is, an allocation $\{c_{it}(i), c_{i+1,t}(i)\}_{t=0}^{\infty}$ for all i is said to be *symmetric* if

$$(31) \qquad c_{it}(i) = c_t^1, \;\; c_{i+1,t}(i) = c_t^2 \qquad t \geqslant 0, \text{ all integers } i.$$

Within the class of such symmetric allocations, then, feasibility is equivalent with

$$(32) \qquad c_t^1 + c_t^2 = 1, \;\; c_t^1 \geqslant 0, \;\; c_t^2 \geqslant 0 \quad t \geqslant 0.$$

It is now claimed that, subject to this symmetry restriction, the unique Pareto optimal allocation may be found as the solution to

<u>*Problem 6:*</u>

$$\max_{\{c_t^1, c_t^2\}_{t=0}^{\infty}} \sum_{t=0}^{\infty} \beta^t V[c_t^1, c_t^2]$$

subject to (32). Since the objective function and constraint sets are time separable, it is obvious that the unique solution $\{c_t^{1*}, c_t^{2*}\}_{t=0}^{\infty}$ to this problem satisfies

$$c_t^{1*} = c^{1*}, \; c_t^{2*} = c^{2*} \qquad \text{all } t \geqslant 0$$

where

$$(33) \qquad \frac{V_1(c^{1*}, c^{2*})}{V_2(c^{1*}, c^{2*})} = 1, \;\; c^{1*} + c^{2*} = 1.$$

(See Figure 8.)

Any symmetric feasible allocation which is supposed to improve upon this solution must satisfy (32) and increase utility in some period t. The choice of c^{1*} and c^{2*} makes this impossible. Similarly, any symmetric feasible allocation which differs from this solution can be improved upon and hence is not an optimum. Finally, note that the unique Pareto optimum is defined completely by intratemporal considerations.

As before, one now seeks to discover the relationship between optimal allocations and monetary equilibria. Thus, suppose at each time $t \geqslant 0$ that households i and $(i+1)$ meet in a competitive market in which commodity $(i+1)$ can be exchanged for fiat money. Thus, let $p_{i+1,t}$ denote the price of commodity $(i+1)$ in terms of fiat money at time $t \geqslant 0$. Also, let $M_t(i)$ denote the

Figure 8
Equilibria in Lucas' Cass-Yaari Model

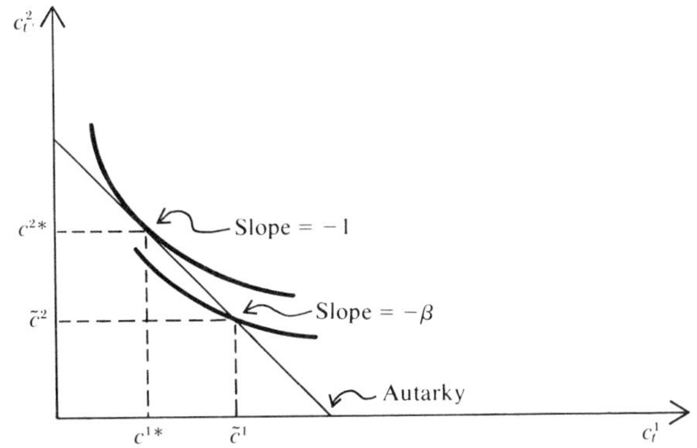

number of units of fiat money held by household i at the beginning of period t, and let $z_t(i)$ denote the lump-sum tax. Finally, let $y_{it}(i)$ denote the endowment of commodity i of household i at time t, so that $y_{it}(i) \equiv 1$. At the beginning of each period t, one member of household i travels to the market $(i, i+1)$ with some of the beginning-of-period money balances and purchases commodity $(i+1)$ at the price $p_{i+1,t}$. Similarly, the other member of household i travels to the market $(i-1, i)$ with some of the endowment of commodity i and sells it for fiat money at the price p_{it}. At the end of each period t, both members of household i return to their original location and consume. Thus, taking the price sequence $\{p_{it}, p_{i+1,t}\}_{t=0}^{\infty}$ and the tax sequence $\{z_t(i)\}_{t=0}^{\infty}$ as given, each household i is confronted with

Problem 7:

$$\max_{\{c_{it}(i), c_{i+1,t}(i)\}_{t=0}^{\infty},\ \{M_t(i)\}_{t=1}^{\infty}} \sum_{t=0}^{\infty} \beta^t V[c_{it}(i), c_{i+1,t}(i)]$$

subject to

$$c_{it}(i) \geqslant 0,\ \ c_{i+1,t}(i) \geqslant 0,\ \ M_t(i) \geqslant 0 \qquad t \geqslant 0$$

(34) $$p_{it}y_{it}(i) + M_t(i) - z_t(i) = p_{it}c_{it}(i) + p_{i+1,t}c_{i+1,t}(i) + M_{t+1}(i) \qquad t \geqslant 0$$

(35) $$p_{i+1,t}c_{i+1,t}(i) \leqslant M_t(i) \qquad t \geqslant 0$$

given $M_0(i) \geqslant 0$, $z_0(i) = 0$.

Here (34) is the money balance accumulation equation, and (35) is the constraint that the valuation of consumption of commodity $(i+1)$ by household i is bounded by beginning-of-period money balances. Thus (35) is very much in the spirit of a Clower constraint. But here this constraint is generated by the underlying exchange technology of the model.[14]

In what follows, attention will be restricted to equilibria which are symmetric across households in that $\{p_{it}\}_{t=0}^{\infty} = \{p_t\}_{t=0}^{\infty}$ for all commodities i; and $\{z_t(i)\}_{t=0}^{\infty} = \{z_t\}_{t=0}^{\infty}$, $\{M_t(i)\}_{t=0}^{\infty} = \{M_t\}_{t=0}^{\infty}$, and $\{c_{it}(i), c_{i+1,t}(i)\}_{t=0}^{\infty} = \{c_t^1, c_t^2\}_{t=0}^{\infty}$ for all households i. Under these symmetry restrictions the problem of each household i is the same, namely, the problem of the representative household,

<u>*Problem 8:*</u>

$$\max_{\{c_t^1, c_t^2\}_{t=0}^{\infty}, \{M_t\}_{t=1}^{\infty}} \sum_{t=0}^{\infty} \beta^t V[c_t^1, c_t^2]$$

subject to

$$c_t^1 \geq 0, \; c_t^2 \geq 0, \; M_t \geq 0 \qquad t \geq 0$$

$$(36) \qquad p_t y_t + M_t - z_t = p_t c_t^1 + p_t c_t^2 + M_{t+1}$$

$$(37) \qquad p_t c_t^2 \leq M_t$$

given $M_0 \geq 0$, $z_0 = 0$ with $y_t \equiv 1$.

The above discussion leads to the following

DEFINITION. *A symmetric monetary equilibrium is a sequence of finite positive prices $\{p_t^*\}_{t=0}^{\infty}$ and sequences of consumptions $\{c_t^{1*}, c_t^{2*}\}_{t=0}^{\infty}$, money balances $\{M_t^*\}_{t=0}^{\infty}$, and taxes $\{z_t^*\}_{t=0}^{\infty}$ such that*

- *Maximization: the sequences $\{c_t^{1*}, c_t^{2*}\}_{t=0}^{\infty}$ and $\{M_t^*\}_{t=1}^{\infty}$ solve Problem 8 relative to $\{p_t^*\}_{t=0}^{\infty}$, $\{z_t^*\}_{t=0}^{\infty}$, and M_0^*.*
- *Market clearing: $c_t^{1*} + c_t^{2*} = 1$, all $t \geq 0$.*

In order to discover the relationship between symmetric monetary equilibria and optimal allocations it is useful to consider the necessary Euler conditions for a maximum to Problem 8. Assuming nonbinding nonnegativity constraints on money balances (and consumption) and following Locay and Palmon 1978, these are of the form

$$(38) \qquad -\beta^t V_1(c_t^1, c_t^2) + \beta^t V_2(c_t^1, c_t^2) - p_t^* \theta_t = 0 \qquad t \geq 0$$

$$(39) \qquad V_1(c_{t-1}^1, c_{t-1}^2) = (p_{t-1}^*/p_t^*)\beta V_2(c_t^1, c_t^2) \qquad t \geq 1$$

where θ_t is the nonnegative Lagrange multiplier associated with the constraint (37). One implication is almost immediate,

PROPOSITION 7. *The optimal allocation c^{1*}, c^{2*} cannot be supported in a noninterventionist symmetric monetary equilibrium, that is, with $z_t^* \equiv 0$.*

[14]It is curious to note that (35) corresponds to the transaction constraint in Grandmont and Younes 1972, 1973 for $k = 0$, a case which is not really analyzed there.

Proof. Suppose the contrary. Then it follows from (39) and the construction of the optimum (33) that in such an equilibrium the rate of deflation must be $1-\beta$, that is,

$$p_t^* = \beta p_{t-1}^* \qquad t \geqslant 1. \tag{40}$$

Also, from the money balance accumulation equation (36) and feasibility of the optimum,

$$M_{t+1}^* - M_t^* = p_t^*(y_t - c^{1*} - c^{2*}) = 0 \qquad t \geqslant 1. \tag{41}$$

Now consider constraint (37) at $t = 0$,

$$p_0^* c^{2*} \leqslant M_0^*. \tag{42}$$

Repeated substitution of (40) and (41) into (42) yields

$$p_t^* c^{2*} < M_t^* \qquad \text{all } t \geqslant 1. \tag{43}$$

Then holding the consumption sequence $\{c_t^1\}_{t=0}^{\infty}$ fixed identically at c^{1*}, the representative household could increase consumption of c_t^2 over c^{2*} in every period $t \geqslant 1$ by spending the surplus money balances. This is the desired contradiction, and it completes the proof. (For an alternative argument see Locay and Palmon 1978.)

Proposition 7 of this model is the analogue of Proposition 1 in the turnpike model. And it seems that Propositions 2 and 4 of the turnpike model have analogues here as well; that is, the optimal allocation can be supported in an interventionist monetary equilibrium, and there exists a noninterventionist monetary equilibrium which is nonoptimal but Pareto superior to autarky.[15] For according to Locay and Palmon (1978), the necessary transversality condition for the maximization problem confronting the representative household is

$$\lim_{t\to\infty} \frac{\beta^t M_t V_2(c_t^1, c_t^2)}{p_t} = 0. \tag{44}$$

Then for the interventionist monetary equilibrium which is to support the optimal allocation c^{1*}, c^{2*}, consider the following specification. Let $M_0^* = p_0^* c^{2*}$ so that the representative household spends all initial money balances on the consumption good with which it is not endowed. Similarly, in each period t let the representative household spend all after-tax money holdings on this commodity, acquiring additional money from the sale of the endowment commodity, $(y_t - c^{1*})$. Also, let the rate of deflation be $1-\beta$. In summary, then, let

$$M_{t+1}^* = p_t^*(y_t - c^{1*}) \qquad t \geqslant 0 \tag{45}$$

$$z_t^* = (M_t^* - p_t^* c^{2*}) > 0 \qquad t \geqslant 1 \tag{46}$$

$$p_t^* = \beta p_{t-1}^* \qquad t \geqslant 1. \tag{47}$$

[15] Grandmont and Younes (1972, 1973) establish all these results for the case $0 < k < 1$ in their transaction constraint.

It is apparent that this specification satisfies the necessary and sufficient conditions for a maximum, (38), (39), and (44), with the nonbinding constraint (37), that is, $\theta_t \equiv 0$.

For the noninterventionist monetary equilibrium, consider the following specification. First, let prices be constant; then, motivated by (39), let $c_t^1 \equiv \bar{c}^1$, $c_t^2 \equiv \bar{c}^2$, where $\bar{c}^1$ and $\bar{c}^2$ are uniquely defined by

(48) $$\frac{V_1(\bar{c}^1,\bar{c}^2)}{V_2(\bar{c}^1,\bar{c}^2)} = \beta, \qquad \bar{c}^1 + \bar{c}^2 = 1.$$

Again, suppose that all beginning-of-period money balances are spent on the other households' consumption good, these being replenished from the sale of the households' own consumption good. That is, let

(49) $$M_{t+1}^* = p_t^*(y_t - \bar{c}^1)$$

(50) $$M_t^* = p_t^* \bar{c}^2$$

(51) $$p_t^* \equiv p^* > 0.$$

Again, the necessary and sufficient first-order conditions for a maximum are satisfied, this time with the binding constraint (37), that is, $\theta_t > 0$. It is clear that this consumption sequence is nonoptimal but Pareto superior to autarky (see Figure 8).

The reader may be struck by the similarity of the above results to those of the turnpike model. To repeat, optimal allocations cannot be supported in a noninterventionist monetary equilibrium, but there exists a monetary equilibrium with constant prices and binding constraints which is Pareto superior to autarky.[16] Yet here, unlike the turnpike model, the imposition of a stronger Clower-type constraint may be sufficient to generate a monetary equilibrium without taxation which is optimal. In fact, the imposition of such a constraint can convert the Cass-Yaari model into Lucas' model of money with certainty (in this volume). These results are now established.

The above scheme is modified in two ways. First, the utility function $V[\cdot,\cdot]$ is assumed to be of the form

$$V[c^1,c^2] = U[(c^1/\alpha_1)^{\alpha_1}(c^2/\alpha_2)^{\alpha_2}]$$

where $\alpha_1 > 0$, $\alpha_2 > 0$, $\alpha_1 + \alpha_2 = 1$, and where $U(\cdot)$ satisfies all the assumptions of the previous two sections. Second, the constraint (37) in Problem 8 is strengthened to

(52) $$p_t c_t^1 + p_t c_t^2 \leq M_t.$$

As in section 2, the idea here is that the member of household i who travels to the market $(i-1, i)$ with the endowment $y_{it}(i) = 1$ must pay cash in advance for any units of commodity i which she or he is to take home. And again, a *Clower-type symmetric monetary equilibrium* may be defined in the obvious

[16] Again one obtains asymptotic welfare results as $\beta \rightarrow 1$ (compare to the discussion at the end of section 2).

way, with (52) replacing (37) in Problem 8, and $z_t^* \equiv 0$. This leads to

PROPOSITION 8. *The optimal allocation c^{1*}, c^{2*} can be supported in a Clower-type symmetric monetary equilibrium with constant prices. In particular, $c_t^{1*} \equiv c^{1*}$, $c_t^{2*} \equiv c^{2*}$, $p_t^* \equiv p^* > 0$, and $M_t^* = p^* y_t$ for all $t > 0$.*

Proof. First let c_t denote real consumption expenditures in period t, that is,

$$p^* c_t^1 + p^* c_t^2 = p^* c_t. \tag{53}$$

Substitution of (53) into the budget constraint (36) yields

$$p^* y_t + M_t - M_{t+1} = p^* c_t. \tag{54}$$

Now fixing M_t and M_{t+1}, the intratemporal period t decision problem of the representative household is of the form

$$\max_{c_t^1 \geq 0,\, c_t^2 \geq 0} \quad U[(c^1/\alpha_1)^{\alpha_1}(c^2/\alpha_2)^{\alpha_2}]$$

subject to

$$p^* c_t^1 + p^* c_t^2 = p^* c_t.$$

The unique solution to this problem is

$$c_t^1 = \alpha_1 c_t, \quad c_t^2 = \alpha_2 c_t$$

so the indirect utility as a function of c_t is just $U(c_t)$. Hence, the problem of the representative household is reduced to

$$\max_{\{M_t\}_{t=1}^{\infty}} \quad \sum_{t=0}^{\infty} \beta^t U(c_t)$$

subject to

$$M_t \geq 0, \quad c_t \geq 0 \qquad t \geq 0$$

$$p^* y + M_t - M_{t+1} = p^* c_t$$

$$p^* c_t \leq M_t$$

given $M_0^* = p^* y$ where $y = 1$. In his paper in this volume, Lucas establishes that $M_t \equiv p^* y$ is the unique solution to this problem. Thus, $p^* c_t = p^* y$ for all $t \geq 0$, and so the solution to the intratemporal problem must be $c_t^{*1} = c^{1*}$, $c_t^{*2} = c^{2*}$ for all $t \geq 0$, the optimum. This completes the proof.

That the imposition of a strong Clower-type constraint generates an optimal allocation in this model and not in the turnpike model is somewhat puzzling. This result seems to turn on the facts that there is only one representative agent in this model, whereas there are two representative agents in the turnpike model, and that optimal allocations are defined accordingly.

5. Circles and Private Debt

As noted in the introduction, there are an infinite number of agents alive at any one date in both the turnpike model and in the version of the Cass-Yaari model just presented. This specification ensured that the exclusion of private debt was indeed endogenous. With the removal of this contemporaneous infinity, the role of private debt can be analyzed. This section is intended to be illustrative of the kind of analysis which may be undertaken.

The contemporaneous infinity is removed from the turnpike model by converting it into a circle. This is done in Figure 9 for an economy with eight agents. As before, arrows indicate the direction of travel, spikes indicate islands or markets, and numbers index the endowment of the agent at the indicated position.

Figure 9
The Turnpike Circle

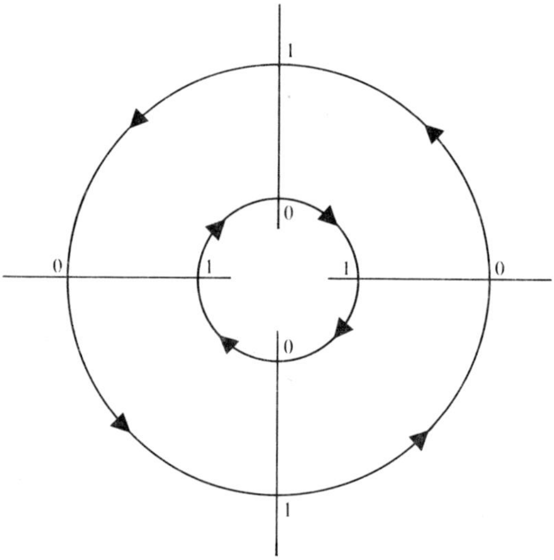

Focusing on the pairings of agents in this model, it becomes clear that the set of agents can be partitioned into two groups or subeconomies, where agents in a subeconomy trade only with other agents of that subeconomy. Thus the essential features of the model depicted in Figure 9 can be captured by the simpler model depicted in Figure 10. Here there are only two markets, labeled L and R, and four agents, labeled a, a', b, and b' at their initial positions. To understand the way agents are paired over time, consider the itinerary of one of the agents. Agent a, of type A, begins in period 0 with 0 units of the consumption good and is paired in market L with agent b, of type B, who has 1 unit. In period 1, agent a is allocated to market R and has 1 unit, being paired with agent b'. Continuing, agent a stays in market R in period 2 and finally moves back to market L in period 3. Period 4 is the same as period 0.

Figure 10
The Debt Model

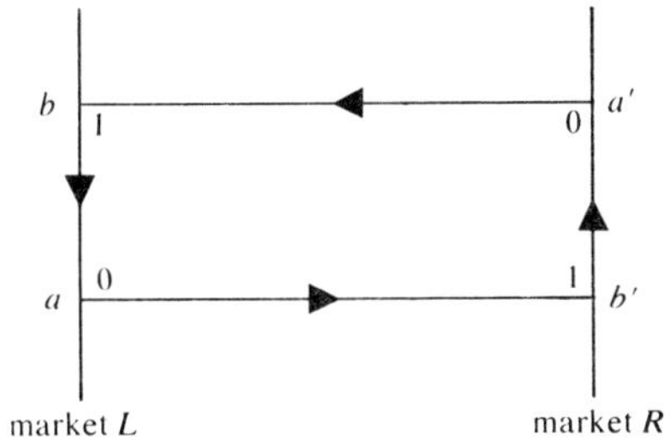

The fact that agents meet repeatedly in this version of the turnpike model has no bearing on the determination of optimal allocations. Under the symmetry condition imposed in section 2, an (interior) optimum has the property that each agent of type A receives λ units of the consumption good in each period. In fact, all the propositions of section 2 apply to this economy if one accepts the exogenous exclusion of debt. Yet now there may be private debt equilibria. That is, debt may be used as a means of payment.

For the purpose of discussing private debt in this economy, attention is restricted first to the obvious four-period version of this model. (Again this has no effect on the properties of optima.) A particular scheme is considered. In the initial period, $t = 0$, each agent of type A is permitted to issue IOUs, where one such IOU is a promise to pay to the holder $(1+r)$ units of the consumption good in period 3. Both the interest rate r and the price $p_0 > 0$ of the consumption good, in terms of such IOUs in period 0, are taken as given by agents a and a'. Thus, the problem confronting each agent of type A in period 0 is

Problem 9:

$$\max_{B_0^A \geq 0,\, c_0^A \geq 0,\, c_3^A \geq 0} \quad U(c_0^A) + \beta^3 U(c_3^A)$$

subject to

(55) $$p_0 c_0^A \leq B_0^A$$

(56) $$c_3^A \leq y_3^A - (B_0^A + z_3^A)(1+r)$$

where B_0^A is the number of IOUs issued by agent type A and $-z_3^A$ is a lump-sum forgiveness (subsidy) of debt in period 3. The above two budget constraints may be assumed to hold as equalities. Here the nonnegativity constraints may be ignored, yielding the necessary first-order condition

(57) $$\frac{U'(c_0^A)}{p_0} = \beta^3 U'(c_3^A)(1+r).$$

In periods 1 and 2 the debt issued by agents a and a' is traded in markets L and R, respectively. In particular, agent a can purchase the debt (of a') in market R in period 1 and sell the debt in market R in period 2. Letting p_1 and p_2 denote the price of the consumption good in terms of IOUs in periods 1 and 2, respectively, the problem confronting each agent type A in period 1 is

Problem 10:

$$\max_{B_2^A \geq 0,\, c_1^A \geq 0,\, c_2^A \geq 0} \beta U(c_1^A) + \beta^2 U(c_2^A)$$

subject to

$$p_1 c_1^A \leqslant p_1 y_1^A - B_2^A \tag{58}$$

$$p_2 c_2^A \leqslant B_2^A - z_2^A \tag{59}$$

where B_2^A is the number of IOUs acquired by agent type a in period 1 and z_2^A is a lump-sum tax (confiscation) of IOUs in period 2. With $z_2^A \geqslant 0$ the nonnegativity constraints may be ignored, yielding the necessary first-order condition

$$\frac{\beta U'(c_1^A)}{p_1} = \frac{\beta^2 U'(c_2^A)}{p_2} \tag{60}$$

It is now obvious that the problem confronting each agent type B in period 0 is

Problem 11:

$$\max_{B_1^B \geq 0,\, c_0^B \geq 0,\, c_1^B \geq 0} U(c_0^B) + \beta U(c_1^B)$$

$$p_0 c_0^B \leqslant p_0 y_0^B - B_1^B \tag{61}$$

$$p_1 c_1^B \leqslant B_1^B - z_1^B \tag{62}$$

where B_1^B is the number of IOUs acquired by agent type B in period 0 and $z_1^B \geqslant 0$ is the lump-sum confiscation in period 1. The necessary first-order condition is

$$\frac{U'(c_0^B)}{p_0} = \frac{\beta U'(c_1^B)}{p_1}. \tag{63}$$

Similarly one obtains

Problem 12:

$$\max_{B_3^B \geq 0,\, c_2^B \geq 0,\, c_3^B \geq 0} \beta^2 U(c_2^B) + \beta^3 U(c_3^B)$$

$$p_2 c_2^B \leqslant p_2 y_2^B - B_3^B \tag{64}$$

$$c_3^B \leqslant (B_3^B - z_3^B)(1+r) \tag{65}$$

with necessary first-order condition

$$(66) \qquad \frac{\beta^2 U'(c_2^B)}{p_2} = \beta^3 U'(c_3^B)\,(1+r).$$

These procedures lead to the following

DEFINITION. *A private debt equilibrium is an interest rate* r^*, *a sequence of finite positive prices* $\{p_t^*\}_{t=0}^2$, *and sequences of lump-sum taxes* $\{z_t^{A*}\}_{t=2,3}$, $\{z_t^{B*}\}_{t=1,3}$; *consumptions* $\{c_t^{A*}\}_{t=0}^3$, $\{c_t^{B*}\}_{t=0}^3$; *and debt decisions* $\{B_t^{A*}\}_{t=0,2}$, $\{B_t^{B*}\}_{t=1,3}$ *such that*

- *Maximization for A:* c_0^{A*}, c_3^{A*}, B_0^{A*} *solve Problem 9 relative to* r^*, p_0^*, z_3^{A*}; *and* c_1^{A*}, c_2^{A*}, B_2^{A*} *solve Problem 10 relative to* p_1^*, p_2^*, z_2^{A*}.
- *Maximization for B:* c_0^{B*}, c_1^{B*}, B_1^{B*} *solve Problem 11 relative to* p_0^*, p_1^*, z_1^{B*}; *and* c_2^{B*}, c_3^{B*}, B_2^{B*} *solve Problem 12 relative to* p_2^*, r^*, z_3^{B*}.
- *Market clearing:* $c_t^{A*} + c_t^{B*} = 1$, $t = 0, 1, 2, 3$.

A major point of this section is that the *decentralization of the turnpike model cannot be overcome with private debt alone*. To see this, suppose for the moment that all four agents of the above model were in the same market in each of the four periods. Then there is a (centralized) Arrow-Debreu competitive equilibrium with

$$p_t^* = \beta p_{t-1}^* \qquad t = 1, 2 \qquad 1 + r^* = \frac{1}{\beta^3}$$

$$c_t^{A*} \equiv \frac{\beta}{1+\beta} \qquad c_t^{B*} \equiv \frac{1}{1+\beta} \qquad t = 0, 1, 2, 3.$$

Of course this allocation is optimal. Yet it turns out that neither this allocation nor any other optimal allocation can be achieved in the decentralized economy under a private debt equilibrium without taxation. More formally, consider

PROPOSITION 9. *No interior optimum* λ *can be supported in a private debt equilibrium without taxation, that is, with* $z_t^{i*} \equiv 0$ *for* $i = A, B$.

Proof. Suppose the contrary. Then from Problem 11 and (63), $p_1^* = \beta p_0^*$. Budget constraint (61) as an equality yields $B_1^{B*} = p_0^*\lambda$. Substitution into (62) yields $\beta = \lambda/(1-\lambda)$. From Problem 10 and (60), $p_2^* = \beta p_1^*$. Budget constraint (58) as an equality yields $B_2^{A*} = p_1^*(1-\lambda)$. Substitution into (59) yields $\beta = (1-\lambda)/\lambda$. Figure 3 makes clear with $\beta < 1$ that these two specifications of β are inconsistent. This completes the proof.

Proposition 9 and its analogue, Proposition 1, suggest that inside money in the turnpike model acts very much like outside money. In fact, the analogue of Proposition 2 may be obtained as well.

PROPOSITION 10. *Any interior optimum* λ *with* $\beta \leq [\lambda/(1-\lambda)]$ *and* $\beta \leq [(1-\lambda)/\lambda]$ *can be supported in a private debt equilibrium with lump-sum taxation and forgiveness of debt.*

Proof. From Problem 9 and (57) let $(1+r^*)p_0^*\beta^3 = 1$. From (55) let $p_0^*\lambda = B_0^{A*}$, and from (56) let $z_3^{A*} = (1-\lambda)\beta^3 p_0^* - \lambda p_0^*$. From Problem 10 and (60) let $p_2^* = \beta p_1^*$.

From (58) let $B_2^{A*} = p_1^*(1-\lambda)$, and from (59) let $0 \leqslant z_2^{A*} = p_1^*[(1-\lambda)-\beta\lambda]$. From Problem 11 and (63) let $p_1^* = \beta p_0^*$. From (61) let $B_1^{B*} = \lambda p_0^*$, and from (62) let $0 \leqslant z_1^{B*} = p_0^*[\lambda-(1-\lambda)\beta]$. Finally, from Problem 12 and (66) let $\beta p_2^*(1+r^*) = 1$. From (64) let $B_3^{B*} = p_2^*\lambda$, and from (65) let $0 \leqslant z_3^{B*} = p_2^*[\lambda-(1-\lambda)\beta]$. Now by construction, all the first-order conditions for maxima are satisfied, with the budget constraints as equalities in every period. This is sufficient for the proposed solution to satisfy the maximizing conditions of an equilibrium. The market-clearing condition is satisfied by construction also. Finally, it may be noted as a check on the above procedure that the sum of the confiscations of debt equals the lump-sum forgiveness in period 3. This completes the proof.

Thus Proposition 10 establishes that an optimal allocation can be achieved with nontrivial intervention in private credit markets. At this point one may well ask whether there exists a private debt equilibrium without such lump-sum taxation and forgiveness of debt which is Pareto nonoptimal but Pareto superior to autarky. In particular, can the allocations of the noninterventionist monetary equilibrium of Proposition 4 be achieved? Perhaps it is now obvious from section 2 and the above analysis that this question may be answered in the affirmative if one is willing to impose an upper bound on the issue of IOUs. That is, in Problem 9 impose the additional exogenous constraint that $B_0^A \leqslant d$ for some constant d and define a *constrained private debt equilibrium* in the obvious way. There follows

PROPOSITION 11. *There exists a constrained private debt equilibrium with a binding constraint on the issue of IOUs in period 0. In particular,*

$$r^* = 0;\; p_t^* = 1, t = 0, 1, 2;\; z_t^{i*} \equiv 0, i = A, B$$

$$c_t^{A*} = c^{**}, c_{t+1}^{A*} = c^*, B_t^{A*} = c^{**} = d, t = 0, 2$$

$$c_t^{B*} = c^*, c_{t+1}^{B} = c^{**}, B_{t+1}^{B*} = c^{**}, t = 0, 2.$$

Proof. The relevant first-order conditions and budget constraints are satisfied for Problems 10, 11, and 12 and modified Problem 9. This completes the proof.

Proposition 11 turns on the fact that the constraint on the issue of inside money plays the role of a nonnegativity constraint on money balances in the same economy with fiat money. This along with Proposition 3 may lead one to the conjecture that there does not exist a private debt equilibrium without taxation and without such exogenously imposed constraints. Yet it can be established that for the simple four-period economy described above there does exist at least one such equilibrium.[17] And clearly one may introduce private debt into an infinite-period economy by duplication of the four-period scheme every four periods. What is not yet clear is the extent to which such equilibria rest on the rather special assumptions which have been loaded into the four-period scheme: that only agents of type A can issue debt in every fourth period, that this debt can only be redeemed four periods after it is issued, and so on. It would seem that a completely unrestricted private debt economy would be plagued by Ponzi schemes. An open and intriguing question is whether relatively unrestricted debt and fiat money can coexist; this is the subject of ongoing research.

[17] The example is due to Neil Wallace.

6. Concluding Remarks

The contention of this paper is obvious: models of money with spatially separated agents should be taken seriously as models of money. Certainly these communication-cost models explain money in a rigorous way, at least subject to the implicit restrictions of the competitive paradigm. But more research is needed. Remaining to be investigated, for example, are the issues of asset dominance and capital over accumulation when storage is allowed. To be looked at also is the problem of multiple monetary equilibria, especially without all the exogenously imposed symmetry restrictions.

Ultimately, though, it is difficult to make judgements on the relative merits of models in the abstract, without reference either to actual observations or to policy questions. One would like to know, for example, whether models with spatially separated agents can be modified to explain the existence of both inside and outside money. In his paper in this volume, Wallace has established that the overlapping generations construct is not subject to this criticism. As for policy issues, the overlapping generations construct has been shown by Bryant and Wallace (1979a, b) and by Kareken and Wallace (1977, 1978) to have strong policy implications for both open market operations and international financial arrangements, respectively. It remains to be seen whether other models can do as well on this account and, if so, whether the implications will be the same.

In closing, let us return to the claim that the three models of this paper explain the use of money. This claim is equivalent with the statement that in each of the models there exists a (noninterventionist) monetary equilibrium, one in which money has value. Thus the approach of this paper relies heavily on the competitive paradigm. Ideally, though, competitive equilibrium allocations should be viewed as the outcome of an explicit game or mechanism (for example, see Shubik 1973, Prescott and Townsend forthcoming, or Townsend 1978b), but this raises an obvious question: why has the competitive mechanism been imposed as opposed to some other?

In this regard, consider the welfare theorems of this paper. These theorems are consistent with the view that the operation of competitive markets is possible though direct redistribution of endowments is not, or at least that the first scheme is less onerous than the second. Putting this in another way, if the agents of the model could agree to direct redistribution of the endowments, then Pareto optimal allocations could be achieved without the use of money. The welfare theorems of this paper are also consistent with the view that the operation of competitive markets along with lump-sum taxation of money is more appealing than direct redistribution. Clearly this second view is even more tenuous than the first. Finally, it may be noted that in Lucas' version of the Cass-Yaari model, optimal allocations can be achieved with either lump-sum taxation or the imposition of a Clower constraint, requiring the use of money to purchase commodities. Is there any sense in which one of these schemes is preferable to the other?

The point of this discussion is that in the context of the specified economic environments of the models of this paper, any criterion used to select from among various schemes is ad hoc and thus unsatisfactory. What is needed is theory in which the choice of social arrangements or games is endogenous. That is, the environment of the model should be sufficiently rich that certain games or constraints are either technically infeasible or too costly (if not impossible) to enforce. Models with moral hazard and asymmetric information may be needed, as was suggested at the outset (compare Harris and Townsend 1978, 1979 or Townsend 1979). It would seem to be particularly important in monetary economics to make the choice of joint arrangements endogenous, that is, to solve Shubik's start-up problem (in his paper in this volume). As Bryant (1979) has emphasized, the seigniorage associated with the issue of money must be allocated.

Appendix

A1. Proof of Proposition 2

First, let $p_t^* = \beta p_{t-1}^*$, all $t \geq 1$. Next, for agent type A let $c_0^{A*} = \lambda$, $(M_0^{A*}/p_0^*) = \lambda$, and $M_1^{A*} = 0$ so that agent type A spends all of her or his initial money balances on consumption. Subsequently, tax as needed to maintain the consumption sequence $c_t^{A*} \equiv \lambda$ with money balances returning to 0 in every other period:

$$y_t^A = 1, \; c_t^{A*} = \lambda, \; z_t^{A*} = 0, \; M_{t+1}^{A*} = p_t^*(1-\lambda) \qquad t \geq 1, t \text{ odd}$$

$$y_t^A = 0, \; c_t^{A*} = \lambda, \; z_t^{A*} = p_t^*\left[\frac{1-\lambda}{\beta} - \lambda\right] \geq 0, \; M_{t+1}^{A*} = 0 \qquad t \geq 2, t \text{ even}.$$

Similarly, for agent type B let $M_0^{B*} = 0$ and

$$y_t^B = 1, \; c_t^{B*} = 1 - \lambda, \; z_t^{B*} = 0, \; M_{t+1}^{B*} = p_t^*\lambda \qquad t \geq 0, t \text{ even}$$

$$y_t^B = 0, \; c_t^{B*} = 1 - \lambda, \; z_t^{B*} = p_t^*\left[\frac{\lambda}{\beta} - (1-\lambda)\right] \geq 0, \; M_{t+1}^{B*} = 0 \qquad t \geq 1, t \text{ odd}.$$

By construction, the market-clearing condition is satisfied, so it remains to verify that the above specification constitutes a solution to the maximization problem confronting each agent type i given M_0^{i*}, $\{p_t^*\}_{t=0}^{\infty}$, $\{z_t^{*i}\}_{t=0}^{\infty}$. This will be done explicitly for agent type B; the argument for agent type A follows immediately.

Consider first any consumption sequence $\{\hat{c}_t^B\}_{t=0}^{\infty}$ and associated money balance sequence $\{\hat{M}_t^B\}_{t=1}^{\infty}$ which are supposed to solve the maximization problem of agent type B. With $p_t^* y_t^B - z_t^{B*} \leq 0$, all $t \geq 1$, t odd, it follows that $\hat{M}_t^B > 0$ for $t \geq 1$, t odd. Hence (7) must hold as an equality at such times, that is,

$$\text{(A1)} \qquad \frac{U'(\hat{c}_{t-1}^B)}{\beta U'(\hat{c}_t^B)} = \frac{p_{t-1}^*}{p_t^*} = \frac{1}{\beta} \qquad t \geq 1, t \text{ odd}.$$

It follows that

(A2) $\hat{c}^B_{t-1} = \hat{c}^B_t \qquad t \geq 1, t \text{ odd}.$

Next, convert the problem of agent type *B* into real terms. In particular, let $w^B_t = (p^*_t y^B_t - z^{B*}_t)/p^*_t$ so that

$$w^B_t = 1 \qquad t \geq 0, t \text{ even}$$

$$w^B_t = -\left[\frac{\lambda}{\beta} - (1-\lambda)\right] \qquad t \geq 1, t \text{ odd}.$$

Also let $m^B_t \equiv M^B_t/p^*_t$ denote real money balances held by agent type *B* at the beginning of period *t*. From the budget constraint (5) as an equality and utilizing the fact that $p^*_t = \beta p^*_{t-1}$, all $t \geq 1$, it follows that

(A3) $c^B_t + \beta m^B_{t+1} = w^B_t + m^B_t \qquad \text{all } t \geq 0.$

Then, from (A2), setting $c^B_t = c^B_{t+1}$ for $t \geq 0$, *t* even, and solving for m^B_{t+1} one obtains

(A4) $(1+\beta)\, m^B_{t+1} = w^B_t - w^B_{t+1} + m^B_t + \beta m^B_{t+2} \qquad t \geq 0, t \text{ even}$

(A5) $(1+\beta)\, c^B_t = (1+\beta)\, c^B_{t+1} = w^B_t + \beta w^B_{t+1} + m^B_t - \beta^2 m^B_{t+2} \qquad t \geq 0, t \text{ even}.$

Following the methods of Lucas and Prescott (1971) it can be established that there exists a bounded continuous function $V(\cdot)$ satisfying the functional equation

$$V(m^B_0) = \max_{m^B_2} \{[U(c^B_0) + \beta U(c^B_1)] + \beta^2 V(m^B_2)\}$$

subject to

$$0 \leq m^B_2 \leq (w^B_1 - w^B_0 - m^B_0)/\beta$$

c^B_0 and c^B_1 satisfy (A5) at $t = 0$

given $m^B_0 \geq 0$. (Here the upper bound on m^B_2 follows from (A4) at $t = 0$ and the constraint $m^B_1 \geq 0$. Note that the constraint set on m^B_2 is compact and the objective function, in brackets above, as an indirect function of m^B_2, is bounded and continuous.) Here, then, the solution $m^B_2 = \Psi(m^B_0)$ is the *stationary policy function* which solves

$$\max_{\{m^B_t\}^\infty_{t=2}} \sum_{\substack{t\geq 0 \\ t \text{ even}}} \beta^t [U(c^B_t) + \beta U(c^B_{t+1})]$$

subject to

$$0 \leqslant m^B_{t+2} \leqslant (w^B_{t+1} - w^B_t - m^B_t)/\beta$$

$$c^B_t \text{ and } c^B_{t+1} \text{ satisfy (A5)}$$

given $m^B_0 \geqslant 0$. Thus there does exist at least one solution to the problem confronting agent type B.

Clearly, the proposed solution

$$c^B_t \equiv 1 - \lambda, \quad m^{B*}_t = 0 \qquad t \geqslant 2, t \text{ even}$$

$$m^{B*}_t = \frac{\lambda}{\beta} \qquad t \geqslant 1, t \text{ odd}$$

satisfies (7) with equality in every period. By construction the budget constraint (5) is also satisfied as an equality in every period. Now suppose there exist a consumption sequence $\{\hat{c}^B_t\}^\infty_{t=0}$ and its associated real money balance sequence $\{\hat{m}^B_t\}^\infty_{t=1}$ which do better than the proposed solution, and consider the first-period τ at which $\hat{c}^B_\tau \neq (1-\lambda)$. [Note from (A2) that τ must be even.] Clearly, $\hat{c}^B_\tau > (1-\lambda)$ is not feasible, for with $\hat{c}^B_{\tau+1} > (1-\lambda)$ also, one obtains $\hat{m}^B_{\tau+2} < 0$. Nor is $\hat{c}^B_\tau < (1-\lambda)$ possible. For in this case $\hat{c}^B_{\tau+1} < (1-\lambda)$, so $\hat{m}^B_{\tau+2} > 0$. Thus (7) would hold as an equality at $t = \tau + 2$, so that $\hat{c}^B_{\tau+2} < (1-\lambda)$ also, and so on. That is, the consumption path would be maintained below the proposed solution for all $t \geqslant \tau$, and this cannot improve matters. Hence the proposed solution is indeed maximizing.

A virtually identical argument establishes that given $c^{A*}_0 = \lambda$, $m^{A*}_0 = \lambda$, and $m^{A*}_1 = 0$, the sequences $\{c^{A*}_t\}^\infty_{t=1}$ and $\{m^{A*}_t\}^\infty_{t=2}$ solve the problem of agent type A from $t = 1$ onward. In particular, by the principle of optimality, at $t = 2$ given

$$m^{A*}_2 = \frac{(1-\lambda)}{\beta}, \quad w^A_2 = -\left[\frac{(1-\lambda)}{\beta} - \lambda\right], \quad m^{A*}_2 + w^A_2 = \lambda$$

the sequences $\{c^{A*}_t\}^\infty_{t=2}$, $\{m^{A*}_t\}^\infty_{t=3}$ solve the problem of agent type A. But given $m^{A*}_0 = \lambda$ this implies that $\{c^{A*}_t\}^\infty_{t=0}$ and $\{m^{A*}_t\}^\infty_{t=1}$ solve the problem of agent type A, as desired.

A2. Proof of Proposition 4

By construction, the market-clearing condition of an equilibrium is satisfied, so it remains to verify that the specification of the proposition is consistent with maximization. This will be done explicitly for agent type A.

Consider first any consumption sequence $\{c^A_t\}^\infty_{t=0}$ and its associated money balance sequence $\{M_t\}^\infty_{t=1}$ which satisfy the budget constraint (5) as an equality, that is,

$$\text{(A6)} \qquad M^A_t = p^* c^A_t + M^A_{t+1} \qquad t \geqslant 0, t \text{ even}$$

$$\text{(A7)} \qquad p^* y^A_{t+1} + M^A_{t+1} = p^* c^A_{t+1} + M^A_{t+2} \qquad t \geqslant 0, t \text{ even.}$$

Solving (A6) for M^A_{t+1} and substituting into (A7) yields

$$\text{(A8)} \qquad p^* c^A_t + p^* c^A_{t+1} = p^* y^A_{t+1} + M^A_t - M^A_{t+2} \qquad t \geqslant 0, t \text{ even.}$$

From (A6) also, with $M_{t+1}^A \geq 0$,

(A9) $\quad p^* c_t^A \leq M_t^A \qquad t \geq 0, t$ even.

Again following the methods of Lucas and Prescott (1971), it can be established that there exists a continuous bounded function $V(\cdot)$ which satisfies the functional equation

$$V(M_0^A) = \max_{M_2^A,\, c_0^A} \left\{ U(c_0^A) + \beta U\left[\frac{M_0^A + p^* y_1^A - M_2^A - p^* c_0^A}{p^*}\right] + \beta^2 V(M_2^A) \right\}$$

subject to

$$0 \leq p^* c_0^A \leq M_0^A$$

$$0 \leq M_2^A \leq p^* y_1^A + M_0^A - p^* c_0^A$$

given $M_0^A \geq 0$. Here, then, the solution $(M_2^A, c_0^A) = \phi(M_0^A)$ is the stationary policy function which solves

$$\max_{\{c_t^A\},\{M_t^A\}} \sum_{\substack{t \geq 0 \\ t \text{ even}}} \beta^t \left[U(c_t^A) + \beta U\left(\frac{M_t^A + p^* y_{t+1}^A - M_{t+2}^A - p^* c_t^A}{p^*}\right)\right]$$

subject to

$$0 \leq p^* c_t^A \leq M_t^A$$

$$0 \leq M_{t+2}^A \leq p^* y_{t+1}^A + M_t^A - p^* c_t^A$$

given $M_0^A \geq 0$. Thus there does exist a solution to the problem of agent A.

Clearly, the proposed solution satisfies (7) as an equality for $t \geq 0$, t even, and as an inequality for $t \geq 1$, t odd, that is,

(A10) $$\frac{U'(c_{t-1}^{A*})}{\beta U'(c_t^{A*})} = \frac{U'(c^{**})}{\beta U'(c^*)} = \frac{1}{\beta^2} > 1 \qquad t \geq 1, t \text{ odd}.$$

Also, the budget constraint is satisfied as an equality in every period. Now fix $\hat{c}_0^A = c_0^{A*}$, $\hat{M}_1^A = M_1^{A*}$, and suppose there exist a consumption sequence $\{\hat{c}_t^A\}_{t=1}^{\infty}$ and an associated money balance sequence $\{\hat{M}_t^A\}_{t=2}^{\infty}$ which do better than the proposed solution from $t = 1$ onward. Consider the first-period τ for which $\hat{c}_\tau^A \neq c_\tau^{A*}$. Since (7) will be satisfied as an equality for $t \geq 2$, t even, it follows that $\tau \geq 1$ and is odd. Clearly, $\hat{c}_\tau^A > c_\tau^{A*}$ is not feasible, for with $\hat{c}_{\tau+1}^A > \hat{c}_{\tau+1}^{A*}$ also, one obtains $\hat{M}_{\tau+2}^A < 0$. Nor is $\hat{c}_\tau^A < c_\tau^{A*}$ possible. For in this case $\hat{c}_{\tau+1}^A < c_{\tau+1}^{A*}$ also, and $\hat{M}_{\tau+2}^A > 0$. Thus (7) must hold as an equality at $t = \tau + 2$, so from (A10), $\hat{c}_{\tau+2}^A < c_{\tau+2}^{A*}$, and so on. This cannot be an improvement. Thus $\{c_t^{A*}\}_{t=1}^{\infty}$, $\{M_t^{A*}\}_{t=2}^{\infty}$ is indeed maximal for agent A from $t = 1$ onward and so, by the principle of optimality, is optimal from $t = 2$ onward with c_1^{A*} and M_2^{A*} given. But this implies $\{c_t^{A*}\}_{t=0}^{\infty}$, $\{M_t^{A*}\}_{t=1}^{\infty}$ is maximal for agent A at $t = 0$, as claimed. A virtually identical argument (without the last step) establishes that the specified solution is maximal for agent type B as well.

Finally, note that for agent A, for example, from (A10) and (6), $\theta_t^{A*} > 0$ for $t \geqslant 1$, t odd. Similarly, $\theta_t^{B*} > 0$ for $t \geqslant 0$, t even.

That the equilibrium allocation is nonoptimal is obvious from the fact that the consumption sequences are not constant. That it is Pareto superior to autarky is also obvious, but it is instructive to note that for agent A, for example, c^{**} dominates 0 in period 0, and the consumption pair (c^*, c^{**}) dominates the endowment pair (1,0) in periods $(t, t+1)$, $t \geqslant 1$, t odd.

A3. Proof of Proposition 6

It is first established that the above specification is maximizing for the agent born at time $t \geqslant 0$. Consider first any consumption sequence $\{c_j(t)\}_{j=0}^{\infty}$ and associated money balance sequence $\{M_j(t)\}_{j=1}^{\infty}$ which satisfy the budget constraints (26) as equalities, $j \geqslant 0$, j even. Substitution for $M_{j+1}(t)$ yields

$$\text{(A11)} \qquad M_j(t) + p_{t+j}^{k*} y_j - M_{j+2}(t) = p_{t+j}^{k*} c_j(t) + p_{t+j+1}^{k*} c_{j+1}(t).$$

Defining real money balances $m_i(t) = M_i(t)/p_{t+i}^{k*}$, $i = j, j+2$, and recalling the specified relationship

$$p_{t+j}^{k*} = p_{t+j+1}^{k*} = (1/\beta^2) p_{t+j+2}^{k*}$$

(A11) then yields

$$m_j(t) + y_j = c_j(t) + c_{j+1}(t) + \beta^2 m_{j+2}(t) \qquad j \geqslant 0, j \text{ even}.$$

Now holding $m_j(t)$ and $m_{j+2}(t)$ fixed, define real disposable income $d_j(t)$ by

$$\text{(A12)} \qquad d_j(t) = m_j(t) + y_j - \beta^2 m_{j+2}(t) \qquad j \geqslant 0, j \text{ even}$$

and consider in isolation the following problem:

$$\max_{c_j(t) \geqslant 0,\, c_{j+1}(t) \geqslant 0} \{U[c_j(t)] + \beta U[c_{j+1}(t)]\}$$

subject to

$$c_j(t) + c_{j+1}(t) = d_j(t).$$

Solving for the maximizing $c_j(t)$ and $c_{j+1}(t)$ as continuous functions of $d_j(t)$, substitution into the objective function then yields the bounded, continuous indirect utility function, denoted here by $W[d_j(t)]$. Thus Problem 4 reduces to

$$\max_{\{m_j(t)\}_j} \sum_{\substack{j \geqslant 0 \\ j \text{ even}}} \beta^j W[d_j(t)]$$

subject to (A12) and

$$m_j(t) \geqslant 0 \qquad j \geqslant 2, j \text{ even, given } m_0(t) \geqslant 0.$$

Again the functional equation approach yields a stationary policy which solves this problem.

It is clear from the discussion preceding the theorem that the specified solution to Problem 4 satisfies the necessary first-order conditions (28) as equalities. (The budget constraints also hold as equalities.) Now suppose there exist a consumption sequence $\{\hat{c}_j(t)\}_{j=0}^{\infty}$ and an associated money balance sequence $\{\hat{m}_j(t)\}_{j=1}^{\infty}$, which do better than the proposed solution, and consider the first age g for which $\hat{c}_g(t) \neq c_g^*(t)$. A now familiar argument leads to a contradiction.

It follows from the principle of optimality that for any $h \geq 1$ the sequences $\{c_j^*(t)\}_{j=h}^{\infty}$, $\{m_j^*(t)\}_{j=h+1}^{\infty}$ are maximal for agent t given $m_h^*(t)$. But then by symmetry the sequences $\{c_j^*(-h)\}_{j=h}^{\infty}$, $\{m_j^*(-h)\}_{j=h+1}^{\infty}$ are maximal for the agent born at each period $-h$, given $m_h^*(-h)$, as we needed to show.

References

Arrow, Kenneth J. 1951. An extension of the basic theorems of classical welfare economics. In *Proceedings of the second Berkeley symposium on mathematical statistics and probability*, ed. Jerzy Neyman. Berkeley: University of California Press.

______. 1964. The role of securities in the optimal allocation of risk-bearing. *Review of Economic Studies* 31 (April): 91–96.

______. 1974. Limited knowledge and economic analysis. *American Economic Review* 64 (March): 1–10.

Arrow, Kenneth J., and Hahn, Frank H. 1971. *General competitive analysis*. San Francisco: Holden-Day.

Bailey, Martin J. 1956. The welfare cost of inflationary finance. *Journal of Political Economy* 64 (April): 93–110.

Barro, Robert J., and Fischer, Stanley. 1976. Recent developments in monetary theory. *Journal of Monetary Economics* 2 (April): 133–67.

Baumol, William J. 1952. The transactions demand for cash: an inventory theoretic approach. *Quarterly Journal of Economics* 66 (November): 545–56.

Benveniste, L. M., and Scheinkman, J. A. 1976. Duality theory for dynamic optimization models of economics: the continuous time case. Manuscript.

______. 1979. On the differentiability of the value function in dynamic models of economics. *Econometrica* 47 (May): 727–32.

Berge, Claude. 1963. *Topological spaces*. New York: Macmillan.

Bewley, Truman. 1977a. The permanent income hypothesis and welfare economics. Manuscript. University of Bonn, Germany.

______. 1977b. The permanent income hypothesis and long-run economic stability. Manuscript. University of Bonn, Germany.

______. 1977c. The permanent income hypothesis and short-run price stability. Manuscript. University of Bonn, Germany.

______. 1977d. The permanent income hypothesis: a theoretical formulation. *Journal of Economic Theory* 16 (December): 252–92.

Black, Fischer. 1974. Uniqueness of the price level in monetary growth models with rational expectations. *Journal of Economic Theory* 7 (January): 53–65.

Blackwell, David. 1965. Discounted dynamic programming. *Annals of Mathematical Statistics* 36: 226–35.

Böhm-Bawerk, Eugen von. 1959. *Positive theory of capital*, trans. G. D. Huncke. Capital and Interest, vol. 2. South Holland, Illinois: Libertarian Press.

Breiman, Leo. 1968. *Probability*. Reading, Mass.: Addison-Wesley.

Brock, William A. 1974. Money and growth: the case of long run perfect foresight. *International Economic Review* 15 (October): 750–77.

______. 1975. A simple perfect foresight monetary model. *Journal of Monetary Economics* 1 (April): 133–50.

______. 1978. A note on hyper-inflationary equilibria in long run perfect foresight monetary models: a correction. Manuscript.

Brock, William A., and Scheinkman, J. A. 1977. Monetary equilibria in overlapping generations models. Manuscript.

Brunner, Karl. 1951. Inconsistency and indeterminacy in classical economics. *Econometrica* 19 (April): 152–73.

Brunner, Karl, and Meltzer, Allan H. 1971. The uses of money: money in the theory of an exchange economy. *American Economic Review* 61 (December): 784–805.

———, eds. 1976. *The Phillips curve and labor markets*. Carnegie-Rochester Conference Series on Public Policy, vol. 1. Amsterdam: North-Holland.

———. 1977. *Stabilization of the domestic and international economy*. Carnegie-Rochester Conference Series on Public Policy, vol. 5. Amsterdam: North-Holland.

Bryant, John. 1978. A simple general equilibrium model of depression. Research Department Staff Report 36. Federal Reserve Bank of Minneapolis, Minnesota.

———. 1979. The political economy of overlapping generations. Research Department Staff Report 43. Federal Reserve Bank of Minneapolis, Minnesota.

Bryant, John, and Wallace, Neil. 1979a. The inefficiency of interest-bearing national debt. *Journal of Political Economy* 87 (April): 365–81.

———. 1979b. Open market operations in a model of regulated, insured intermediaries. Research Department Staff Report 34. Federal Reserve Bank of Minneapolis, Minnesota. Also forthcoming, *Journal of Political Economy*.

Cagan, Phillip. 1956. The monetary dynamics of hyperinflation. In *Studies in the quantity theory of money,* ed. Milton Friedman, pp. 25–117. Chicago: University of Chicago Press.

Calvo, Guillermo. 1978. On the indeterminacy of interest rates and wages with perfect foresight. *Journal of Economic Theory* 19 (December): 321–37.

———. 1979. On models of money and perfect foresight. *International Economic Review* 20 (February): 83–103.

Cass, David, and Shell, Karl. Undated. Notes on the role of money in rational-expectations, intergenerational macromodels. Manuscript.

Cass, David, and Yaari, Menahem. 1966a. A re-examination of the pure consumption loans model. *Journal of Political Economy* 74 (August): 353–67.

———. 1966b. A note on the role of money in providing sufficient intermediation. Cowles Foundation for Research in Economics Discussion Paper 215. Yale University.

Clower, Robert W. 1967. A reconsideration of the microfoundations of monetary theory. *Western Economic Journal* 6 (December): 1–8.

———. 1968. Comment: the optimal growth rate of money. *Journal of Political Economy* 76 (July-August): 876–80.

———. 1970. Is there an optimal money supply? *Journal of Finance* 25 (May): 425–33.

Clower, Robert W., and Howitt, Peter W. 1978. The transactions theory of the demand for money: a reconsideration. *Journal of Political Economy* 86 (June): 449–66.

Debreu, Gerard. 1954. Valuation equilibrium and Pareto optimum. *Proceedings of the National Academy of Science* 40: 588–92.

———. 1959. *The theory of value*. New York: Wiley.
———. 1974. Excess demand functions. *Journal of Mathematical Economics* 1: 15–21.
Diamond, Peter A. 1965. National debt in a neoclassical growth model. *American Economic Review* 55 (December): 1126–50.
Doob, Joseph L. 1953. *Stochastic processes*. New York: Wiley.
Dornbusch, Rudiger, and Fischer, Stanley. 1978. *Macroeconomics*. New York: McGraw-Hill.
Drandrakis, Emmanuel M. 1966. On the competitive equilibrium in a monetary economy. *International Economic Review* 7 (September): 304–28.
Drèze, Jacques H., ed. 1974. *Allocation under uncertainty: equilibrium and optimality*. Edinburgh: Macmillan.
Dubey, P., and Shubik, M. 1977a. Bankruptcy and optimality in a closed trading mass economy modelled as a noncooperative game. A theory of money and financial institutions, pt. 35. Cowles Foundation for Research in Economics Discussion Paper 448. Yale University.
———. 1977b. A closed economic system with production and exchange modelled as a game strategy. *Journal of Mathematical Economics* 4.
———. 1978. The money rate of interest: a multi-period nonatomic trading and production economy with outside money and optimal bankruptcy rules. A theory of money and financial institutions, pt. 36. Cowles Foundation for Research in Economics Discussion Paper 454. Yale University.
Eden, B. 1975. Aspects of uncertainty in simple monetary models. Ph.D. dissertation. University of Chicago.
Feige, Edgar L., and Parkin, Michael. 1971. The optimal quantity of money, bonds, commodity inventories, and capital. *American Economic Review* 61 (June): 335–49.
Feige, E. L.; Parkin, M.; Avery, R.; and Stones, C. 1973. The roles of money in an economy and the optimum quantity of money. *Economica* 40 (November): 416–31.
Feldman, Allan M. 1973. Bilateral trading processes, pairwise optimality, and Pareto optimality. *Review of Economic Studies* 40 (October): 463–73.
Feller, William. 1966. *An introduction to probability theory and its applications,* vol. 2. New York: Wiley.
Fischer, Stanley. 1975. Recent developments in monetary theory. *American Economic Review* 65 (May): 157–66.
Foley, Duncan K., and Hellwig, Martin. 1975. Asset management with trading uncertainty. *Review of Economic Studies* 42 (July): 327–46.
Friedman, Milton. 1953. *Essays in positive economics*. Chicago: University of Chicago Press.
———. 1956. The quantity theory of money: a restatement. In *Studies in the quantity theory of money,* ed. Milton Friedman, pp. 3–21. Chicago: University of Chicago Press.
———. 1959. The demand for money: some theoretical and empirical results. *Journal of Political Economy* 67 (August): 327–51.
———. 1960. *A program for monetary stability*. New York: Fordham University Press.
———. 1969. *The optimum quantity of money and other essays*. Chicago: Aldine.

Futia, Carl. Undated. A stochastic approach to economic dynamics. Bell Laboratories Working Paper.

Gale, David. 1973. Pure exchange equilibrium of dynamic economic models. *Journal of Economic Theory* 6 (February): 12–36.

Grandmont, Jean Michel. 1974. On the short-run equilibrium in a monetary economy. In *Allocation under uncertainty: equilibrium and optimality,* ed. Jacques H. Drèze. Edinburgh: Macmillan.

———. 1977. Temporary general equilibrium theory. *Econometrica* 45 (April): 535–72.

Grandmont, Jean Michel, and Laroque, Guy. 1973. Money in the pure consumption loan model. *Journal of Economic Theory* 6 (August): 382–95.

Grandmont, Jean Michel, and Younes, Yves. 1972. On the role of money and the existence of a monetary equilibrium. *Review of Economic Studies* 39 (July): 355–72.

———. 1973. On the efficiency of a monetary equilibrium. *Review of Economic Studies* 40 (April): 149–65.

Guthrie, Harold W. 1963. Intergeneration transfers of wealth and the theory of saving. *Journal of Business* 1 (January): 97–108.

Hahn, Frank H. 1965. On some problems of proving the existence of an equilibrium in a monetary economy. In *The theory of interest rates,* ed. Frank H. Hahn and F. P. R. Brechling, pp. 126–35. London: Macmillan.

———. 1971a. Professor Friedman's views on money. *Economica* 38 (February): 61–80.

———. 1971b. Equilibrium with transaction costs. *Econometrica* 39 (May): 417–39.

———. 1973a. On the foundations of monetary theory. In *Essays in modern economics,* ed. Michael Parkin and A. R. Nobay, pp. 230–42. New York: Harper & Row.

———. 1973b. On transaction costs, inessential sequence economies and money. *Review of Economic Studies* 40 (October): 449–61.

Hahn, Frank H., and Brechling, F. P. R., eds. 1965. *The theory of interest rates*. London: Macmillan.

Harcourt, G. C., ed. 1977. *The microeconomic foundations of macroeconomics*. London: Macmillan.

Harris, M. Forthcoming. Expectations and money in a dynamic exchange economy. *Econometrica*.

Harris, M., and Townsend, R. M. 1978. Allocation mechanisms for asymmetrically informed agents. Working Paper 35-76-77. Carnegie-Mellon University.

———. 1979. Resource allocation under asymmetric information. Working Paper 43-77-78. Carnegie-Mellon University.

Heller, Walter P. 1974. The holding of money balances in general equilibrium. *Journal of Economic Theory* 7 (January): 93–108.

Heller, Walter P., and Starr, Ross M. 1976. Equilibrium with non-convex transactions costs: monetary and non-monetary economies. *Review of Economic Studies* 43 (June): 195–215.

Helpman, Elhanan, and Sadka, Efraim. 1979. Optimal financing of the government's budget: taxes, bonds, or money? *American Economic Review* 69 (March): 152–60.

Hicks, John R. 1937. Mr. Keynes and the "classics": a suggested interpretation. *Econometrica* 5 (April): 147–59.

Honkapohja, Seppo. 1978. A reexamination of the store of value in a sequence economy with transaction costs. *Journal of Economic Theory* 18 (August): 278–93.

Hool, Bryce. 1976. Money, expectations and the existence of a temporary equilibrium. *Review of Economic Studies* 43 (October): 439–45.

Hurwicz, Leonid. 1951. Comment on Arthur Smithies' Business cycle analysis and public policy. In *Conference on business cycles*, pp. 416–20. New York: National Bureau of Economic Research.

______. 1953. What has happened to the theory of games? *American Economic Review* 43 (May): 398–405.

Jevons, W. S. 1875. *Money and the mechanism of exchange*. London: Appleton.

Johnson, Harry G. 1963. Equilibrium under fixed exchanges. *American Economic Review* 53 (May): 112–19.

______. 1967. Money in a neo-classical one-sector growth model. In *Essays in monetary economics*, pp. 143–78. London: Allen & Unwin.

______. 1970. Is there an optimal money supply? *Journal of Finance* 25 (May): 435–42.

Jones, Robert A. 1976. The origin and development of media of exchange. *Journal of Political Economy* 84 (August): 757–75.

Kareken, John H.; Muench, Thomas; and Wallace, Neil. 1973. Optimal open market strategy: the use of information variables. *American Economic Review* 63 (March): 156–72.

Kareken, John H., and Wallace, Neil. 1977. Portfolio autarky: a welfare analysis. *Journal of International Economics* 7 (February): 19–43.

______. 1978. Samuelson's consumption-loan model with country-specific fiat monies. Research Department Staff Report 24. Federal Reserve Bank of Minneapolis, Minnesota.

Kaulla, Rudolf. 1920. *Grundlagen des geldwerts*. Stuttgart, Germany.

Keynes, John M. 1936. *The general theory of employment, interest, and money*. New York: Harcourt, Brace.

Koopmans, Tjalling C. 1960. Stationary ordinal utility and impatience. *Econometrica* 28 (April): 287–309.

______. 1972. Representation of preference orderings over time. In *Decision and organization*, ed. C. B. McGuire and Roy Radner. Studies in Mathematical and Managerial Economics 12: 79–100. Amsterdam: North-Holland.

______. 1977. Examples of production relations based on microdata. In *The microeconomic foundations of macroeconomics*, ed. G. C. Harcourt. London: Macmillan.

Kurz, Mordecai. 1974a. Equilibrium in a finite sequence of markets with transaction cost. *Econometrica* 42 (January): 1–20.

______. 1974b. Equilibrium with transaction cost and money in a single market exchange economy. *Journal of Economic Theory* 7 (April): 418–52.

Lancaster, Kelvin J. 1966. A new approach to consumer theory. *Journal of Political Economy* 74 (April): 132–57.

Lerner, Abba P. 1947. Money as a creature of the state. *American Economic Review* 37 (May): 312–17.

Levhari, David, and Patinkin, Don. 1968. The role of money in a simple growth model. *American Economic Review* 58 (September): 713–53.

Locay, Luis, and Palmon, Oded. 1978. The optimum quantity of money in a perfect foresight monetary model. Working paper. University of Chicago.

Lucas, Robert E., Jr. 1972. Expectations and the neutrality of money. *Journal of Economic Theory* 4 (April): 103–24.

______. 1976. Econometric policy evaluation: a critique. In *The Phillips curve and labor markets,* ed. Karl Brunner and Allan H. Meltzer. Carnegie-Rochester Conference Series on Public Policy 1: 19–46. Amsterdam: North-Holland.

______. 1977. Understanding business cycles. In *Stabilization of the domestic and international economy,* ed. Karl Brunner and Allan H. Meltzer. Carnegie-Rochester Conference Series on Public Policy 5: 7–29. Amsterdam: North-Holland.

______. 1978a. Two illustrations of the quantity theory of money. Manuscript. Department of Economics, University of Chicago.

______. 1978b. Asset prices in an exchange economy. *Econometrica* 46 (November): 1429–46.

Lucas, Robert E., Jr., and Prescott, Edward C. 1971. Investment under uncertainty. *Econometrica* 39 (September): 659–81.

______. 1974. Equilibrium search and unemployment. *Journal of Economic Theory* 7 (February): 188–209.

Lutz, Friedrich A. 1968. *The theory of interest.* Trans. C. Wittich. Chicago: Aldine.

Madden, Paul J. 1975. Efficient sequences of non-monetary exchange. *Review of Economic Studies* 42 (October): 581–96.

Malinvaud, Edmond. 1953. Capital accumulation and efficient allocation of resources. *Econometrica* 21 (April): 233–68.

Mantel, Rolf R. 1974. On the characterization of aggregate excess demand. *Journal of Economic Theory* 7 (March): 348–53.

Martins, A. C. 1975. The private and the social optimum quantity of public debt in a pure consumption loans model. Ph.D. dissertation. University of Chicago.

Marty, Alvin L. 1968. The optimal rate of growth of money. *Journal of Political Economy* 76 (July-August, pt. 2): 860–73.

McFadden, D.; Majumdar, M.; and Mitra, T. Forthcoming. Pareto optimality in infinite horizon reachable economies. *Journal of Mathematical Economics*.

McGuinness, P. P. 1977. The economy isn't about statistics, but how people react. *Australian National Times,* June 20–25.

McGuire, C. B., and Radner, Roy, eds. 1972. *Decision and organization.* Studies in Mathematical and Managerial Economics, vol. 12. Amsterdam: North-Holland.

McKenzie, L. W. 1959. On the existence of general equilibrium for a competitive market. *Econometrica* 27 (January): 54–71.

Meltzer, Allan H. 1963. The demand for money: a cross-section study of business firms. *Quarterly Journal of Economics* 77 (August): 405–22.

Miller, Merton, and Orr, D. 1966. A model of the demand for money by firms. *Quarterly Journal of Economics* 80 (August): 413–35.

Modigliani, Franco, and Miller, M. H. 1958. The cost of capital, corporation finance and the theory of investment. *American Economic Review* 48 (June): 261–97.

Muench, Thomas J. 1977. Optimality, the interaction of spot and futures markets, and the nonneutrality of money in the Lucas model. *Journal of Economic Theory* 15 (August): 325–44.

Müller, Heinz, and Schweizer, Urs. 1978. Temporary equilibrium in a money economy. *Journal of Economic Theory* 19 (December): 267–86.

Neyman, Jerzy, ed. 1951. *Proceedings of the second Berkeley symposium on mathematical statistics and probability*. Berkeley: University of California Press.

Niehans, Jürg. 1969. Money in a static theory of optimal payment arrangements. *Journal of Money, Credit and Banking* 1 (November): 706–26.

______. 1971. Money and barter in general equilibrium with transactions costs. *American Economic Review* 61 (December): 773–83.

______. 1975. Interest and credit in general equilibrium with transactions costs. *American Economic Review* 65 (September): 548–66.

Okun, A. M., and Perry, G. L., eds. 1978. *Brookings Papers on Economic Activity*, vol. 2. Washington, D.C.: Brookings Institution.

Okuno, Masahiro, and Zilcha, Itzhak. 1977. On the efficiency of competitive equilibrium in infinite horizon monetary economies. Manuscript. Department of Economics, University of Illinois, Urbana.

Ostroy, Joseph M. 1973. The informational efficiency of monetary exchange. *American Economic Review* 63 (September): 597–610.

Ostroy, Joseph M., and Starr, Ross M. 1974. Money and the decentralization of exchange. *Econometrica* 42 (November): 1093–113.

Parkin, Michael, and Nobay, A. R., eds. 1973. *Essays in modern economics*. New York: Harper & Row.

Perlman, Morris. 1971. The roles of money in an economy and the optimum quantity of money. *Economica* 38 (August): 233–52.

______. 1973. The roles of money in an economy and the optimum quantity of money: reply. *Economica* 40 (November): 432–41.

Perry, G. L. 1978. Slowing the wage-price spiral: the macroeconomic view. In *Brookings Papers on Economic Activity*, ed. A. M. Okun and G. L. Perry, 2: 259–300. Washington, D. C.: Brookings Institution.

Phelps, Edmund S. 1966. *Golden rules of economic growth*. New York: Norton.

______. 1972. *Inflation policy and unemployment theory: the cost-benefit approach to monetary planning*. New York: Norton.

______. 1973. Inflation in the theory of public finance. *Swedish Journal of Economics* 75 (March): 67–82.

Poole, William. 1970. Optimal choice of monetary policy instruments in a simple stochastic macro model. *Quarterly Journal of Economics* 84 (May): 197–216.

Prescott, E. C., and Townsend, R. M. Forthcoming. Equilibrium under uncertainty: multi-agent statistical decision theory. In *Studies in Bayesian econometrics and statistics in honor of Harold Jeffreys*, ed. Arnold Zellner. Amsterdam: North-Holland.

Ramsey, Frank P. 1928. A mathematical theory of saving. *Economic Journal* 38 (December): 543–59.

Russell, Thomas. 1974. Feige and Parkin on the optimal quantity of money. *American Economic Review* 64 (December): 1074–76.

Samuelson, Paul A. 1958. An exact consumption-loan model of interest with or without the social contrivance of money. *Journal of Political Economy* 66 (December): 467–82.

———. 1963. D. H. Robertson (1890–1963). *Quarterly Journal of Economics* 77 (November): 517–36.

———. 1968. What classical and neoclassical monetary theory really was. *Canadian Journal of Economics* 1 (February): 1–15.

———. 1969. Nonoptimality of money holding under laissez faire. *Canadian Journal of Economics* 2 (May): 303–8.

Saving, Thomas R. 1971. Transactions costs and the demand for money. *American Economic Review* 61 (June): 407–20.

Schechtman, Jack. 1976. An income fluctuation problem. *Journal of Economic Theory* 12 (April): 218–41.

Shapley, Lloyd, and Shubik, Martin. 1977. Trade using one commodity as a means of payment. *Journal of Political Economy* 85 (October): 937–68.

Shell, Karl. 1971. Notes on the economics of infinity. *Journal of Political Economy* 79 (September-October): 1002–11.

Shiller, R. J. 1978. Rational expectations and the dynamic structure of macroeconomic models. *Journal of Monetary Economics* 4 (January): 1–44.

Shubik, Martin. 1959. *Strategy and market structure: competition, oligopoly, and the theory of games*. New York: Wiley.

———. 1973. Commodity money, oligopoly, credit and bankruptcy in a general equilibrium model. *Western Economic Journal* 11 (March): 24–38.

Sidrauski, Miguel. 1967. Inflation and economic growth. *Journal of Political Economy* 75 (December): 796–810.

Solow, Robert M. 1963. *Capital theory and the rate of return*. Amsterdam: North-Holland.

Sonnenschein, Hugo. 1972. Market excess demand functions. *Econometrica* 40 (May): 549–63.

———. 1973. Do Walras' identity and continuity characterize the class of community excess demand functions? *Journal of Economic Theory* 6 (August): 345–54.

Sontheimer, Kevin. 1972. On the determination of money prices. *Journal of Money, Credit and Banking* 4 (August): 489–508.

Starr, Ross M. 1972. The structure of exchange in barter and monetary economies. *Quarterly Journal of Economics* 86 (May): 290–302.

———. 1974. The price of money in a pure exchange monetary economy with taxation. *Econometrica* 42 (January): 45–54.

———. 1976. Decentralized nonmonetary trade. *Econometrica* 44 (September): 1087–89.

Starrett, David A. 1972. On golden rules, the "biological theory of interest," and competitive inefficiency. *Journal of Political Economy* 80 (March-April): 276–91.

———. 1973. Inefficiency and the demand for "money" in a sequence economy. *Review of Economic Studies* 40 (October): 437–48.

Stein, Jerome L. 1970. Monetary growth theory in perspective. *American Economic Review* 60 (March): 85–106.

———. 1976. Inside the monetarist black box. In *Monetarism*, ed. Jerome L. Stein. Studies in Monetary Economics 1: 183–232. Amsterdam: North-Holland.

Stiglitz, Joseph E. 1969. A re-examination of the Modigliani-Miller theorem. *American Economic Review* 59 (December): 784–93.

Tobin, James. 1956. The interest-elasticity of transactions demand for cash. *Review of Economics and Statistics* 38 (August): 241–47.

———. 1958. Liquidity preference as behavior towards risk. *Review of Economic Studies* 25 (February): 65–86.

———. 1965. Money and economic growth. *Econometrica* 33 (October): 671–84.

———. 1968. Notes on optimal monetary growth. *Journal of Political Economy* 76 (July-August, pt. 2): 833–59.

———. 1969. A general equilibrium approach to monetary theory. *Journal of Money, Credit and Banking* 1 (February): 15–29.

Tobin, James, and Brainard, W. C. 1963. Financial intermediaries and the effectiveness of monetary controls. *American Economic Review* 53 (May): 383–400.

Townsend, Robert M. 1978a. Intermediation with costly bilateral exchange. *Review of Economic Studies* 45 (October): 417–25.

———. 1978b. Equilibrium with endogenous marketeers. Working Paper. Carnegie-Mellon University.

———. 1979. Optimal contracts and competitive markets with costly state verification. Working Paper. Carnegie-Mellon University. Also forthcoming, *Journal of Economic Theory*.

Tsiang, S. C. 1969. A critical note on the optimum supply of money. *Journal of Money, Credit and Banking* 1 (May): 266–80.

Wallace, Neil. 1977. A payments mechanism without Fed involvement and Fed monetary policy without required reserves. Research Department Staff Report 15. Federal Reserve Bank of Minneapolis, Minnesota. Also manuscript, Department of Economics, University of Minnesota.

Wilson, Charles. 1978a. A perfect foresight model with transactions demand for money. Social Science Research Institute Discussion Paper 7808. University of Wisconsin, Madison.

———. 1978b. An infinite horizon model with money. Social Science Research Institute Discussion Paper 7814. University of Wisconsin, Madison.

Zellner, Arnold, ed. Forthcoming. *Studies in Bayesian econometrics and statistics in honor of Harold Jeffreys*. Amsterdam: North-Holland.